高橋　和希

WHEN THIS GRAPHIC NOVEL FIRST CAME OUT IN JAPAN, THE
JAPANESE YU-GI-OH! ANIME WAS JUST STARTING. WHEN THEY
OFFERED TO ANIMATE YU-GI-OH!, I WAS HALF EXCITED AND HALF
SCARED! IT MEANT HANDING OVER SOMETHING THAT MEANS SO
MUCH TO ME TO SOMEBODY ELSE. "WILL THE THEMES TRANSLATE
PROPERLY TO THE SCREEN?" THAT WAS MY MAIN CONCERN AS I
HEADED TO THE ANIME POST-RECORDING SESSION. .BUT WHEN I
GOT THERE, THE PERFORMANCE OF THE VOICE ACTORS RELIEVED
MY DOUBTS. THESE PROS NOT ONLY GAVE THE CHARACTERS A
VOICE, THEY GAVE THEM LIFE! I WAS MOVED!
　　　　　　　　—KAZUKI TAKAHASHI. 1998

Artist/author Kazuki Takahashi first tried to break into
the manga business in 1982, but success eluded him
until **Yu-Gi-Oh!** debuted in the Japanese **Weekly
Shonen Jump** magazine in 1996. **Yu-Gi-Oh!**'s themes
of friendship and fighting, together with Takahashi's
weird and wonderful art, soon became enormously
successful, spawning a real-world card game, video
games, and two anime series. A lifelong gamer,
Takahashi enjoys Shogi (Japanese chess), Mahjong,
card games, and tabletop RPGs, among other games.

YU-GI-OH!: DUELIST VOL. 1
The SHONEN JUMP Graphic Novel Edition

STORY AND ART BY
KAZUKI TAKAHASHI

Translation & English Adaptation/Anita Sengupta
Touch-up Art & Lettering/Jim Keefe
Design/Sean Lee
Editor/Jason Thompson

Managing Editor/Elizabeth Kawasaki
Director of Production/Noboru Watanabe
Editorial Director/Alvin Lu
Executive Vice President & Editor in Chief/Hyoe Narita
Sr. Director of Licensing & Acquisitions/Rika Inouye
Vice President of Sales & Marketing/Liza Coppola
Vice President of Strategic Development/Yumi Hoashi
Publisher/Seiji Horibuchi

In the original Japanese edition, YU-GI-OH! and YU-GI-OH!: DUELIST are known
collectively as YU-GI-OH!. The English YU-GI-OH!: DUELIST was originally
volumes 8-31 of the Japanese YU-GI-OH!.

Printed in the U.S.A.

Published by VIZ, LLC
P.O. Box 77010
San Francisco, CA 94107

SHONEN JUMP Graphic Novel Edition
10 9 8 7 6 5 4 3 2 1
First printing, January 2005

PARENTAL ADVISORY
YU-GI-OH! is rated T for Teen. It contains
fantasy violence. It is recommended for
ages 13 and up.

THE WORLD'S
MOST POPULAR MANGA

SHONEN JUMP
GRAPHIC NOVEL

www.viz.com

www.shonenjump.com

SHONEN JUMP GRAPHIC NOVEL

Vol. 1

DUELIST KINGDOM

STORY AND ART BY
KAZUKI TAKAHASHI

《MAIN CAST》

メイン キャスト

THE STORY SO FAR...

Shy 10th-grader Yugi spent most of his time alone playing games... until he solved the Millennium Puzzle, a mysterious Egyptian artifact passed down from his grandfather. Possessed by the puzzle, Yugi became Yu-Gi-Oh, the King of Games, and challenged bullies and criminals to the "Shadow Games"... magical games of life and death! But one of the many games which Yugi has played is about to come back with a vengeance...

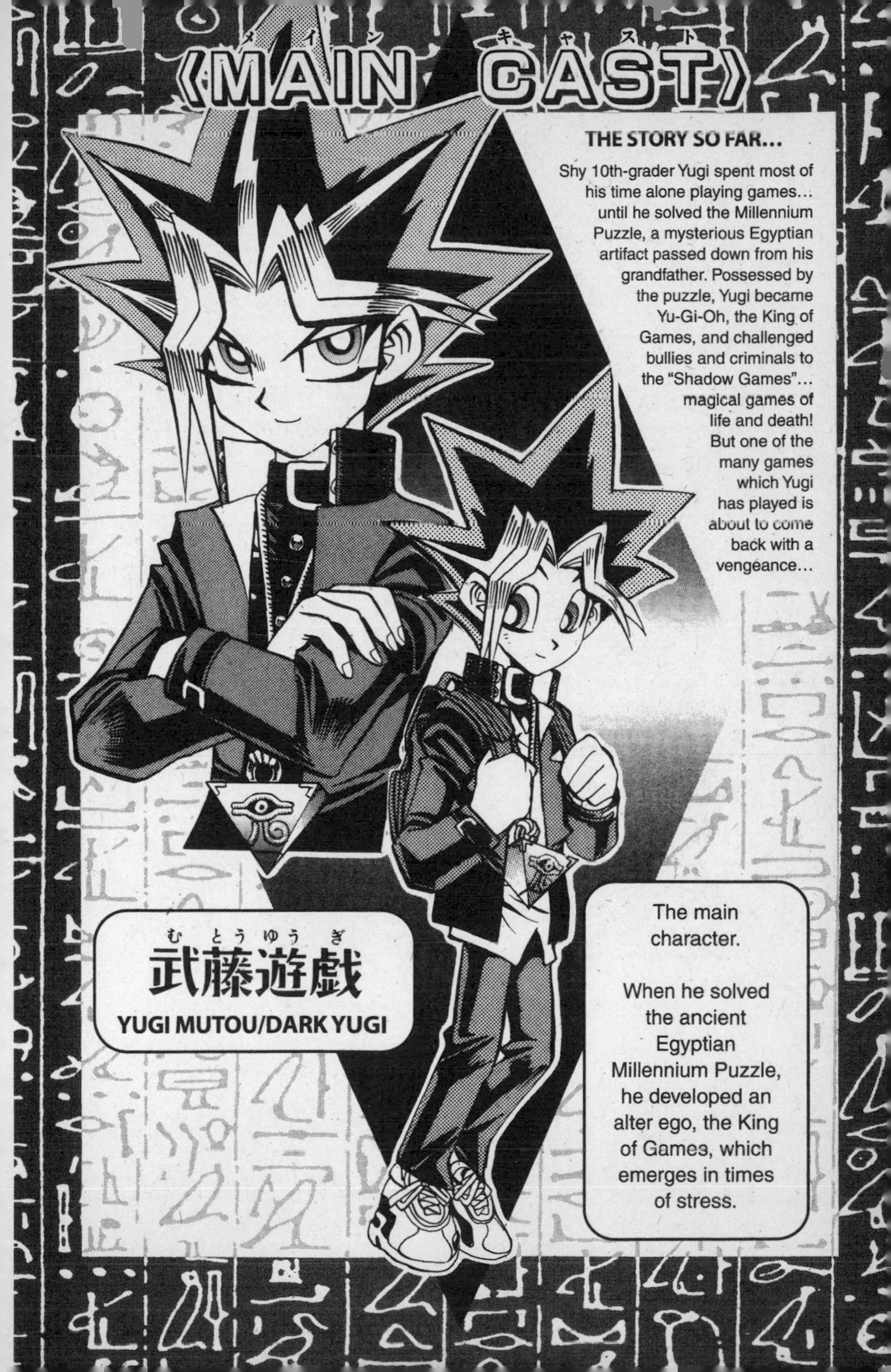

むとうゆうぎ

武藤遊戯

YUGI MUTOU/DARK YUGI

The main character.

When he solved the ancient Egyptian Millennium Puzzle, he developed an alter ego, the King of Games, which emerges in times of stress.

城之内克也
KATSUYA JONOUCHI

Yugi's classmate, a tough guy who used to get in lots of fights. He used to think Yugi was a wimp, but now they are good friends. In the English anime he's known as "Joey Wheeler."

武藤双六
SUGOROKU MUTOU

Yugi's grandfather, the owner of the Kame ("Turtle") game store. His first name, Sugoroku, is a Japanese game similar to backgammon.

本田ヒロト
HIROTO HONDA

Yugi's classmate, a friend of Jonouchi. In the English anime he's known as "Tristan Taylor."

真崎杏子
ANZU MAZAKI

Yugi's classmate and childhood friend. Her first name means "Peach." In the English anime she's known as "Téa Gardner."

獏良 了
RYO BAKURA

Like Yugi, Bakura owns a Millennium Item: the Millennium Ring. Unfortunately for him, it's possessed by an evil spirit.

ペガサス・J・クロフォード
MAXIMILLION J. PEGASUS

A brilliant, wealthy American game designer who shows up on page 18 of this graphic novel. In the original Japanese manga he's called "Pegasus J. Crawford."

Vol. 1

CONTENTS

Duel 1 Challenge!!	7
Duel 2 Don't Draw that Card!!	27
Duel 3 Countdown!!	47
Duel 4 I Won't Lose!!	67
Duel 5 Fate on the High Seas!!	89
Duel 6 Let the Duel Begin!	111
Duel 7 The Trap	129
Duel 8 The Ultimate Great Moth	148
Duel 9 Demon Lightning	170
Duel 10 The Siren	191
Master of the Cards	210
Previews	214

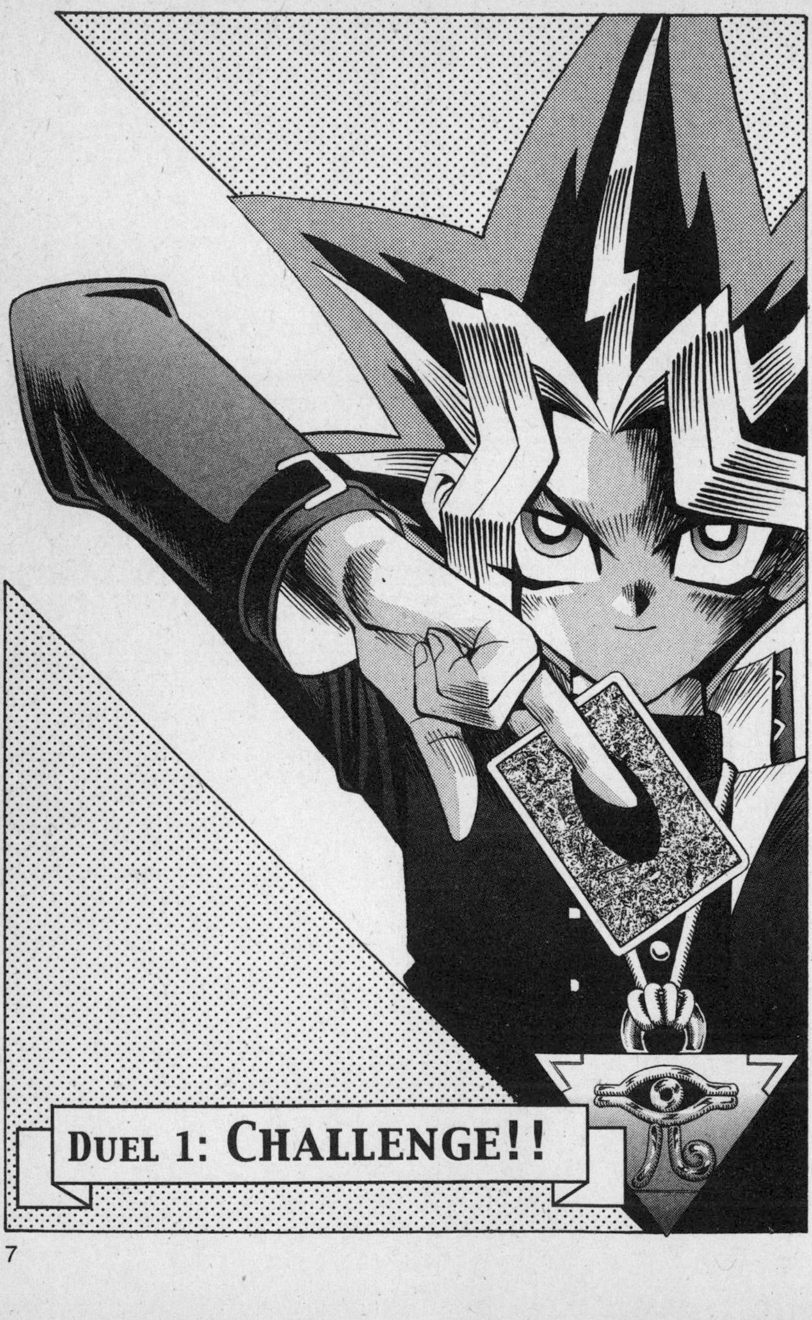
Duel 1: Challenge!!

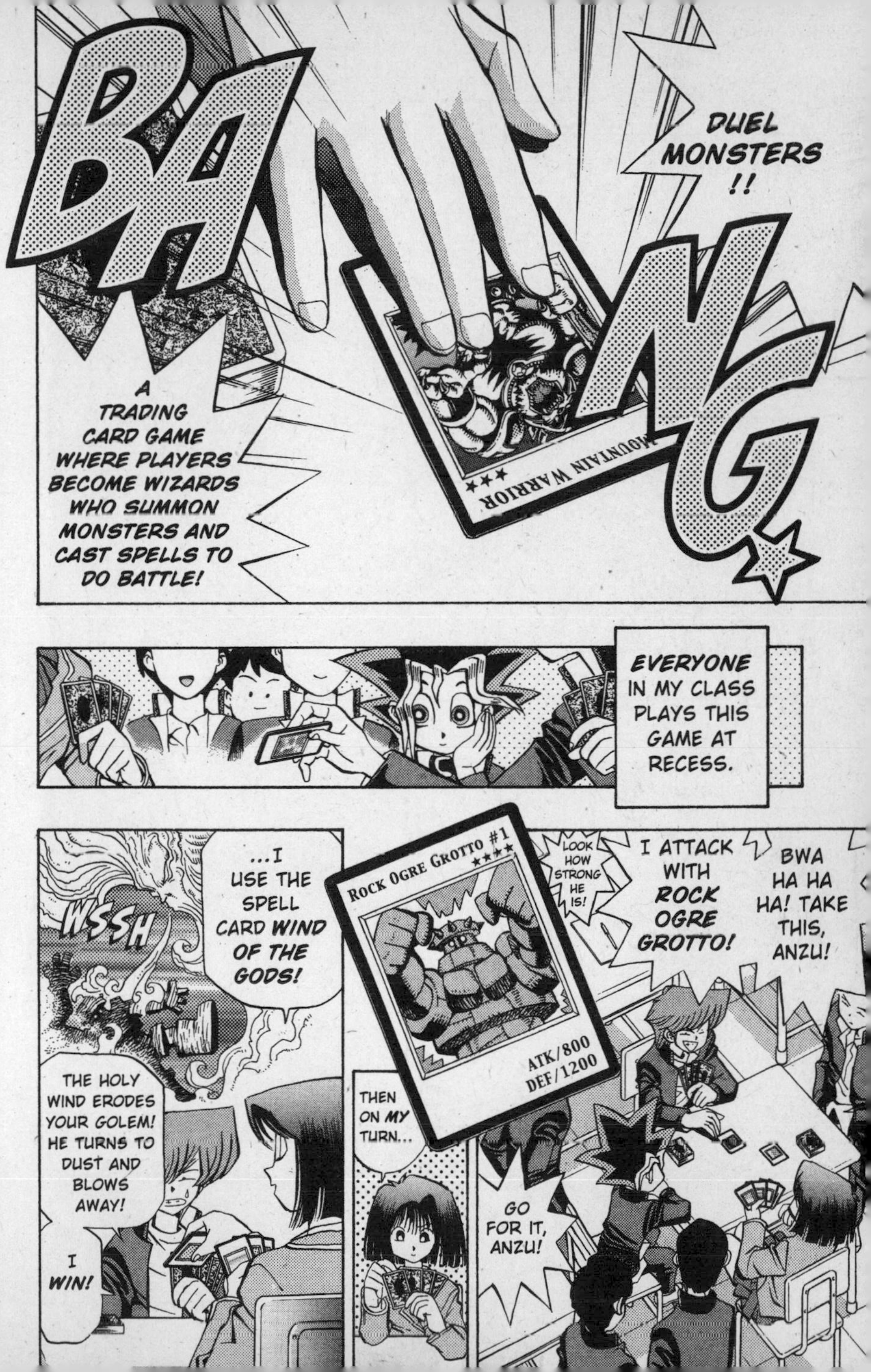
DUEL MONSTERS !!
BANG
MOUNTAIN WARRIOR
A TRADING CARD GAME WHERE PLAYERS BECOME WIZARDS WHO SUMMON MONSTERS AND CAST SPELLS TO DO BATTLE!
EVERYONE IN MY CLASS PLAYS THIS GAME AT RECESS.
BWA HA HA HA! TAKE THIS, ANZU!
I ATTACK WITH ROCK OGRE GROTTO!
LOOK HOW STRONG HE IS!
ROCK OGRE GROTTO #1
ATK/800
DEF/1200
GO FOR IT, ANZU!
THEN ON MY TURN...
...I USE THE SPELL CARD WIND OF THE GODS!
WSSH
THE HOLY WIND ERODES YOUR GOLEM! HE TURNS TO DUST AND BLOWS AWAY!
I WIN!

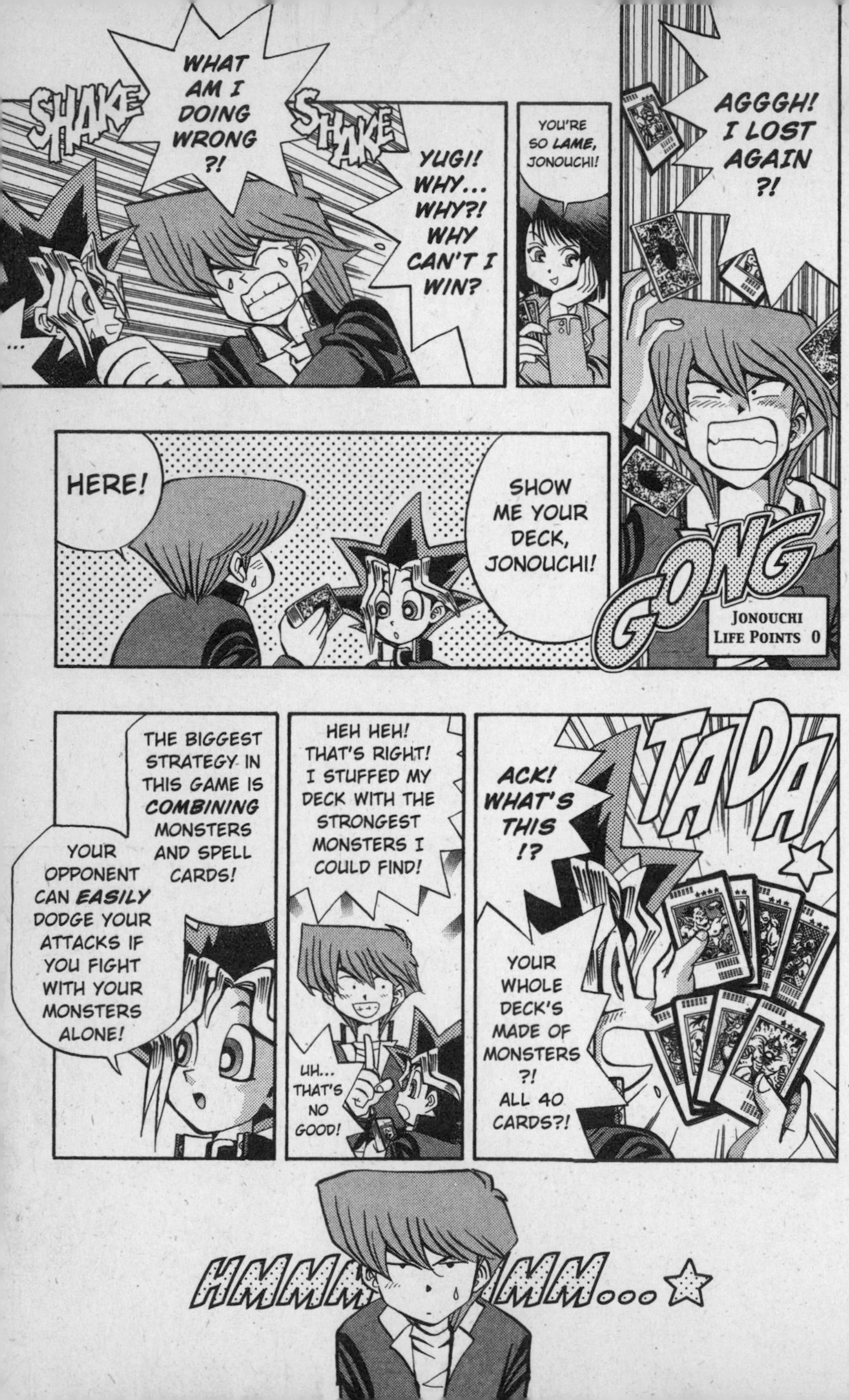
AGGGH! I LOST AGAIN?!
GONG
JONOUCHI LIFE POINTS 0
YOU'RE SO LAME, JONOUCHI!
SHAKE
YUGI! WHY... WHY?! WHY CAN'T I WIN?
WHAT AM I DOING WRONG?!
SHAKE
...
SHOW ME YOUR DECK, JONOUCHI!
HERE!
TADA
ACK! WHAT'S THIS!?
YOUR WHOLE DECK'S MADE OF MONSTERS?! ALL 40 CARDS?!
HEH HEH! THAT'S RIGHT! I STUFFED MY DECK WITH THE STRONGEST MONSTERS I COULD FIND!
UH... THAT'S NO GOOD!
THE BIGGEST STRATEGY IN THIS GAME IS COMBINING MONSTERS AND SPELL CARDS!
YOUR OPPONENT CAN EASILY DODGE YOUR ATTACKS IF YOU FIGHT WITH YOUR MONSTERS ALONE!
HMMMM MMM...☆

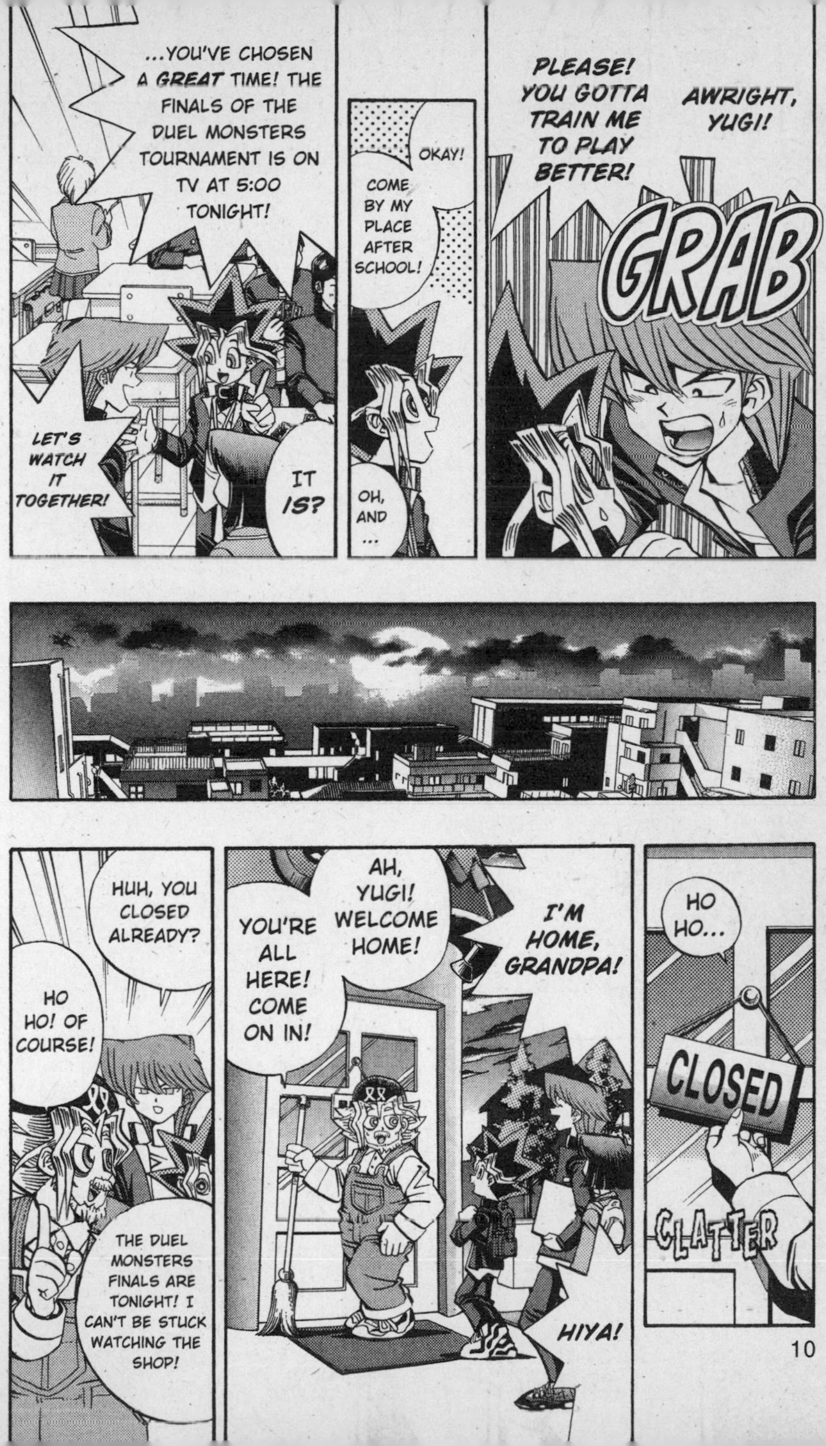

AWRIGHT, YUGI!
PLEASE! YOU GOTTA TRAIN ME TO PLAY BETTER!
GRAB
OKAY!
COME BY MY PLACE AFTER SCHOOL!
OH, AND ...
...YOU'VE CHOSEN A GREAT TIME! THE FINALS OF THE DUEL MONSTERS TOURNAMENT IS ON TV AT 5:00 TONIGHT!
IT IS?
LET'S WATCH IT TOGETHER!
HO HO...
CLOSED
CLATTER
I'M HOME, GRANDPA!
HIYA!
AH, YUGI! WELCOME HOME!
YOU'RE ALL HERE! COME ON IN!
HUH, YOU CLOSED ALREADY?
HO HO! OF COURSE!
THE DUEL MONSTERS FINALS ARE TONIGHT! I CAN'T BE STUCK WATCHING THE SHOP!

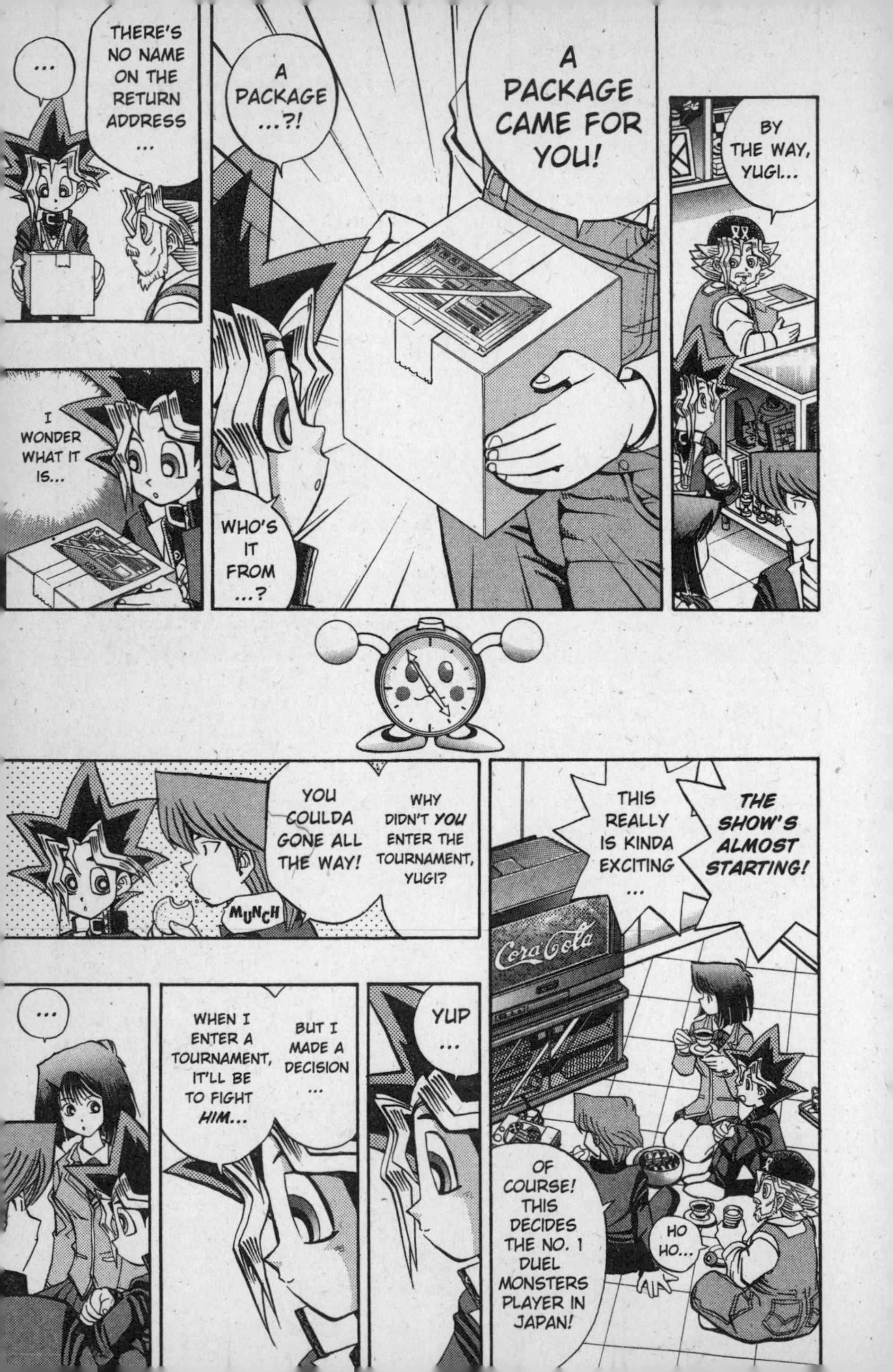
BY THE WAY, YUGI...
A PACKAGE CAME FOR YOU!
A PACKAGE ...?!
WHO'S IT FROM ...?
THERE'S NO NAME ON THE RETURN ADDRESS ...
...
I WONDER WHAT IT IS...
THE SHOW'S ALMOST STARTING!
THIS REALLY IS KINDA EXCITING ...
OF COURSE! THIS DECIDES THE NO. 1 DUEL MONSTERS PLAYER IN JAPAN!
HO HO...
WHY DIDN'T YOU ENTER THE TOURNAMENT, YUGI?
YOU COULDA GONE ALL THE WAY!
MUNCH
YUP ...
BUT I MADE A DECISION ...
WHEN I ENTER A TOURNAMENT, IT'LL BE TO FIGHT HIM...
...

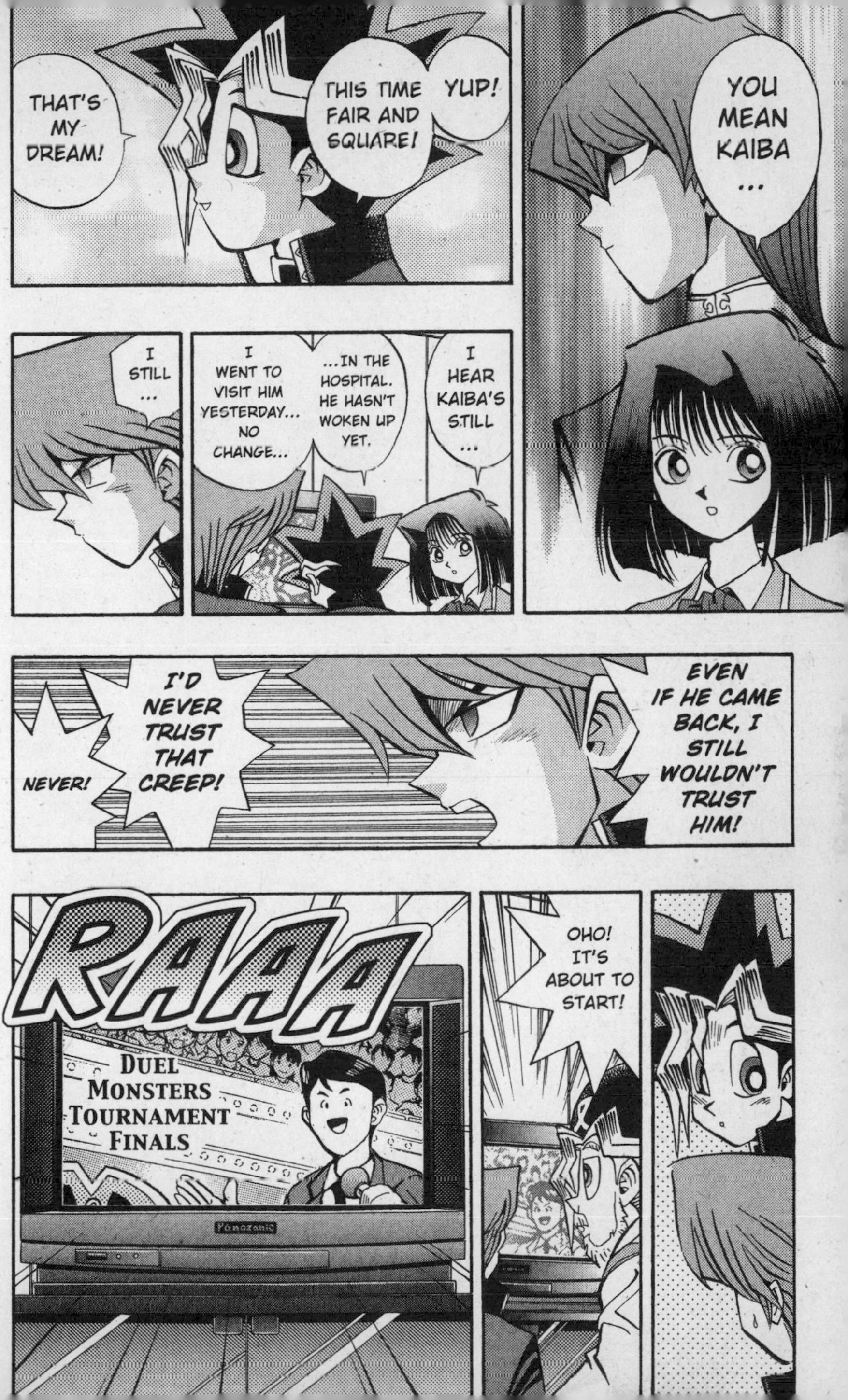
YOU MEAN KAIBA ...
YUP!
THIS TIME FAIR AND SQUARE!
THAT'S MY DREAM!
I HEAR KAIBA'S STILL ...
...IN THE HOSPITAL. HE HASN'T WOKEN UP YET.
I WENT TO VISIT HIM YESTERDAY... NO CHANGE...
I STILL ...
EVEN IF HE CAME BACK, I STILL WOULDN'T TRUST HIM!
I'D NEVER TRUST THAT CREEP!
NEVER!
OHO! IT'S ABOUT TO START!
RAAA
DUEL MONSTERS TOURNAMENT FINALS

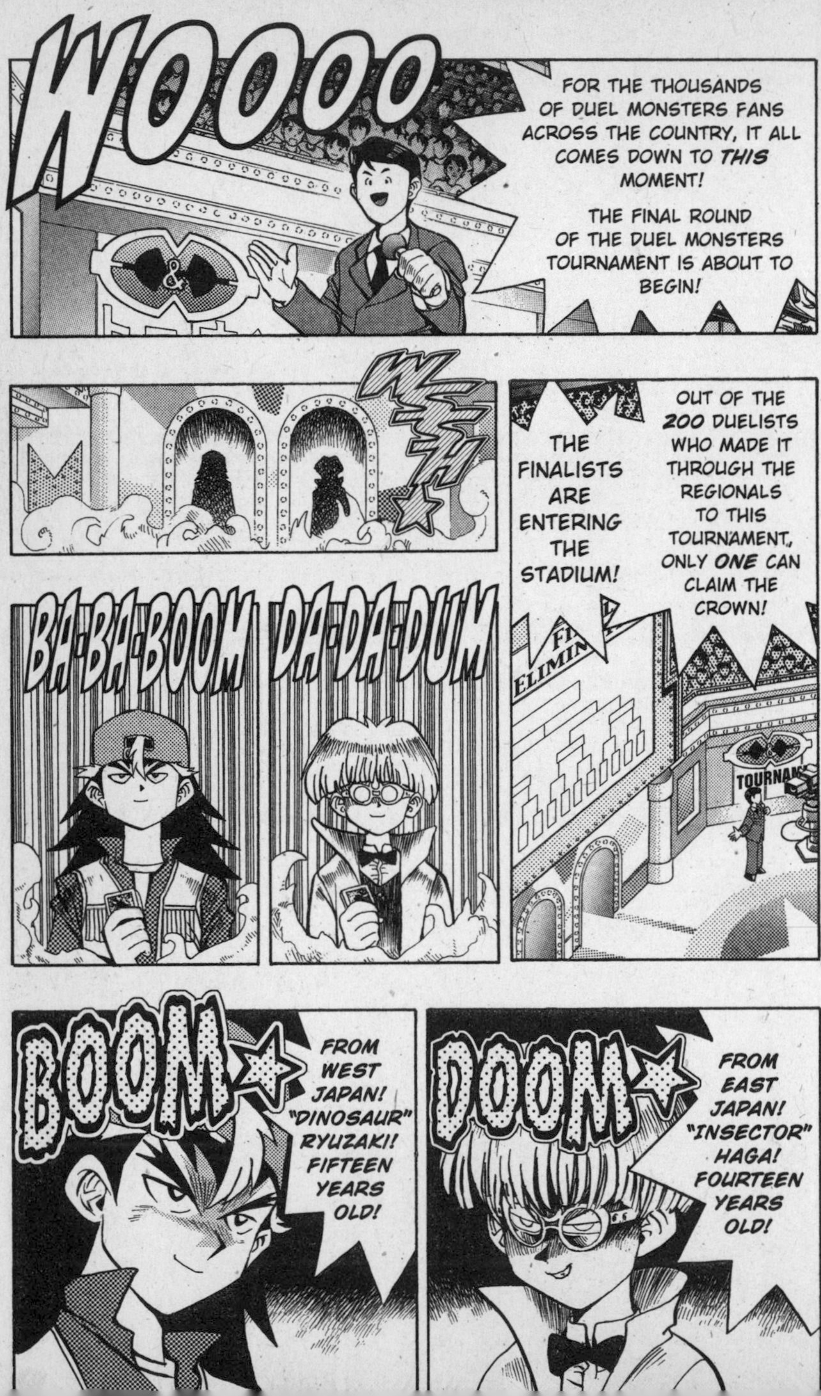
WOOOO
FOR THE THOUSANDS OF DUEL MONSTERS FANS ACROSS THE COUNTRY, IT ALL COMES DOWN TO *THIS* MOMENT!
THE FINAL ROUND OF THE DUEL MONSTERS TOURNAMENT IS ABOUT TO BEGIN!
OUT OF THE *200* DUELISTS WHO MADE IT THROUGH THE REGIONALS TO THIS TOURNAMENT, ONLY *ONE* CAN CLAIM THE CROWN!
THE FINALISTS ARE ENTERING THE STADIUM!
WSSH
DA-DA-DUM
BA-BA-BOOM
DOOM
FROM EAST JAPAN! "INSECTOR" HAGA! FOURTEEN YEARS OLD!
BOOM
FROM WEST JAPAN! "DINOSAUR" RYUZAKI! FIFTEEN YEARS OLD!

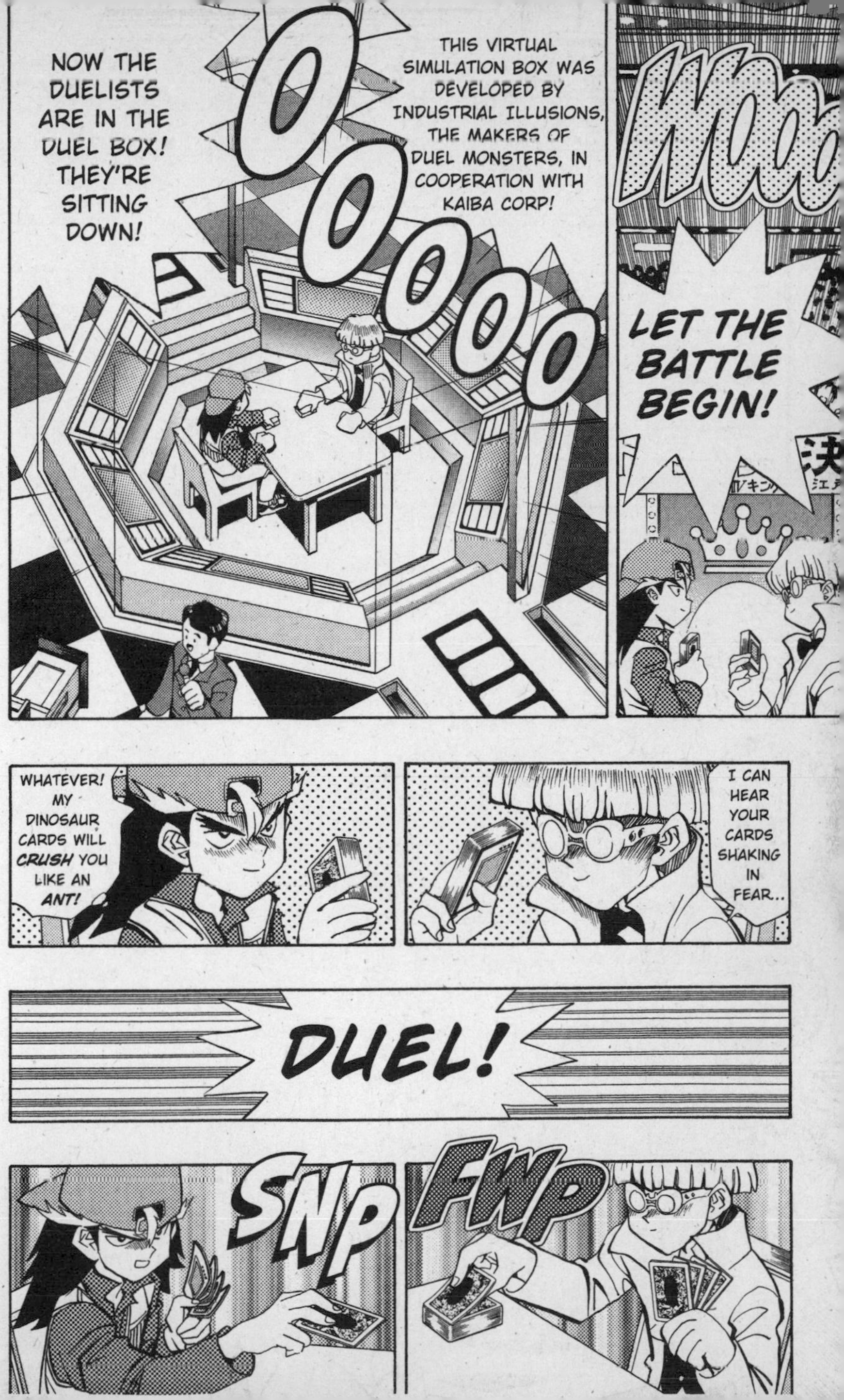
WOOO
LET THE BATTLE BEGIN!
THIS VIRTUAL SIMULATION BOX WAS DEVELOPED BY INDUSTRIAL ILLUSIONS, THE MAKERS OF DUEL MONSTERS, IN COOPERATION WITH KAIBA CORP!
OOOOO
NOW THE DUELISTS ARE IN THE DUEL BOX! THEY'RE SITTING DOWN!
I CAN HEAR YOUR CARDS SHAKING IN FEAR...
WHATEVER! MY DINOSAUR CARDS WILL *CRUSH* YOU LIKE AN *ANT!*
DUEL!
FWP
SNP

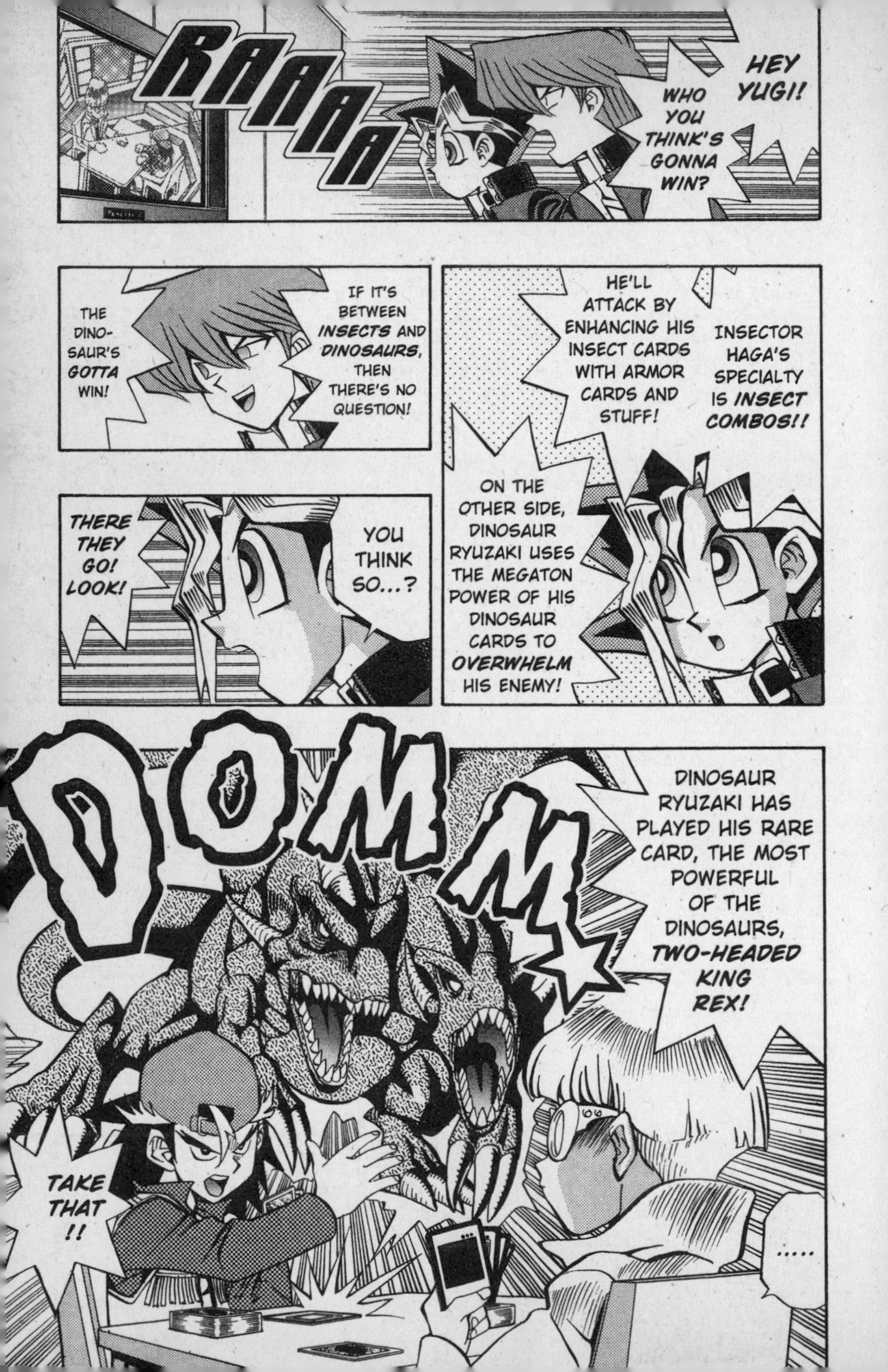
HEY YUGI!
WHO YOU THINK'S GONNA WIN?
RAAAAA
INSECTOR HAGA'S SPECIALTY IS INSECT COMBOS!!
HE'LL ATTACK BY ENHANCING HIS INSECT CARDS WITH ARMOR CARDS AND STUFF!
ON THE OTHER SIDE, DINOSAUR RYUZAKI USES THE MEGATON POWER OF HIS DINOSAUR CARDS TO OVERWHELM HIS ENEMY!
IF IT'S BETWEEN INSECTS AND DINOSAURS, THEN THERE'S NO QUESTION!
THE DINOSAUR'S GOTTA WIN!
YOU THINK SO...?
THERE THEY GO! LOOK!
DINOSAUR RYUZAKI HAS PLAYED HIS RARE CARD, THE MOST POWERFUL OF THE DINOSAURS, TWO-HEADED KING REX!
DOMM
.....
TAKE THAT!!

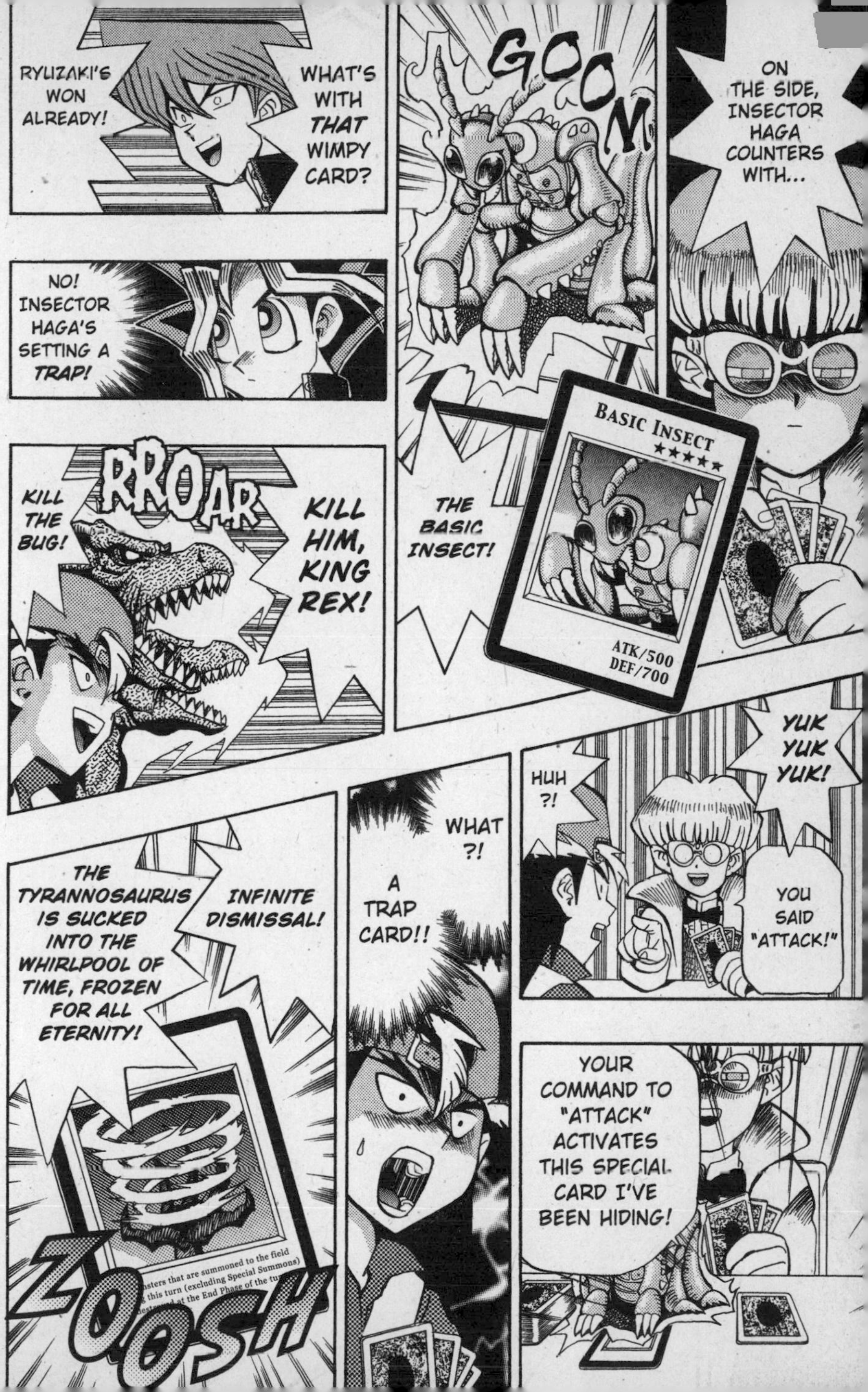
ON THE SIDE, INSECTOR HAGA COUNTERS WITH...
GOOON
THE BASIC INSECT!
BASIC INSECT
ATK/500
DEF/700
WHAT'S WITH THAT WIMPY CARD?
RYUZAKI'S WON ALREADY!
NO! INSECTOR HAGA'S SETTING A TRAP!
KILL HIM, KING REX!
RROAR
KILL THE BUG!
YUK YUK YUK!
HUH ?!
YOU SAID "ATTACK!"
YOUR COMMAND TO "ATTACK" ACTIVATES THIS SPECIAL CARD I'VE BEEN HIDING!
WHAT ?!
A TRAP CARD!!
INFINITE DISMISSAL!
THE TYRANNOSAURUS IS SUCKED INTO THE WHIRLPOOL OF TIME, FROZEN FOR ALL ETERNITY!
ZOOSH

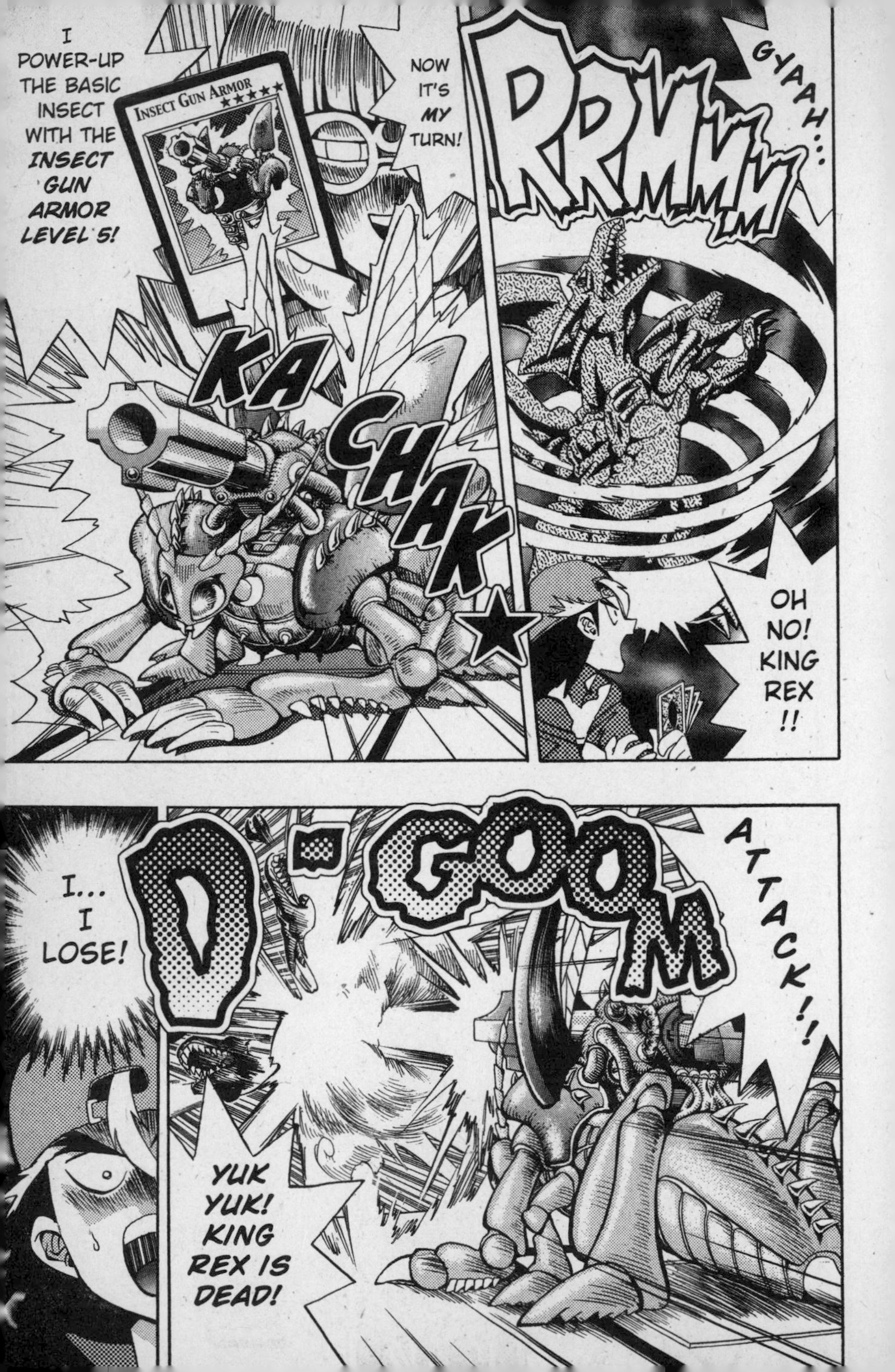
RRMMMMM
GYAAH...
OH NO! KING REX !!
NOW IT'S MY TURN!
I POWER-UP THE BASIC INSECT WITH THE INSECT GUN ARMOR LEVEL 5!
INSECT GUN ARMOR
KA CHAK
D-GOOM
ATTACK!!
YUK YUK! KING REX IS DEAD!
I... I LOSE!

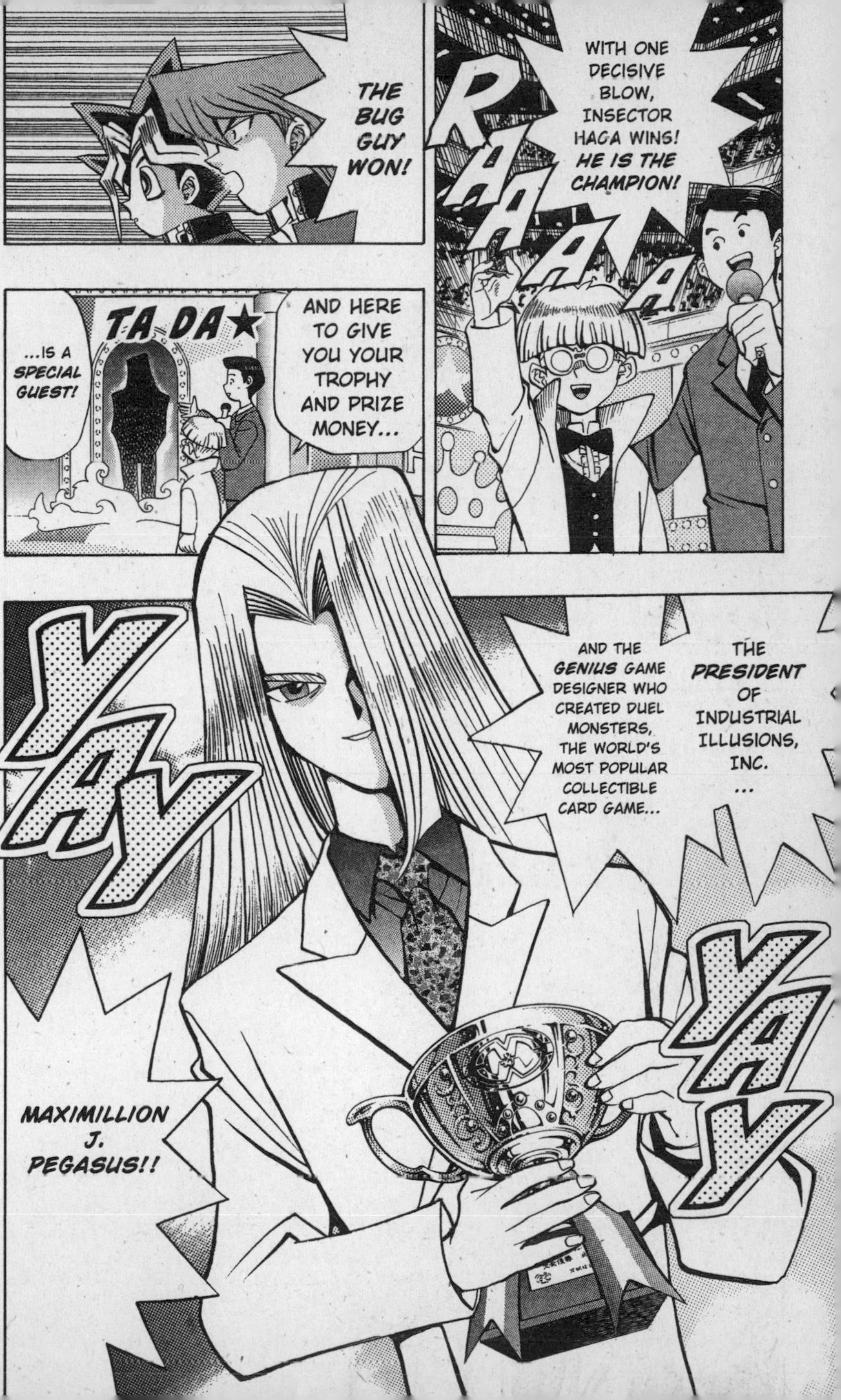
RAAAA
WITH ONE DECISIVE BLOW, INSECTOR HAGA WINS! HE IS THE CHAMPION!
THE BUG GUY WON!
TA DA★
AND HERE TO GIVE YOU YOUR TROPHY AND PRIZE MONEY...
...IS A SPECIAL GUEST!
YAY
THE PRESIDENT OF INDUSTRIAL ILLUSIONS, INC. ...
AND THE GENIUS GAME DESIGNER WHO CREATED DUEL MONSTERS, THE WORLD'S MOST POPULAR COLLECTIBLE CARD GAME...
YAY
MAXIMILLION J. PEGASUS!!

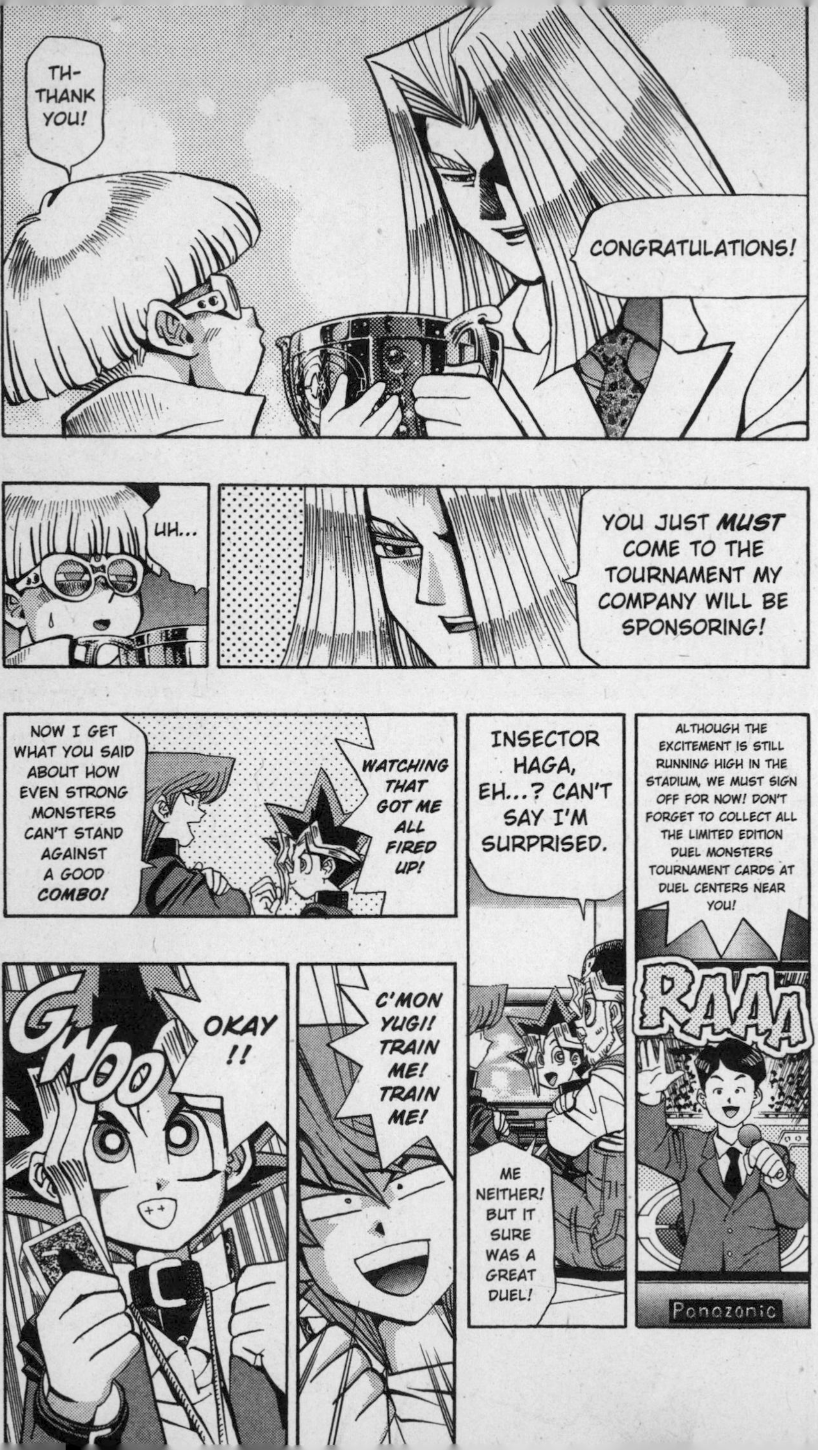
CONGRATULATIONS!
TH- THANK YOU!
YOU JUST MUST COME TO THE TOURNAMENT MY COMPANY WILL BE SPONSORING!
UH...
ALTHOUGH THE EXCITEMENT IS STILL RUNNING HIGH IN THE STADIUM, WE MUST SIGN OFF FOR NOW! DON'T FORGET TO COLLECT ALL THE LIMITED EDITION DUEL MONSTERS TOURNAMENT CARDS AT DUEL CENTERS NEAR YOU!
RAAA
Panazonic
INSECTOR HAGA, EH...? CAN'T SAY I'M SURPRISED.
ME NEITHER! BUT IT SURE WAS A GREAT DUEL!
WATCHING THAT GOT ME ALL FIRED UP!
NOW I GET WHAT YOU SAID ABOUT HOW EVEN STRONG MONSTERS CAN'T STAND AGAINST A GOOD COMBO!
C'MON YUGI! TRAIN ME! TRAIN ME!
OKAY !!
GWOO

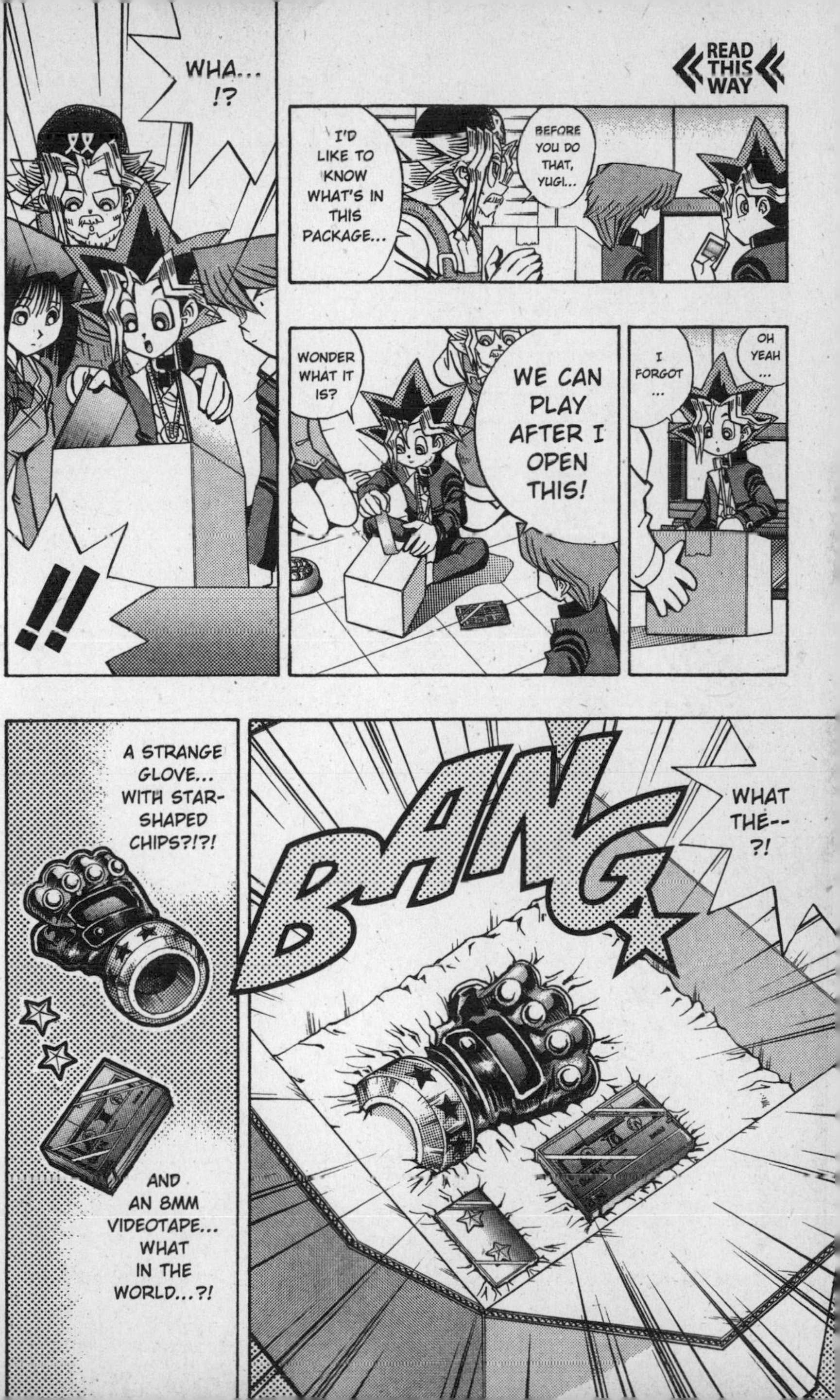

READ THIS WAY
BEFORE YOU DO THAT, YUGI...
I'D LIKE TO KNOW WHAT'S IN THIS PACKAGE...
OH YEAH...
I FORGOT...
WE CAN PLAY AFTER I OPEN THIS!
WONDER WHAT IT IS?
WHA... !?
!!
BANG
WHAT THE-- ?!
A STRANGE GLOVE... WITH STAR-SHAPED CHIPS?!?!
AND AN 8MM VIDEOTAPE... WHAT IN THE WORLD...?!

READ THIS WAY

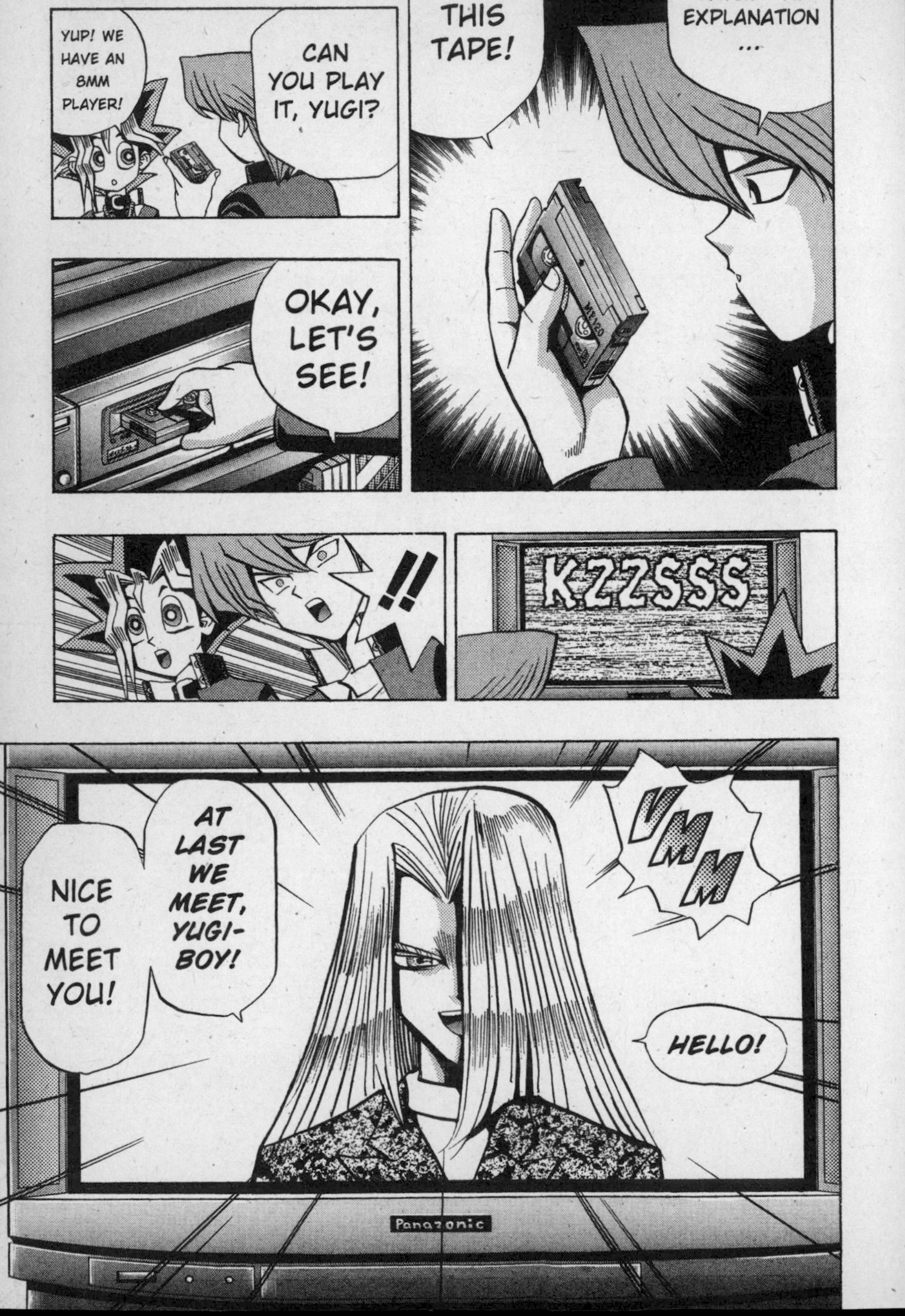
MAYBE THE EXPLANATION ...
IS ON THIS TAPE!
CAN YOU PLAY IT, YUGI?
YUP! WE HAVE AN 8MM PLAYER!
OKAY, LET'S SEE!
KZZSSS
!!
VMM
HELLO!
AT LAST WE MEET, YUGI-BOY!
NICE TO MEET YOU!
Panazonic

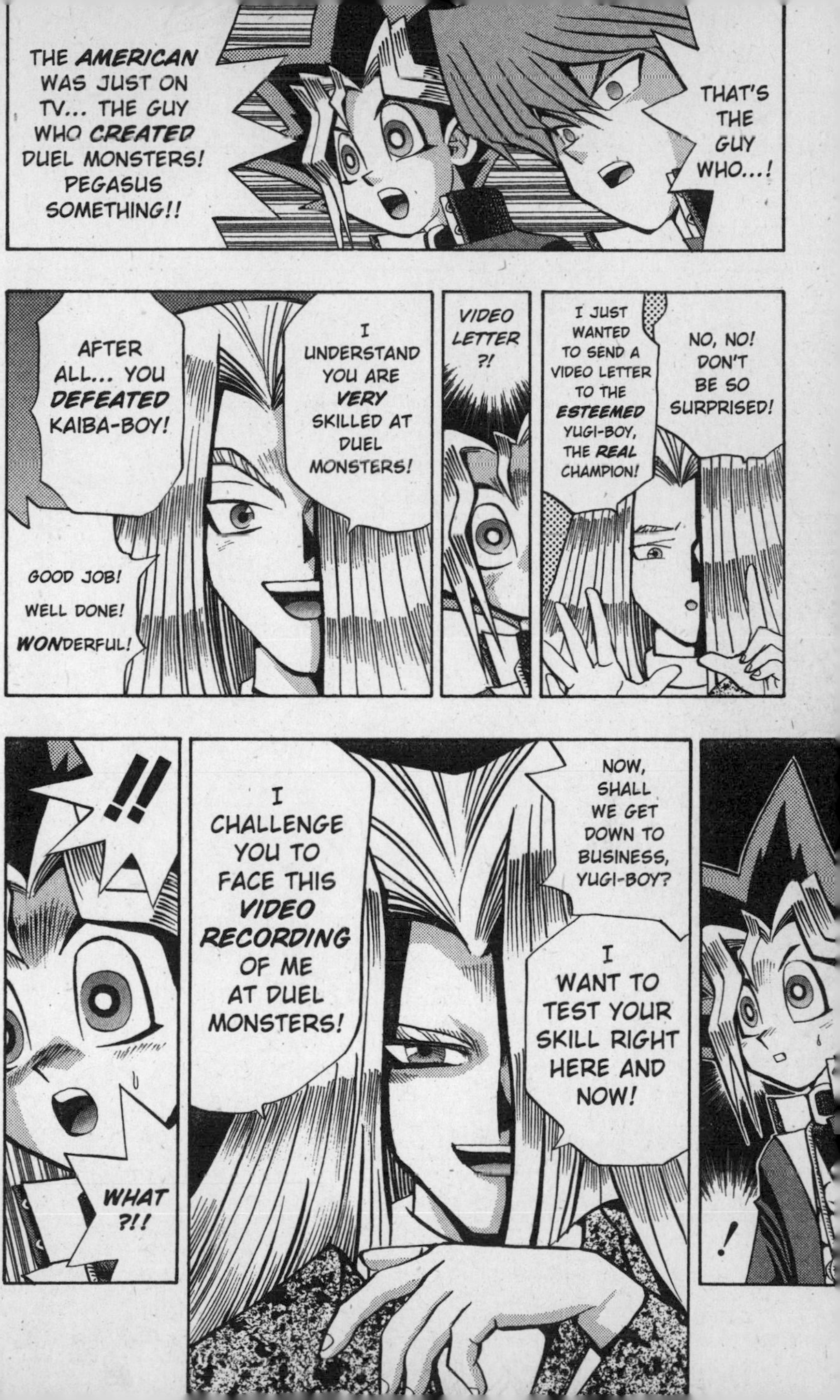
THAT'S THE GUY WHO...!
THE AMERICAN WAS JUST ON TV... THE GUY WHO CREATED DUEL MONSTERS! PEGASUS SOMETHING!!
NO, NO! DON'T BE SO SURPRISED!
I JUST WANTED TO SEND A VIDEO LETTER TO THE ESTEEMED YUGI-BOY, THE REAL CHAMPION!
VIDEO LETTER ?!
I UNDERSTAND YOU ARE VERY SKILLED AT DUEL MONSTERS!
AFTER ALL... YOU DEFEATED KAIBA-BOY!
GOOD JOB!
WELL DONE!
WONDERFUL!
!
NOW, SHALL WE GET DOWN TO BUSINESS, YUGI-BOY?
I WANT TO TEST YOUR SKILL RIGHT HERE AND NOW!
I CHALLENGE YOU TO FACE THIS VIDEO RECORDING OF ME AT DUEL MONSTERS!
!!
WHAT ?!!

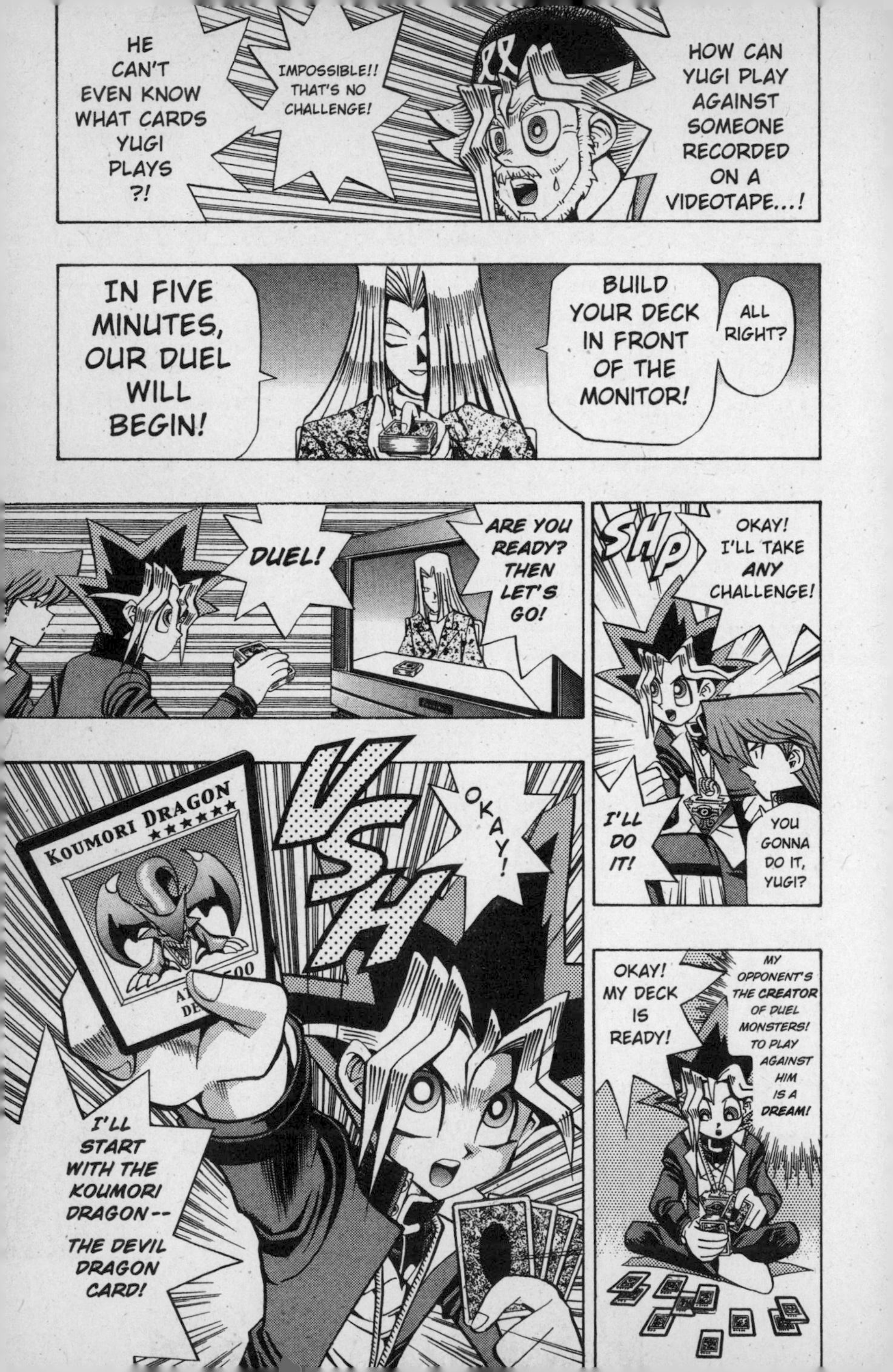

HOW CAN YUGI PLAY AGAINST SOMEONE RECORDED ON A VIDEOTAPE...!
IMPOSSIBLE!! THAT'S NO CHALLENGE!
HE CAN'T EVEN KNOW WHAT CARDS YUGI PLAYS ?!
ALL RIGHT?
BUILD YOUR DECK IN FRONT OF THE MONITOR!
IN FIVE MINUTES, OUR DUEL WILL BEGIN!
OKAY! I'LL TAKE ANY CHALLENGE!
SHP
YOU GONNA DO IT, YUGI?
I'LL DO IT!
ARE YOU READY? THEN LET'S GO!
DUEL!
MY OPPONENT'S THE CREATOR OF DUEL MONSTERS! TO PLAY AGAINST HIM IS A DREAM!
OKAY! MY DECK IS READY!
OKAY!
VSH
KOUMORI DRAGON
I'LL START WITH THE KOUMORI DRAGON-- THE DEVIL DRAGON CARD!

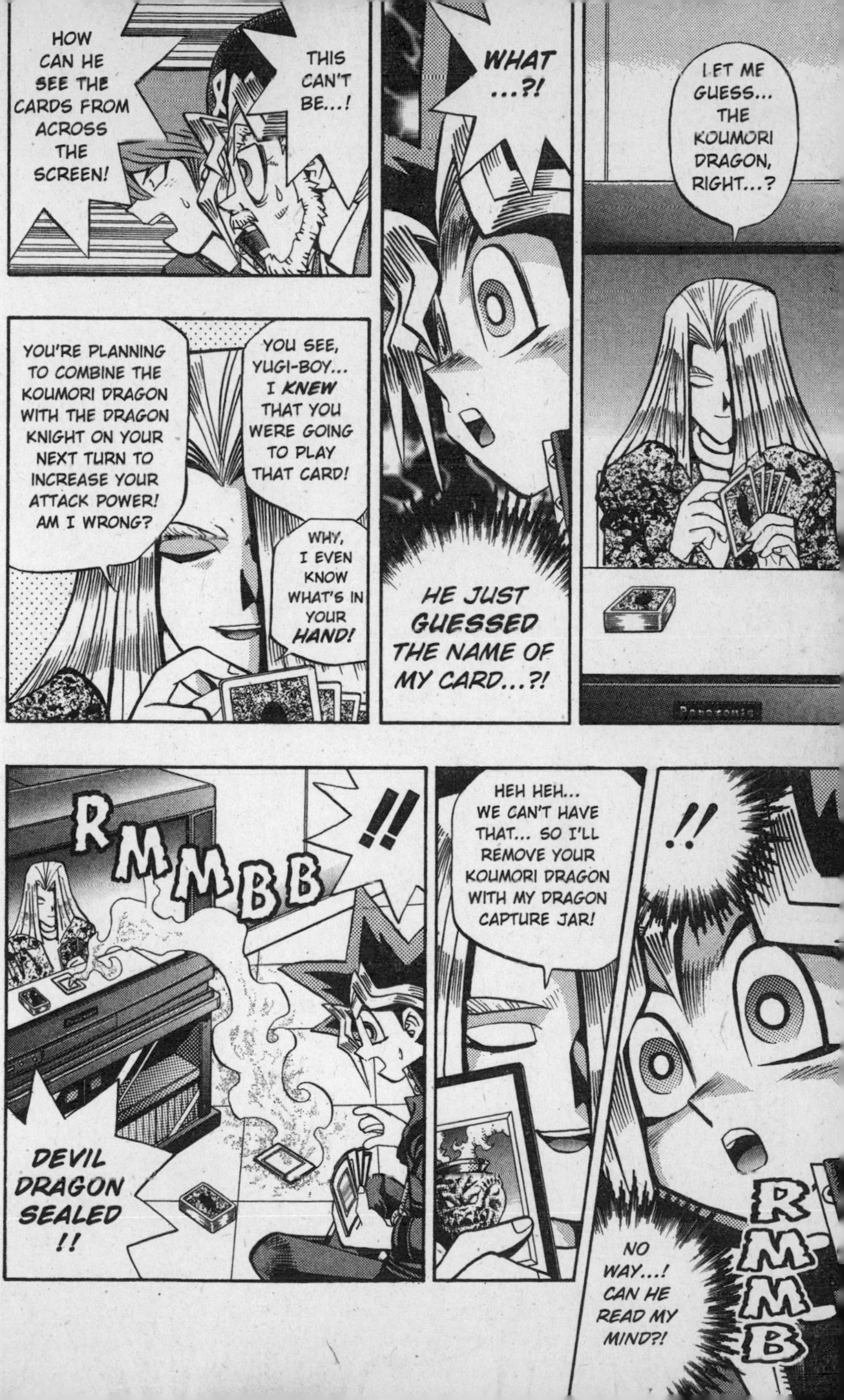
LET ME GUESS... THE KOUMORI DRAGON, RIGHT...?
WHAT ...?!
HE JUST GUESSED THE NAME OF MY CARD...?!
THIS CAN'T BE...!
HOW CAN HE SEE THE CARDS FROM ACROSS THE SCREEN!
YOU SEE, YUGI-BOY... I KNEW THAT YOU WERE GOING TO PLAY THAT CARD!
WHY, I EVEN KNOW WHAT'S IN YOUR HAND!
YOU'RE PLANNING TO COMBINE THE KOUMORI DRAGON WITH THE DRAGON KNIGHT ON YOUR NEXT TURN TO INCREASE YOUR ATTACK POWER! AM I WRONG?
!!
RMMB
NO WAY...! CAN HE READ MY MIND?!
HEH HEH... WE CAN'T HAVE THAT... SO I'LL REMOVE YOUR KOUMORI DRAGON WITH MY DRAGON CAPTURE JAR!
!!
RMMBB
DEVIL DRAGON SEALED !!

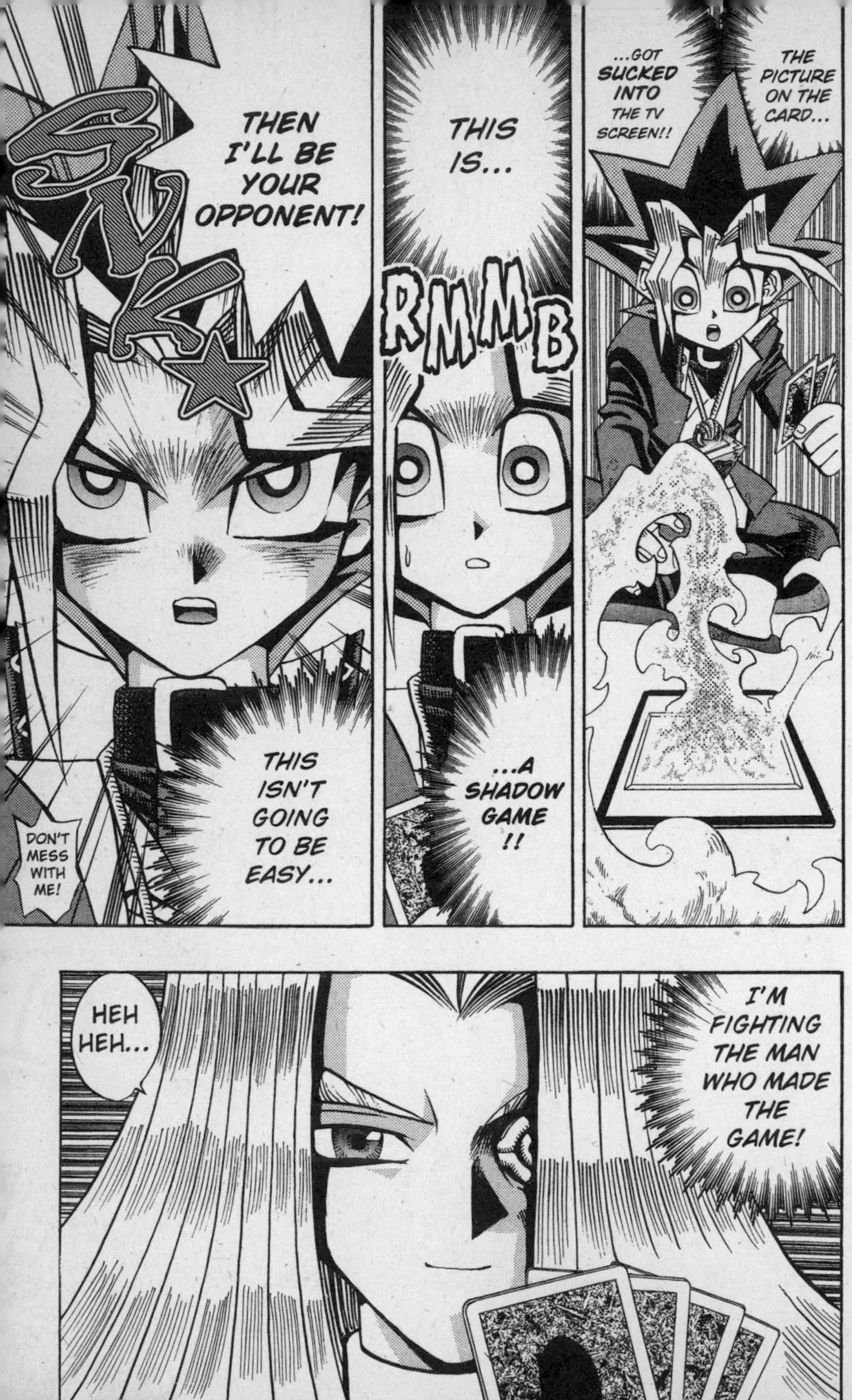
THE PICTURE ON THE CARD...
...GOT SUCKED INTO THE TV SCREEN!!
THIS IS...
RMMB
...A SHADOW GAME!!
THEN I'LL BE YOUR OPPONENT!
THIS ISN'T GOING TO BE EASY...
DON'T MESS WITH ME!
I'M FIGHTING THE MAN WHO MADE THE GAME!
HEH HEH...

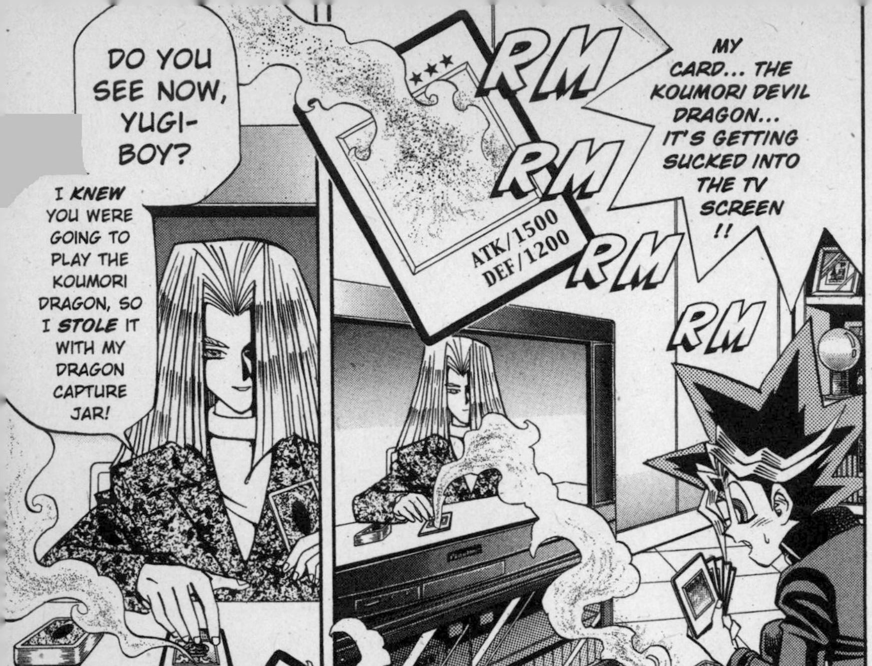
MY CARD... THE KOUMORI DEVIL DRAGON... IT'S GETTING SUCKED INTO THE TV SCREEN !!
RM RM RM RM
ATK/1500 DEF/1200
DO YOU SEE NOW, YUGI-BOY?
I KNEW YOU WERE GOING TO PLAY THE KOUMORI DRAGON, SO I STOLE IT WITH MY DRAGON CAPTURE JAR!
WSSSHHT
All Dragon-Type monsters on the field are switched to Defense Position and remain in this position as long as this card is active.
THIS IS A SHADOW GAME!
D-D-DOOM

Duel 2: Don't Draw That Card!!

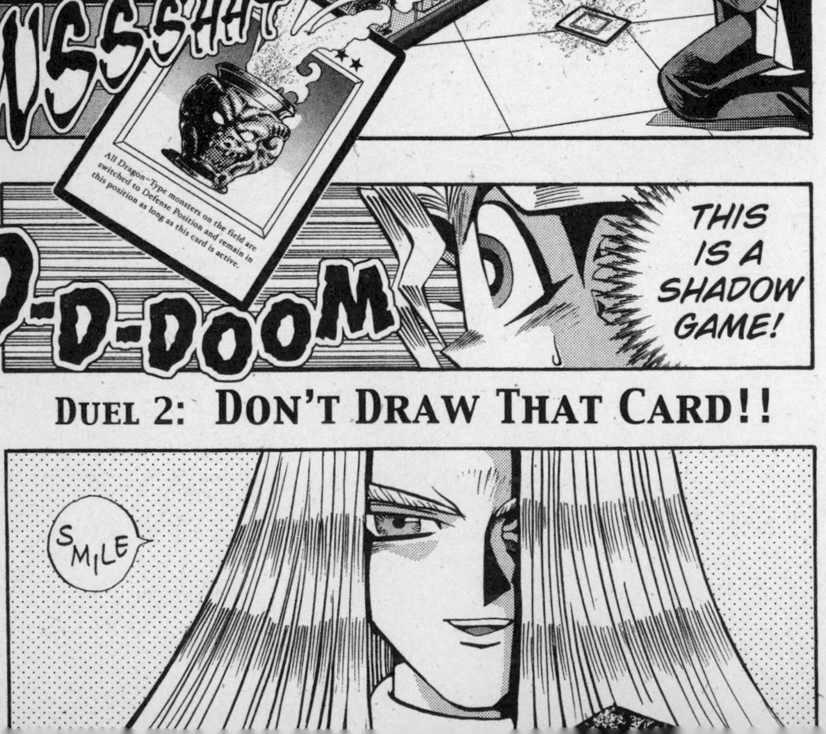
SMILE

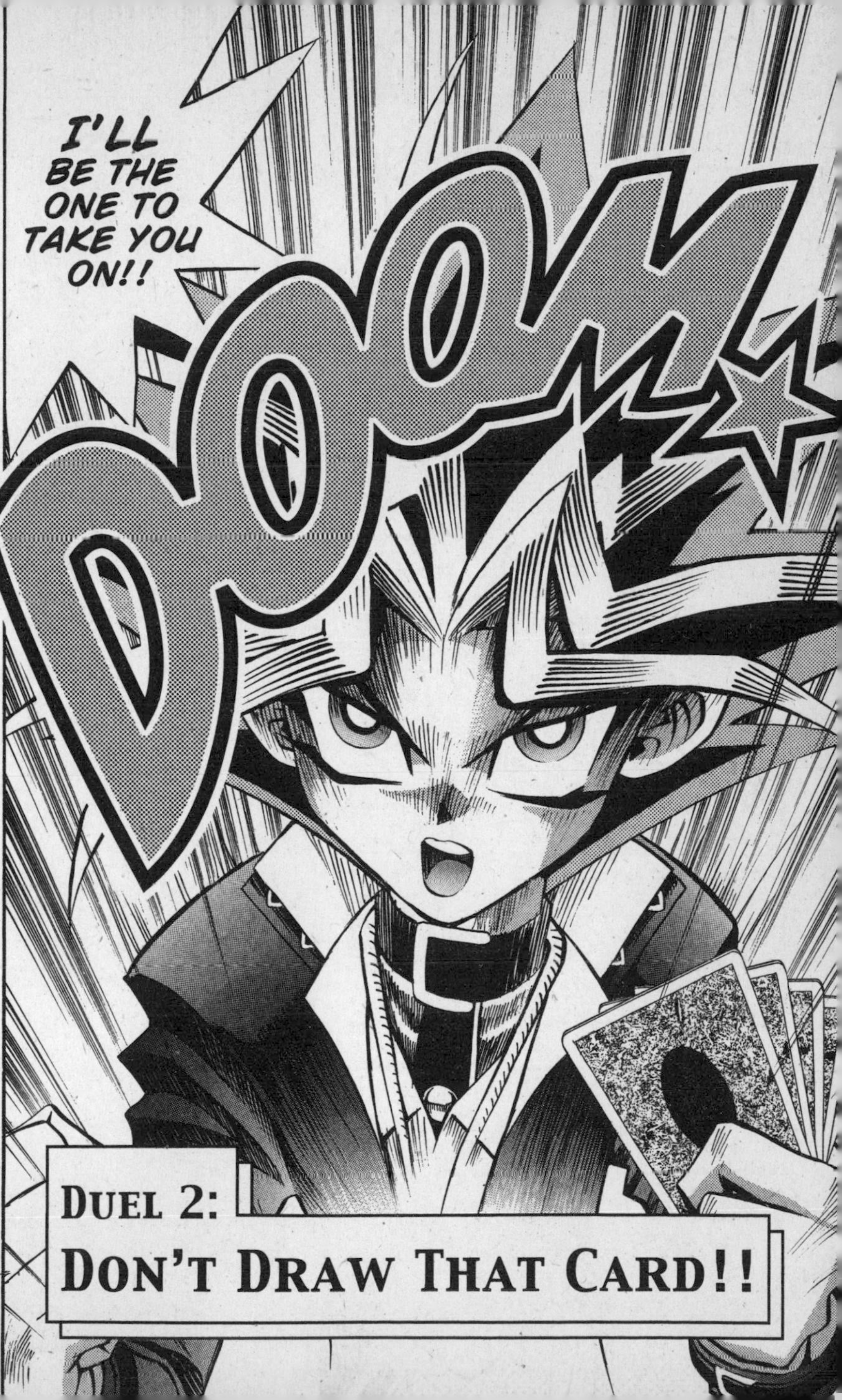
I'LL BE THE ONE TO TAKE YOU ON!!
DOOM
DUEL 2:
DON'T DRAW THAT CARD!!

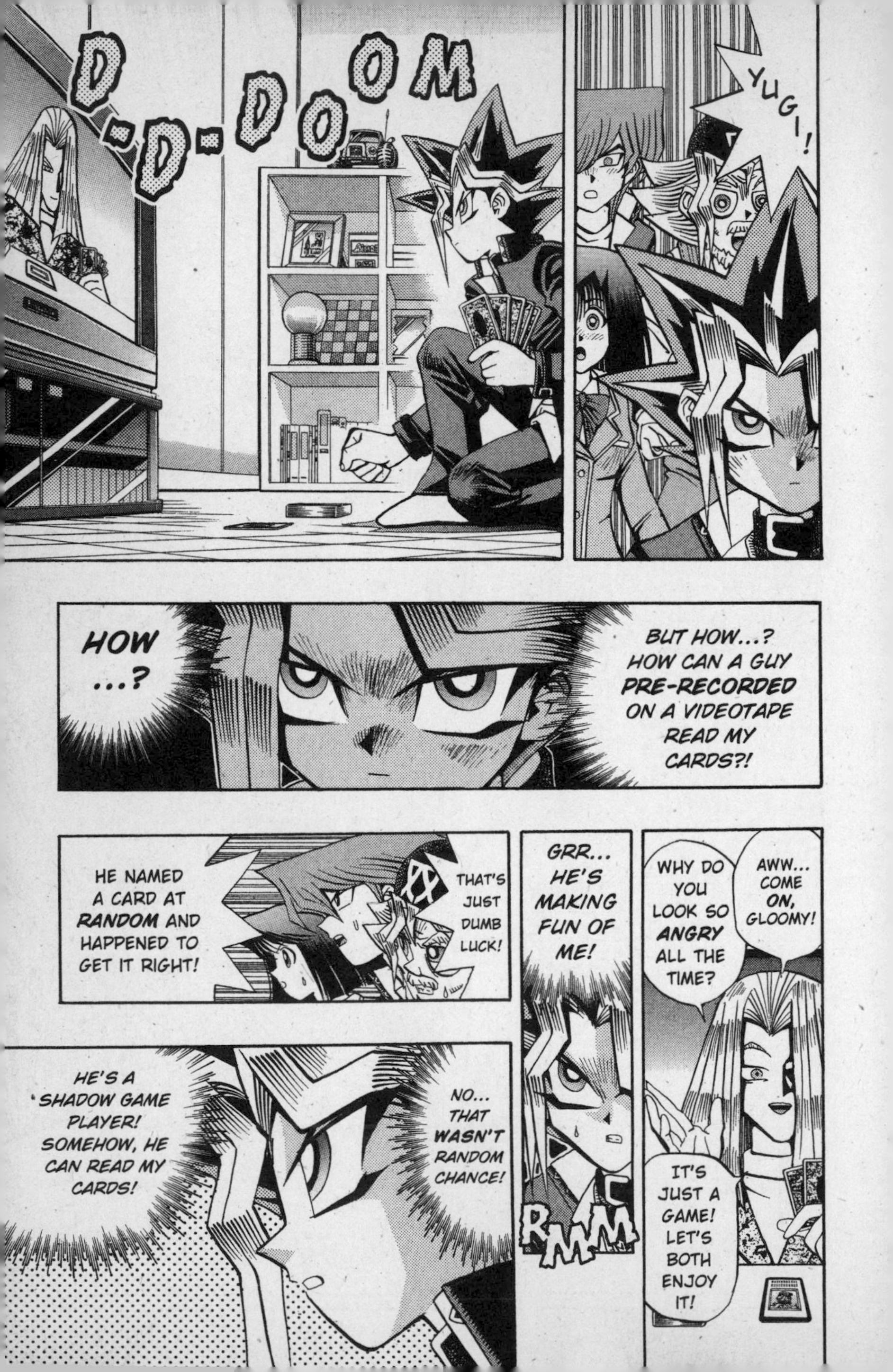
YUGI!
D-D-DOOM
BUT HOW...? HOW CAN A GUY PRE-RECORDED ON A VIDEOTAPE READ MY CARDS?!
HOW ...?
AWW... COME ON, GLOOMY!
WHY DO YOU LOOK SO ANGRY ALL THE TIME?
IT'S JUST A GAME! LET'S BOTH ENJOY IT!
GRR... HE'S MAKING FUN OF ME!
RMM
THAT'S JUST DUMB LUCK!
HE NAMED A CARD AT RANDOM AND HAPPENED TO GET IT RIGHT!
NO... THAT WASN'T RANDOM CHANCE!
HE'S A SHADOW GAME PLAYER! SOMEHOW, HE CAN READ MY CARDS!

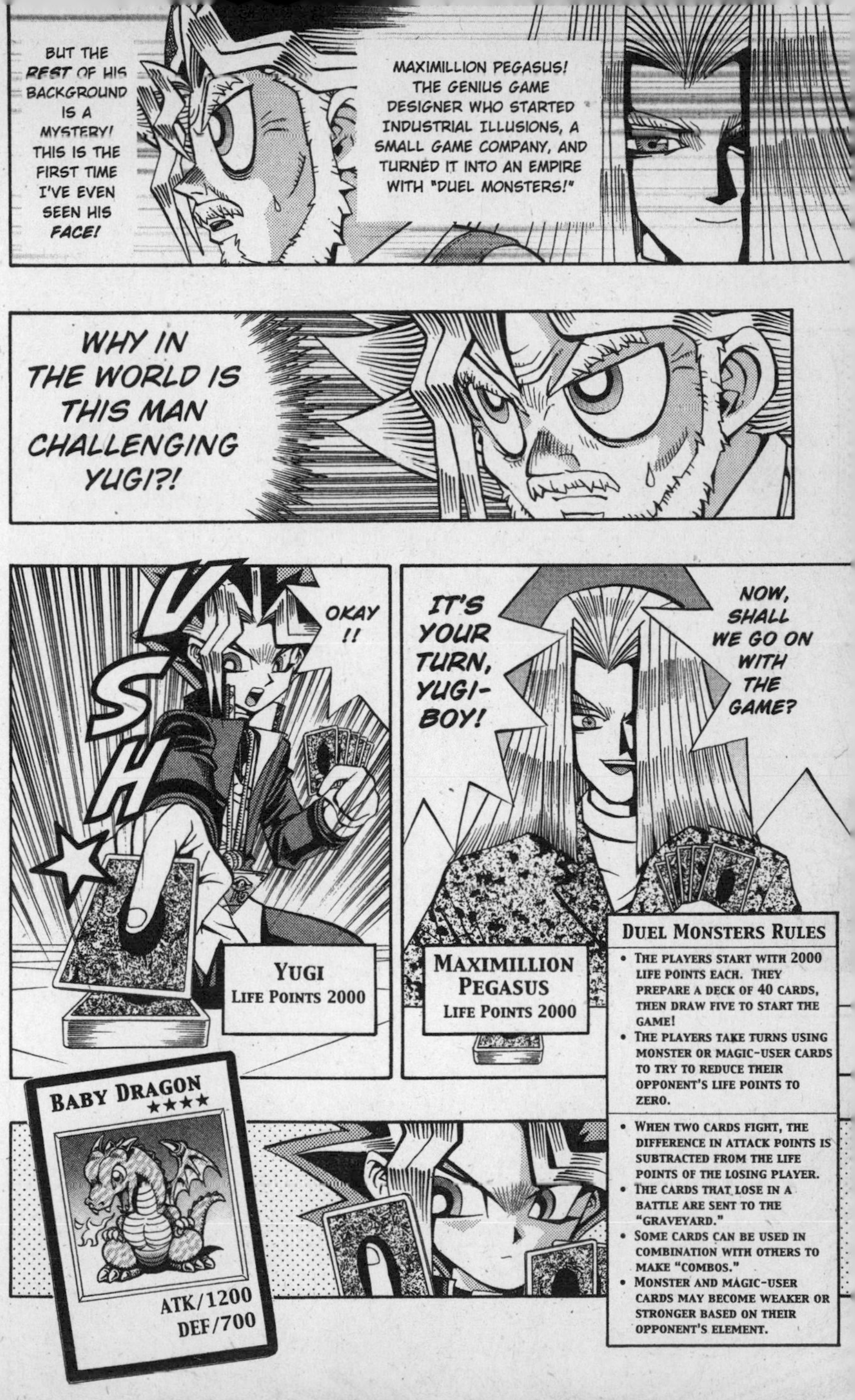
MAXIMILLION PEGASUS! THE GENIUS GAME DESIGNER WHO STARTED INDUSTRIAL ILLUSIONS, A SMALL GAME COMPANY, AND TURNED IT INTO AN EMPIRE WITH "DUEL MONSTERS!"
BUT THE REST OF HIS BACKGROUND IS A MYSTERY! THIS IS THE FIRST TIME I'VE EVEN SEEN HIS FACE!
WHY IN THE WORLD IS THIS MAN CHALLENGING YUGI?!
NOW, SHALL WE GO ON WITH THE GAME?
IT'S YOUR TURN, YUGI-BOY!
MAXIMILLION PEGASUS
LIFE POINTS 2000
DUEL MONSTERS RULES
• THE PLAYERS START WITH 2000 LIFE POINTS EACH. THEY PREPARE A DECK OF 40 CARDS, THEN DRAW FIVE TO START THE GAME!
• THE PLAYERS TAKE TURNS USING MONSTER OR MAGIC-USER CARDS TO TRY TO REDUCE THEIR OPPONENT'S LIFE POINTS TO ZERO.
• WHEN TWO CARDS FIGHT, THE DIFFERENCE IN ATTACK POINTS IS SUBTRACTED FROM THE LIFE POINTS OF THE LOSING PLAYER.
• THE CARDS THAT LOSE IN A BATTLE ARE SENT TO THE "GRAVEYARD."
• SOME CARDS CAN BE USED IN COMBINATION WITH OTHERS TO MAKE "COMBOS."
• MONSTER AND MAGIC-USER CARDS MAY BECOME WEAKER OR STRONGER BASED ON THEIR OPPONENT'S ELEMENT.
OKAY !!
YUGI
LIFE POINTS 2000
BABY DRAGON
★★★★
ATK/1200
DEF/700

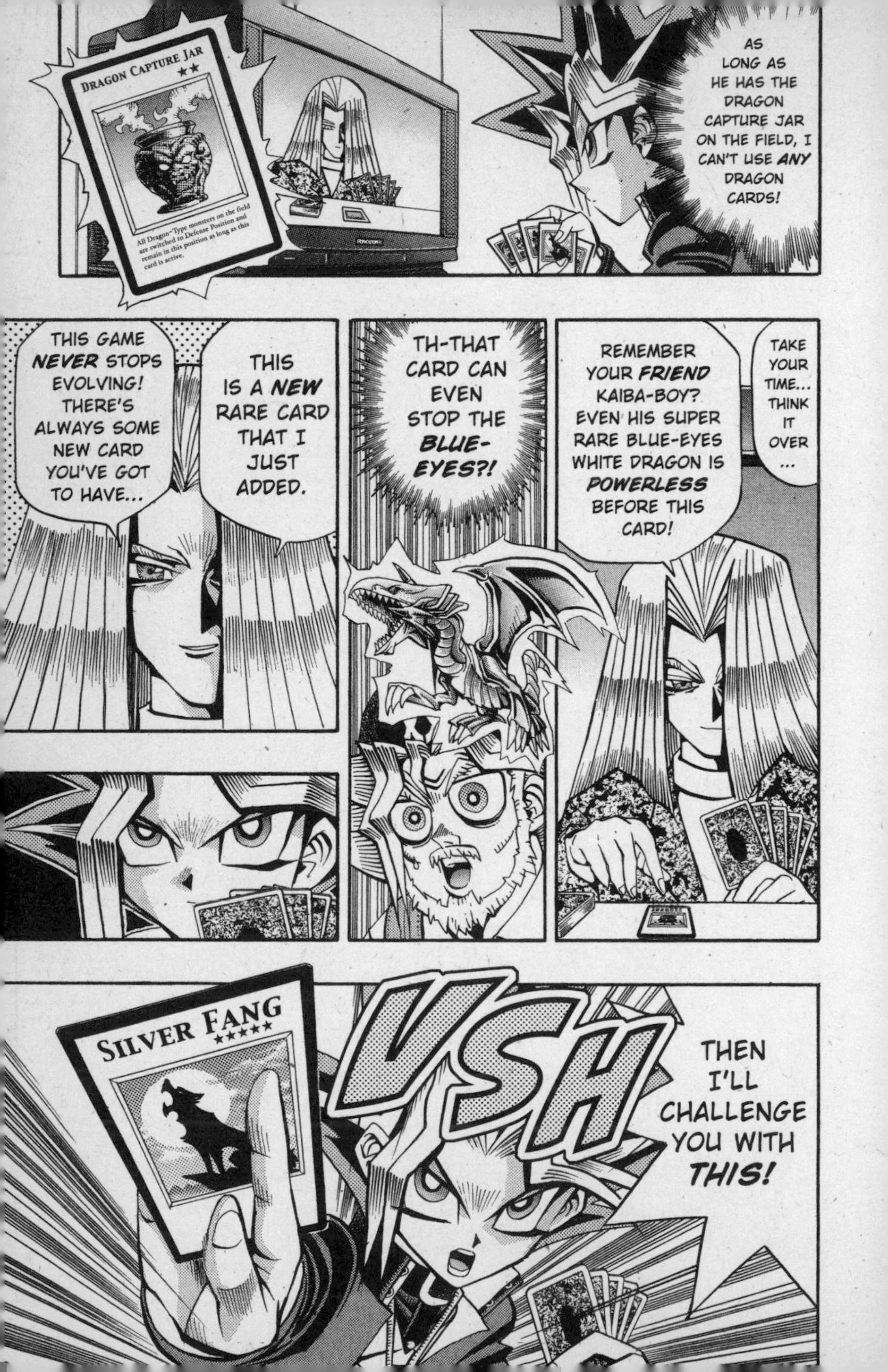
AS LONG AS HE HAS THE DRAGON CAPTURE JAR ON THE FIELD, I CAN'T USE *ANY* DRAGON CARDS!
DRAGON CAPTURE JAR ★★
All Dragon-Type monsters on the field are switched to Defense Position and remain in this position as long as this card is active.
TAKE YOUR TIME... THINK IT OVER...
REMEMBER YOUR *FRIEND* KAIBA-BOY? EVEN HIS SUPER RARE BLUE-EYES WHITE DRAGON IS *POWERLESS* BEFORE THIS CARD!
TH-THAT CARD CAN EVEN STOP THE *BLUE-EYES?!*
THIS IS A *NEW* RARE CARD THAT I JUST ADDED.
THIS GAME *NEVER* STOPS EVOLVING! THERE'S ALWAYS SOME NEW CARD YOU'VE GOT TO HAVE...
THEN I'LL CHALLENGE YOU WITH *THIS!*
VSH
SILVER FANG ★★★★★

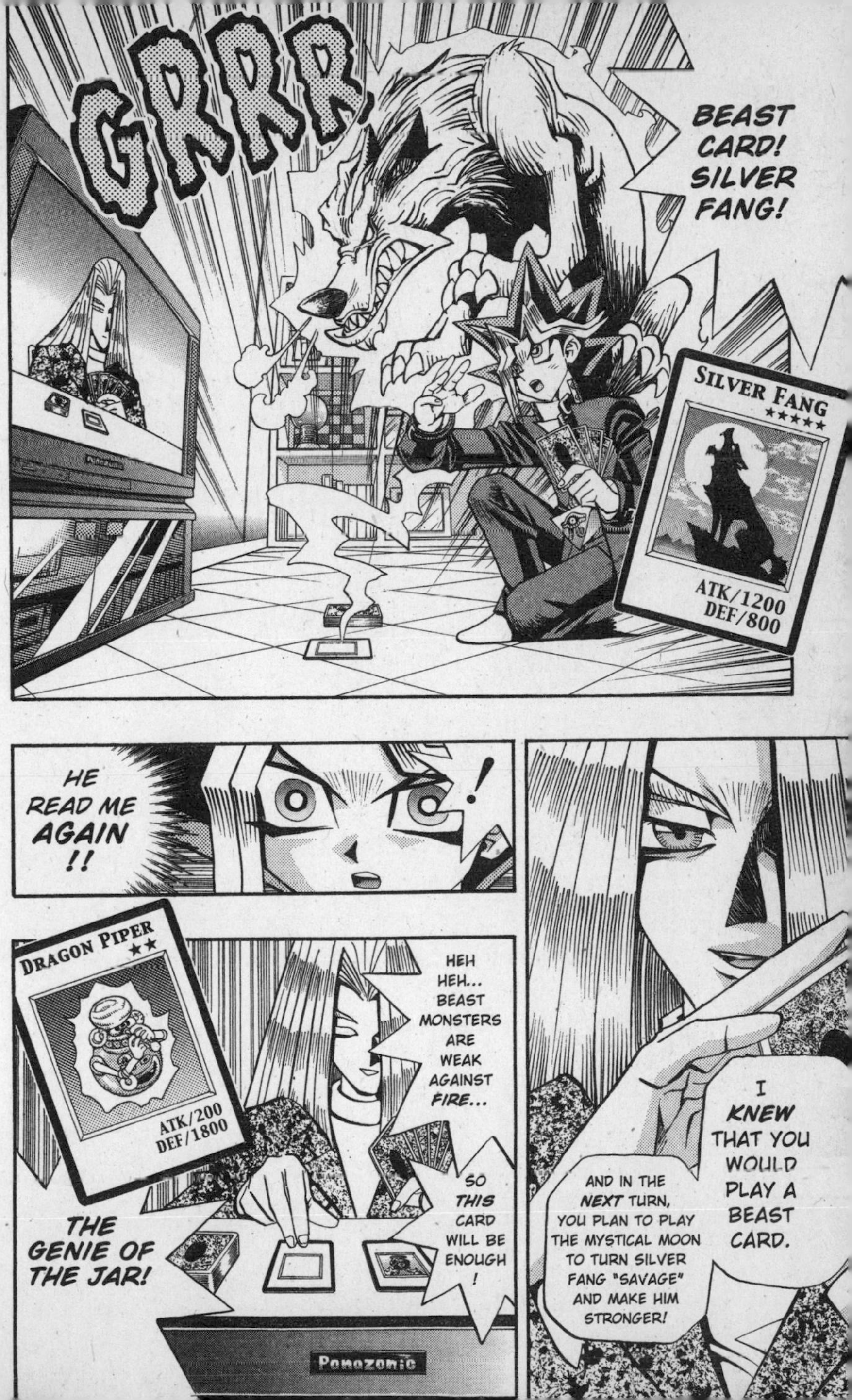
GRRR
BEAST CARD! SILVER FANG!
SILVER FANG ★★★★★
ATK/1200 DEF/800
I KNEW THAT YOU WOULD PLAY A BEAST CARD.
AND IN THE NEXT TURN, YOU PLAN TO PLAY THE MYSTICAL MOON TO TURN SILVER FANG "SAVAGE" AND MAKE HIM STRONGER!
!
HE READ ME AGAIN !!
HEH HEH... BEAST MONSTERS ARE WEAK AGAINST FIRE...
SO THIS CARD WILL BE ENOUGH !
DRAGON PIPER ★★
ATK/200 DEF/1800
THE GENIE OF THE JAR!
Panazonic

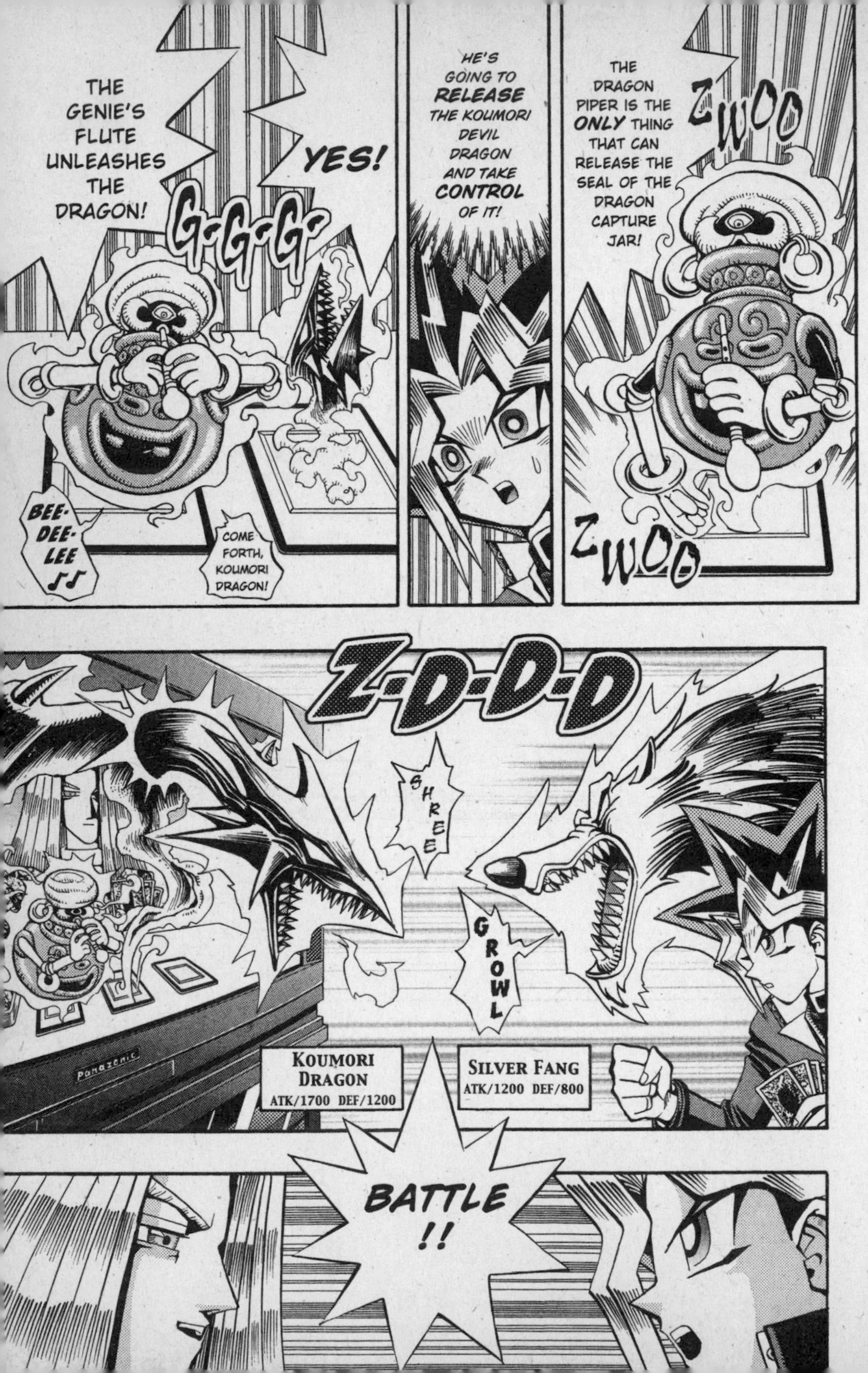
THE DRAGON PIPER IS THE ONLY THING THAT CAN RELEASE THE SEAL OF THE DRAGON CAPTURE JAR!
ZWOO
ZWOO
HE'S GOING TO RELEASE THE KOUMORI DEVIL DRAGON AND TAKE CONTROL OF IT!
YES!
THE GENIE'S FLUTE UNLEASHES THE DRAGON!
G-G-G
COME FORTH, KOUMORI DRAGON!
BEE-DEE-LEE ♪♪
Z-D-D-D
SHREE
GROWL
SILVER FANG ATK/1200 DEF/800
KOUMORI DRAGON ATK/1700 DEF/1200
BATTLE!!

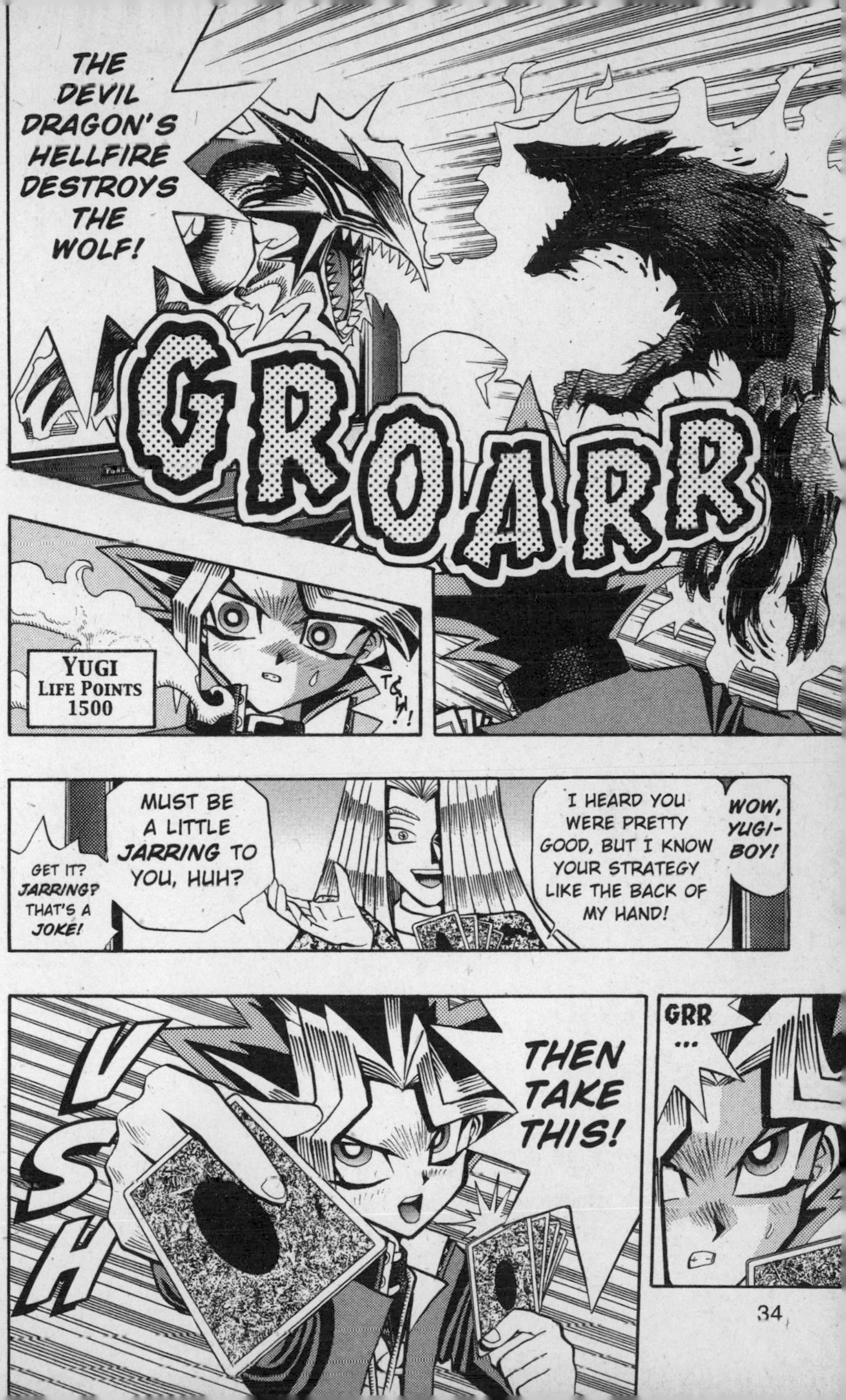
THE DEVIL DRAGON'S HELLFIRE DESTROYS THE WOLF!
GROARR
YUGI LIFE POINTS 1500
TCH!
WOW, YUGI-BOY!
I HEARD YOU WERE PRETTY GOOD, BUT I KNOW YOUR STRATEGY LIKE THE BACK OF MY HAND!
MUST BE A LITTLE *JARRING* TO YOU, HUH?
GET IT? *JARRING?* THAT'S A *JOKE!*
GRR ...
THEN TAKE THIS!
VSSH

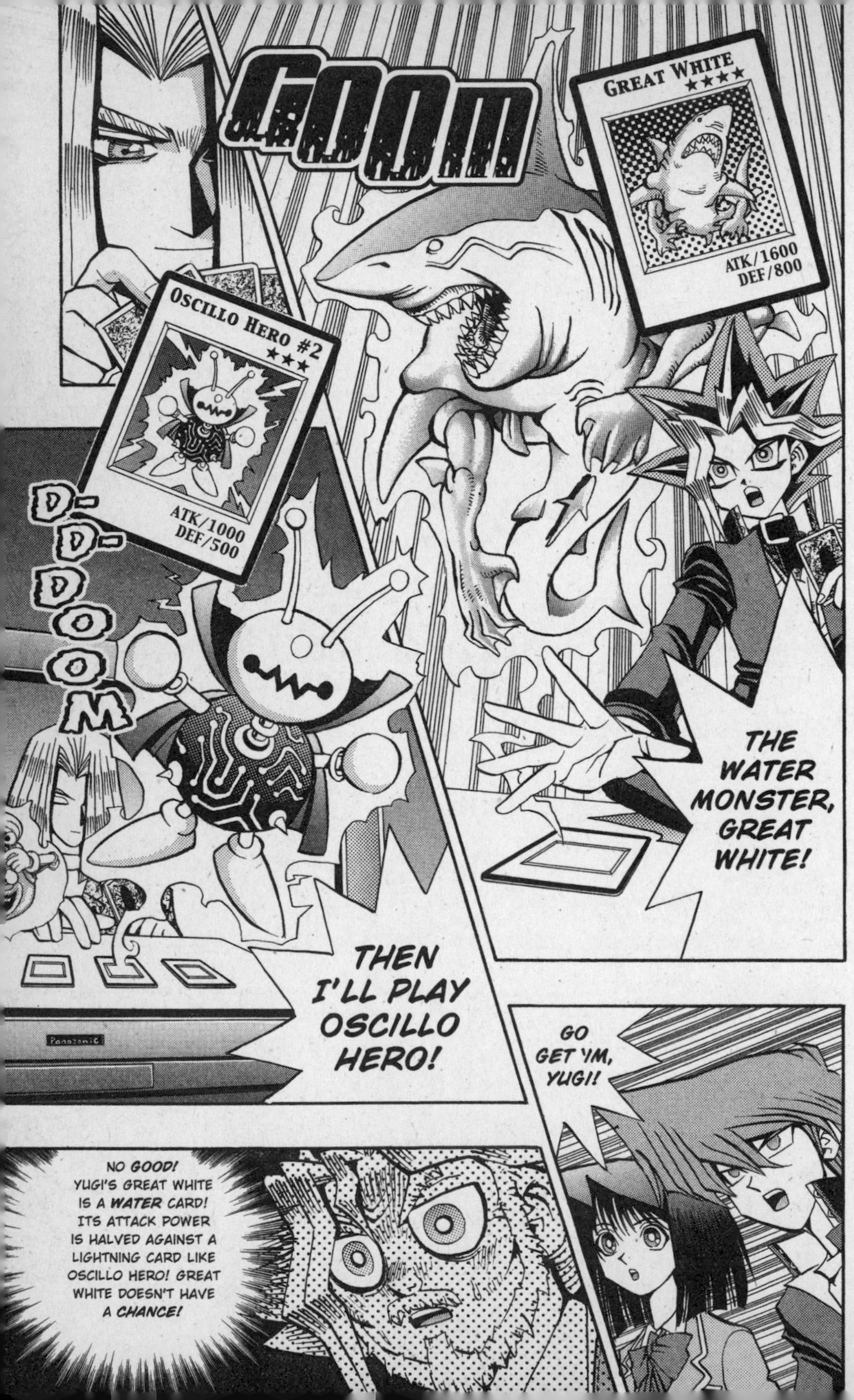

GOOM
GREAT WHITE ★★★★
ATK/1600 DEF/800
THE WATER MONSTER, GREAT WHITE!
OSCILLO HERO #2 ★★★
ATK/1000 DEF/500
D-D-DOOOM
THEN I'LL PLAY OSCILLO HERO!
GO GET 'IM, YUGI!
NO GOOD! YUGI'S GREAT WHITE IS A WATER CARD! ITS ATTACK POWER IS HALVED AGAINST A LIGHTNING CARD LIKE OSCILLO HERO! GREAT WHITE DOESN'T HAVE A CHANCE!

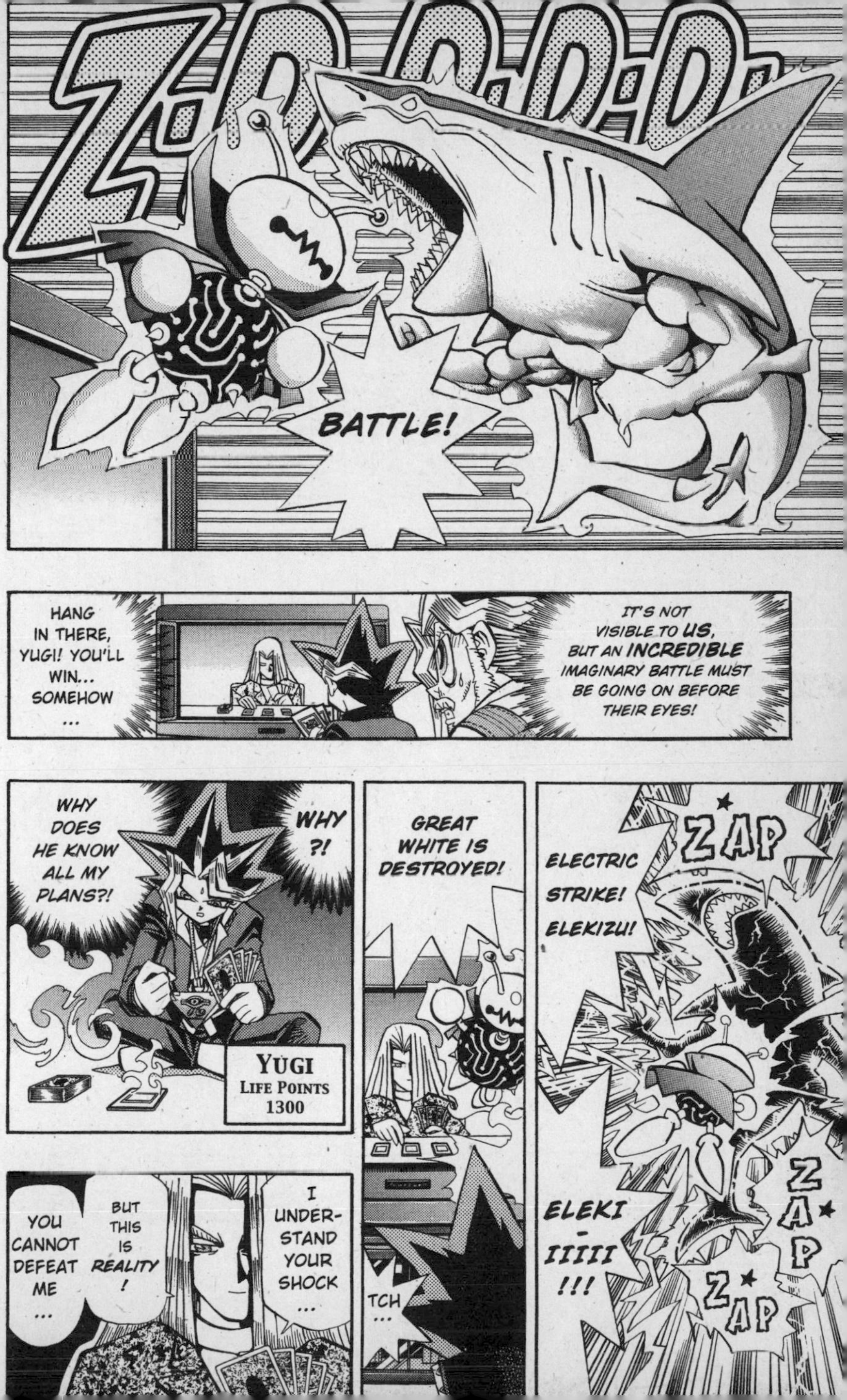
BATTLE!
IT'S NOT VISIBLE TO US, BUT AN INCREDIBLE IMAGINARY BATTLE MUST BE GOING ON BEFORE THEIR EYES!
HANG IN THERE, YUGI! YOU'LL WIN... SOMEHOW...
ZAP
ELECTRIC STRIKE! ELEKIZU!
ELEKI-IIIII!!!
ZAP
ZAP
GREAT WHITE IS DESTROYED!
TCH...
WHY?!
WHY DOES HE KNOW ALL MY PLANS?!
YUGI
LIFE POINTS
1300
I UNDER-STAND YOUR SHOCK...
BUT THIS IS REALITY!
YOU CANNOT DEFEAT ME...

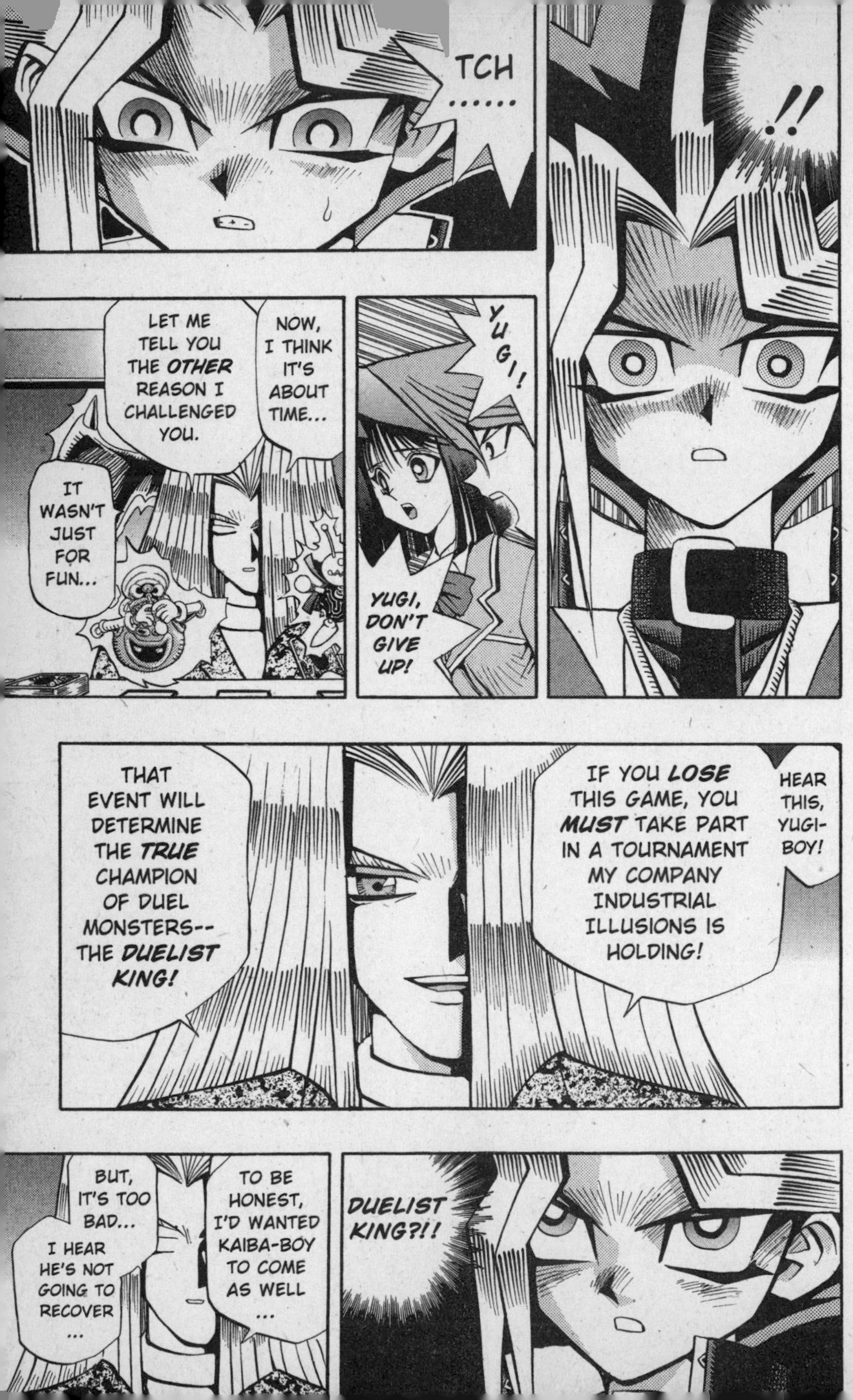
!!
TCH ......
YUGI!
YUGI, DON'T GIVE UP!
NOW, I THINK IT'S ABOUT TIME...
LET ME TELL YOU THE OTHER REASON I CHALLENGED YOU.
IT WASN'T JUST FOR FUN...
HEAR THIS, YUGI-BOY!
IF YOU LOSE THIS GAME, YOU MUST TAKE PART IN A TOURNAMENT MY COMPANY INDUSTRIAL ILLUSIONS IS HOLDING!
THAT EVENT WILL DETERMINE THE TRUE CHAMPION OF DUEL MONSTERS--THE DUELIST KING!
DUELIST KING?!!
TO BE HONEST, I'D WANTED KAIBA-BOY TO COME AS WELL ...
BUT, IT'S TOO BAD...
I HEAR HE'S NOT GOING TO RECOVER ...

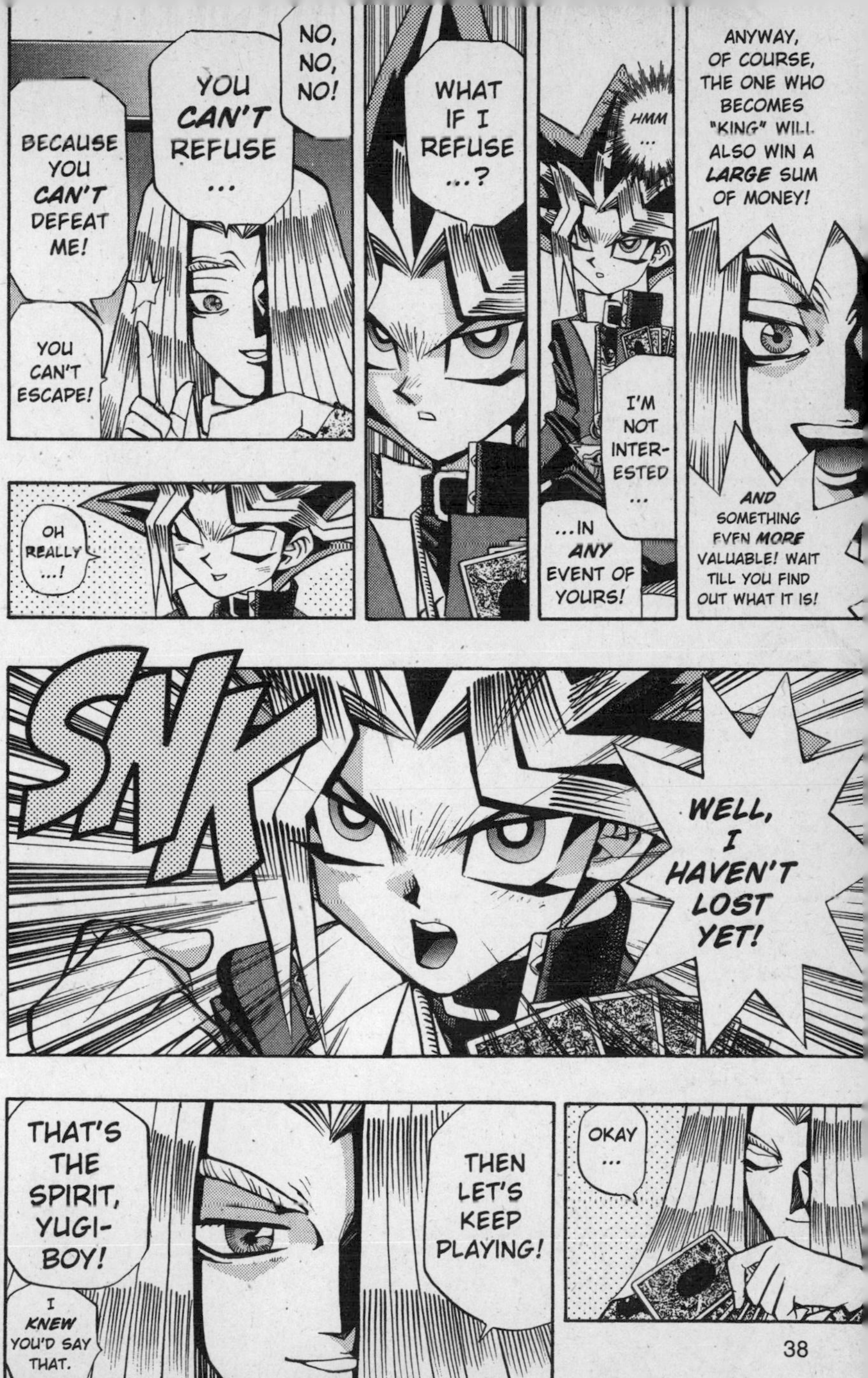
ANYWAY, OF COURSE, THE ONE WHO BECOMES "KING" WILL ALSO WIN A LARGE SUM OF MONEY!
AND SOMETHING EVEN MORE VALUABLE! WAIT TILL YOU FIND OUT WHAT IT IS!
HMM...
I'M NOT INTERESTED...
...IN ANY EVENT OF YOURS!
WHAT IF I REFUSE...?
NO, NO, NO!
YOU CAN'T REFUSE...
BECAUSE YOU CAN'T DEFEAT ME!
YOU CAN'T ESCAPE!
OH REALLY...!
SNK
WELL, I HAVEN'T LOST YET!
OKAY...
THEN LET'S KEEP PLAYING!
THAT'S THE SPIRIT, YUGI-BOY!
I KNEW YOU'D SAY THAT.

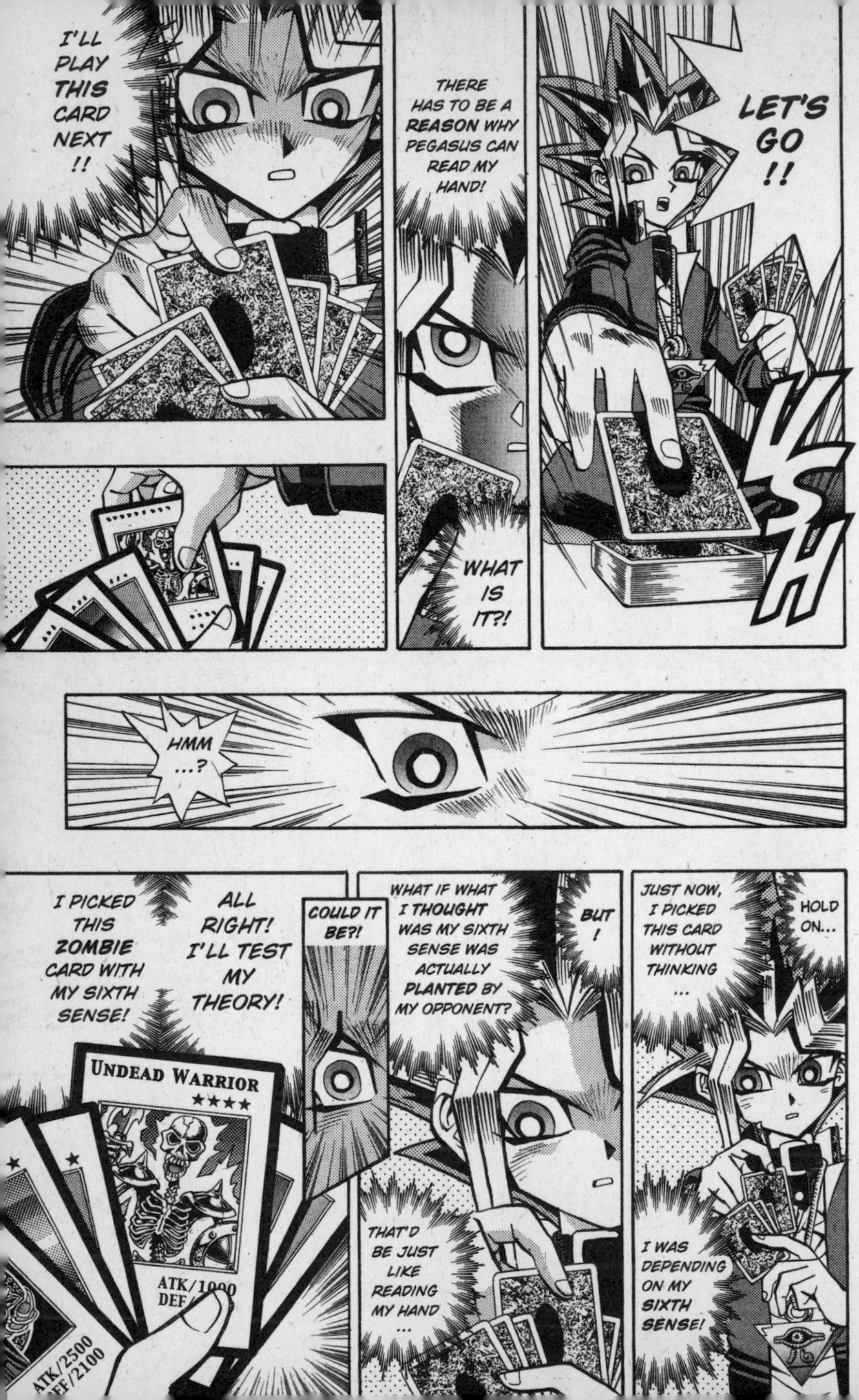
LET'S GO !!
WSH
THERE HAS TO BE A REASON WHY PEGASUS CAN READ MY HAND!
WHAT IS IT?!
I'LL PLAY THIS CARD NEXT !!
HMM ...?
HOLD ON...
JUST NOW, I PICKED THIS CARD WITHOUT THINKING ...
I WAS DEPENDING ON MY SIXTH SENSE!
BUT !
WHAT IF WHAT I THOUGHT WAS MY SIXTH SENSE WAS ACTUALLY PLANTED BY MY OPPONENT?
THAT'D BE JUST LIKE READING MY HAND ...
COULD IT BE?!
ALL RIGHT! I'LL TEST MY THEORY!
I PICKED THIS ZOMBIE CARD WITH MY SIXTH SENSE!
UNDEAD WARRIOR
ATK/1000
ATK/2500

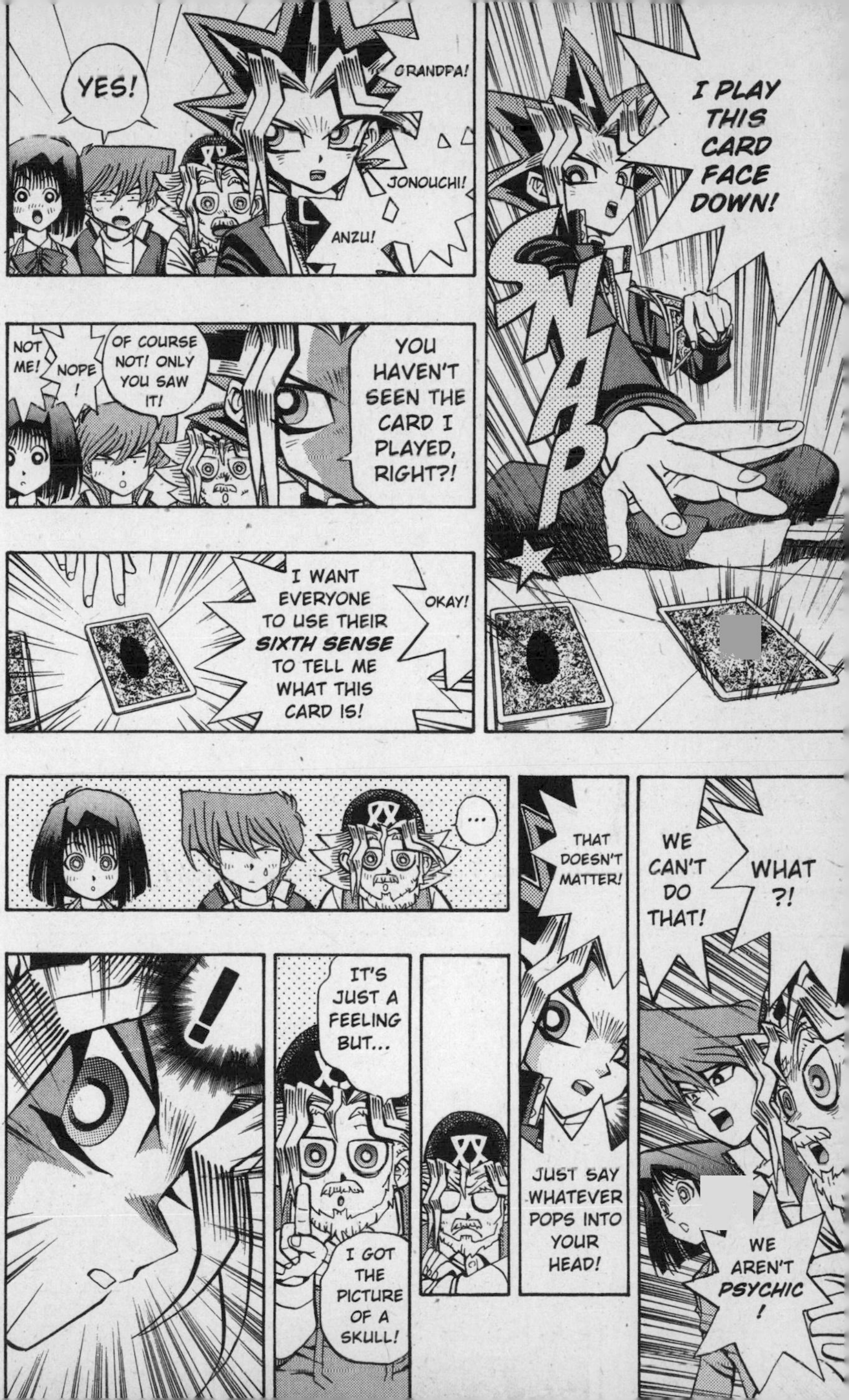

I PLAY THIS CARD FACE DOWN!
SNAP
GRANDPA!
JONOUCHI!
ANZU!
YES!
YOU HAVEN'T SEEN THE CARD I PLAYED, RIGHT?!
OF COURSE NOT! ONLY YOU SAW IT!
NOPE!
NOT ME!
OKAY!
I WANT EVERYONE TO USE THEIR *SIXTH SENSE* TO TELL ME WHAT THIS CARD IS!
WHAT?!
WE CAN'T DO THAT!
WE AREN'T *PSYCHIC*!
THAT DOESN'T MATTER!
JUST SAY WHATEVER POPS INTO YOUR HEAD!
...
IT'S JUST A FEELING BUT...
I GOT THE PICTURE OF A SKULL!
!

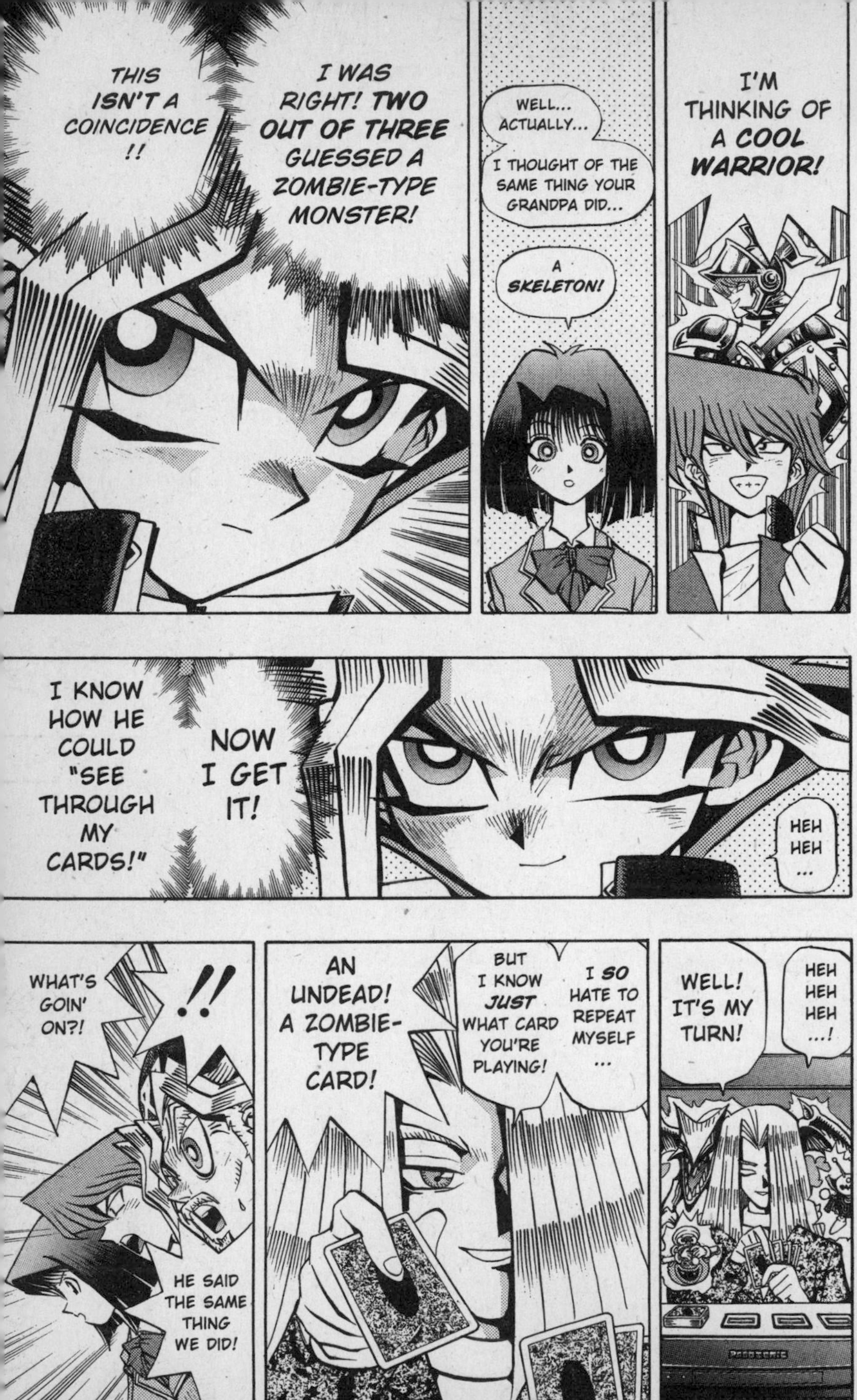
I'M THINKING OF A COOL WARRIOR!
WELL... ACTUALLY...
I THOUGHT OF THE SAME THING YOUR GRANDPA DID...
A SKELETON!
I WAS RIGHT! TWO OUT OF THREE GUESSED A ZOMBIE-TYPE MONSTER!
THIS ISN'T A COINCIDENCE !!
HEH HEH ...
NOW I GET IT!
I KNOW HOW HE COULD "SEE THROUGH MY CARDS!"
HEH HEH HEH ...!
WELL! IT'S MY TURN!
I SO HATE TO REPEAT MYSELF ...
BUT I KNOW JUST WHAT CARD YOU'RE PLAYING!
AN UNDEAD! A ZOMBIE-TYPE CARD!
!!
WHAT'S GOIN' ON?!
HE SAID THE SAME THING WE DID!

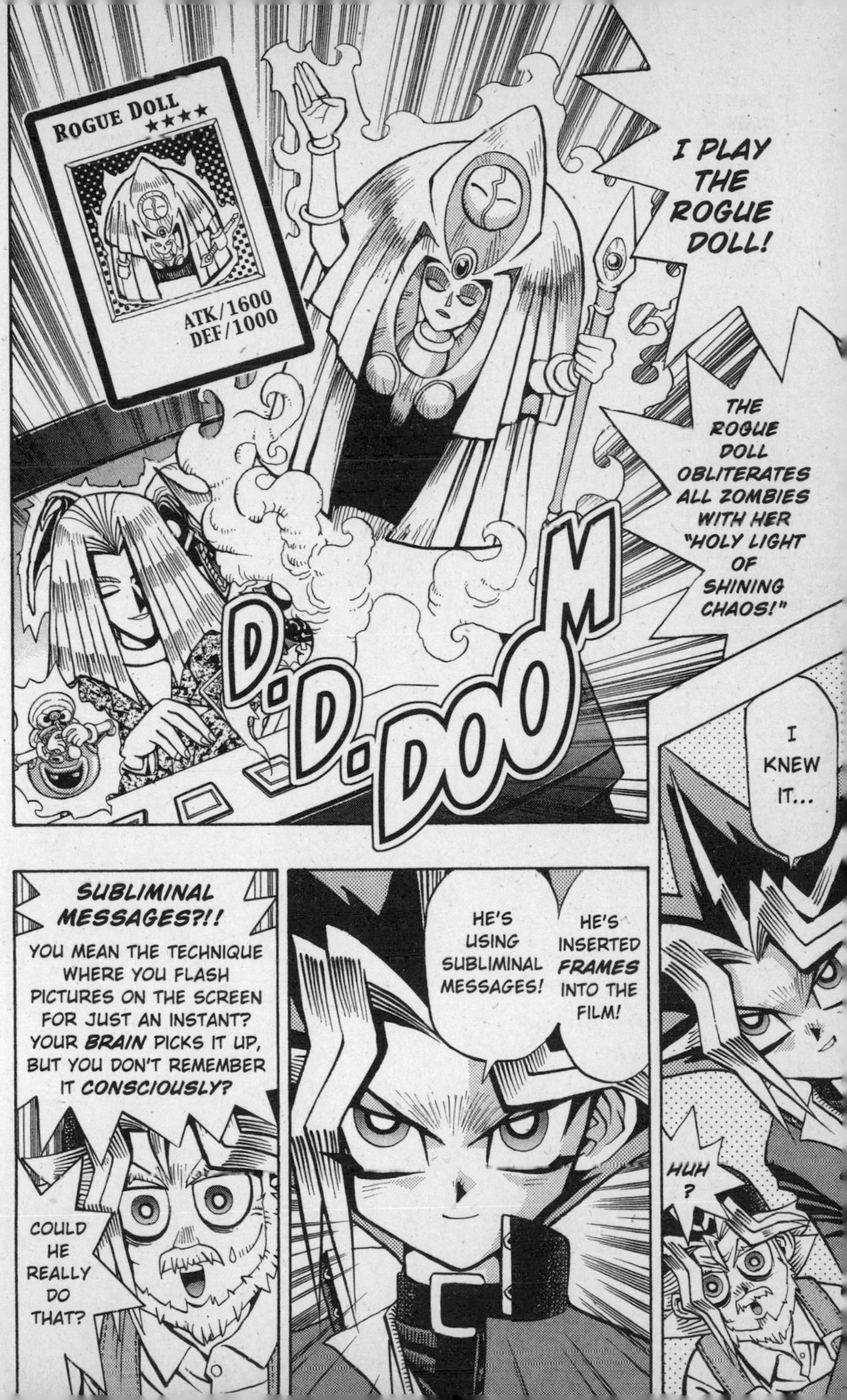
ROGUE DOLL ★★★★
ATK/1600 DEF/1000
I PLAY THE ROGUE DOLL!
THE ROGUE DOLL OBLITERATES ALL ZOMBIES WITH HER "HOLY LIGHT OF SHINING CHAOS!"
D.D.DOOM
I KNEW IT...
HUH ?
HE'S USING SUBLIMINAL MESSAGES!
HE'S INSERTED FRAMES INTO THE FILM!
SUBLIMINAL MESSAGES?!!
YOU MEAN THE TECHNIQUE WHERE YOU FLASH PICTURES ON THE SCREEN FOR JUST AN INSTANT? YOUR BRAIN PICKS IT UP, BUT YOU DON'T REMEMBER IT CONSCIOUSLY?
COULD HE REALLY DO THAT?

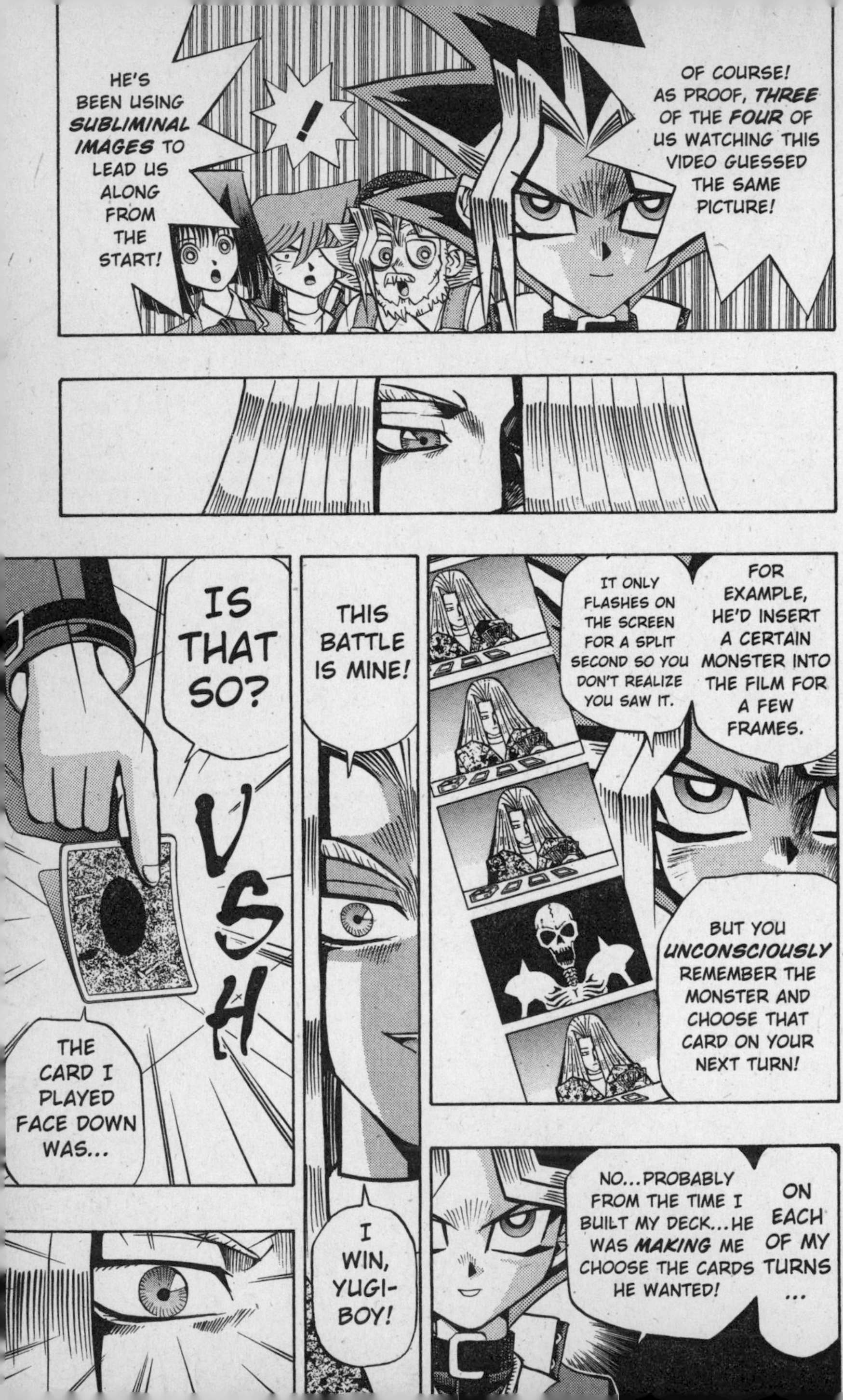

OF COURSE! AS PROOF, THREE OF THE FOUR OF US WATCHING THIS VIDEO GUESSED THE SAME PICTURE!
!
HE'S BEEN USING SUBLIMINAL IMAGES TO LEAD US ALONG FROM THE START!
FOR EXAMPLE, HE'D INSERT A CERTAIN MONSTER INTO THE FILM FOR A FEW FRAMES.
IT ONLY FLASHES ON THE SCREEN FOR A SPLIT SECOND SO YOU DON'T REALIZE YOU SAW IT.
BUT YOU UNCONSCIOUSLY REMEMBER THE MONSTER AND CHOOSE THAT CARD ON YOUR NEXT TURN!
ON EACH OF MY TURNS ...
NO...PROBABLY FROM THE TIME I BUILT MY DECK...HE WAS MAKING ME CHOOSE THE CARDS HE WANTED!
THIS BATTLE IS MINE!
I WIN, YUGI-BOY!
IS THAT SO?
VSH
THE CARD I PLAYED FACE DOWN WAS...

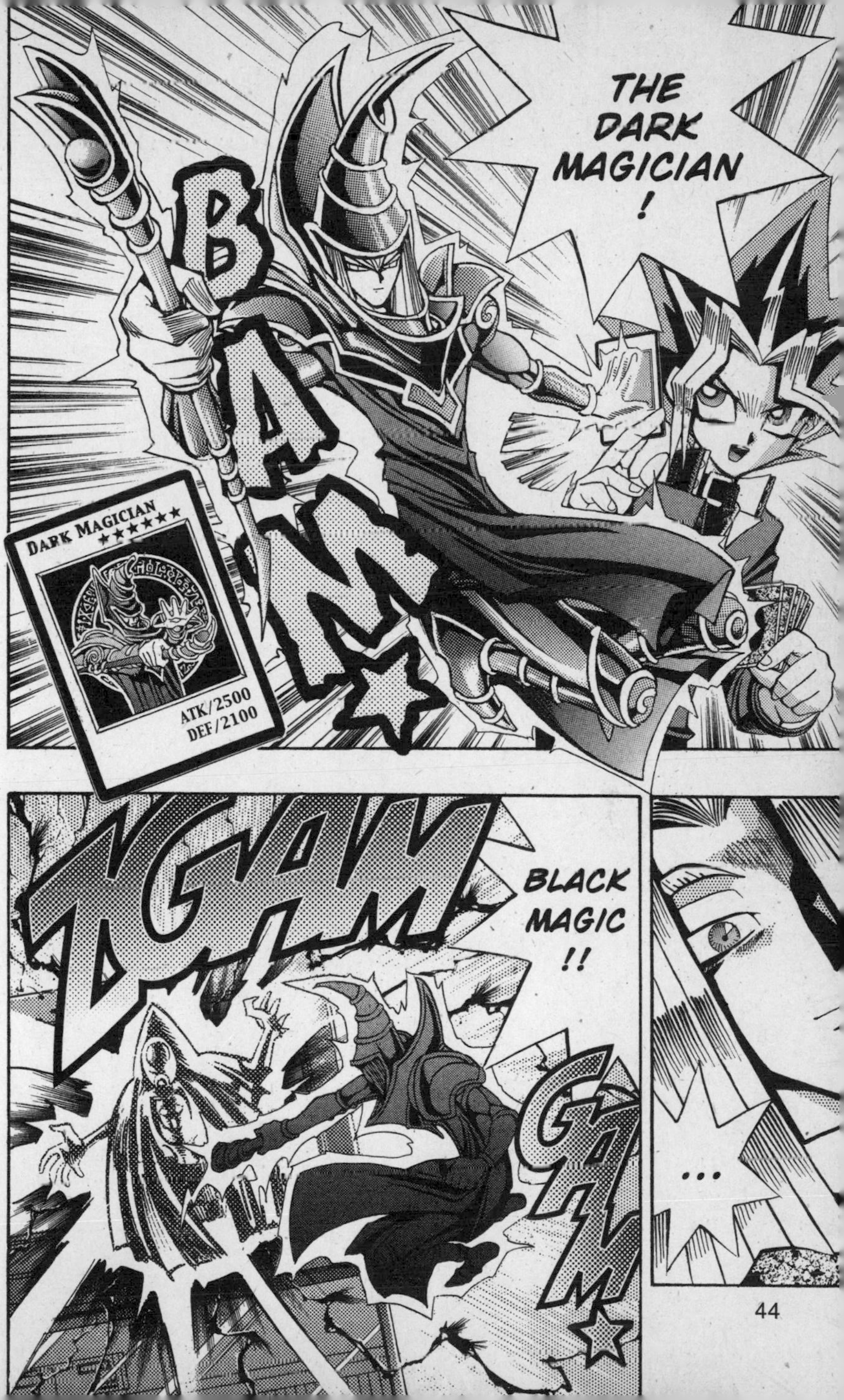
THE DARK MAGICIAN !
BAM
DARK MAGICIAN
ATK/2500
DEF/2100
...
BLACK MAGIC !!
GAM

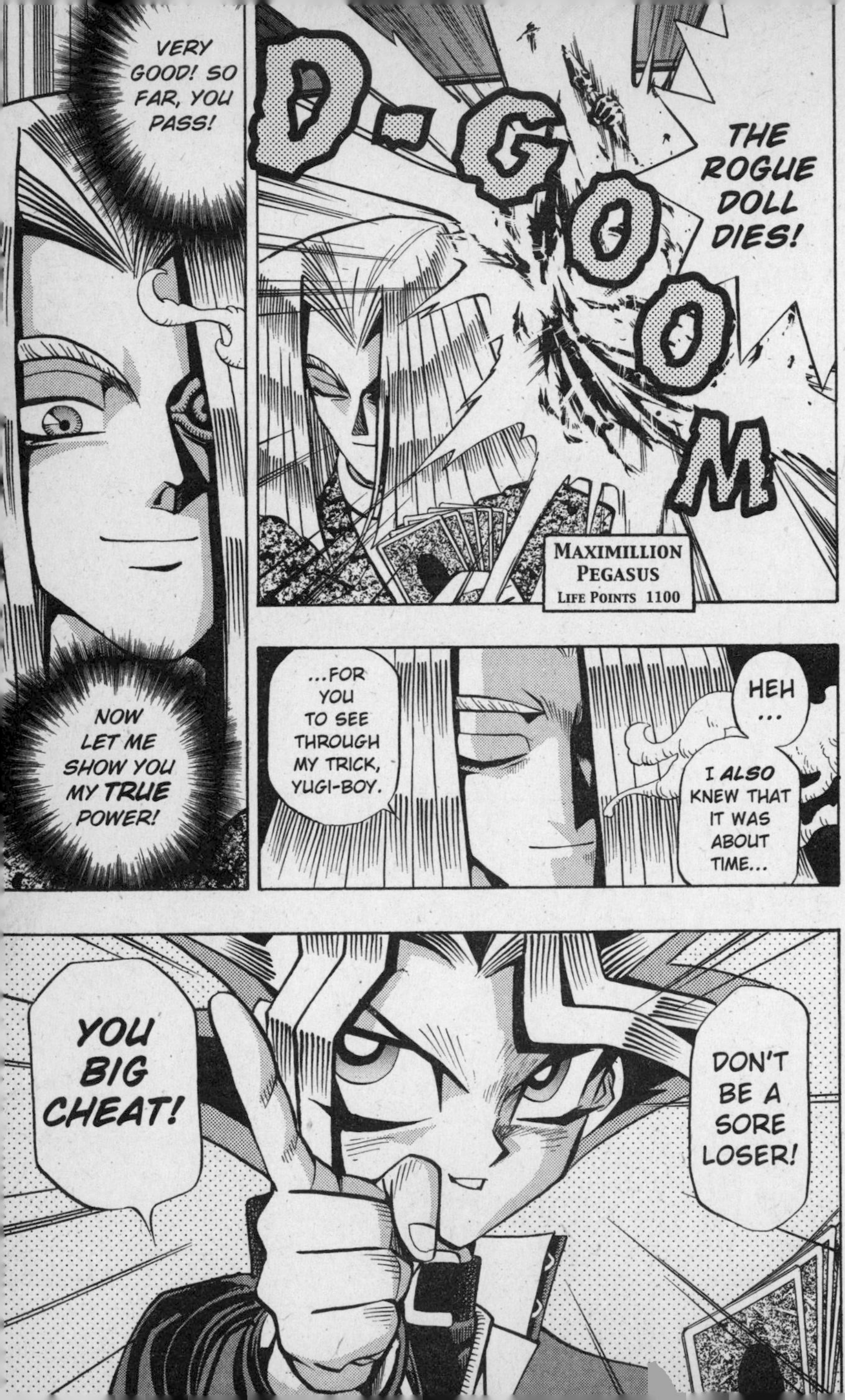
D-GOOOM
THE ROGUE DOLL DIES!
MAXIMILLION PEGASUS LIFE POINTS 1100
HEH...
I ALSO KNEW THAT IT WAS ABOUT TIME...
...FOR YOU TO SEE THROUGH MY TRICK, YUGI-BOY.
VERY GOOD! SO FAR, YOU PASS!
NOW LET ME SHOW YOU MY TRUE POWER!
DON'T BE A SORE LOSER!
YOU BIG CHEAT!

DUEL 3: COUNTDOWN!!

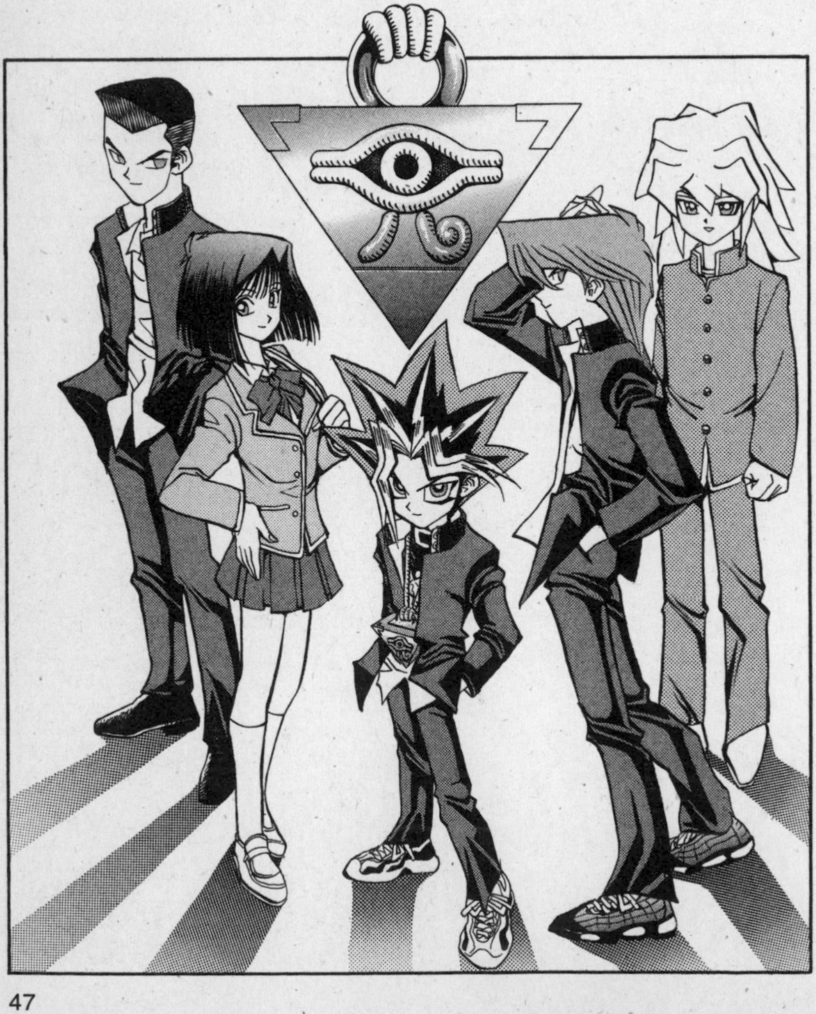

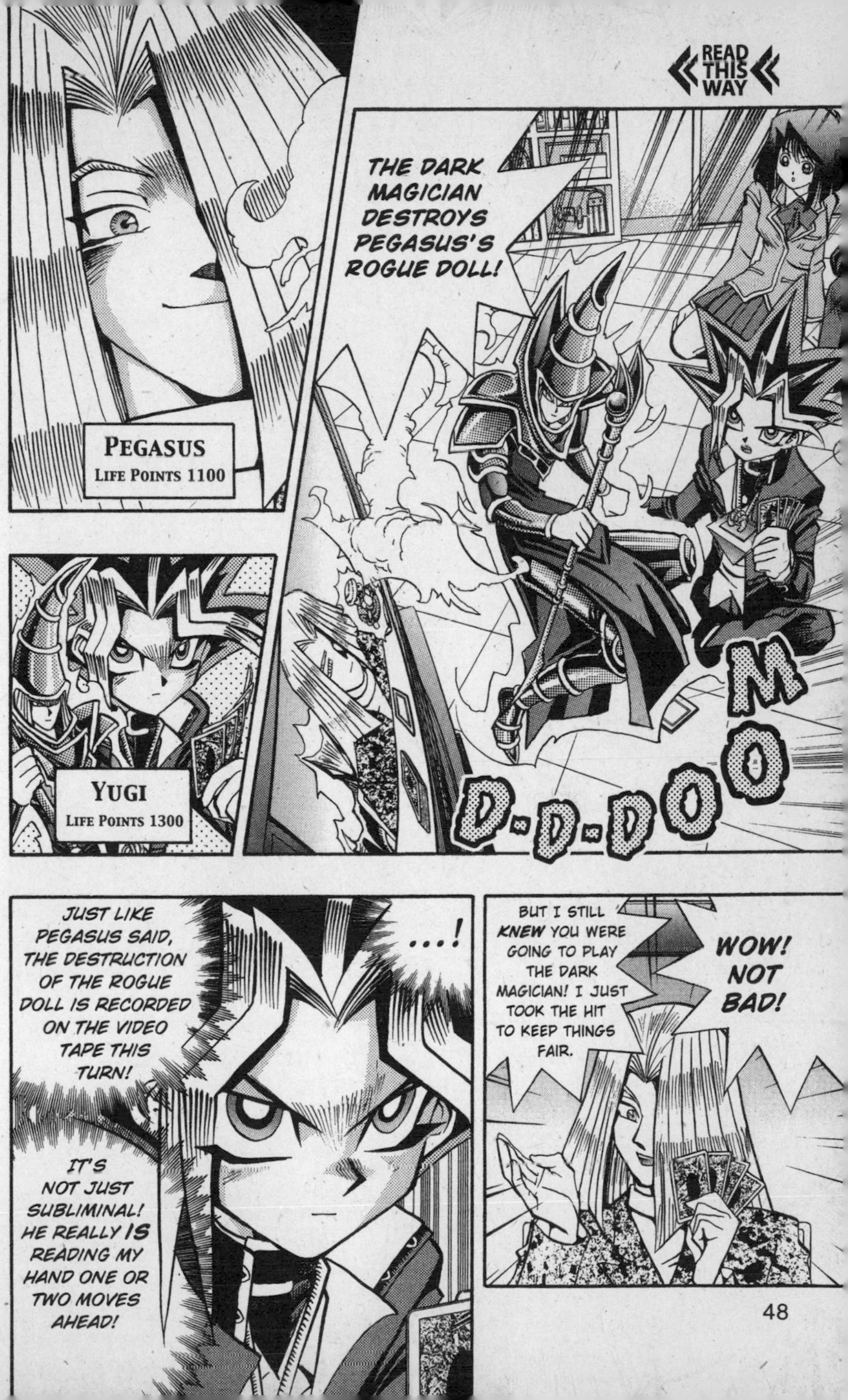
READ THIS WAY
THE DARK MAGICIAN DESTROYS PEGASUS'S ROGUE DOLL!
D-D-DOOOM
PEGASUS
LIFE POINTS 1100
YUGI
LIFE POINTS 1300
WOW! NOT BAD!
BUT I STILL KNEW YOU WERE GOING TO PLAY THE DARK MAGICIAN! I JUST TOOK THE HIT TO KEEP THINGS FAIR.
...!
JUST LIKE PEGASUS SAID, THE DESTRUCTION OF THE ROGUE DOLL IS RECORDED ON THE VIDEO TAPE THIS TURN!
IT'S NOT JUST SUBLIMINAL! HE REALLY IS READING MY HAND ONE OR TWO MOVES AHEAD!

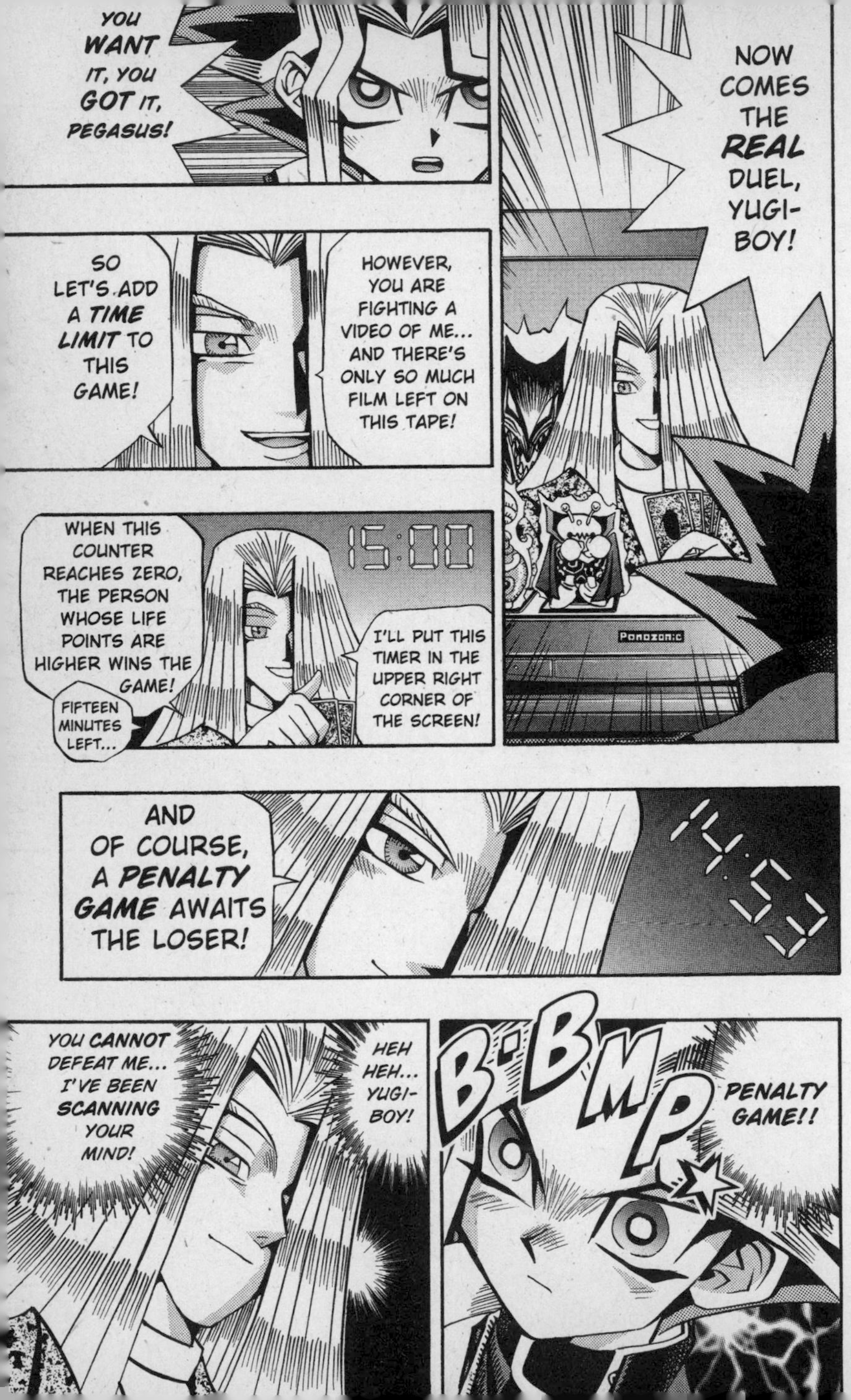
NOW COMES THE REAL DUEL, YUGI-BOY!
YOU WANT IT, YOU GOT IT, PEGASUS!
HOWEVER, YOU ARE FIGHTING A VIDEO OF ME... AND THERE'S ONLY SO MUCH FILM LEFT ON THIS TAPE!
SO LET'S ADD A TIME LIMIT TO THIS GAME!
15:00
I'LL PUT THIS TIMER IN THE UPPER RIGHT CORNER OF THE SCREEN!
WHEN THIS COUNTER REACHES ZERO, THE PERSON WHOSE LIFE POINTS ARE HIGHER WINS THE GAME!
FIFTEEN MINUTES LEFT...
14:59
AND OF COURSE, A PENALTY GAME AWAITS THE LOSER!
B-BMP
PENALTY GAME!!
HEH HEH... YUGI-BOY!
YOU CANNOT DEFEAT ME... I'VE BEEN SCANNING YOUR MIND!

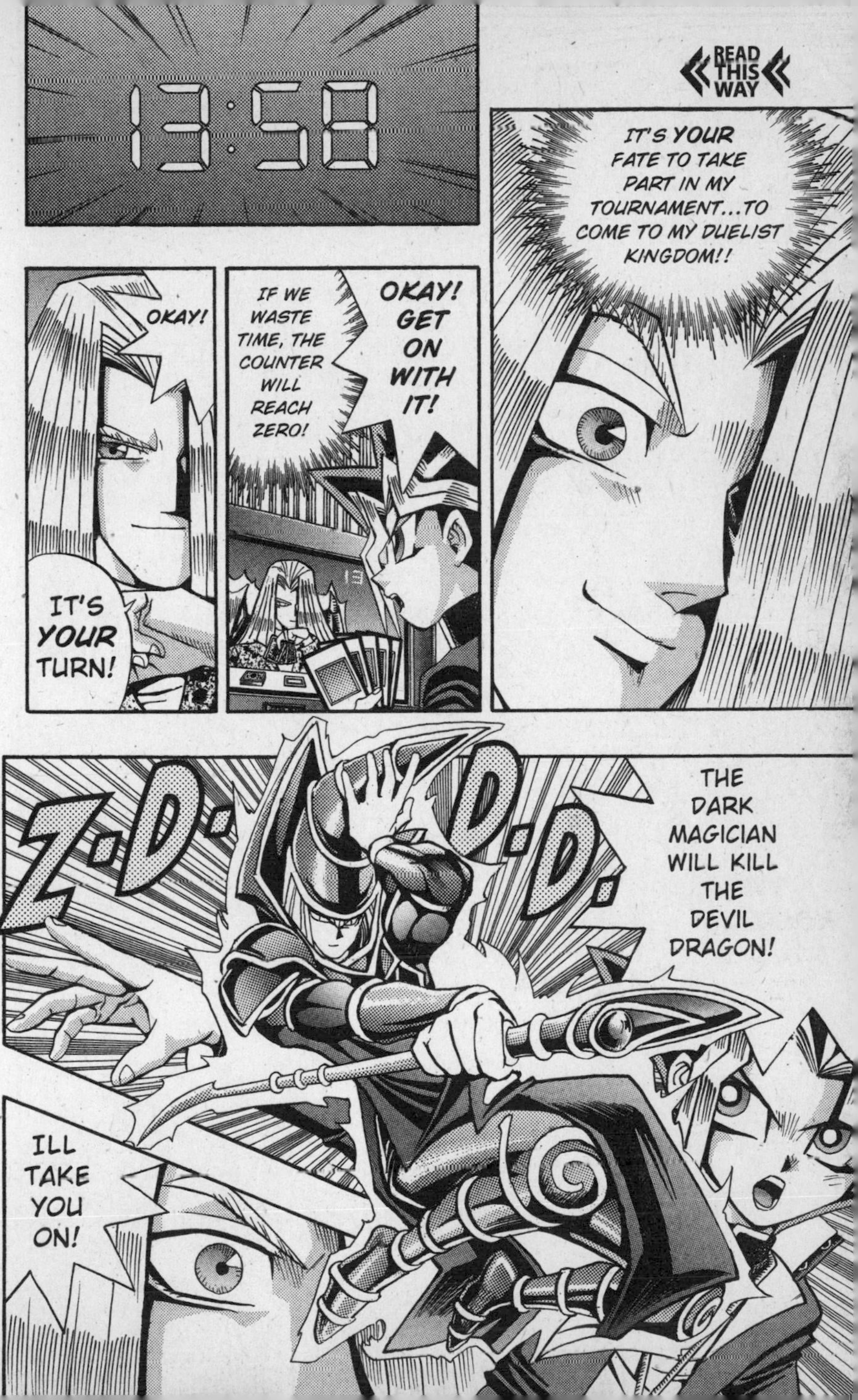
READ THIS WAY
IT'S YOUR FATE TO TAKE PART IN MY TOURNAMENT...TO COME TO MY DUELIST KINGDOM!!
13:58
OKAY! GET ON WITH IT!
IF WE WASTE TIME, THE COUNTER WILL REACH ZERO!
OKAY!
IT'S YOUR TURN!
THE DARK MAGICIAN WILL KILL THE DEVIL DRAGON!
Z-D-D-D
ILL TAKE YOU ON!

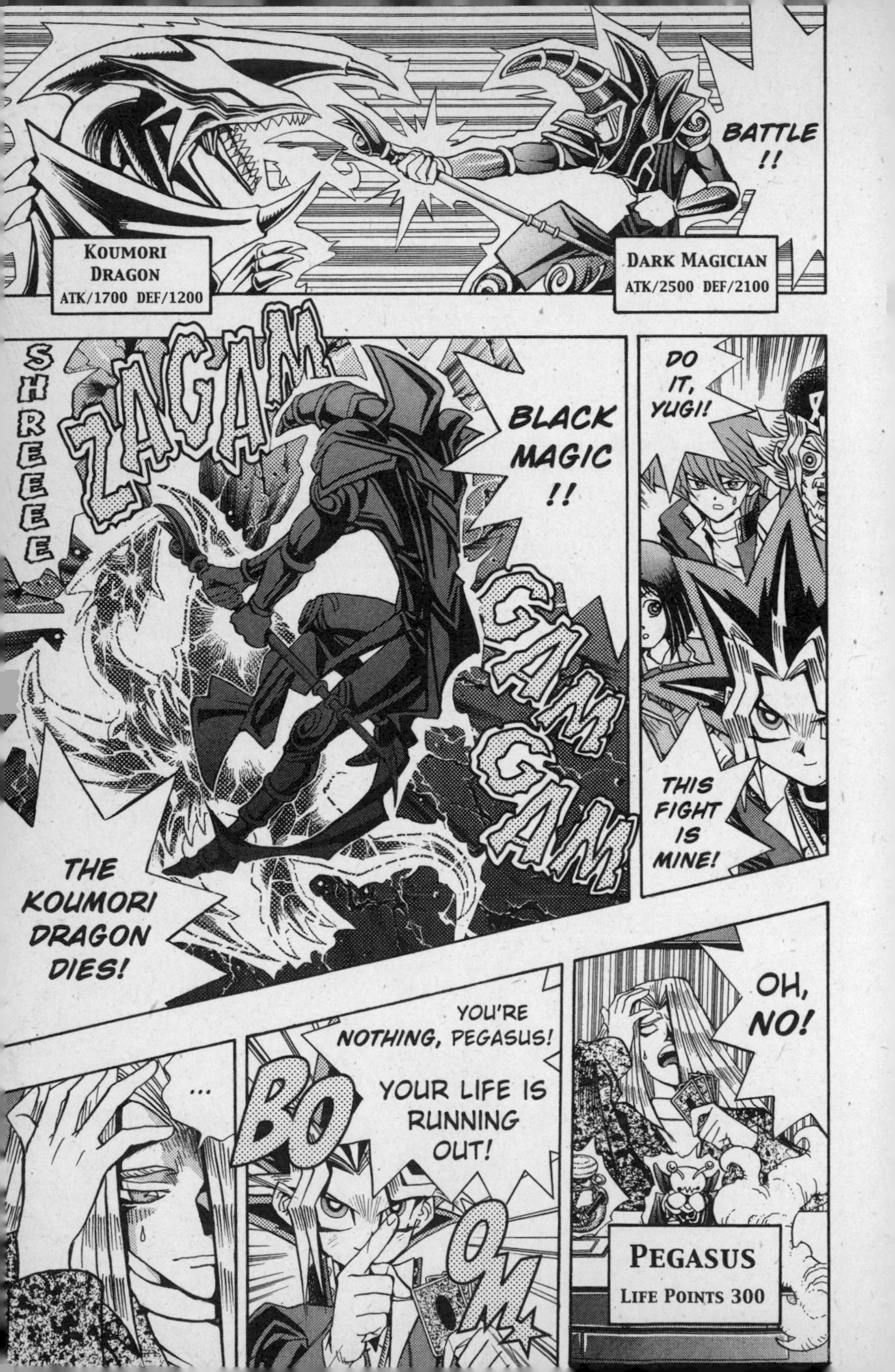
BATTLE !!
DARK MAGICIAN ATK/2500 DEF/2100
KOUMORI DRAGON ATK/1700 DEF/1200
DO IT, YUGI!
THIS FIGHT IS MINE!
BLACK MAGIC !!
ZAGAM
SHREEEE
GAM GAM
THE KOUMORI DRAGON DIES!
OH, NO!
PEGASUS LIFE POINTS 300
YOU'RE NOTHING, PEGASUS!
YOUR LIFE IS RUNNING OUT!
BOOM
...

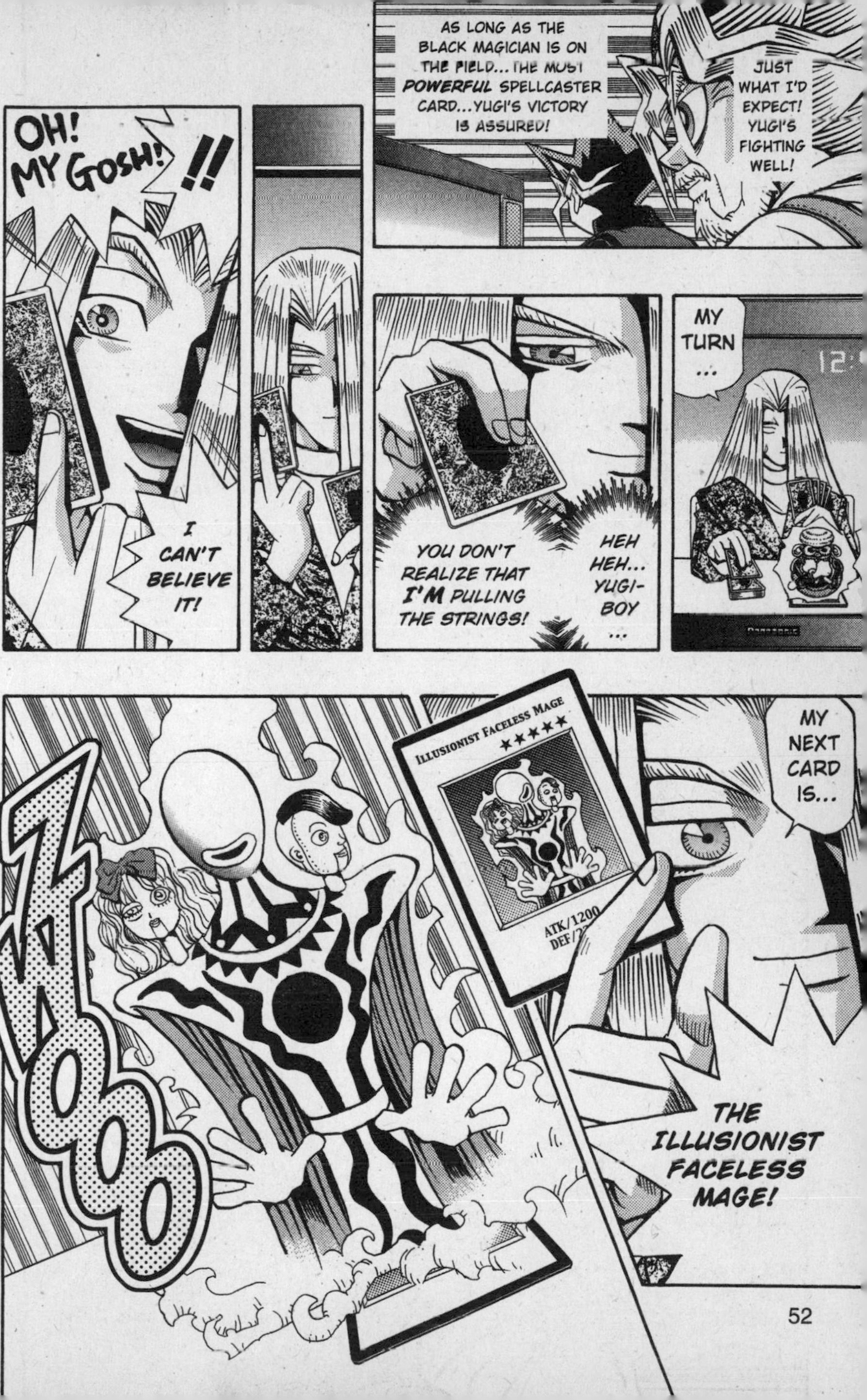
JUST WHAT I'D EXPECT! YUGI'S FIGHTING WELL!
AS LONG AS THE BLACK MAGICIAN IS ON THE FIELD... THE MOST POWERFUL SPELLCASTER CARD...YUGI'S VICTORY IS ASSURED!
MY TURN ...
HEH HEH... YUGI-BOY ...
YOU DON'T REALIZE THAT I'M PULLING THE STRINGS!
OH! MY GOSH!!
I CAN'T BELIEVE IT!
MY NEXT CARD IS...
ILLUSIONIST FACELESS MAGE
ATK/1200
THE ILLUSIONIST FACELESS MAGE!
ZOOOO

READ THIS WAY

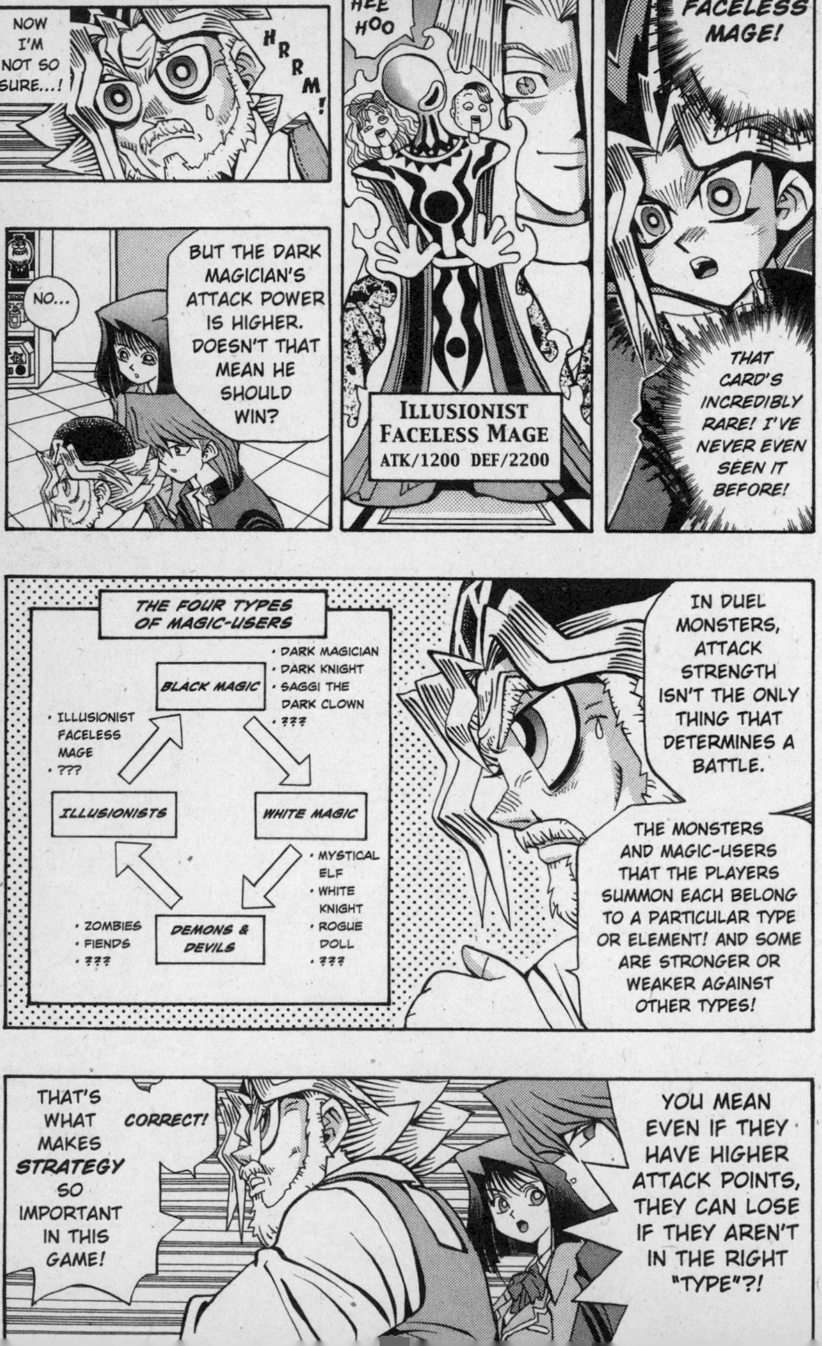
THE FACELESS MAGE!
THAT CARD'S INCREDIBLY RARE! I'VE NEVER EVEN SEEN IT BEFORE!
HEE HOO HEE HOO
ILLUSIONIST FACELESS MAGE
ATK/1200 DEF/2200
HRRM!
NOW I'M NOT SO SURE...!
BUT THE DARK MAGICIAN'S ATTACK POWER IS HIGHER. DOESN'T THAT MEAN HE SHOULD WIN?
NO...
IN DUEL MONSTERS, ATTACK STRENGTH ISN'T THE ONLY THING THAT DETERMINES A BATTLE.
THE MONSTERS AND MAGIC-USERS THAT THE PLAYERS SUMMON EACH BELONG TO A PARTICULAR TYPE OR ELEMENT! AND SOME ARE STRONGER OR WEAKER AGAINST OTHER TYPES!
THE FOUR TYPES OF MAGIC-USERS
BLACK MAGIC
• DARK MAGICIAN
• DARK KNIGHT
• SAGGI THE DARK CLOWN
• ???
WHITE MAGIC
• MYSTICAL ELF
• WHITE KNIGHT
• ROGUE DOLL
• ???
DEMONS & DEVILS
• ZOMBIES
• FIENDS
• ???
ILLUSIONISTS
• ILLUSIONIST FACELESS MAGE
• ???
YOU MEAN EVEN IF THEY HAVE HIGHER ATTACK POINTS, THEY CAN LOSE IF THEY AREN'T IN THE RIGHT "TYPE"?!
CORRECT!
THAT'S WHAT MAKES STRATEGY SO IMPORTANT IN THIS GAME!

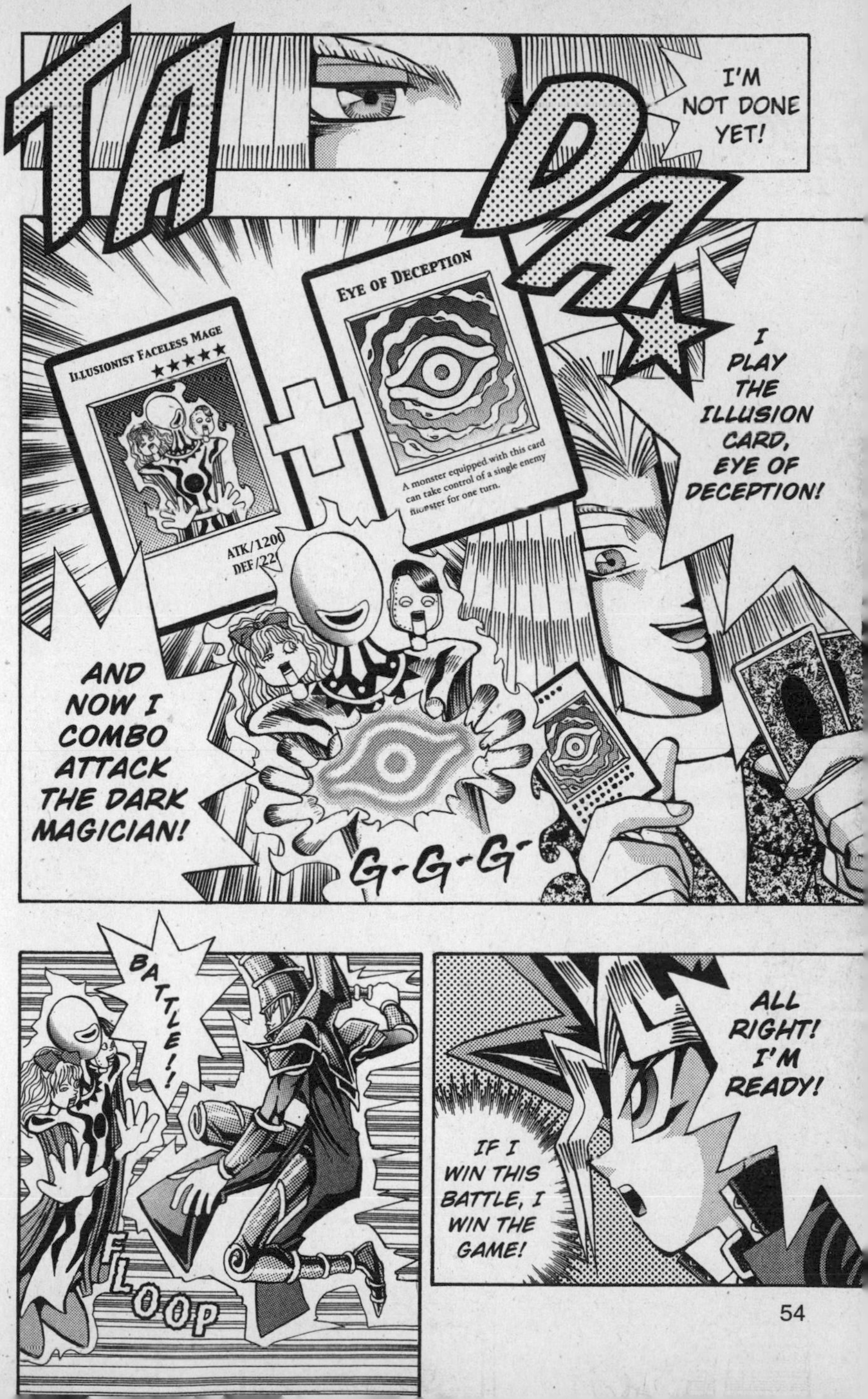
TA DA
I'M NOT DONE YET!
I PLAY THE ILLUSION CARD, EYE OF DECEPTION!
EYE OF DECEPTION
A monster equipped with this card can take control of a single enemy monster for one turn.
ILLUSIONIST FACELESS MAGE
ATK/1200
DEF/22
AND NOW I COMBO ATTACK THE DARK MAGICIAN!
G-G-G
ALL RIGHT! I'M READY!
IF I WIN THIS BATTLE, I WIN THE GAME!
BATTLE!!
FLOOOP

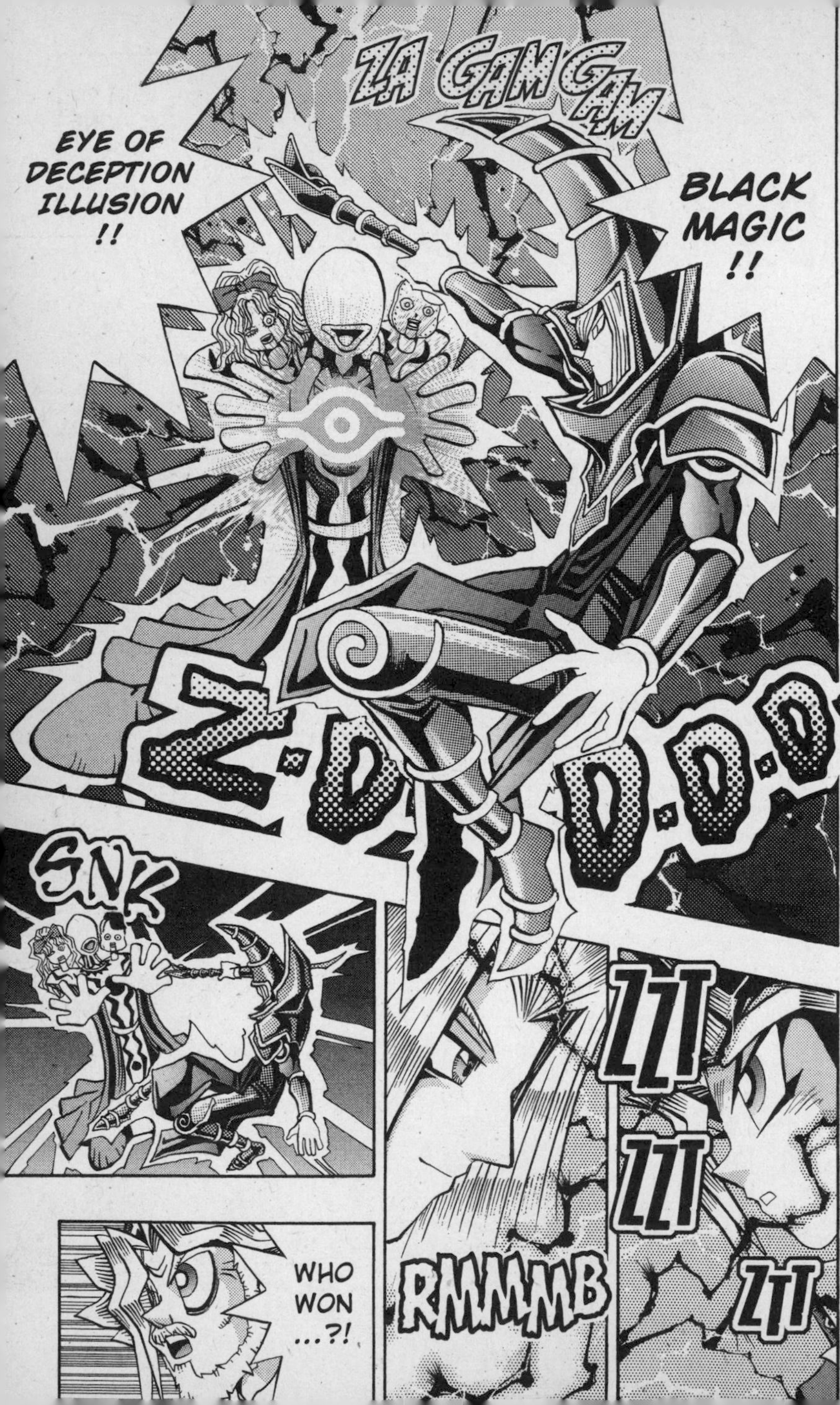

ZA GAM GAM
BLACK MAGIC !!
EYE OF DECEPTION ILLUSION !!
Z-D-D-D-D
ZZT
ZZT
ZZT
RMMMB
SNK
WHO WON ...?!

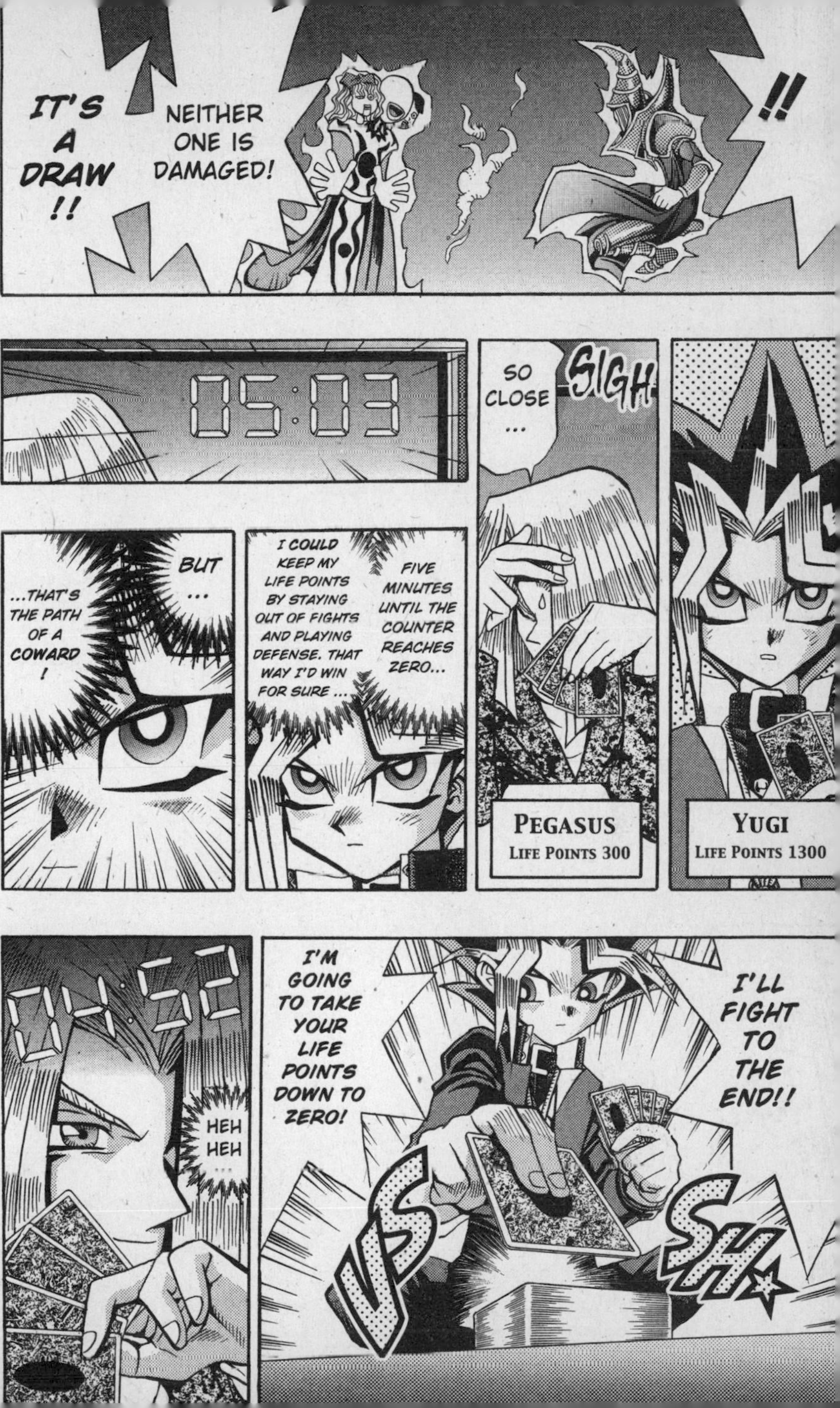
!!
NEITHER ONE IS DAMAGED!
IT'S A DRAW!!
YUGI
LIFE POINTS 1300
SIGH
SO CLOSE ...
PEGASUS
LIFE POINTS 300
05:03
FIVE MINUTES UNTIL THE COUNTER REACHES ZERO...
I COULD KEEP MY LIFE POINTS BY STAYING OUT OF FIGHTS AND PLAYING DEFENSE. THAT WAY I'D WIN FOR SURE ...
BUT ...
...THAT'S THE PATH OF A COWARD!
I'LL FIGHT TO THE END!!
I'M GOING TO TAKE YOUR LIFE POINTS DOWN TO ZERO!
VSSH
04:52
HEH HEH ...

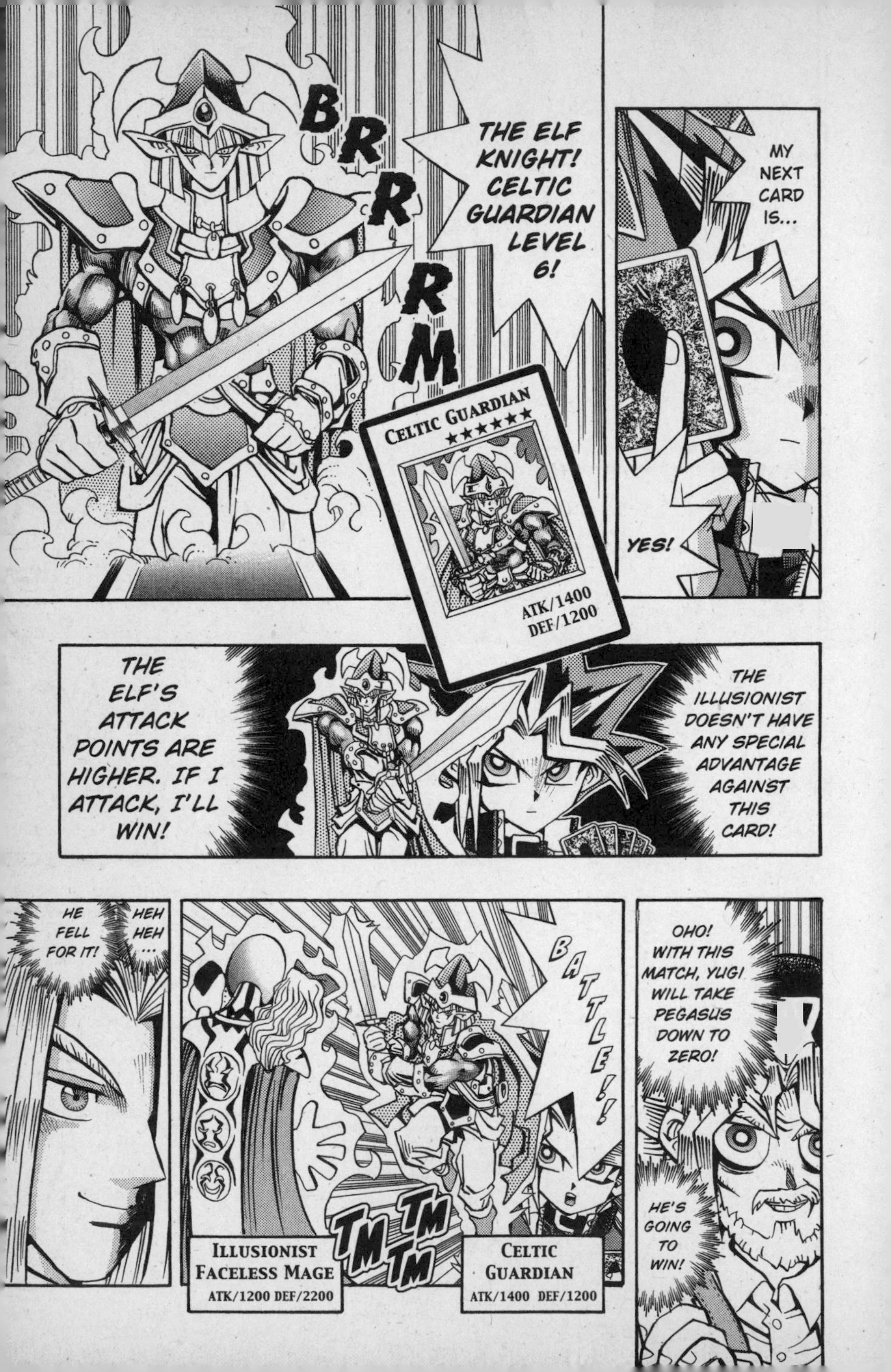
MY NEXT CARD IS...
YES!
BRRRM
THE ELF KNIGHT! CELTIC GUARDIAN LEVEL 6!
CELTIC GUARDIAN ★★★★★★
ATK/1400 DEF/1200
THE ILLUSIONIST DOESN'T HAVE ANY SPECIAL ADVANTAGE AGAINST THIS CARD!
THE ELF'S ATTACK POINTS ARE HIGHER. IF I ATTACK, I'LL WIN!
OHO! WITH THIS MATCH, YUGI WILL TAKE PEGASUS DOWN TO ZERO!
HE'S GOING TO WIN!
BATTLE!!
TM TM TM TM
CELTIC GUARDIAN
ATK/1400 DEF/1200
ILLUSIONIST FACELESS MAGE
ATK/1200 DEF/2200
HEH HEH ...
HE FELL FOR IT!

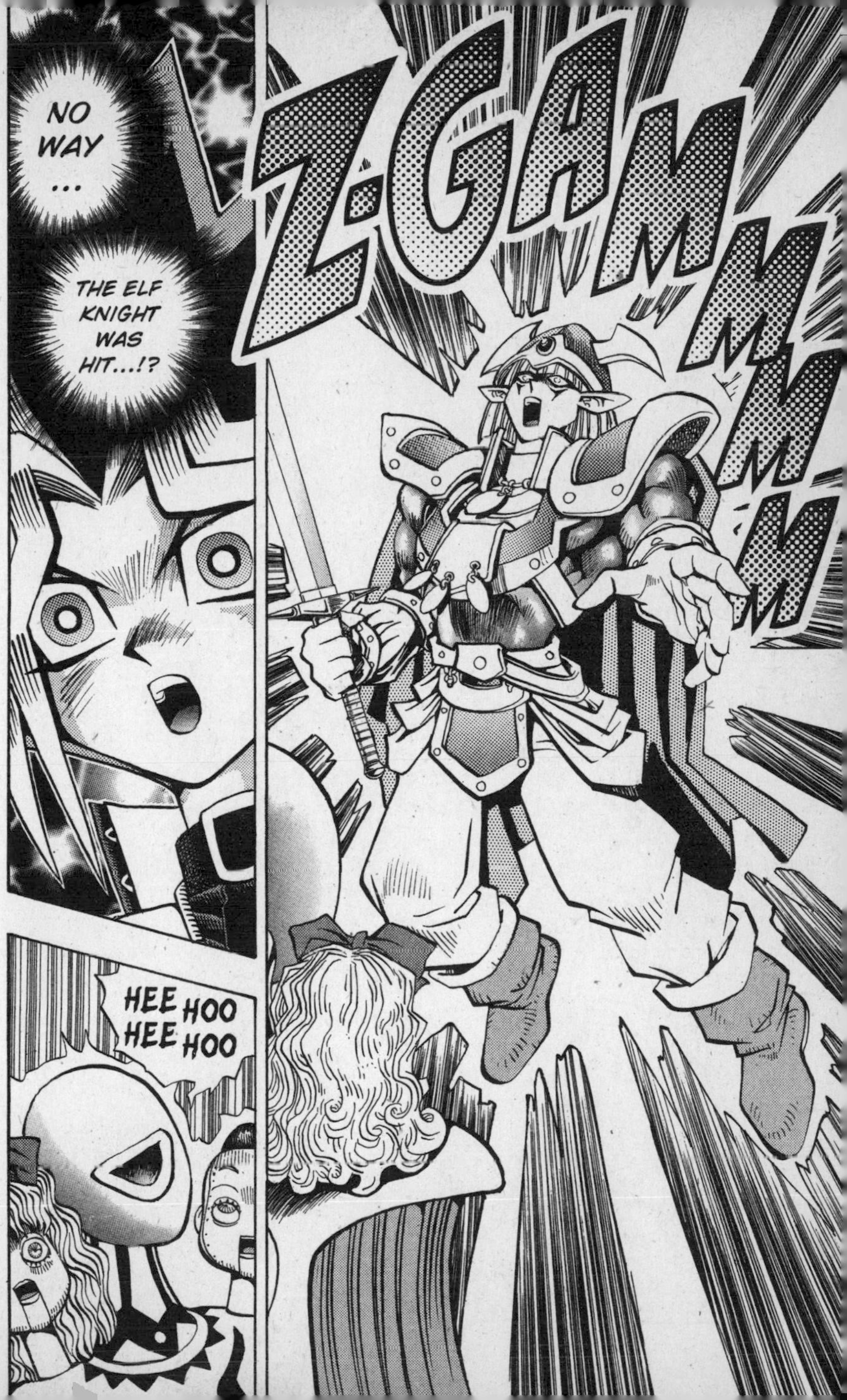

Z-GAMMMMMM
NO WAY ...
THE ELF KNIGHT WAS HIT...!?
HEE HOO HEE HOO

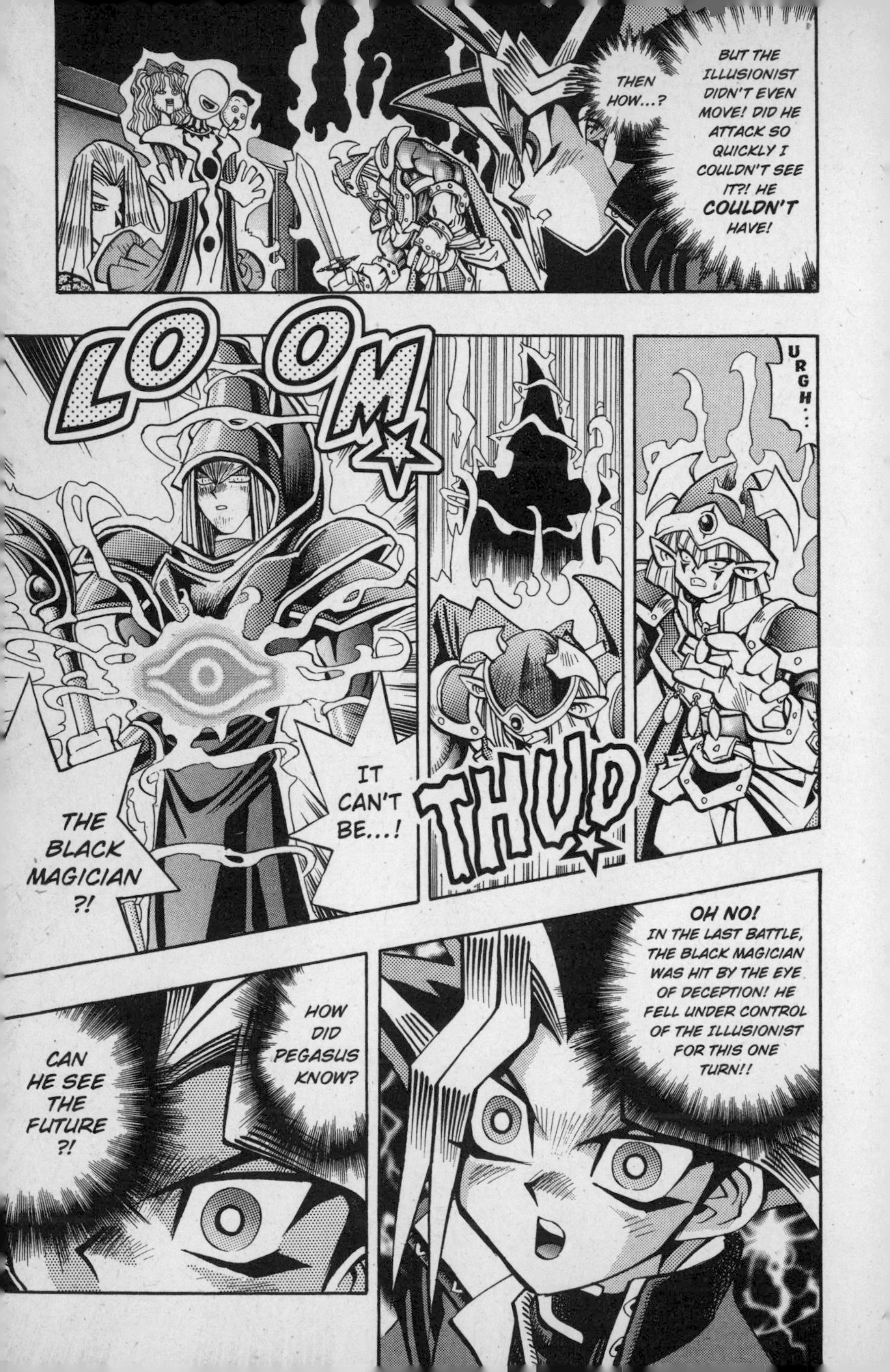
BUT THE ILLUSIONIST DIDN'T EVEN MOVE! DID HE ATTACK SO QUICKLY I COULDN'T SEE IT?! HE **COULDN'T** HAVE!
THEN HOW...?
URGH...
THUD
LO-OM
IT CAN'T BE...!
THE BLACK MAGICIAN ?!
OH NO! IN THE LAST BATTLE, THE BLACK MAGICIAN WAS HIT BY THE EYE OF DECEPTION! HE FELL UNDER CONTROL OF THE ILLUSIONIST FOR THIS ONE TURN!!
HOW DID PEGASUS KNOW?
CAN HE SEE THE FUTURE ?!

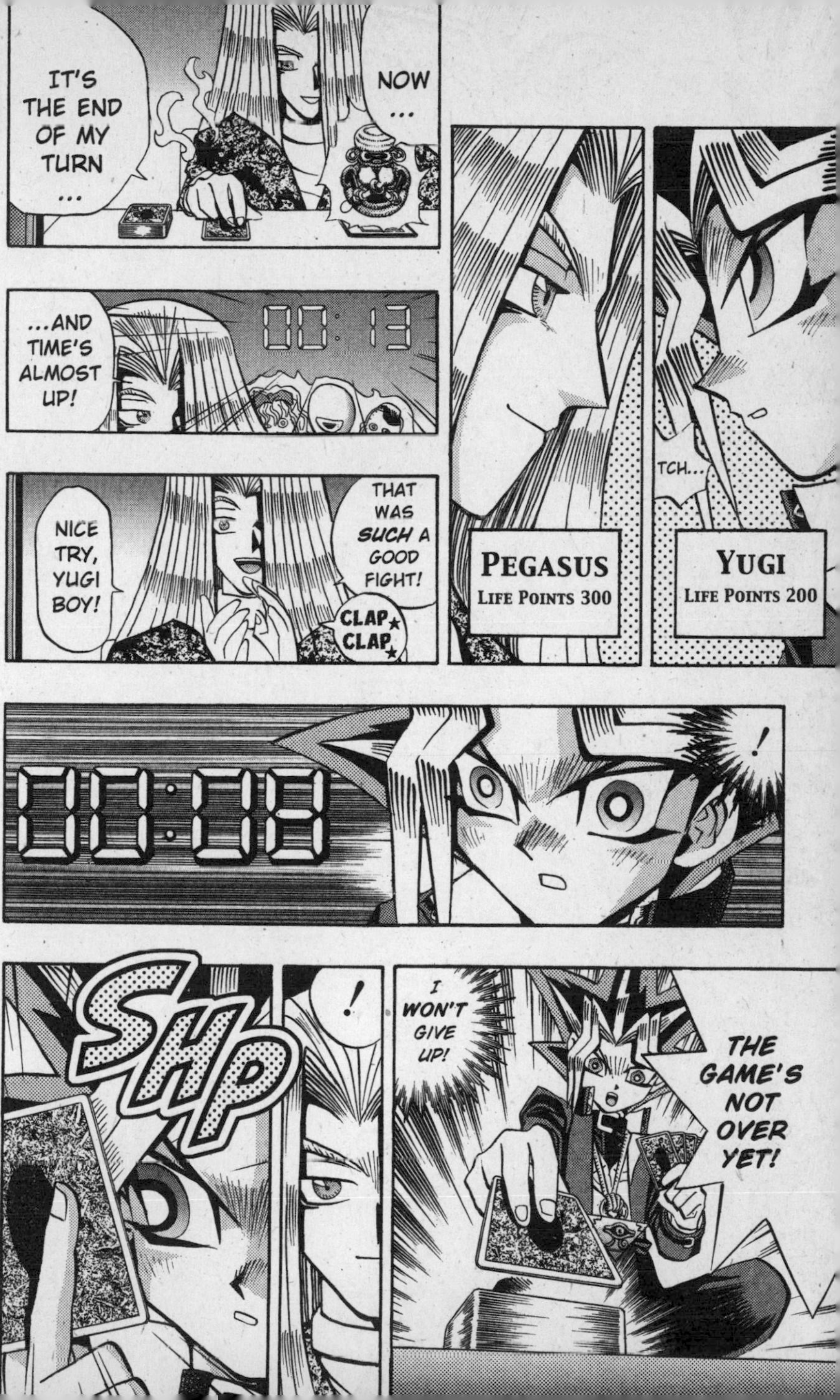
TCH...
YUGI
LIFE POINTS 200
PEGASUS
LIFE POINTS 300
NOW ...
IT'S THE END OF MY TURN ...
00:13
...AND TIME'S ALMOST UP!
THAT WAS SUCH A GOOD FIGHT!
NICE TRY, YUGI BOY!
CLAP★ CLAP★
!
00:08
THE GAME'S NOT OVER YET!
I WON'T GIVE UP!
!
SHP

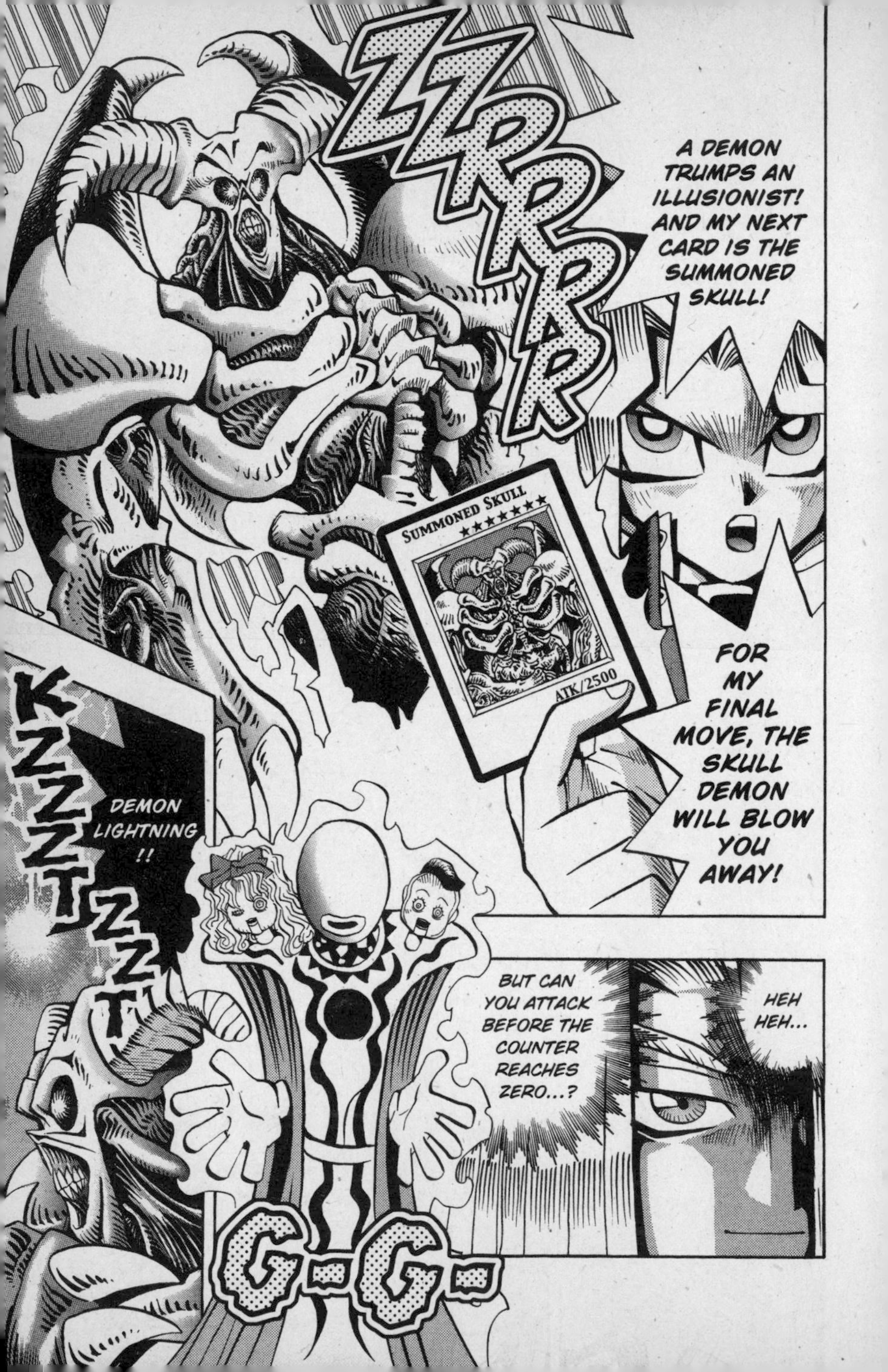
ZZRRR
A DEMON TRUMPS AN ILLUSIONIST! AND MY NEXT CARD IS THE SUMMONED SKULL!
SUMMONED SKULL
ATK/2500
FOR MY FINAL MOVE, THE SKULL DEMON WILL BLOW YOU AWAY!
HEH HEH...
BUT CAN YOU ATTACK BEFORE THE COUNTER REACHES ZERO...?
KZZZT ZZZT
DEMON LIGHTNING !!
G-G-

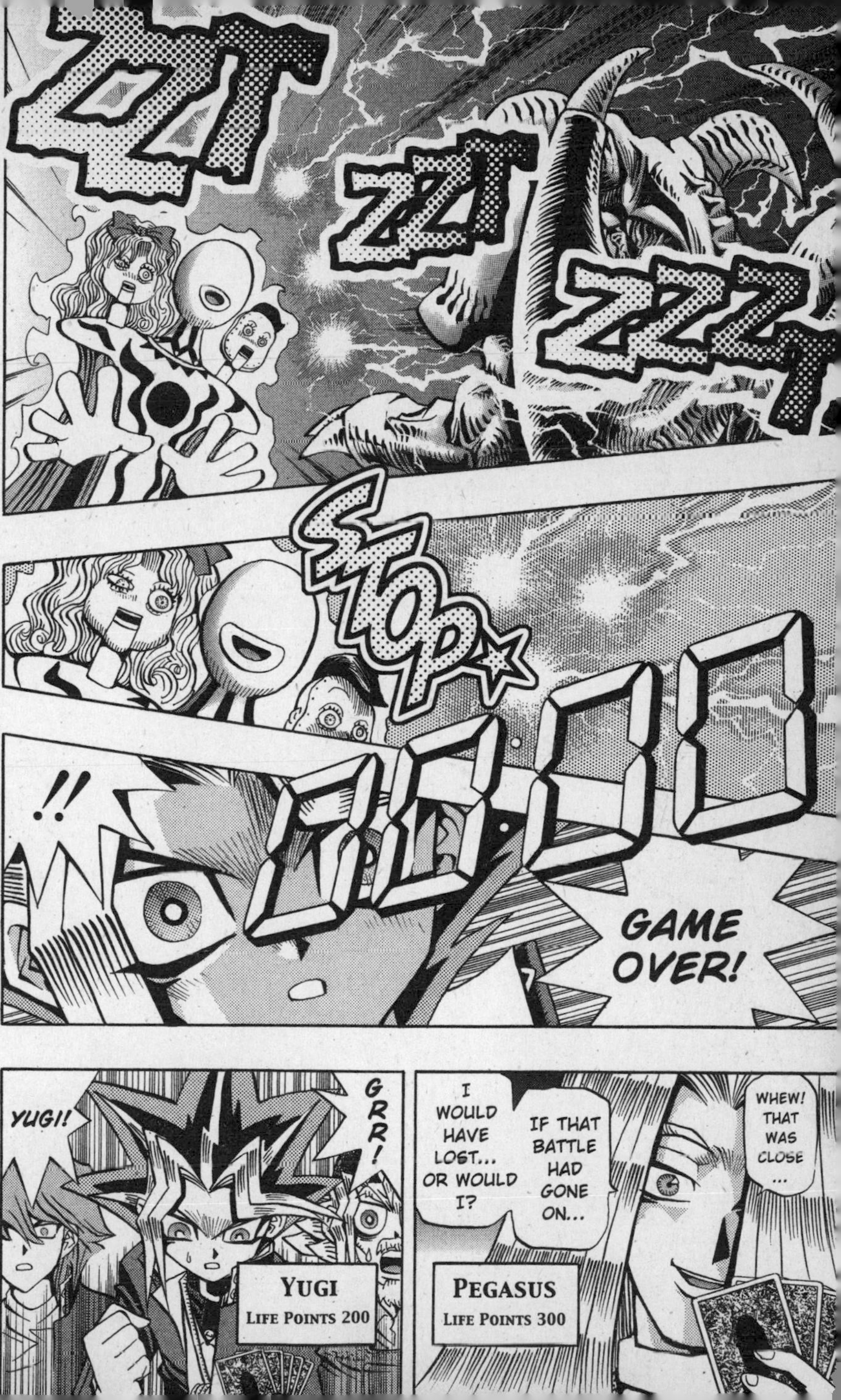
ZZZZT
ZZT
ZT
STOP
!!
GAME OVER!
WHEW! THAT WAS CLOSE ...
IF THAT BATTLE HAD GONE ON...
I WOULD HAVE LOST... OR WOULD I?
PEGASUS
LIFE POINTS 300
GRR!
YUGI!
YUGI
LIFE POINTS 200

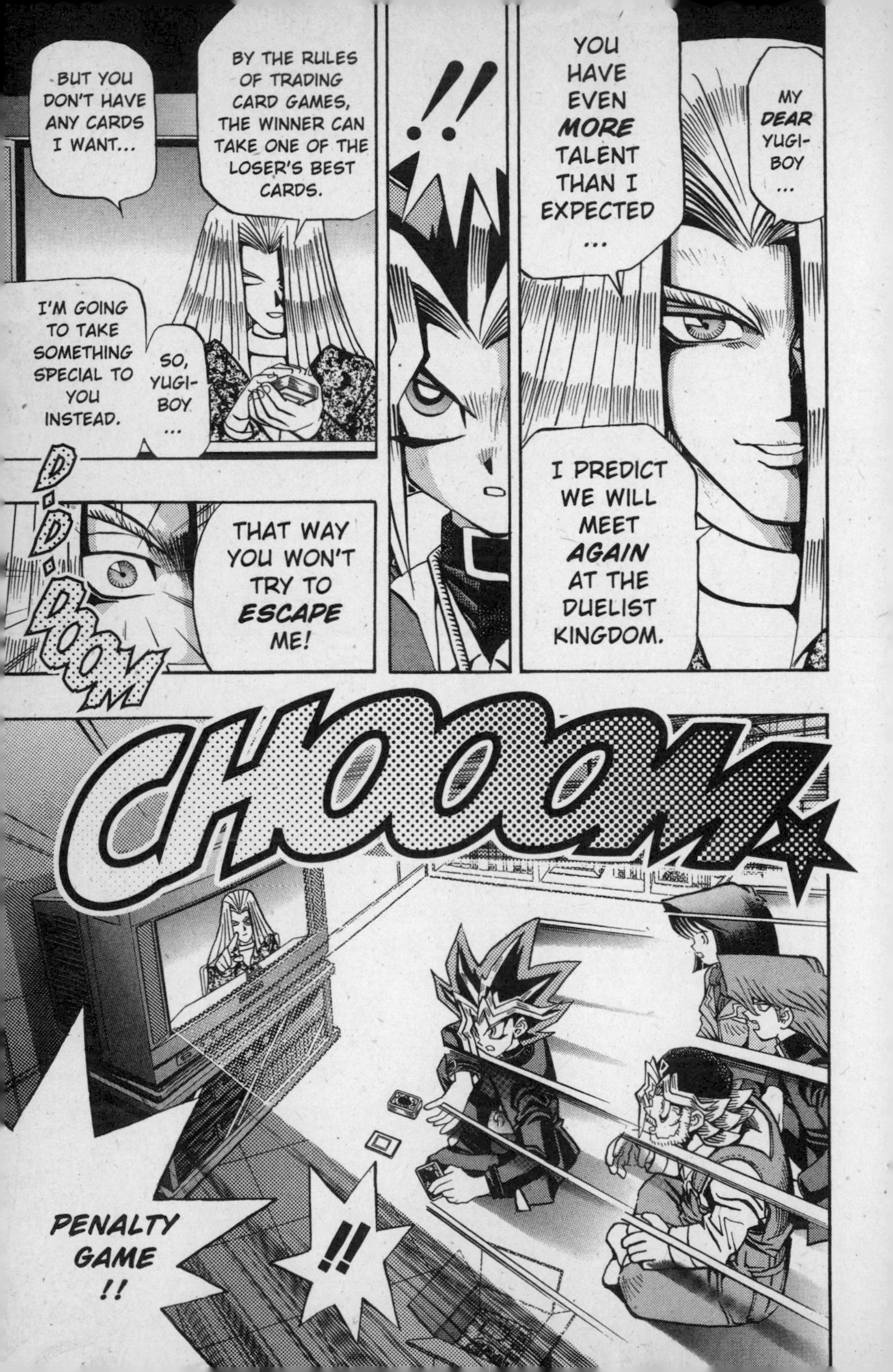
MY DEAR YUGI-BOY ...
YOU HAVE EVEN MORE TALENT THAN I EXPECTED ...
I PREDICT WE WILL MEET AGAIN AT THE DUELIST KINGDOM.
!!
BY THE RULES OF TRADING CARD GAMES, THE WINNER CAN TAKE ONE OF THE LOSER'S BEST CARDS.
BUT YOU DON'T HAVE ANY CARDS I WANT...
SO, YUGI-BOY ...
I'M GOING TO TAKE SOMETHING SPECIAL TO YOU INSTEAD.
THAT WAY YOU WON'T TRY TO ESCAPE ME!
D D DOOOM
CHOOOM
!!
PENALTY GAME !!

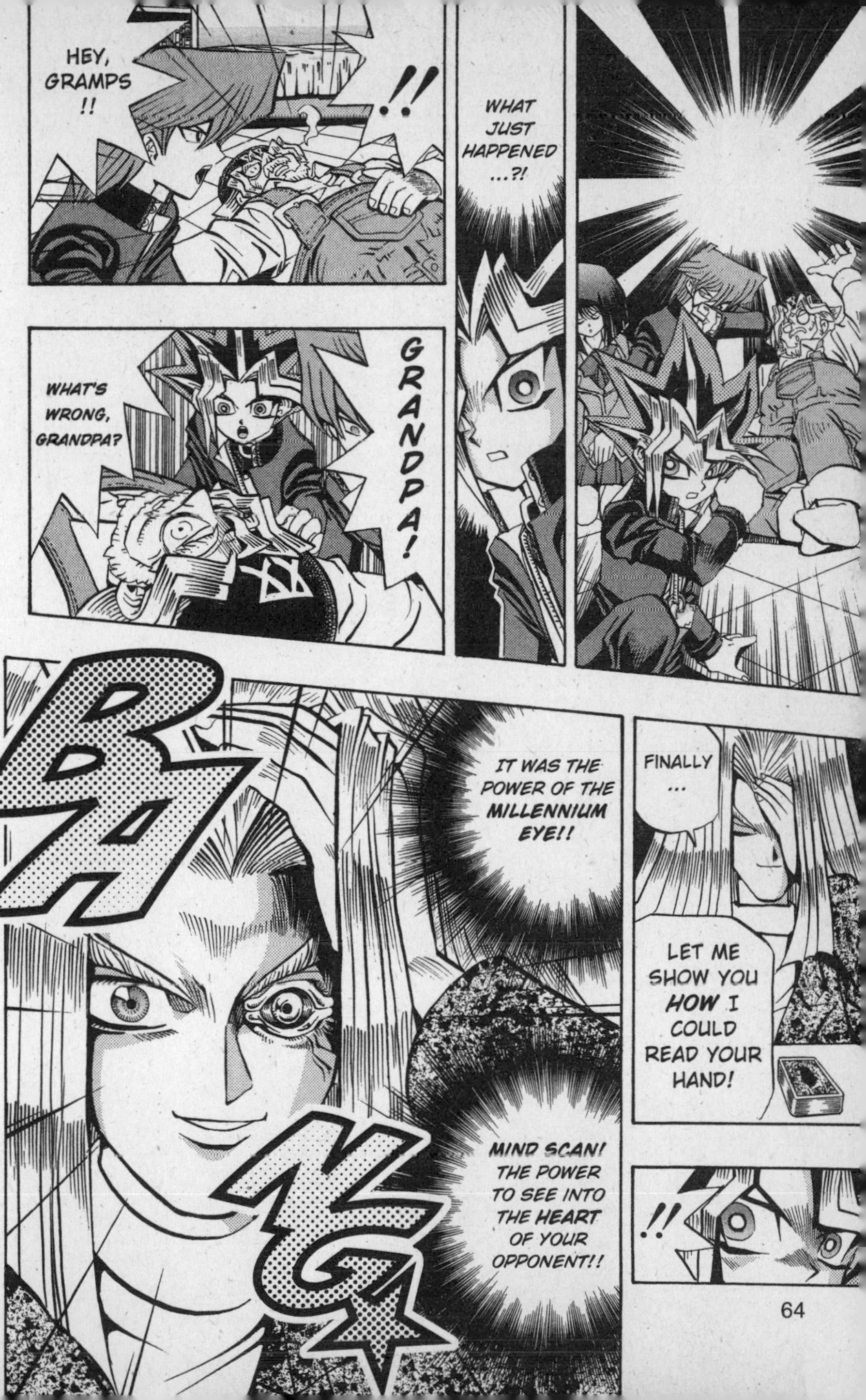
WHAT JUST HAPPENED ...?!
HEY, GRAMPS !!
!!
GRANDPA!
WHAT'S WRONG, GRANDPA?
FINALLY ...
LET ME SHOW YOU HOW I COULD READ YOUR HAND!
!!
IT WAS THE POWER OF THE MILLENNIUM EYE!!
BA
MIND SCAN! THE POWER TO SEE INTO THE HEART OF YOUR OPPONENT!!
NG

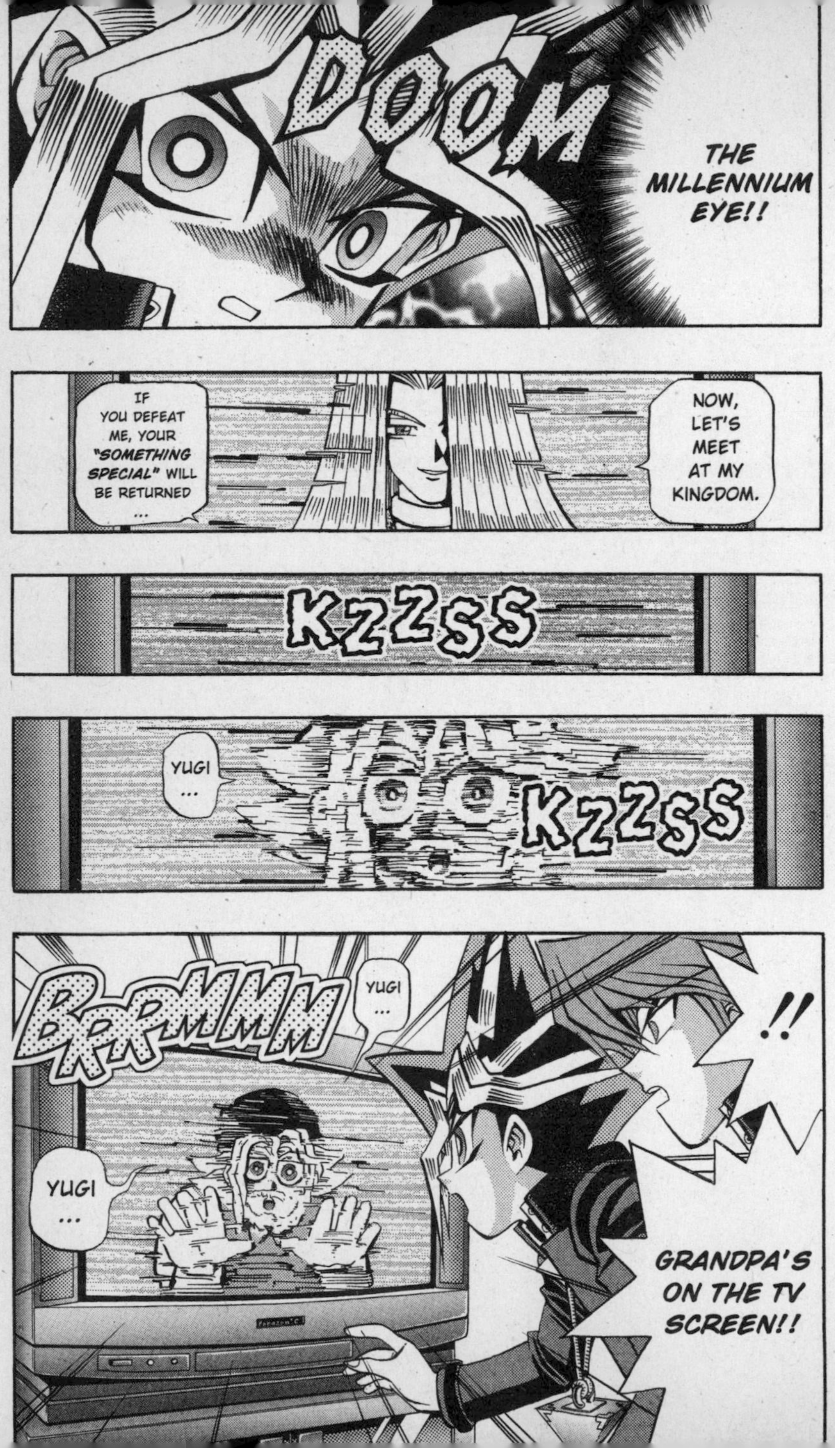
DOOM
THE MILLENNIUM EYE!!
NOW, LET'S MEET AT MY KINGDOM.
IF YOU DEFEAT ME, YOUR "SOMETHING SPECIAL" WILL BE RETURNED ...
KZZSS
KZZSS
YUGI ...
!!
YUGI ...
GRANDPA'S ON THE TV SCREEN!!
YUGI ...

DUEL 4: I WON'T LOSE!!

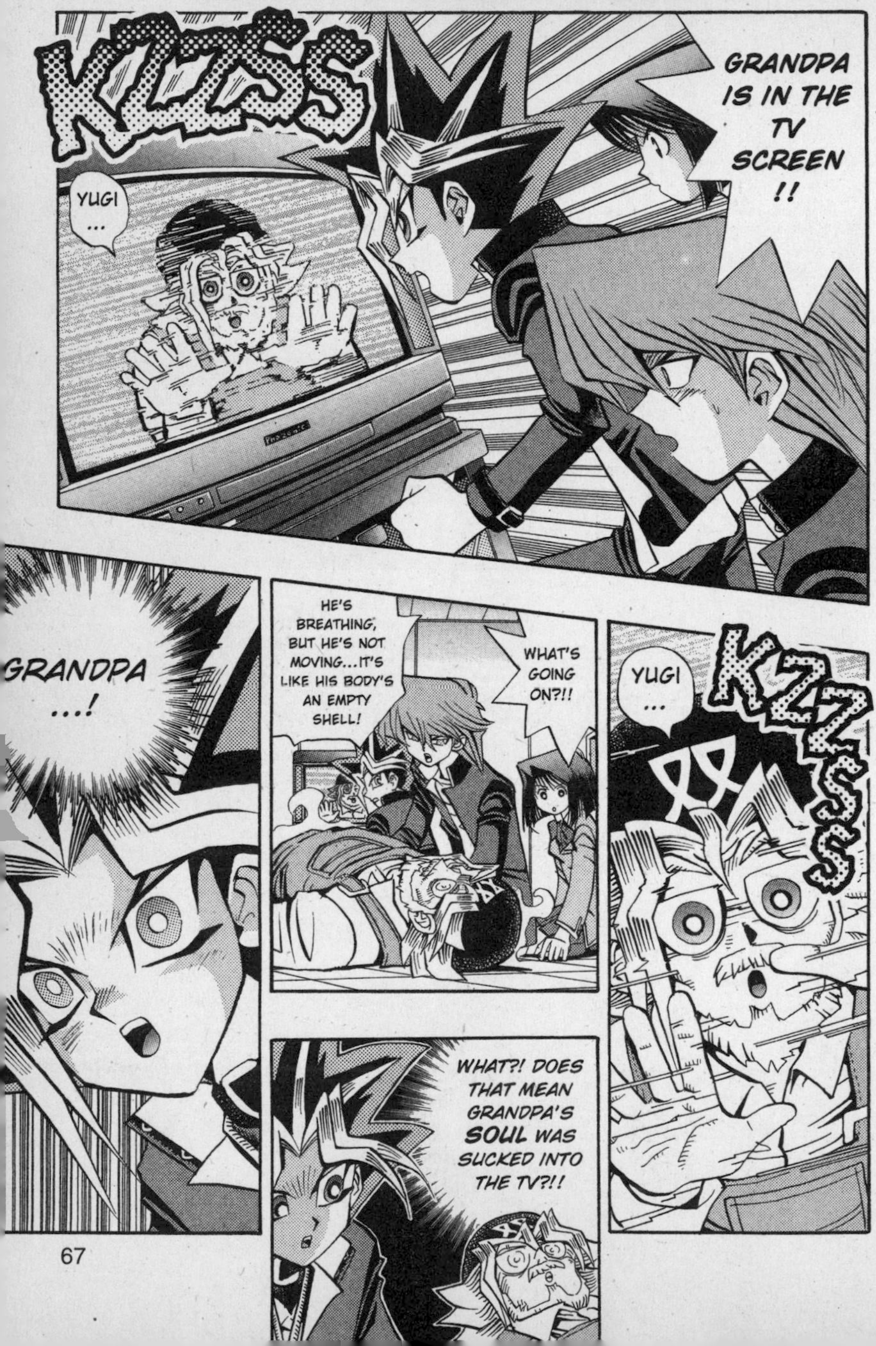

GRANDPA IS IN THE TV SCREEN!!
KZZSS
YUGI ...
YUGI ...
KZZSSS
WHAT'S GOING ON?!!
HE'S BREATHING, BUT HE'S NOT MOVING...IT'S LIKE HIS BODY'S AN EMPTY SHELL!
GRANDPA ...!
WHAT?! DOES THAT MEAN GRANDPA'S SOUL WAS SUCKED INTO THE TV?!!

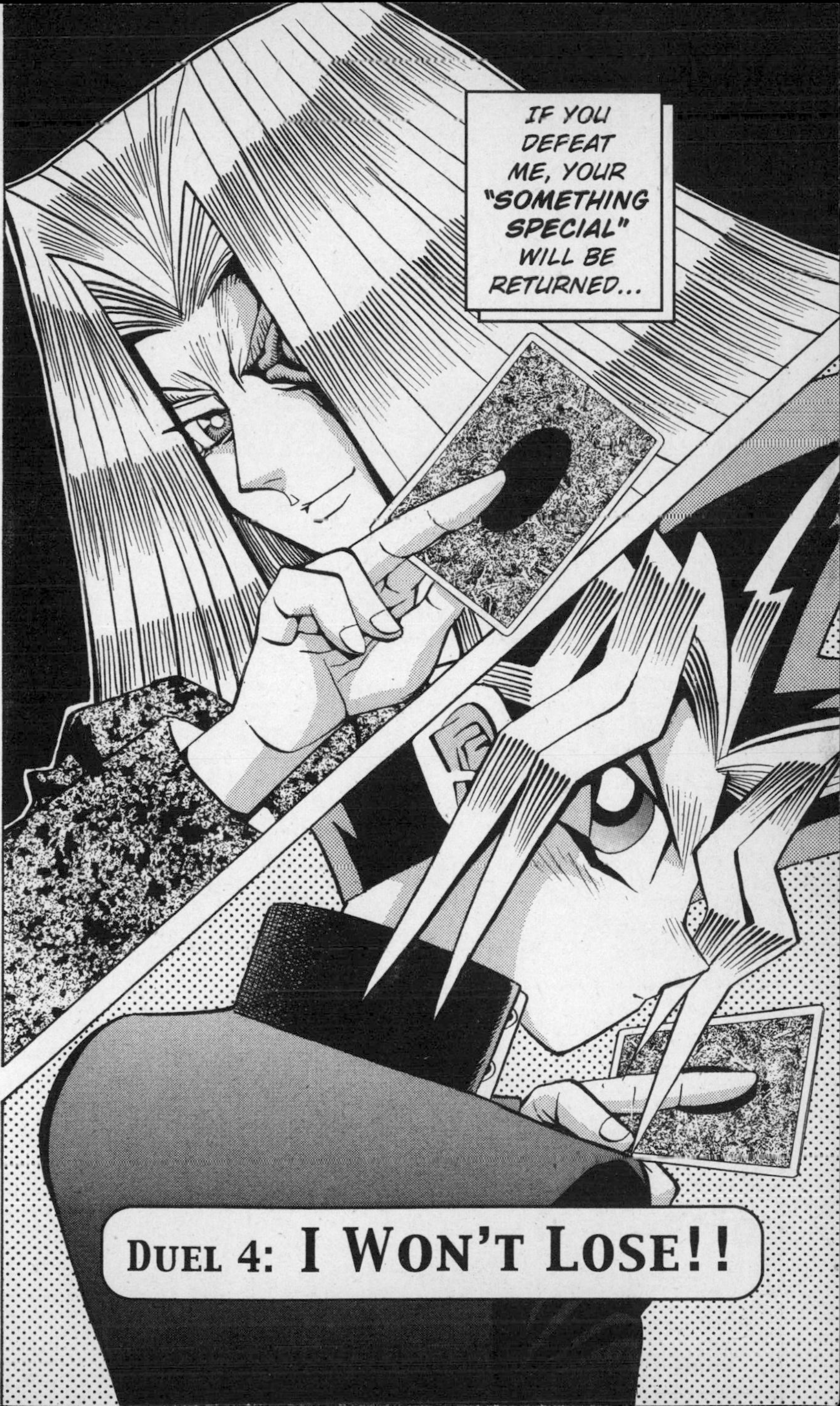
IF YOU DEFEAT ME, YOUR "SOMETHING SPECIAL" WILL BE RETURNED...
Duel 4: I Won't Lose!!

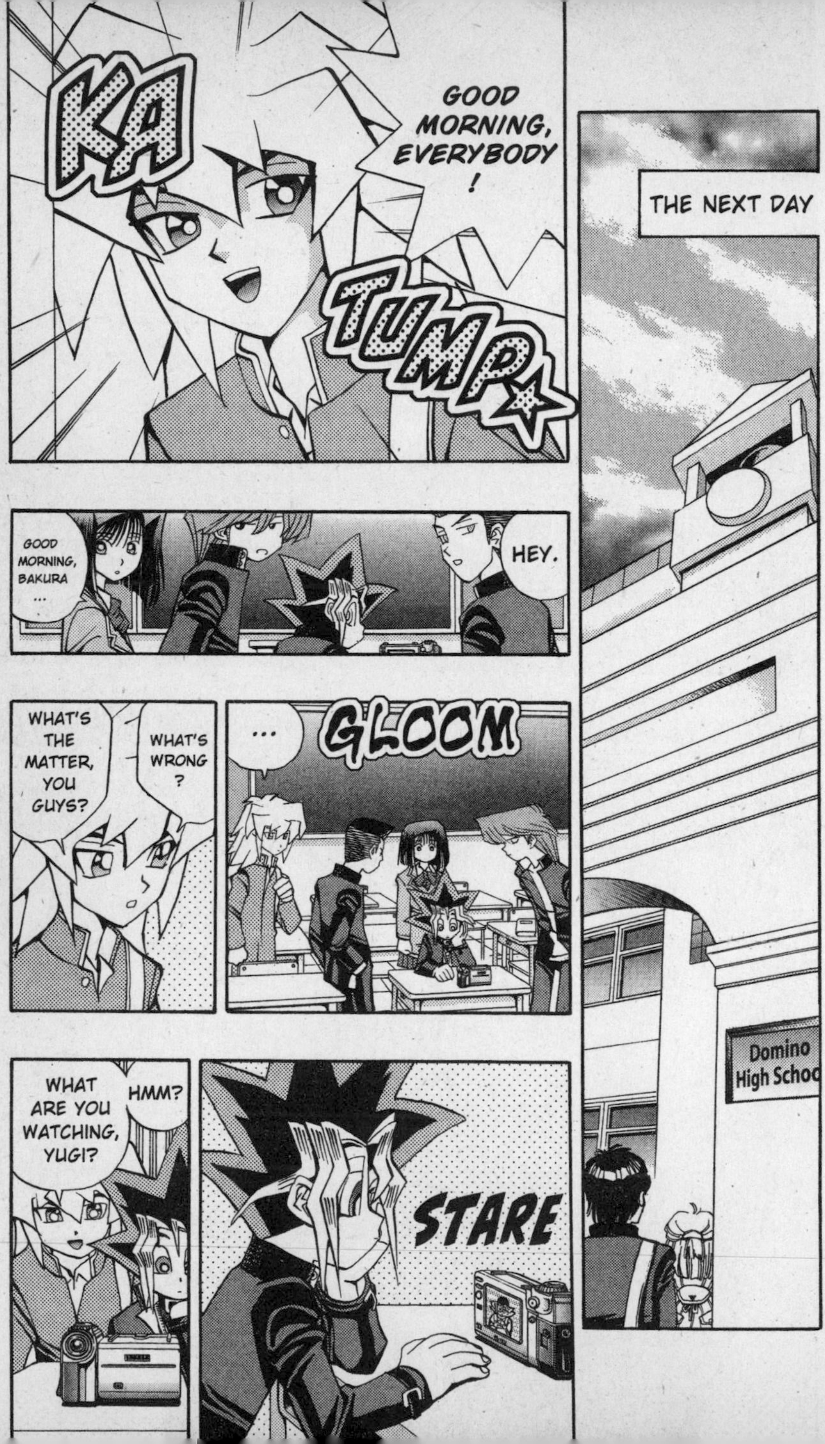
THE NEXT DAY
Domino
High Schoo
GOOD MORNING, EVERYBODY!
KA
TUMP
HEY.
GOOD MORNING, BAKURA...
...
GLOOM
WHAT'S WRONG?
WHAT'S THE MATTER, YOU GUYS?
STARE
HMM?
WHAT ARE YOU WATCHING, YUGI?

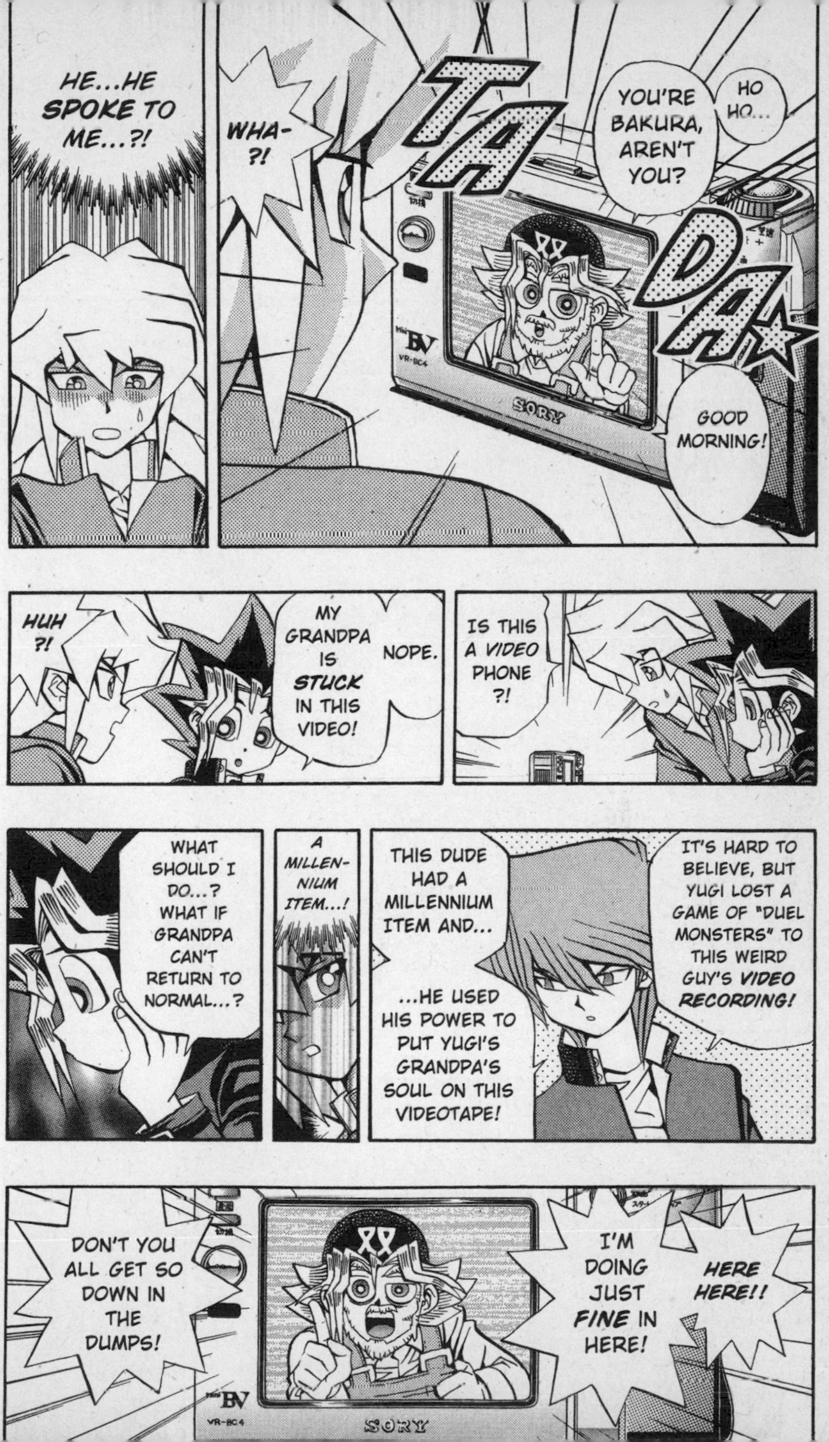
HO HO...
YOU'RE BAKURA, AREN'T YOU?
TA DA☆
SORY
GOOD MORNING!
WHA-?!
HE...HE SPOKE TO ME...?!
IS THIS A VIDEO PHONE?!
NOPE.
MY GRANDPA IS STUCK IN THIS VIDEO!
HUH?!
IT'S HARD TO BELIEVE, BUT YUGI LOST A GAME OF "DUEL MONSTERS" TO THIS WEIRD GUY'S VIDEO RECORDING!
THIS DUDE HAD A MILLENNIUM ITEM AND...
...HE USED HIS POWER TO PUT YUGI'S GRANDPA'S SOUL ON THIS VIDEOTAPE!
A MILLENNIUM ITEM...!
WHAT SHOULD I DO...? WHAT IF GRANDPA CAN'T RETURN TO NORMAL...?
HERE HERE!!
I'M DOING JUST FINE IN HERE!
DON'T YOU ALL GET SO DOWN IN THE DUMPS!
SORY

READ THIS WAY

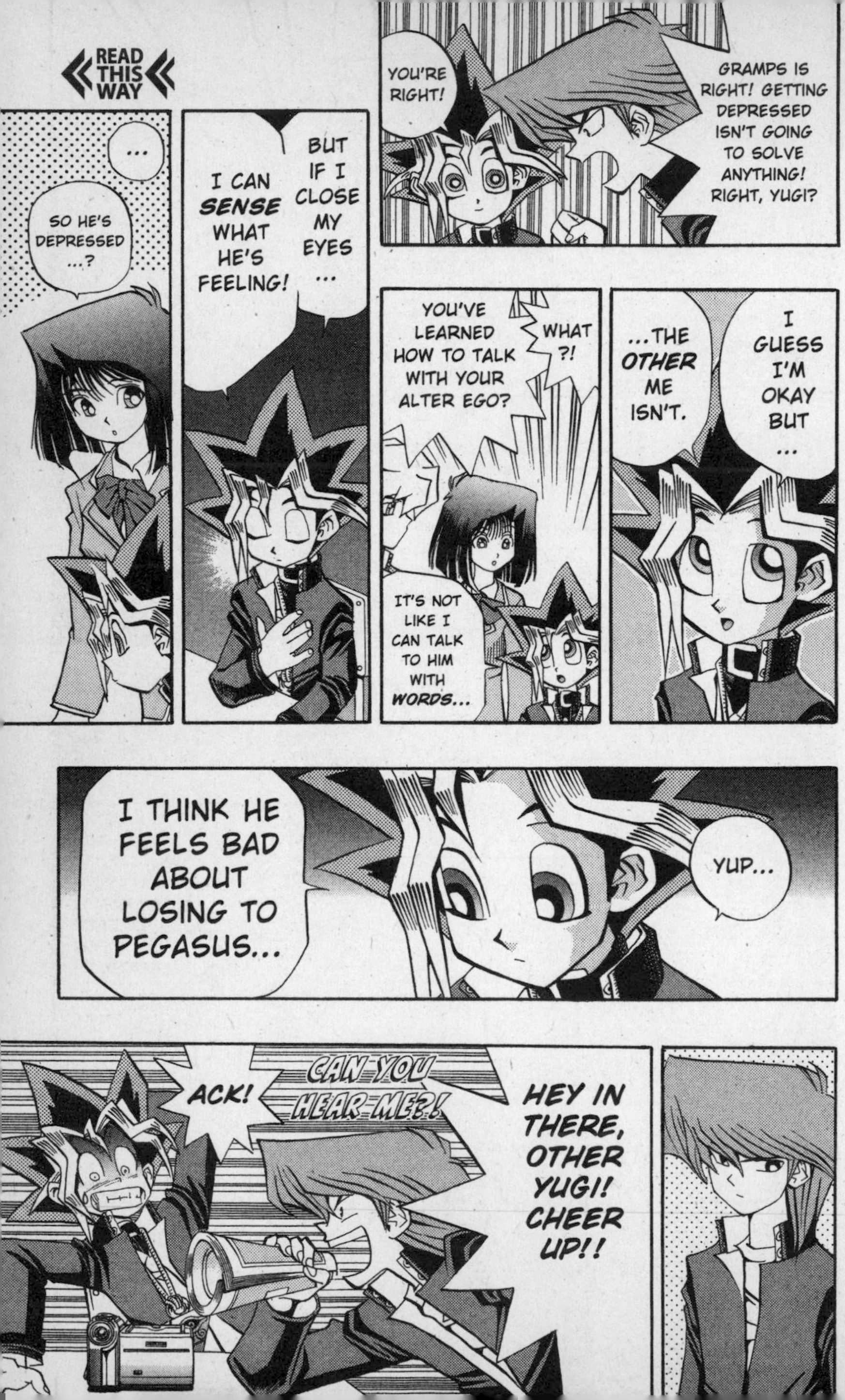
GRAMPS IS RIGHT! GETTING DEPRESSED ISN'T GOING TO SOLVE ANYTHING! RIGHT, YUGI?
YOU'RE RIGHT!
I GUESS I'M OKAY BUT ...
...THE OTHER ME ISN'T.
WHAT ?!
YOU'VE LEARNED HOW TO TALK WITH YOUR ALTER EGO?
IT'S NOT LIKE I CAN TALK TO HIM WITH WORDS...
BUT IF I CLOSE MY EYES ...
I CAN SENSE WHAT HE'S FEELING!
...
SO HE'S DEPRESSED ...?
YUP...
I THINK HE FEELS BAD ABOUT LOSING TO PEGASUS...
HEY IN THERE, OTHER YUGI! CHEER UP!!
CAN YOU HEAR ME?!
ACK!

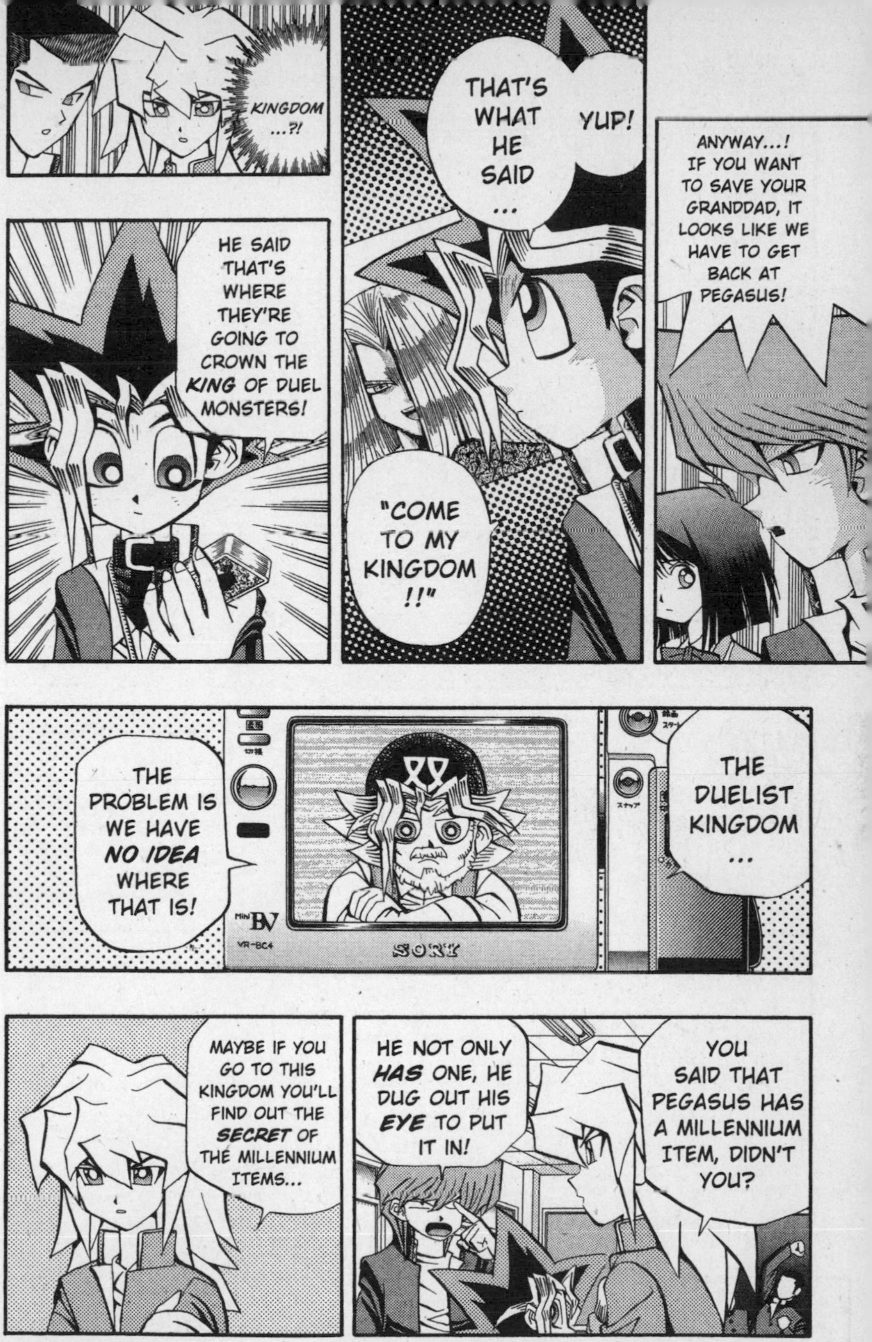
ANYWAY...! IF YOU WANT TO SAVE YOUR GRANDDAD, IT LOOKS LIKE WE HAVE TO GET BACK AT PEGASUS!
YUP!
THAT'S WHAT HE SAID ...
"COME TO MY KINGDOM !!"
KINGDOM ...?!
HE SAID THAT'S WHERE THEY'RE GOING TO CROWN THE KING OF DUEL MONSTERS!
THE DUELIST KINGDOM ...
THE PROBLEM IS WE HAVE NO IDEA WHERE THAT IS!
YOU SAID THAT PEGASUS HAS A MILLENNIUM ITEM, DIDN'T YOU?
HE NOT ONLY HAS ONE, HE DUG OUT HIS EYE TO PUT IT IN!
MAYBE IF YOU GO TO THIS KINGDOM YOU'LL FIND OUT THE SECRET OF THE MILLENNIUM ITEMS...

READ THIS WAY

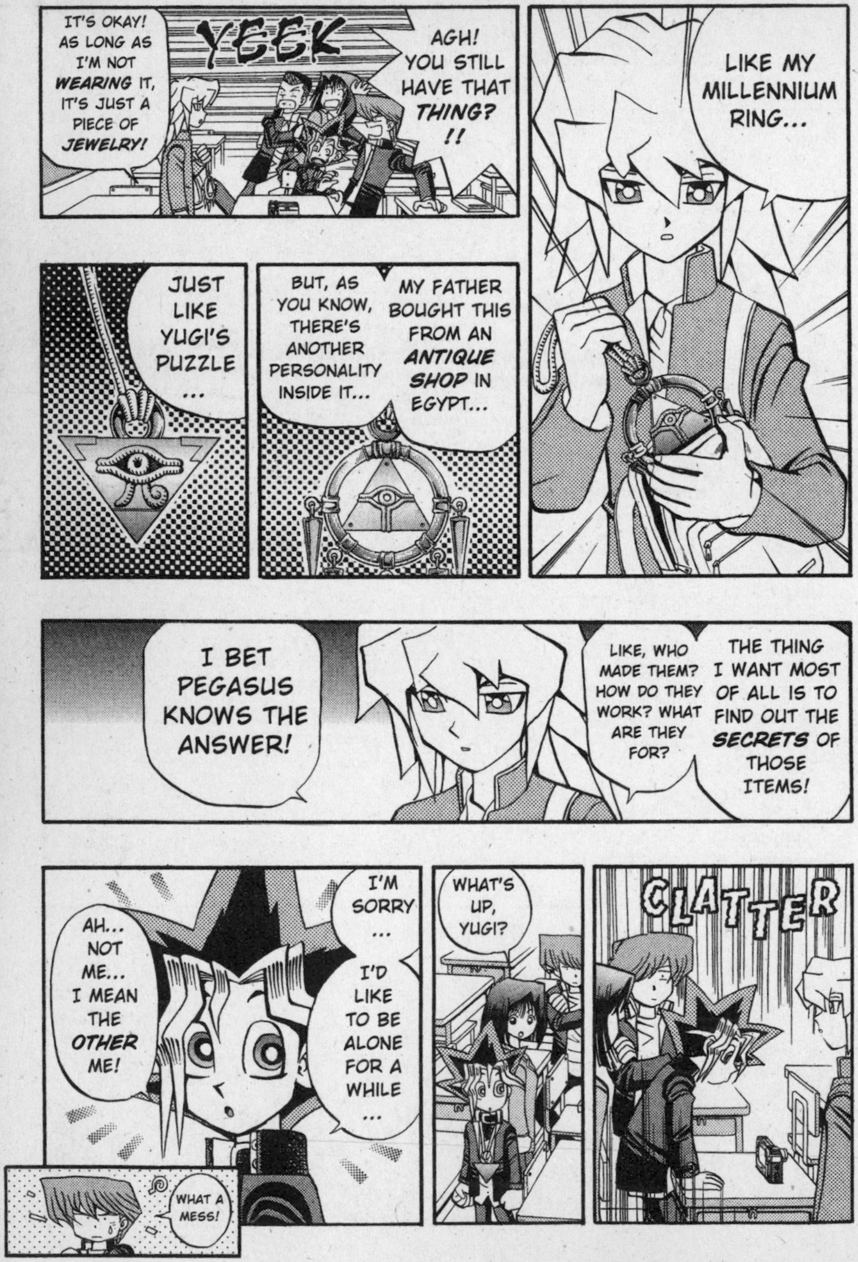
LIKE MY MILLENNIUM RING...
AGH! YOU STILL HAVE THAT THING? !!
YEEK
IT'S OKAY! AS LONG AS I'M NOT WEARING IT, IT'S JUST A PIECE OF JEWELRY!
MY FATHER BOUGHT THIS FROM AN ANTIQUE SHOP IN EGYPT...
BUT, AS YOU KNOW, THERE'S ANOTHER PERSONALITY INSIDE IT...
JUST LIKE YUGI'S PUZZLE ...
THE THING I WANT MOST OF ALL IS TO FIND OUT THE SECRETS OF THOSE ITEMS!
LIKE, WHO MADE THEM? HOW DO THEY WORK? WHAT ARE THEY FOR?
I BET PEGASUS KNOWS THE ANSWER!
CLATTER
WHAT'S UP, YUGI?
I'M SORRY ... I'D LIKE TO BE ALONE FOR A WHILE ...
AH... NOT ME... I MEAN THE OTHER ME!
WHAT A MESS!

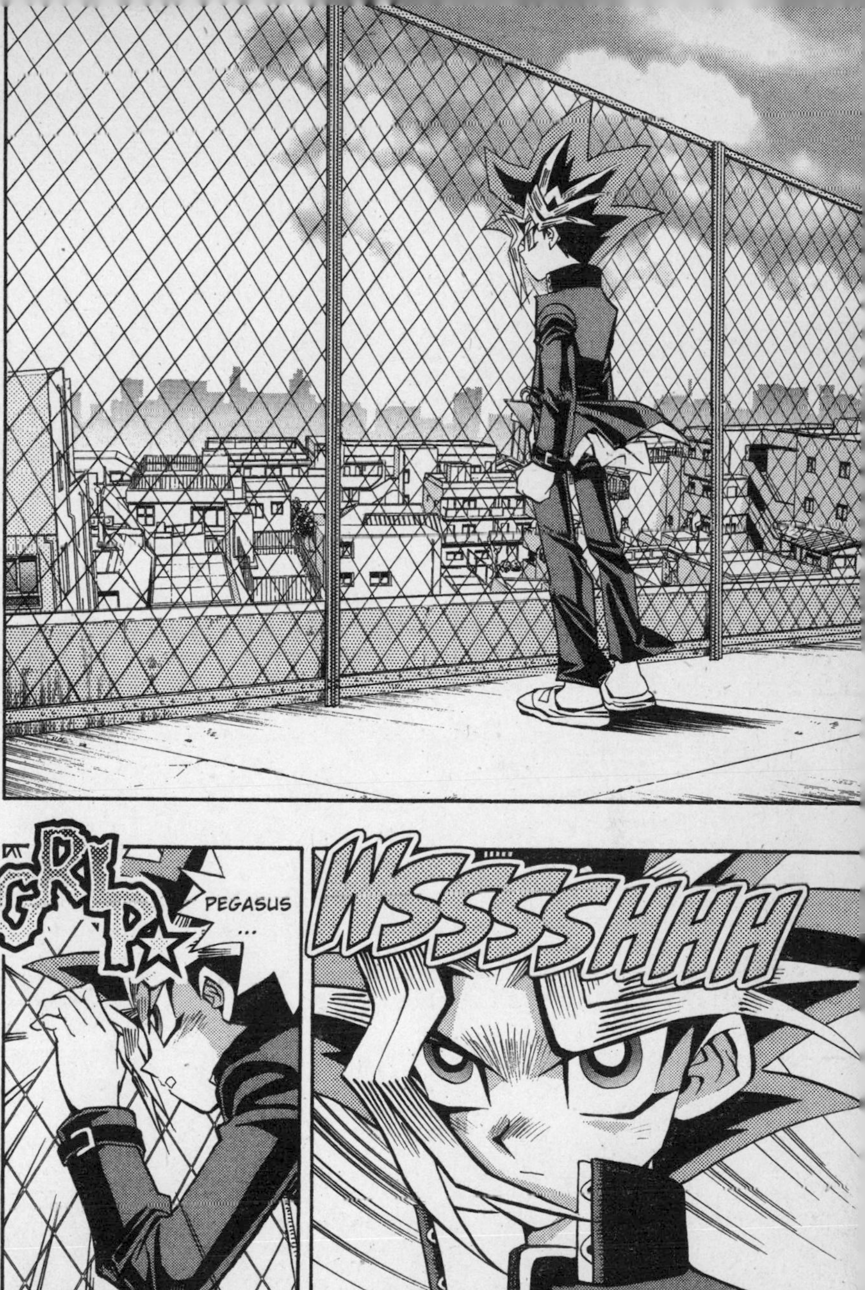
WSSSSHHH
PEGASUS ...
GRIP

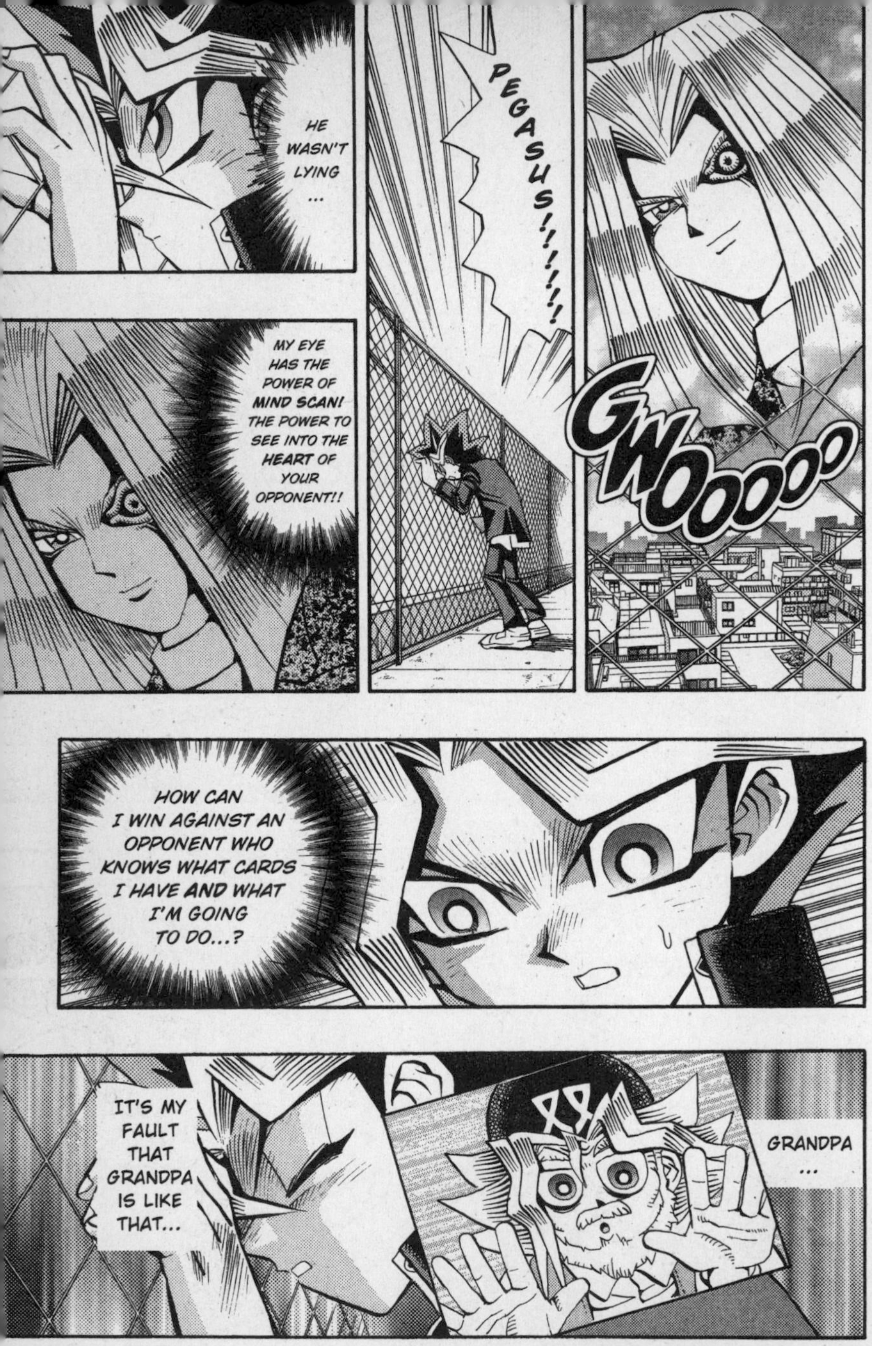
GWOOOOOO
PEGASUS!!!!!!
HE WASN'T LYING ...
MY EYE HAS THE POWER OF MIND SCAN! THE POWER TO SEE INTO THE HEART OF YOUR OPPONENT!!
HOW CAN I WIN AGAINST AN OPPONENT WHO KNOWS WHAT CARDS I HAVE AND WHAT I'M GOING TO DO...?
GRANDPA ...
IT'S MY FAULT THAT GRANDPA IS LIKE THAT...

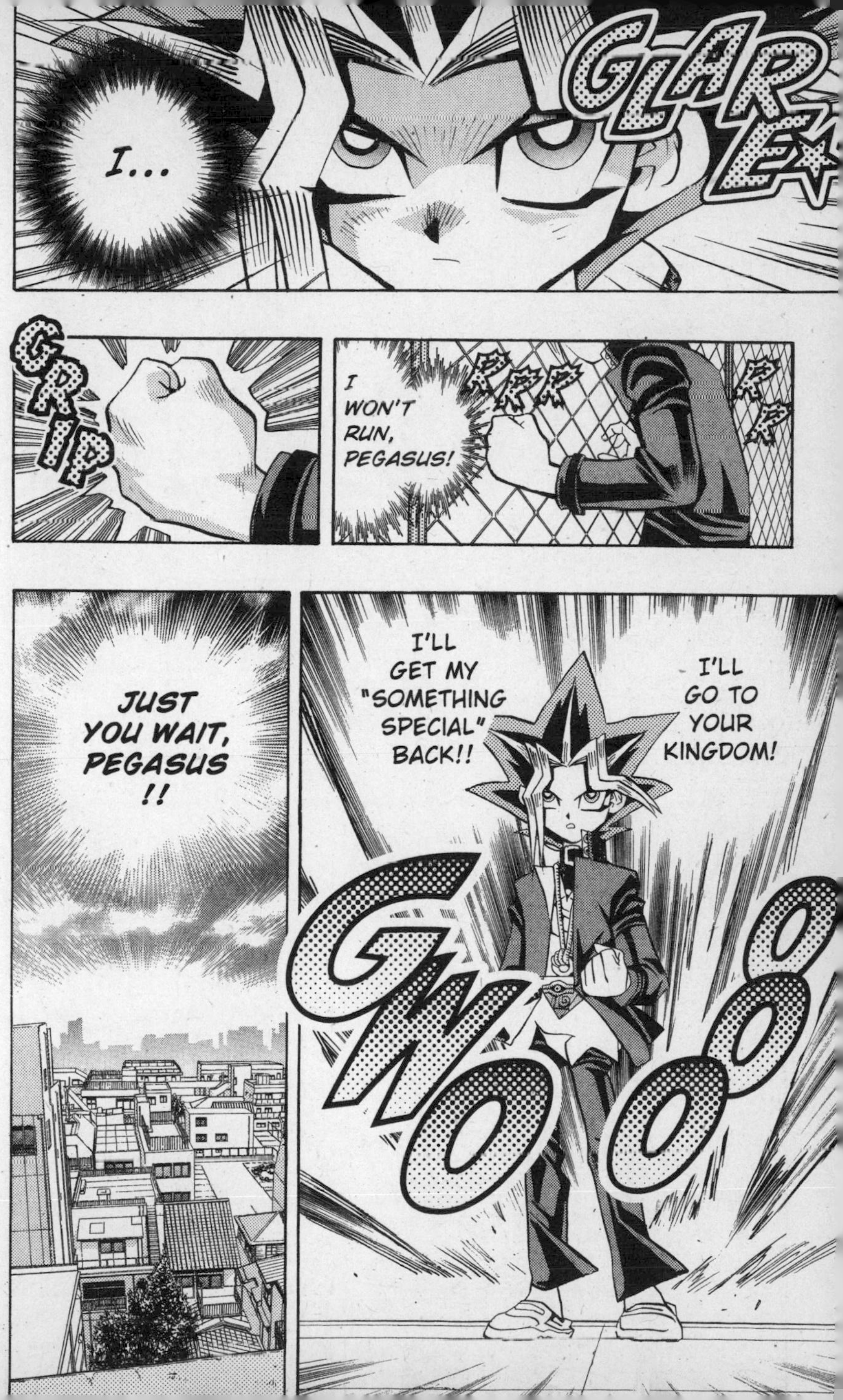
GLARE☆
I...
RRR
I WON'T RUN, PEGASUS!
RRR
GRIP
I'LL GO TO YOUR KINGDOM!
I'LL GET MY "SOMETHING SPECIAL" BACK!!
GWOOOOO
JUST YOU WAIT, PEGASUS!!

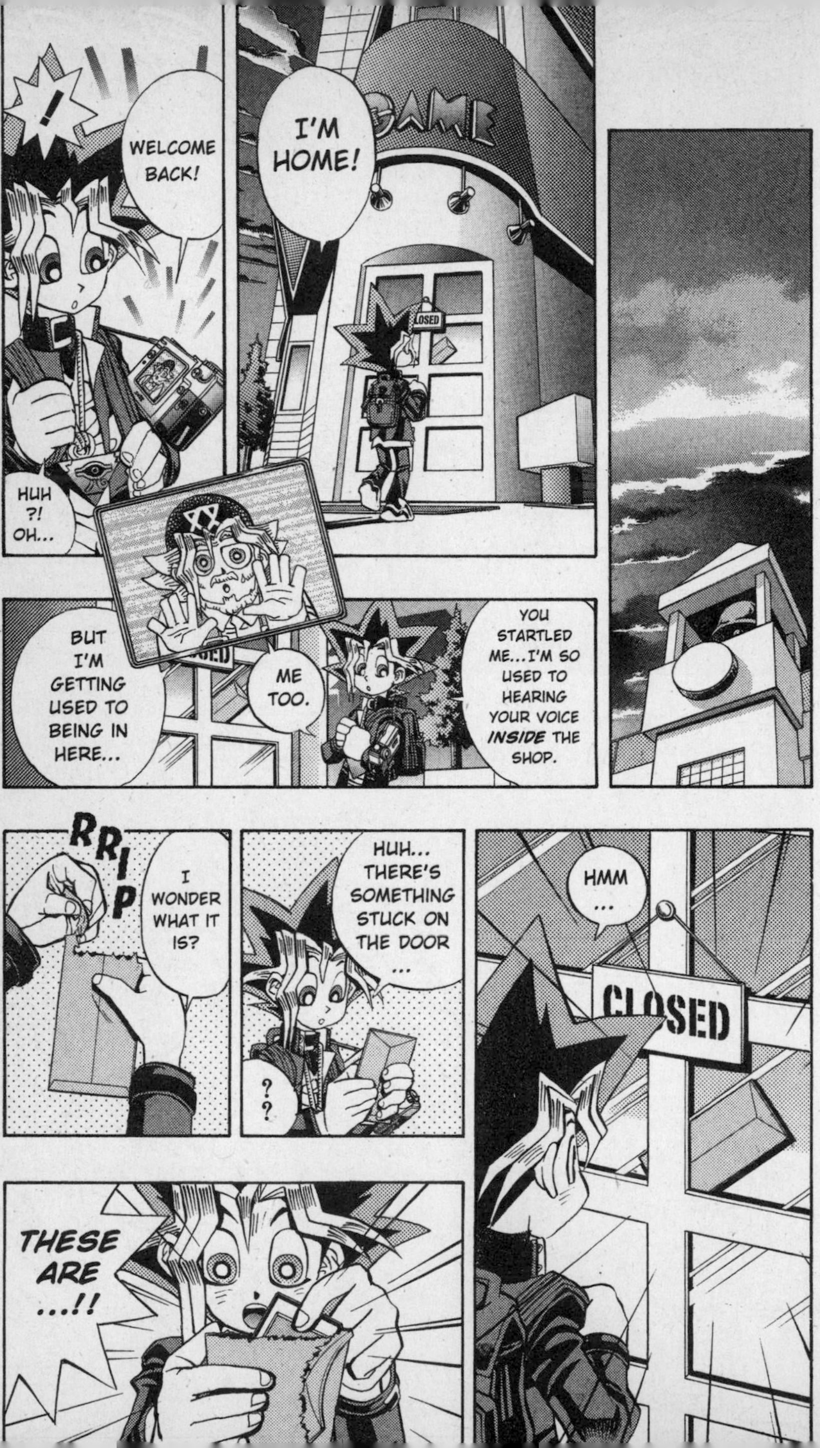
GAME
I'M HOME!
CLOSED
!
WELCOME BACK!
HUH ?! OH...
YOU STARTLED ME...I'M SO USED TO HEARING YOUR VOICE *INSIDE* THE SHOP.
ME TOO.
BUT I'M GETTING USED TO BEING IN HERE...
CLOSED
HMM ...
HUH... THERE'S SOMETHING STUCK ON THE DOOR ...
??
RRIP
I WONDER WHAT IT IS?
THESE ARE ...!!

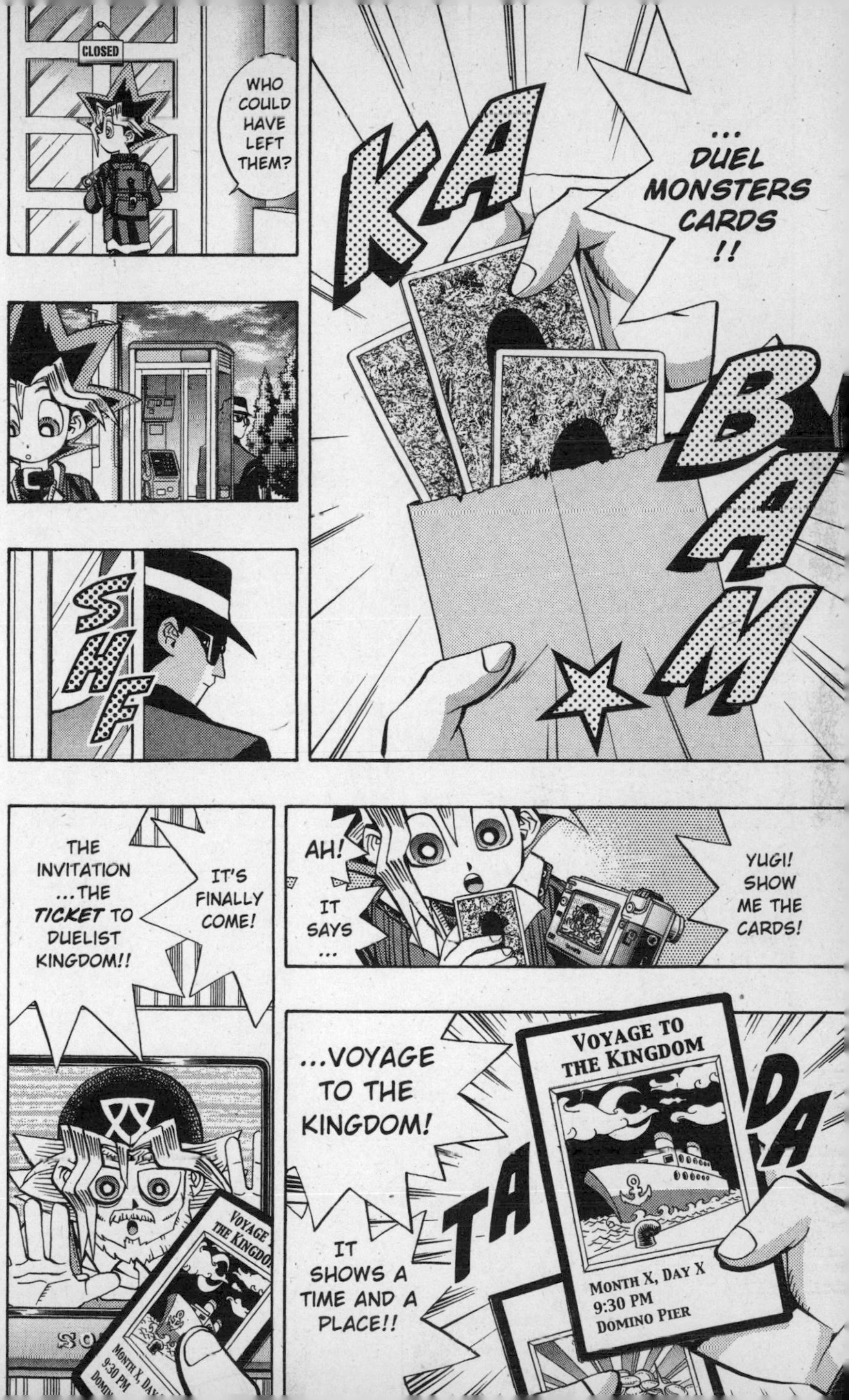

KA BAM
... DUEL MONSTERS CARDS !!
CLOSED
WHO COULD HAVE LEFT THEM?
SHF
YUGI! SHOW ME THE CARDS!
AH!
IT SAYS ...
...VOYAGE TO THE KINGDOM!
VOYAGE TO THE KINGDOM
MONTH X, DAY X
9:30 PM
DOMINO PIER
TA DA
IT SHOWS A TIME AND A PLACE!!
THE INVITATION ...THE TICKET TO DUELIST KINGDOM!!
IT'S FINALLY COME!

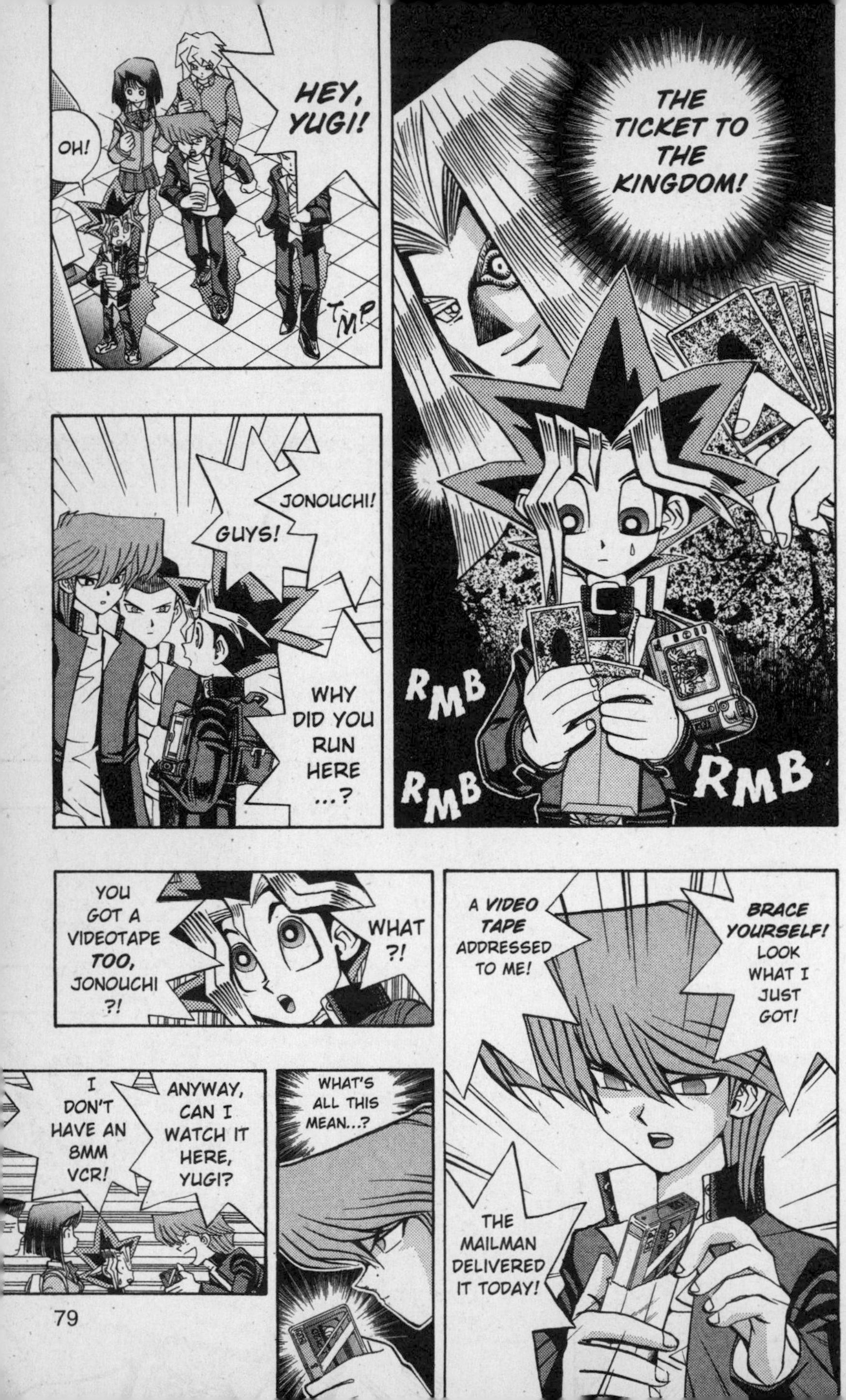
THE TICKET TO THE KINGDOM!
RMB
RMB
RMB
HEY, YUGI!
OH!
TMP
JONOUCHI!
GUYS!
WHY DID YOU RUN HERE ...?
BRACE YOURSELF! LOOK WHAT I JUST GOT!
A VIDEO TAPE ADDRESSED TO ME!
THE MAILMAN DELIVERED IT TODAY!
WHAT ?!
YOU GOT A VIDEOTAPE TOO, JONOUCHI ?!
WHAT'S ALL THIS MEAN...?
ANYWAY, CAN I WATCH IT HERE, YUGI?
I DON'T HAVE AN 8MM VCR!

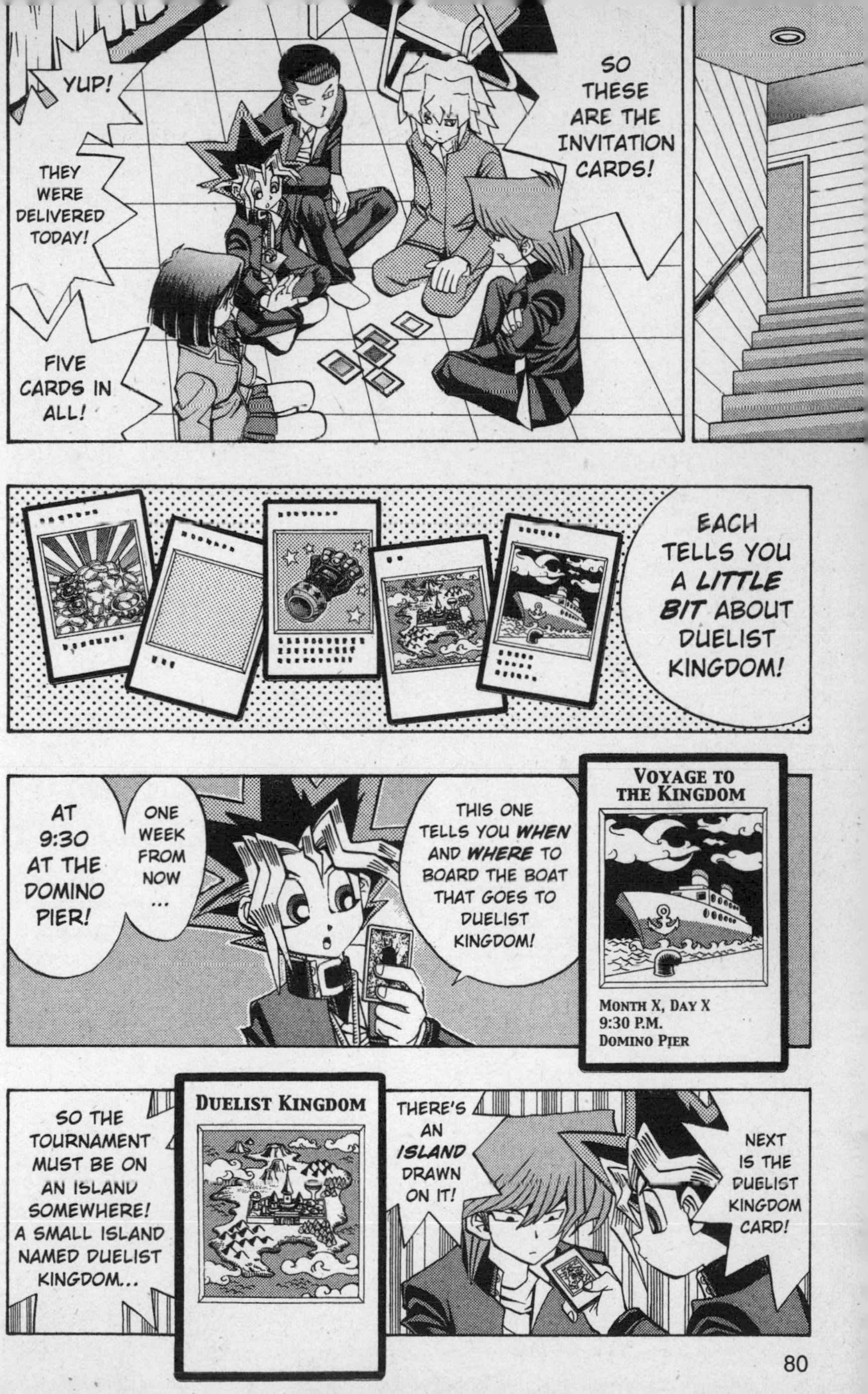
SO THESE ARE THE INVITATION CARDS!
YUP!
THEY WERE DELIVERED TODAY!
FIVE CARDS IN ALL!
EACH TELLS YOU A *LITTLE BIT* ABOUT DUELIST KINGDOM!
VOYAGE TO THE KINGDOM
MONTH X, DAY X
9:30 P.M.
DOMINO PIER
THIS ONE TELLS YOU *WHEN* AND *WHERE* TO BOARD THE BOAT THAT GOES TO DUELIST KINGDOM!
ONE WEEK FROM NOW ...
AT 9:30 AT THE DOMINO PIER!
NEXT IS THE DUELIST KINGDOM CARD!
THERE'S AN *ISLAND* DRAWN ON IT!
DUELIST KINGDOM
SO THE TOURNAMENT MUST BE ON AN ISLAND SOMEWHERE! A SMALL ISLAND NAMED DUELIST KINGDOM...

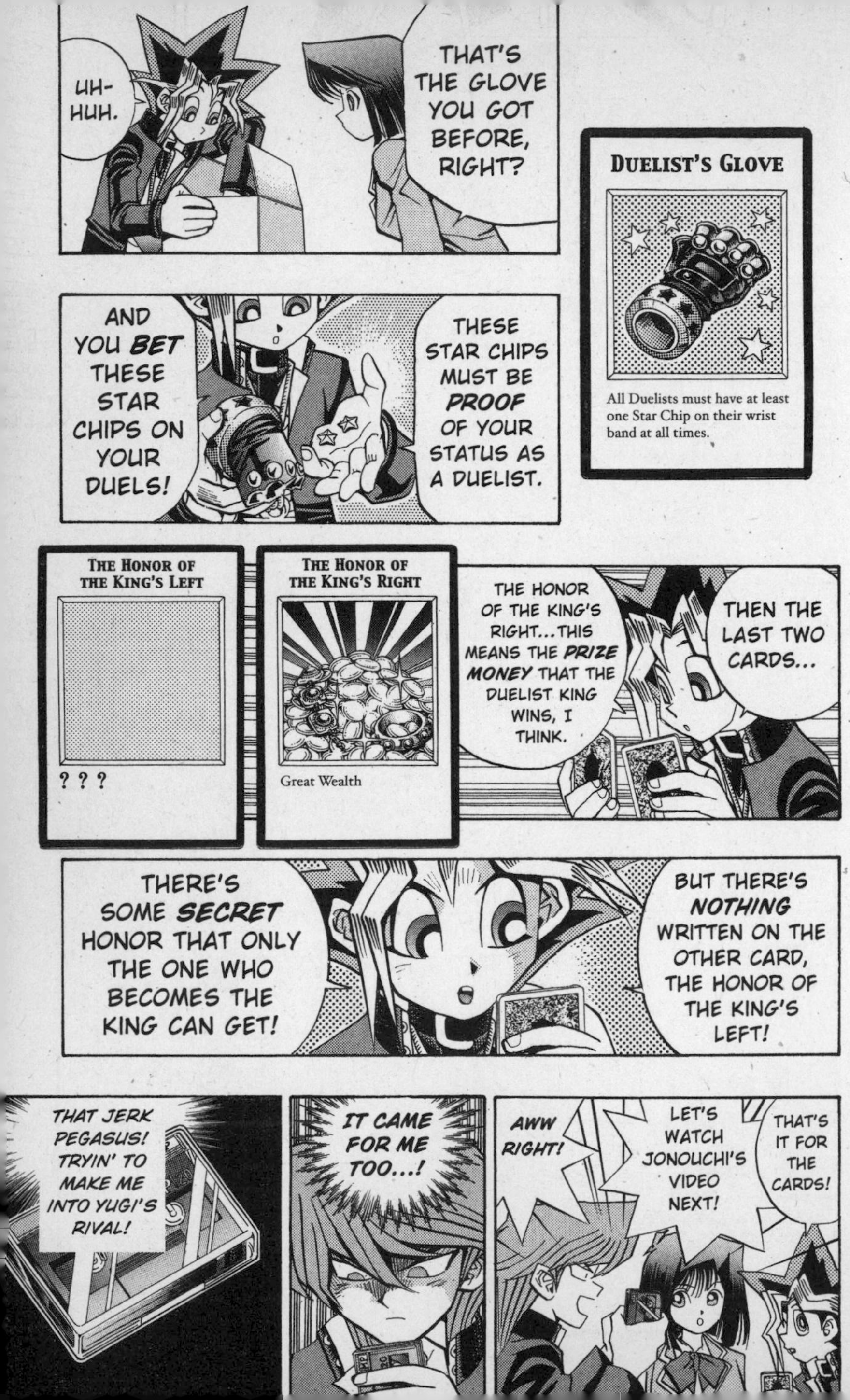
DUELIST'S GLOVE
All Duelists must have at least one Star Chip on their wrist band at all times.
THAT'S THE GLOVE YOU GOT BEFORE, RIGHT?
UH-HUH.
THESE STAR CHIPS MUST BE PROOF OF YOUR STATUS AS A DUELIST.
AND YOU BET THESE STAR CHIPS ON YOUR DUELS!
THEN THE LAST TWO CARDS...
THE HONOR OF THE KING'S RIGHT...THIS MEANS THE PRIZE MONEY THAT THE DUELIST KING WINS, I THINK.
THE HONOR OF THE KING'S RIGHT
Great Wealth
THE HONOR OF THE KING'S LEFT
? ? ?
BUT THERE'S NOTHING WRITTEN ON THE OTHER CARD, THE HONOR OF THE KING'S LEFT!
THERE'S SOME SECRET HONOR THAT ONLY THE ONE WHO BECOMES THE KING CAN GET!
THAT'S IT FOR THE CARDS!
LET'S WATCH JONOUCHI'S VIDEO NEXT!
AWW RIGHT!
IT CAME FOR ME TOO...!
THAT JERK PEGASUS! TRYIN' TO MAKE ME INTO YUGI'S RIVAL!

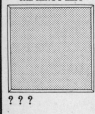

READ THIS WAY

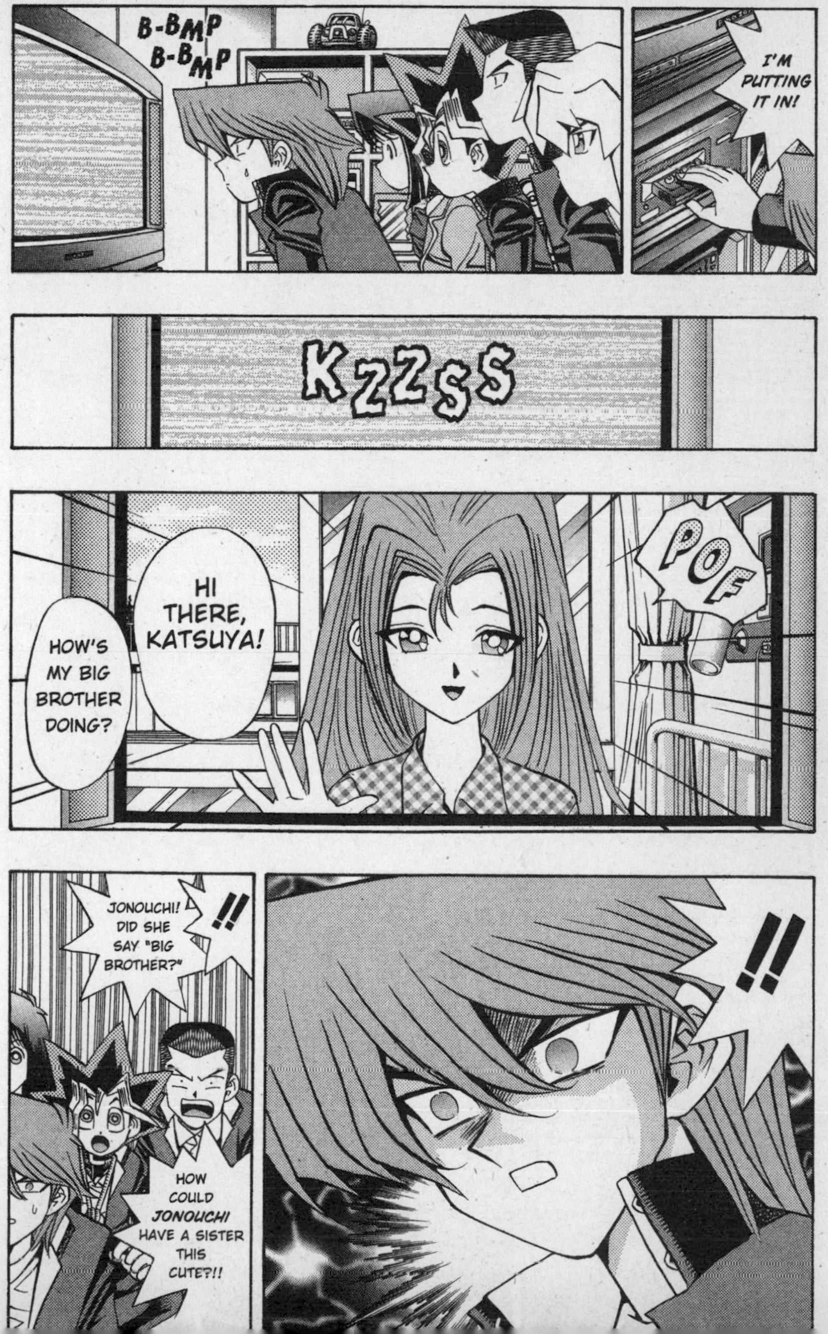
I'M PUTTING IT IN!
B-BMP B-BMP
KZZSS
POF
HI THERE, KATSUYA!
HOW'S MY BIG BROTHER DOING?
!!
JONOUCHI! DID SHE SAY "BIG BROTHER?"
!!
HOW COULD JONOUCHI HAVE A SISTER THIS CUTE?!!

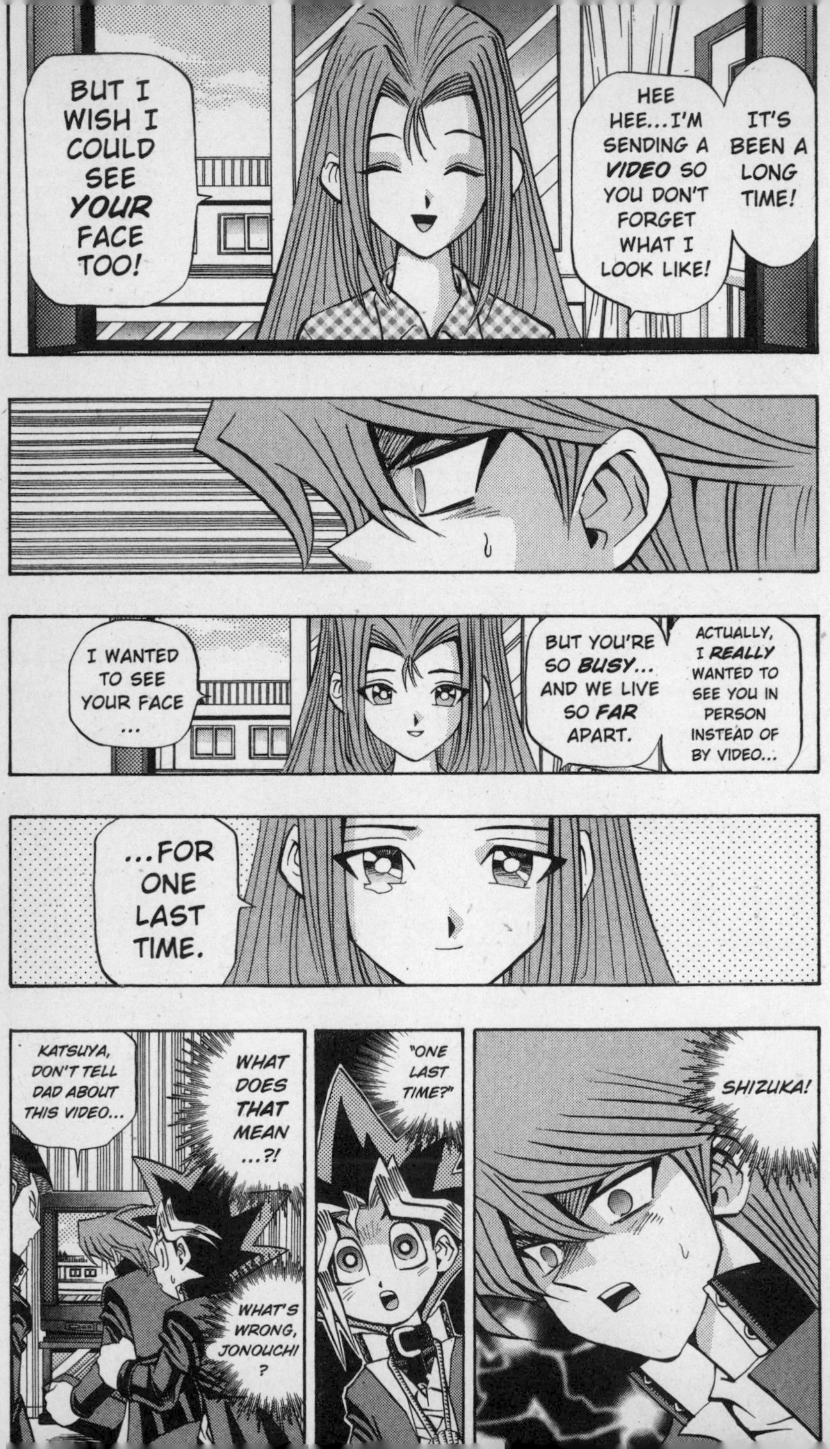
IT'S BEEN A LONG TIME!
HEE HEE...I'M SENDING A VIDEO SO YOU DON'T FORGET WHAT I LOOK LIKE!
BUT I WISH I COULD SEE YOUR FACE TOO!
ACTUALLY, I REALLY WANTED TO SEE YOU IN PERSON INSTEAD OF BY VIDEO...
BUT YOU'RE SO BUSY... AND WE LIVE SO FAR APART.
I WANTED TO SEE YOUR FACE ...
...FOR ONE LAST TIME.
SHIZUKA!
"ONE LAST TIME?"
WHAT'S WRONG, JONOUCHI?
WHAT DOES THAT MEAN ...?!
KATSUYA, DON'T TELL DAD ABOUT THIS VIDEO...

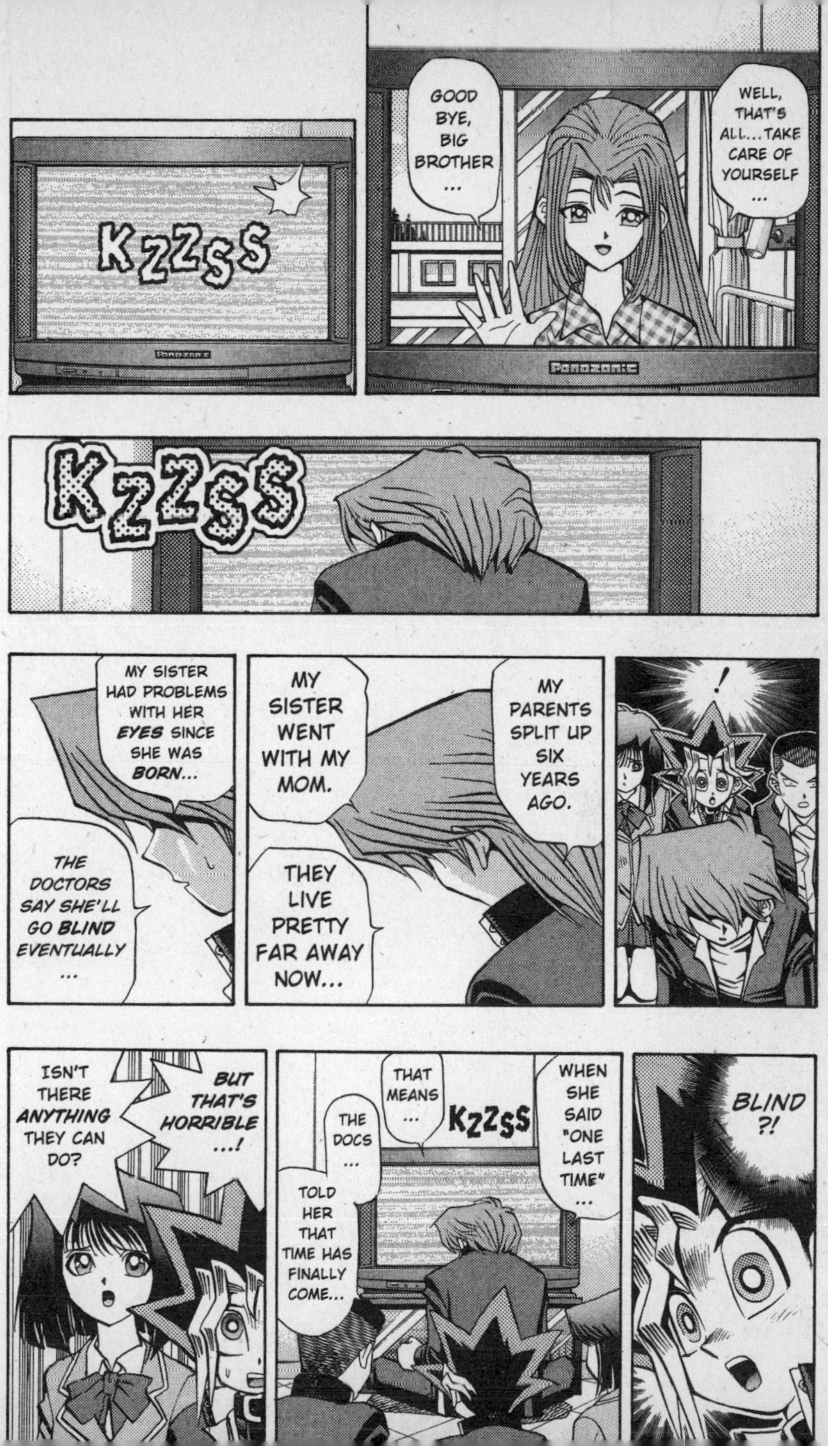
WELL, THAT'S ALL...TAKE CARE OF YOURSELF ...
GOOD BYE, BIG BROTHER ...
KZZSS
KZZSS
!
MY PARENTS SPLIT UP SIX YEARS AGO.
MY SISTER WENT WITH MY MOM.
THEY LIVE PRETTY FAR AWAY NOW...
MY SISTER HAD PROBLEMS WITH HER EYES SINCE SHE WAS BORN...
THE DOCTORS SAY SHE'LL GO BLIND EVENTUALLY ...
BLIND ?!
WHEN SHE SAID "ONE LAST TIME" ...
KZZSS
THAT MEANS ...
THE DOCS ...
TOLD HER THAT TIME HAS FINALLY COME...
BUT THAT'S HORRIBLE ...!
ISN'T THERE ANYTHING THEY CAN DO?

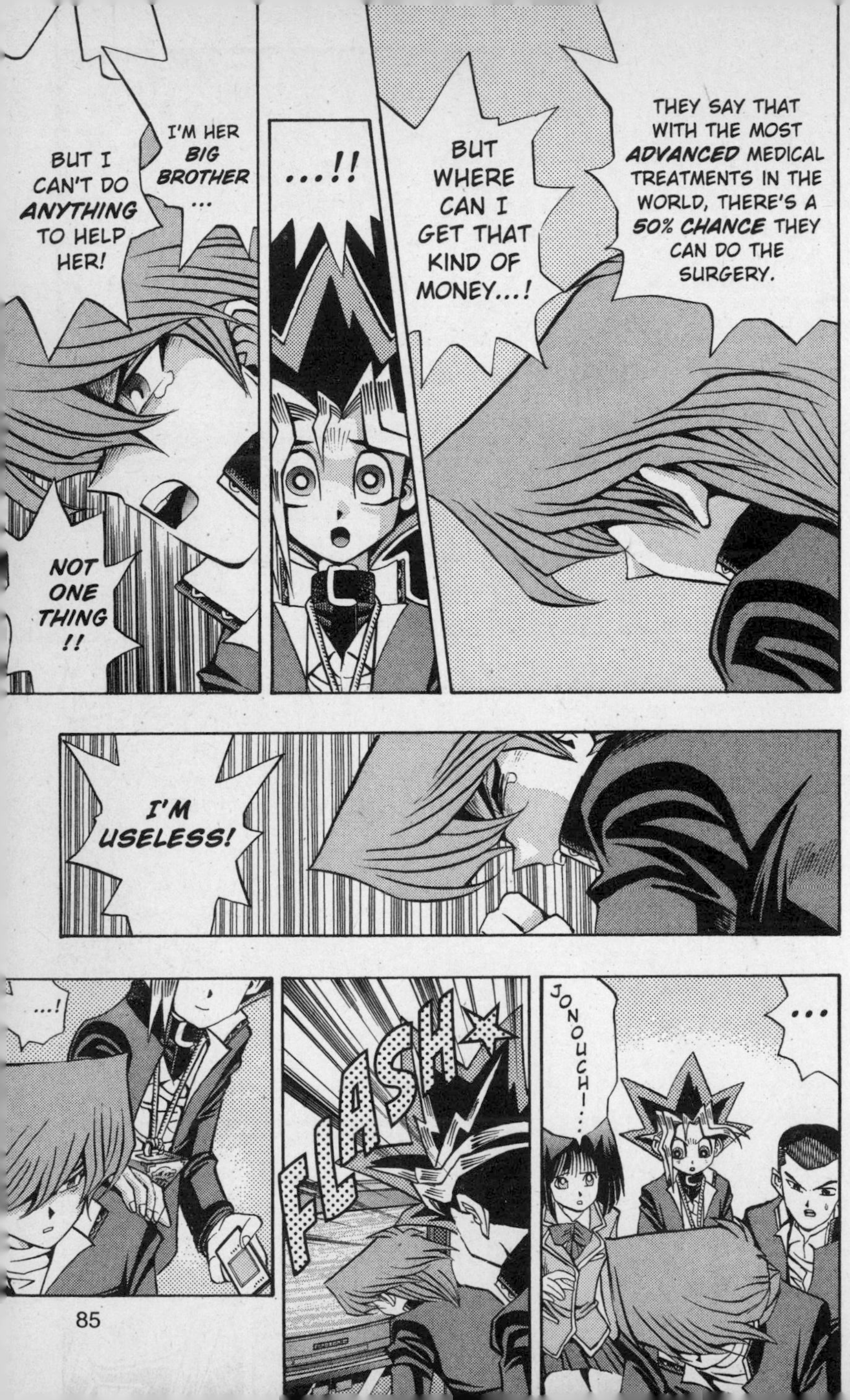

THEY SAY THAT WITH THE MOST ADVANCED MEDICAL TREATMENTS IN THE WORLD, THERE'S A 50% CHANCE THEY CAN DO THE SURGERY.
BUT WHERE CAN I GET THAT KIND OF MONEY...!
...!!
I'M HER BIG BROTHER ...
BUT I CAN'T DO ANYTHING TO HELP HER!
NOT ONE THING !!
I'M USELESS!
...
JONOUCHI...
FLASH
...!

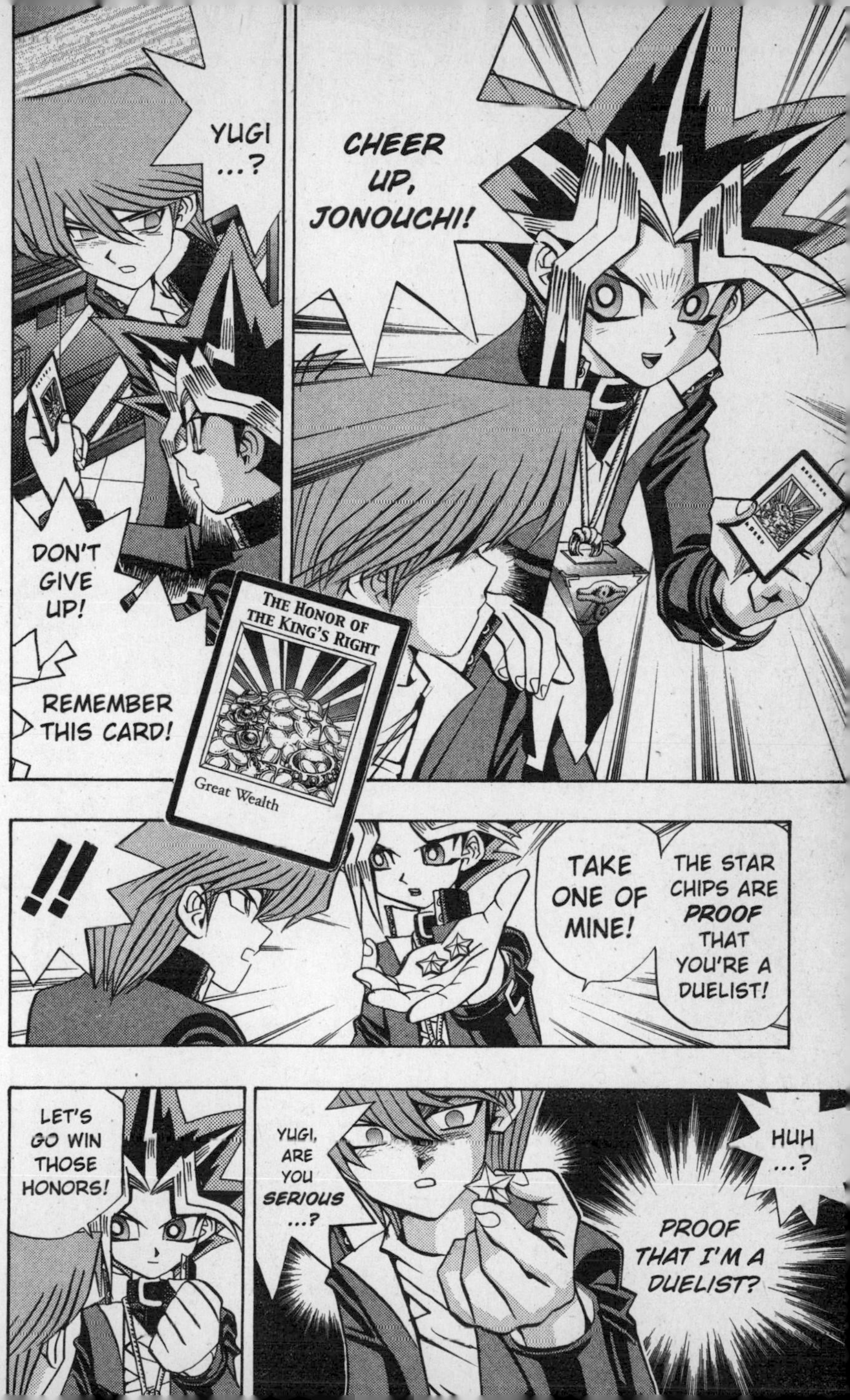
CHEER UP, JONOUCHI!
YUGI ...?
DON'T GIVE UP!
THE HONOR OF THE KING'S RIGHT
Great Wealth
REMEMBER THIS CARD!
THE STAR CHIPS ARE PROOF THAT YOU'RE A DUELIST!
TAKE ONE OF MINE!
!!
HUH ...?
YUGI, ARE YOU SERIOUS ...?
PROOF THAT I'M A DUELIST?
LET'S GO WIN THOSE HONORS!

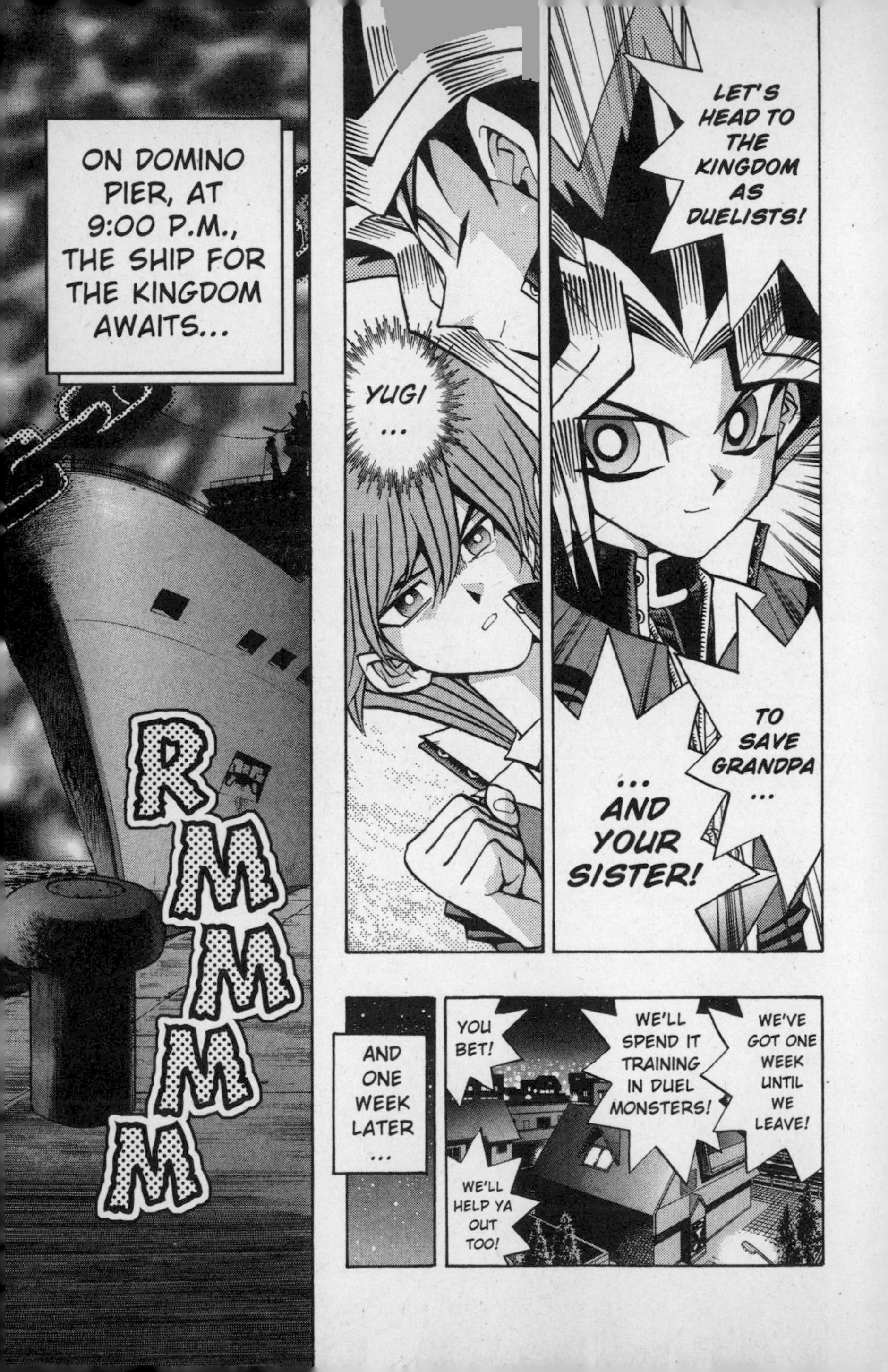

LET'S HEAD TO THE KINGDOM AS DUELISTS!
TO SAVE GRANDPA ...
... AND YOUR SISTER!
YUGI ...
WE'VE GOT ONE WEEK UNTIL WE LEAVE!
WE'LL SPEND IT TRAINING IN DUEL MONSTERS!
YOU BET!
WE'LL HELP YA OUT TOO!
AND ONE WEEK LATER ...
ON DOMINO PIER, AT 9:00 P.M., THE SHIP FOR THE KINGDOM AWAITS...
RMMMM

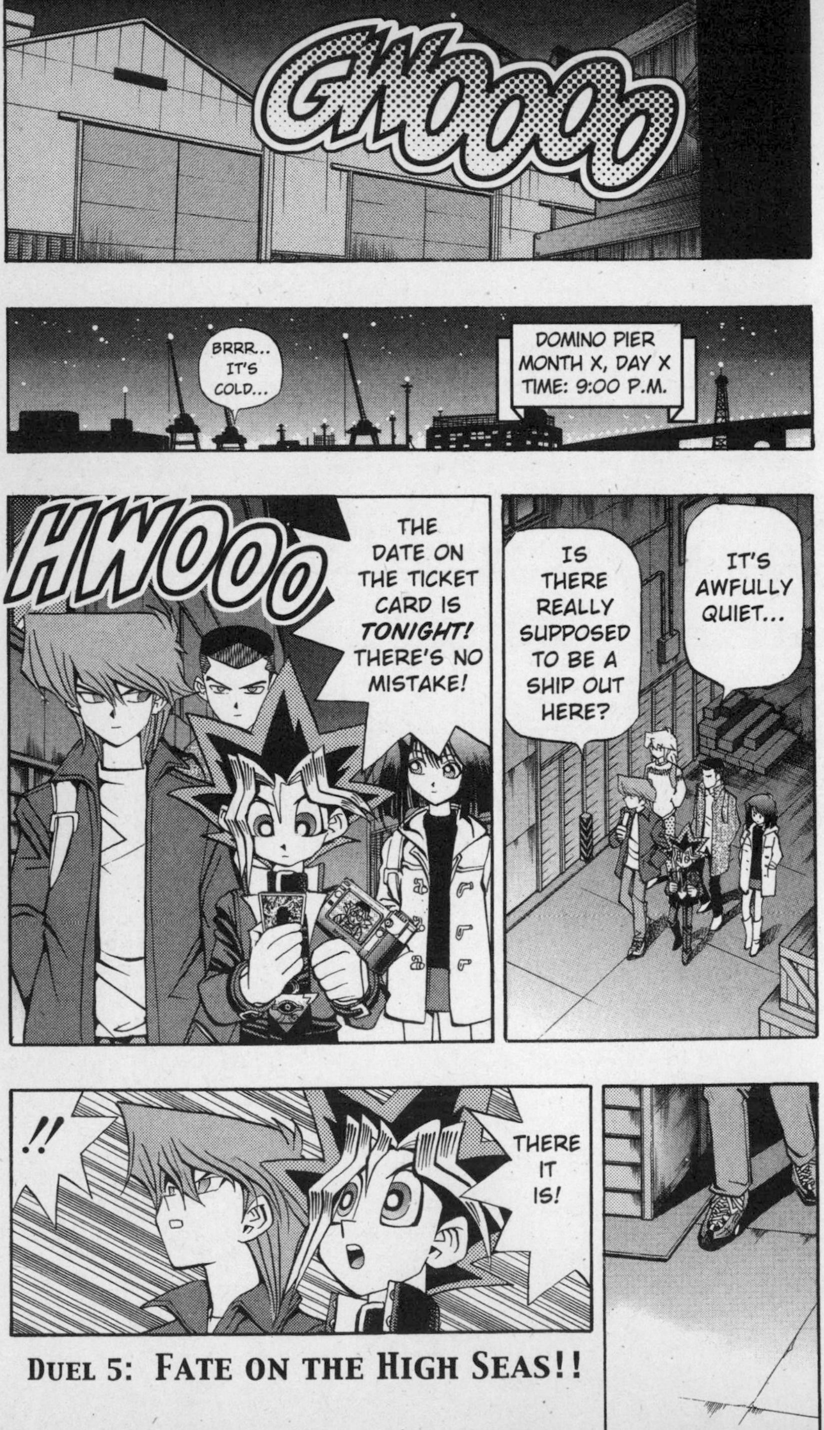
GWOOOO
DOMINO PIER MONTH X, DAY X TIME: 9:00 P.M.
BRRR... IT'S COLD...
IT'S AWFULLY QUIET...
IS THERE REALLY SUPPOSED TO BE A SHIP OUT HERE?
THE DATE ON THE TICKET CARD IS *TONIGHT!* THERE'S NO MISTAKE!
HWOOO
THERE IT IS!
!!

Duel 5: Fate on the High Seas!!

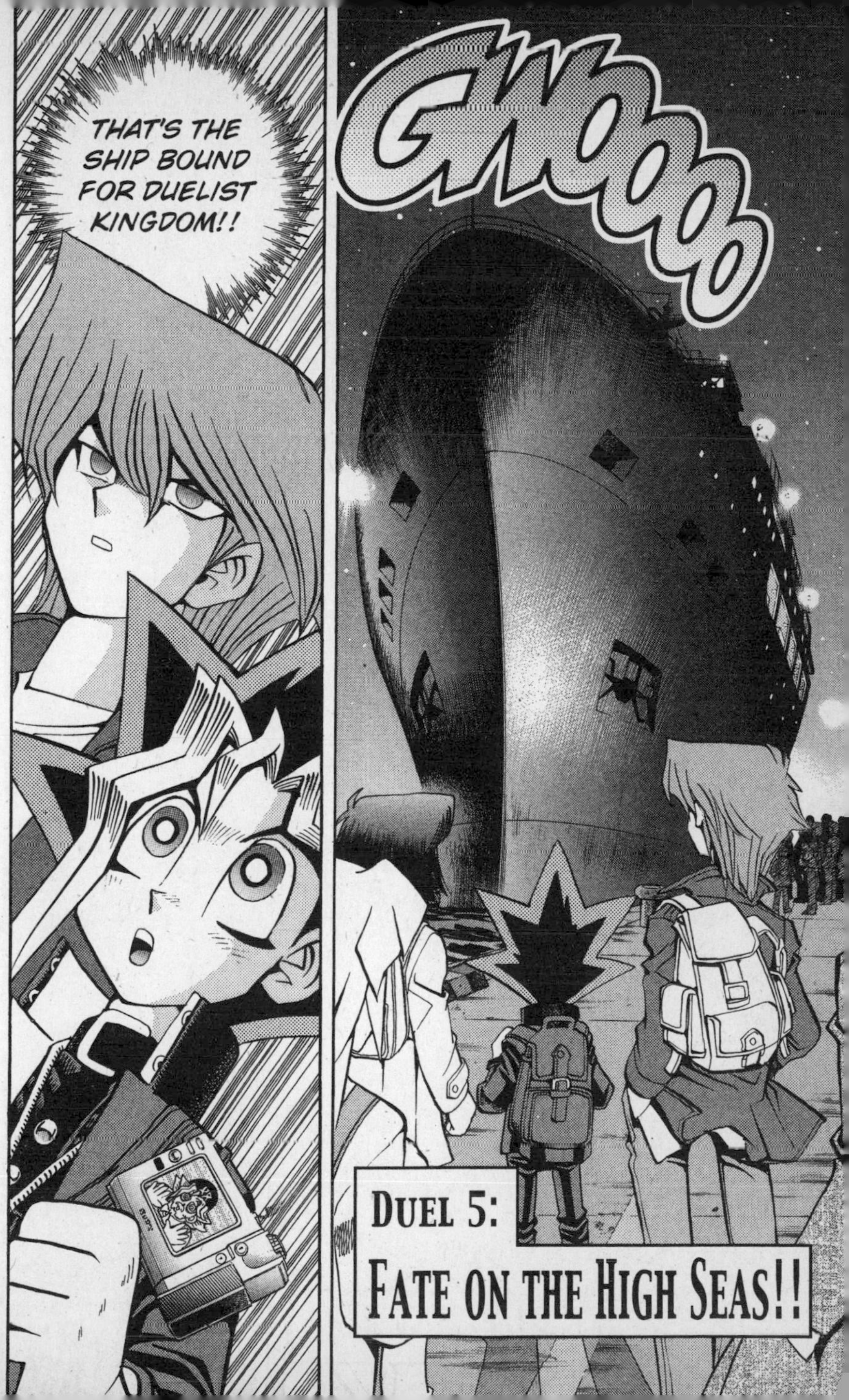
GWOOOOO
DUEL 5:
FATE ON THE HIGH SEAS!!
THAT'S THE SHIP BOUND FOR DUELIST KINGDOM!!

READ THIS WAY

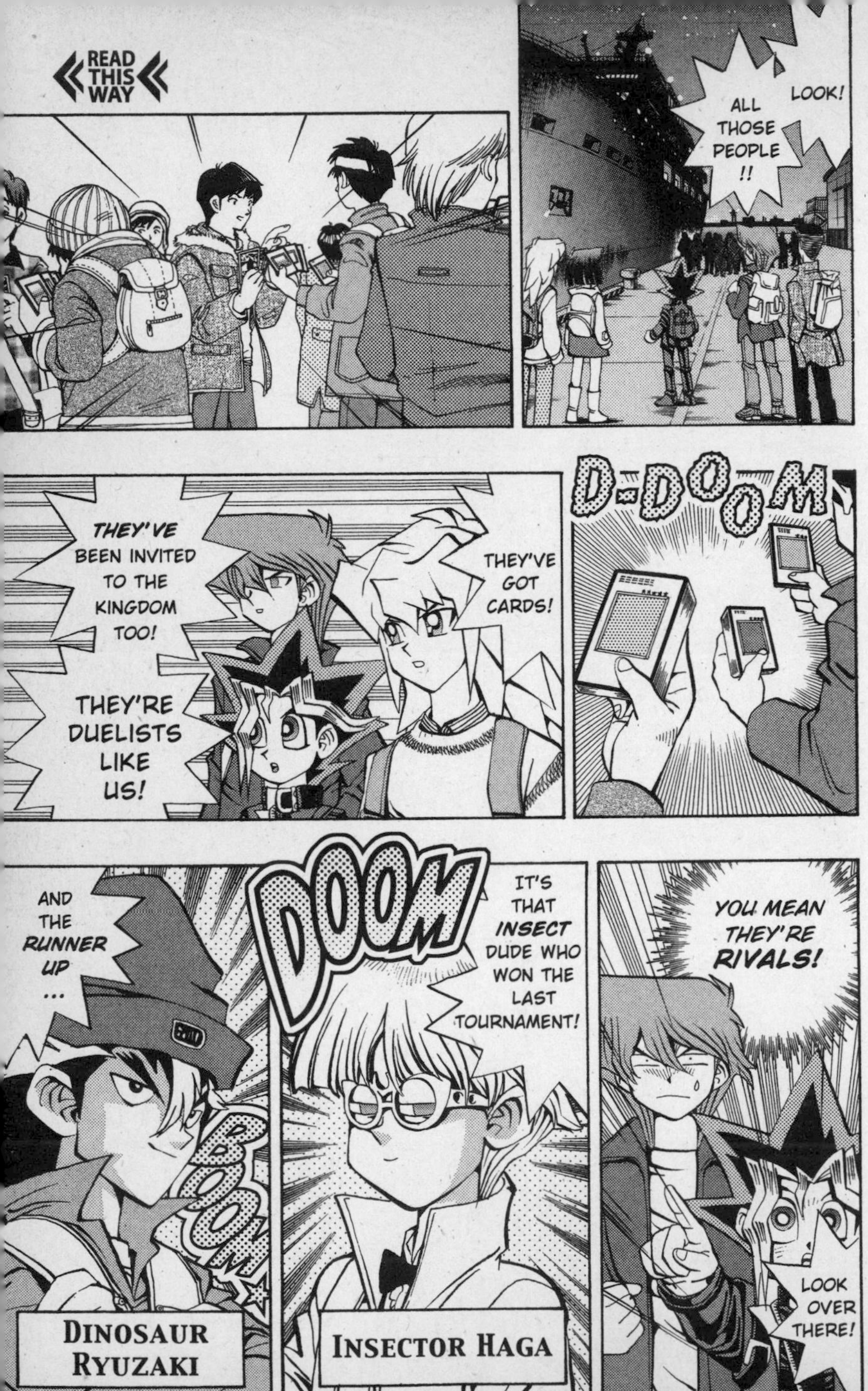
LOOK!
ALL THOSE PEOPLE !!
D-DOOOM
THEY'VE GOT CARDS!
THEY'VE BEEN INVITED TO THE KINGDOM TOO!
THEY'RE DUELISTS LIKE US!
YOU MEAN THEY'RE RIVALS!
LOOK OVER THERE!
IT'S THAT INSECT DUDE WHO WON THE LAST TOURNAMENT!
DOOM
INSECTOR HAGA
AND THE RUNNER UP ...
BOOM
DINOSAUR RYUZAKI

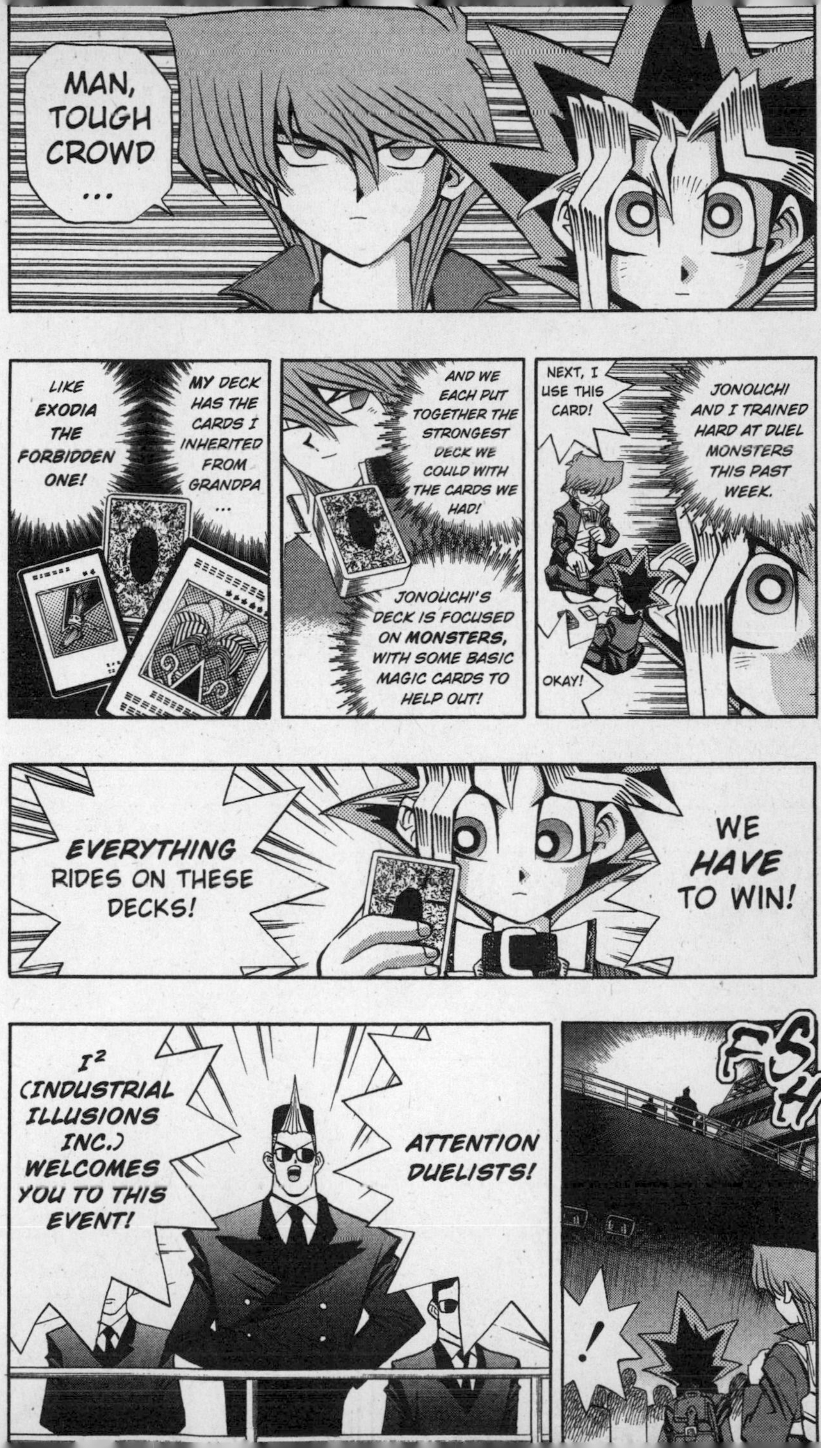
MAN, TOUGH CROWD ...
JONOUCHI AND I TRAINED HARD AT DUEL MONSTERS THIS PAST WEEK.
NEXT, I USE THIS CARD!
OKAY!
AND WE EACH PUT TOGETHER THE STRONGEST DECK WE COULD WITH THE CARDS WE HAD!
JONOUCHI'S DECK IS FOCUSED ON MONSTERS, WITH SOME BASIC MAGIC CARDS TO HELP OUT!
MY DECK HAS THE CARDS I INHERITED FROM GRANDPA ...
LIKE EXODIA THE FORBIDDEN ONE!
WE HAVE TO WIN!
EVERYTHING RIDES ON THESE DECKS!
FSH
!
ATTENTION DUELISTS!
I^2 (INDUSTRIAL ILLUSIONS INC.) WELCOMES YOU TO THIS EVENT!

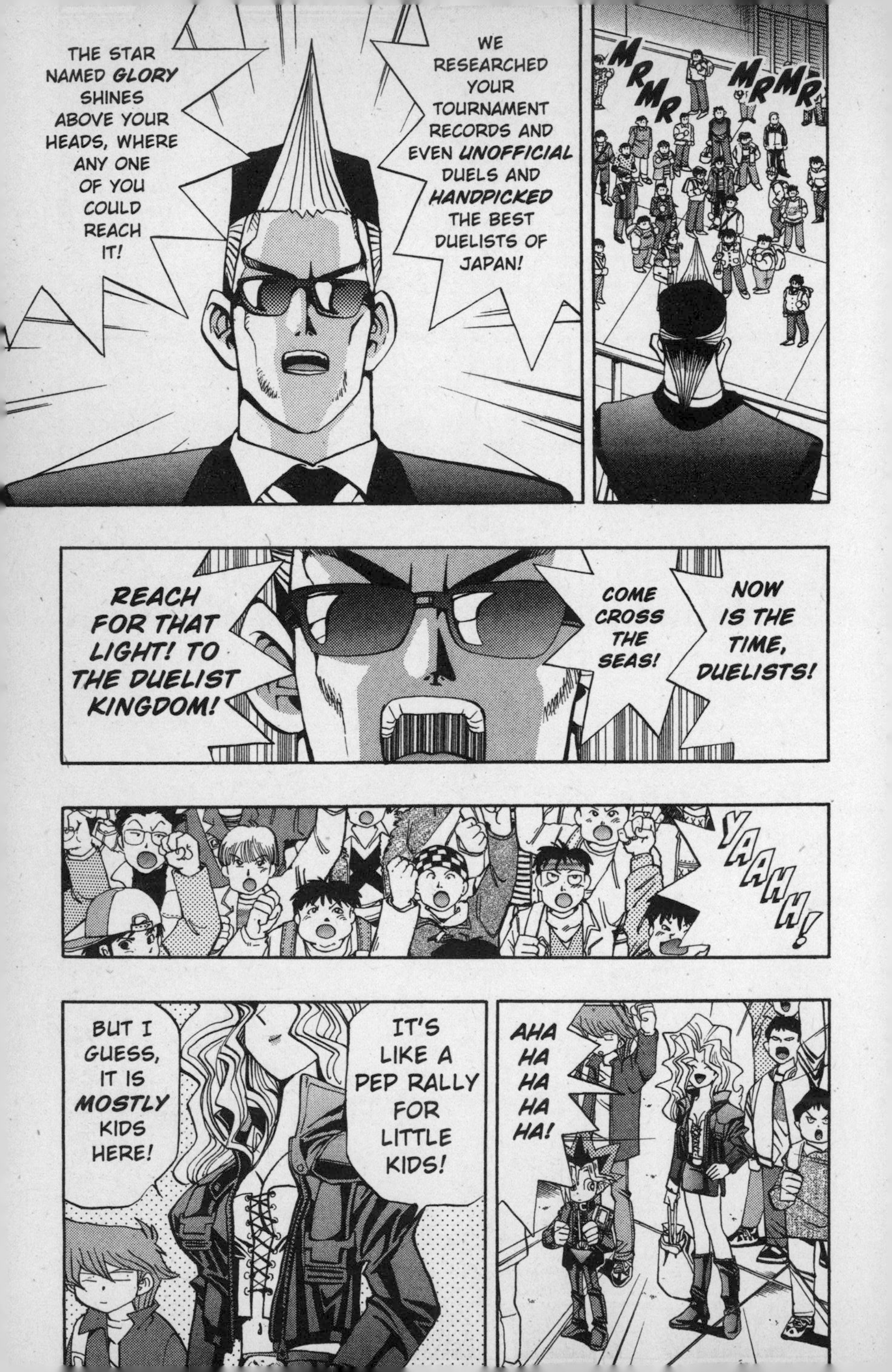
MRMR
MRMR
WE RESEARCHED YOUR TOURNAMENT RECORDS AND EVEN UNOFFICIAL DUELS AND HANDPICKED THE BEST DUELISTS OF JAPAN!
THE STAR NAMED GLORY SHINES ABOVE YOUR HEADS, WHERE ANY ONE OF YOU COULD REACH IT!
NOW IS THE TIME, DUELISTS!
COME CROSS THE SEAS!
REACH FOR THAT LIGHT! TO THE DUELIST KINGDOM!
YAAHH!
AHA HA HA HA HA!
IT'S LIKE A PEP RALLY FOR LITTLE KIDS!
BUT I GUESS, IT IS MOSTLY KIDS HERE!

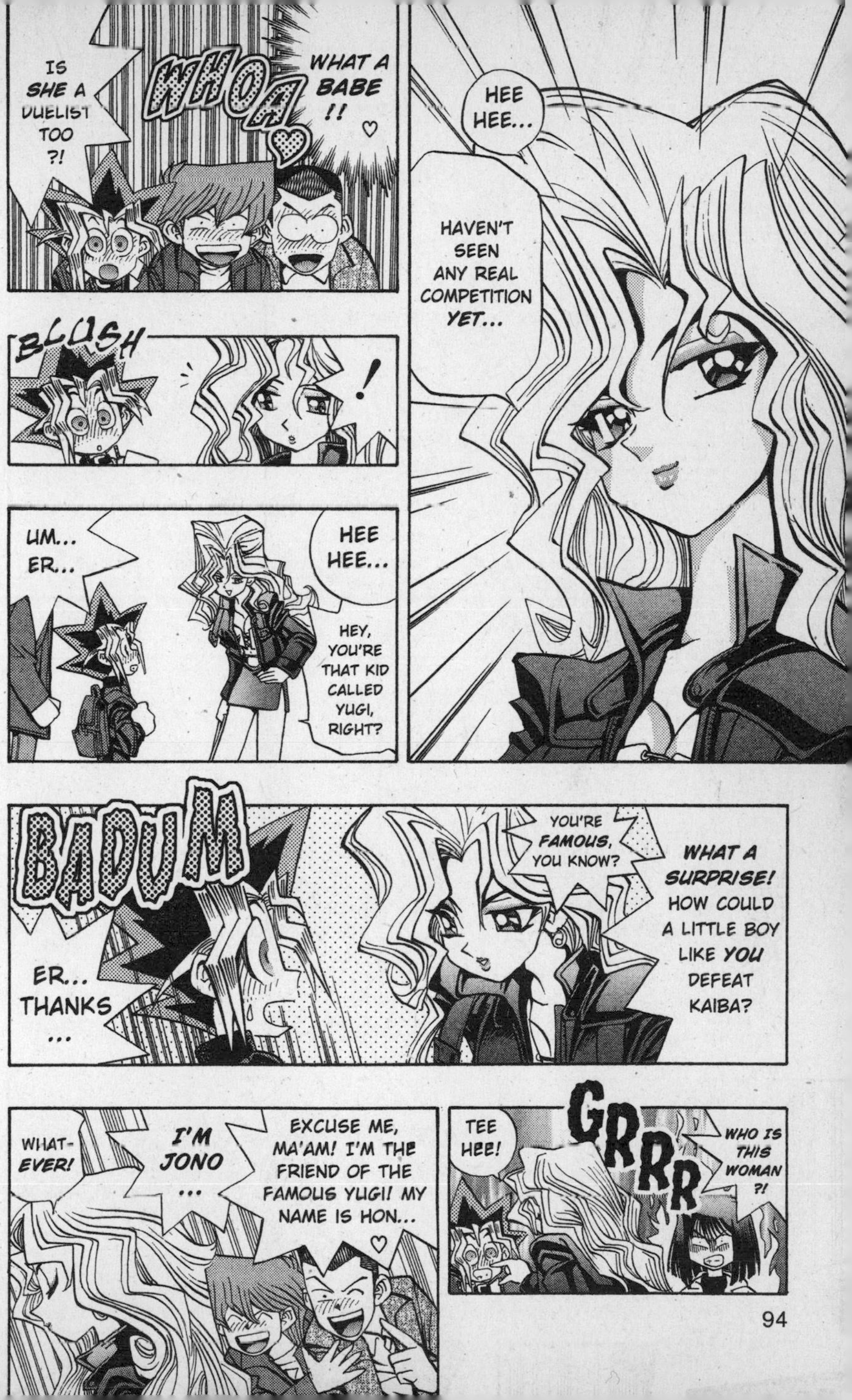
HEE HEE...
HAVEN'T SEEN ANY REAL COMPETITION YET...
WHAT A BABE !! ♡
WHOA
IS SHE A DUELIST TOO ?!
BLUSH
!
HEE HEE...
HEY, YOU'RE THAT KID CALLED YUGI, RIGHT?
UM... ER...
WHAT A SURPRISE! HOW COULD A LITTLE BOY LIKE YOU DEFEAT KAIBA?
YOU'RE FAMOUS, YOU KNOW?
BADUM
ER... THANKS ...
WHO IS THIS WOMAN ?!
GRRR
TEE HEE!
EXCUSE ME, MA'AM! I'M THE FRIEND OF THE FAMOUS YUGI! MY NAME IS HON... ♡
I'M JONO ...
WHAT-EVER!

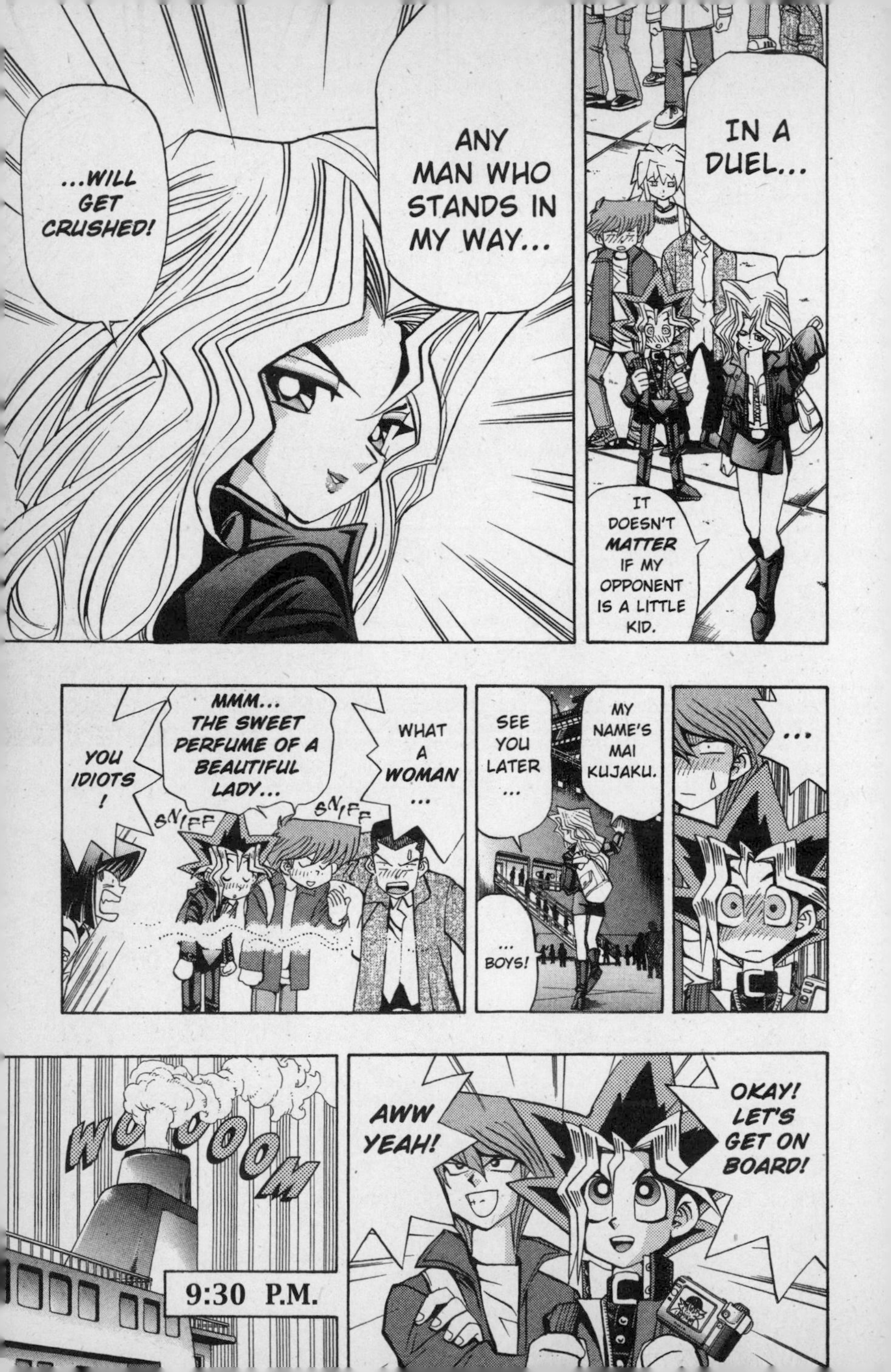
IN A DUEL...
IT DOESN'T MATTER IF MY OPPONENT IS A LITTLE KID.
ANY MAN WHO STANDS IN MY WAY...
...WILL GET CRUSHED!
...
MY NAME'S MAI KUJAKU.
SEE YOU LATER ...
... BOYS!
WHAT A WOMAN ...
SNIFF
MMM... THE SWEET PERFUME OF A BEAUTIFUL LADY...
SNIFF
YOU IDIOTS !
OKAY! LET'S GET ON BOARD!
AWW YEAH!
WOOOOOM
9:30 P.M.

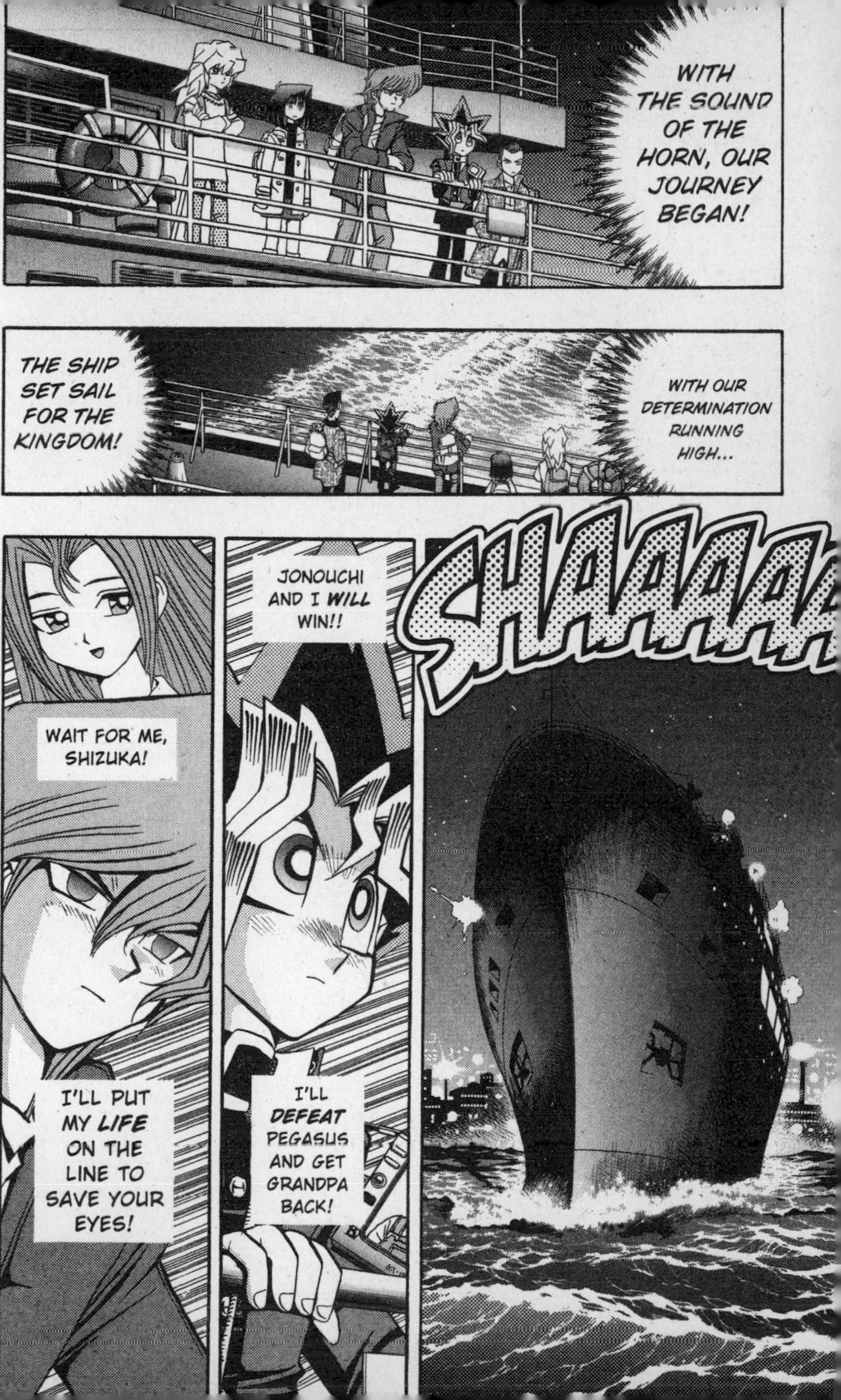
WITH THE SOUND OF THE HORN, OUR JOURNEY BEGAN!
WITH OUR DETERMINATION RUNNING HIGH...
THE SHIP SET SAIL FOR THE KINGDOM!
SHAAAAA
JONOUCHI AND I WILL WIN!!
I'LL DEFEAT PEGASUS AND GET GRANDPA BACK!
WAIT FOR ME, SHIZUKA!
I'LL PUT MY LIFE ON THE LINE TO SAVE YOUR EYES!

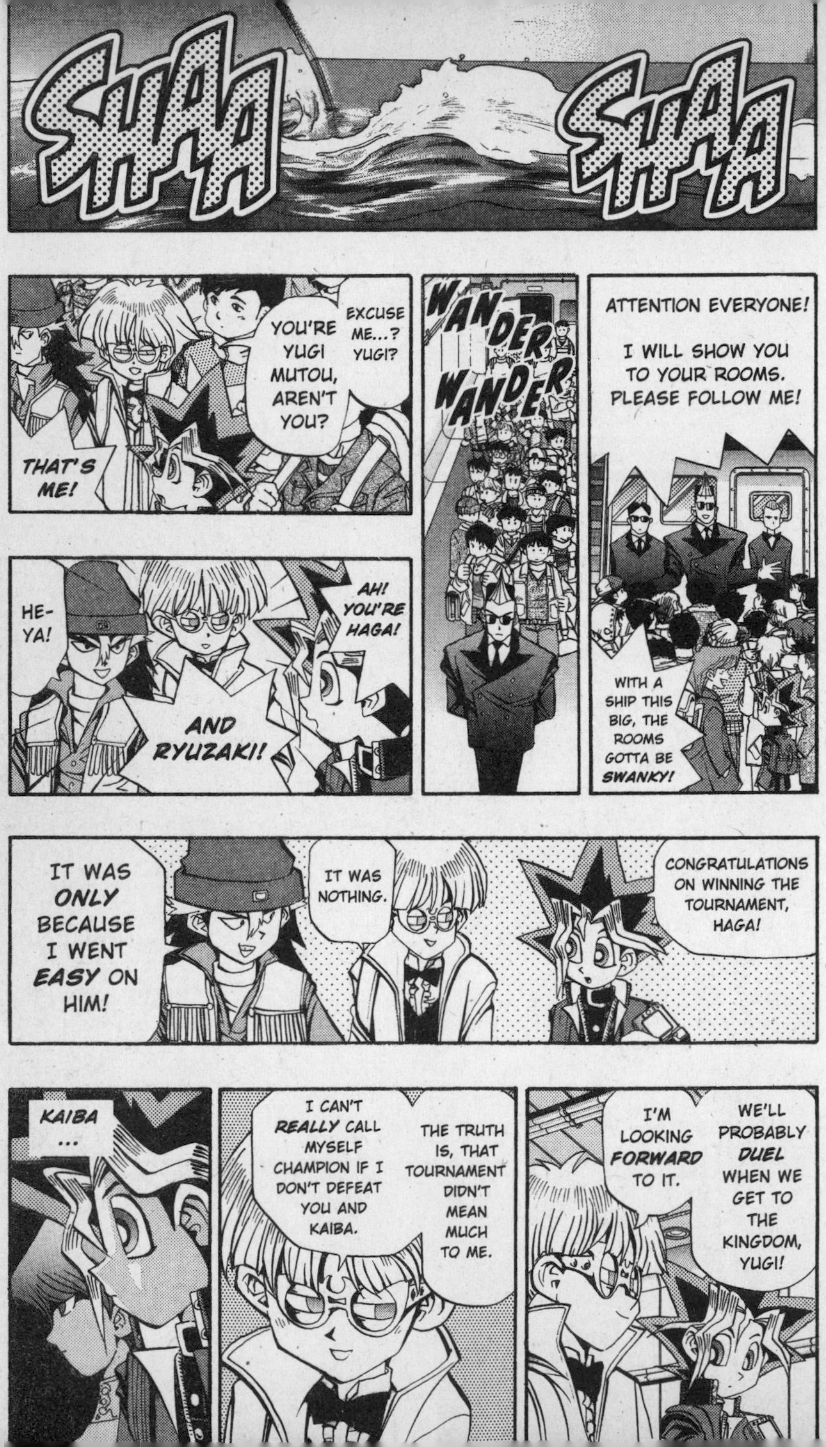
SHAA
SHAA
ATTENTION EVERYONE! I WILL SHOW YOU TO YOUR ROOMS. PLEASE FOLLOW ME!
WITH A SHIP THIS BIG, THE ROOMS GOTTA BE SWANKY!
WANDER WANDER
EXCUSE ME...? YUGI?
YOU'RE YUGI MUTOU, AREN'T YOU?
THAT'S ME!
AH! YOU'RE HAGA!
AND RYUZAKI!
HE-YA!
CONGRATULATIONS ON WINNING THE TOURNAMENT, HAGA!
IT WAS NOTHING.
IT WAS ONLY BECAUSE I WENT EASY ON HIM!
WE'LL PROBABLY DUEL WHEN WE GET TO THE KINGDOM, YUGI!
I'M LOOKING FORWARD TO IT.
THE TRUTH IS, THAT TOURNAMENT DIDN'T MEAN MUCH TO ME.
I CAN'T REALLY CALL MYSELF CHAMPION IF I DON'T DEFEAT YOU AND KAIBA.
KAIBA ...

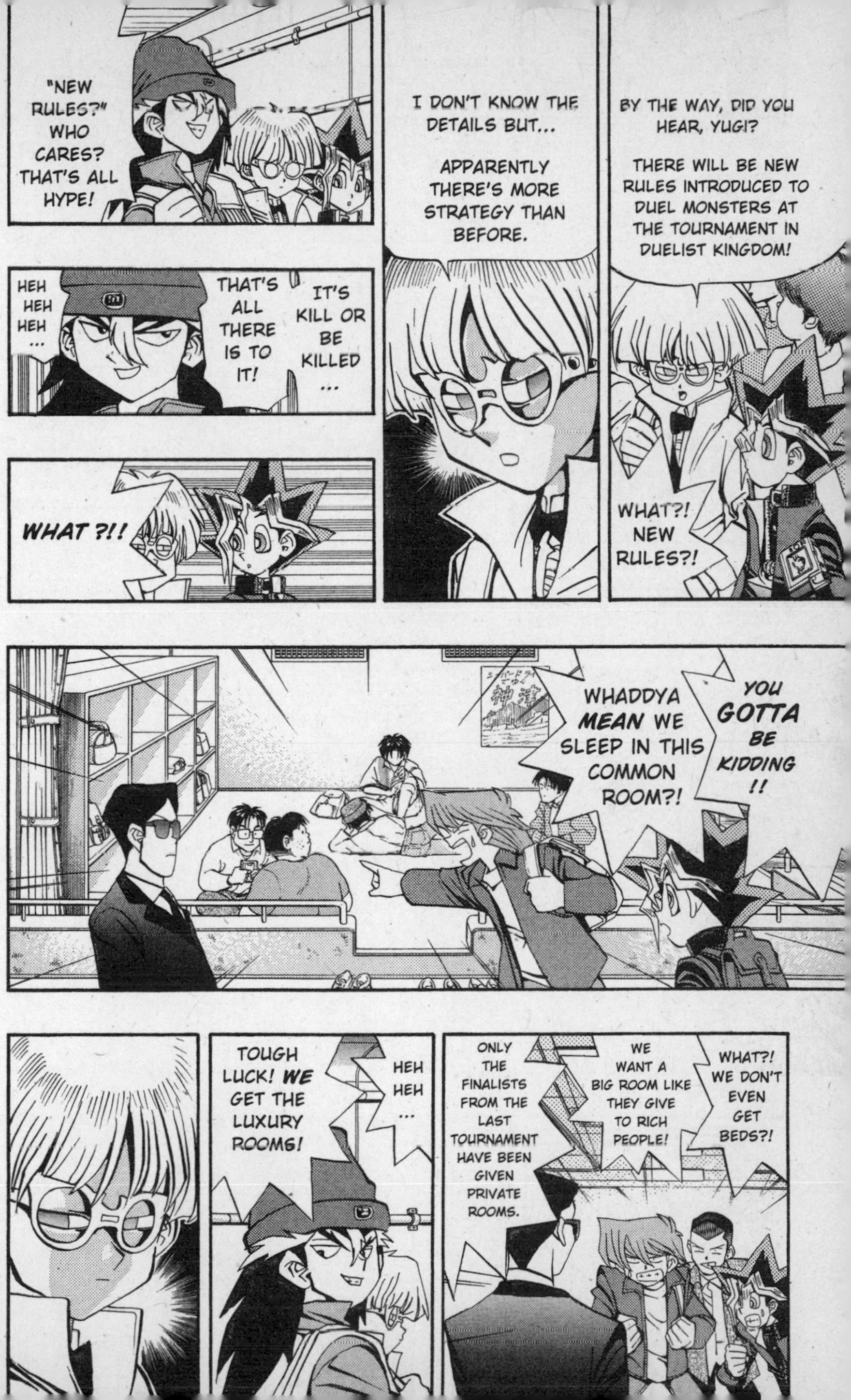
BY THE WAY, DID YOU HEAR, YUGI?
THERE WILL BE NEW RULES INTRODUCED TO DUEL MONSTERS AT THE TOURNAMENT IN DUELIST KINGDOM!
WHAT?! NEW RULES?!
I DON'T KNOW THE DETAILS BUT...
APPARENTLY THERE'S MORE STRATEGY THAN BEFORE.
"NEW RULES?" WHO CARES? THAT'S ALL HYPE!
IT'S KILL OR BE KILLED...
THAT'S ALL THERE IS TO IT!
HEH HEH HEH...
WHAT ?!!
YOU GOTTA BE KIDDING!!
WHADDYA MEAN WE SLEEP IN THIS COMMON ROOM?!
WHAT?! WE DON'T EVEN GET BEDS?!
WE WANT A BIG ROOM LIKE THEY GIVE TO RICH PEOPLE!
ONLY THE FINALISTS FROM THE LAST TOURNAMENT HAVE BEEN GIVEN PRIVATE ROOMS.
HEH HEH...
TOUGH LUCK! WE GET THE LUXURY ROOMS!

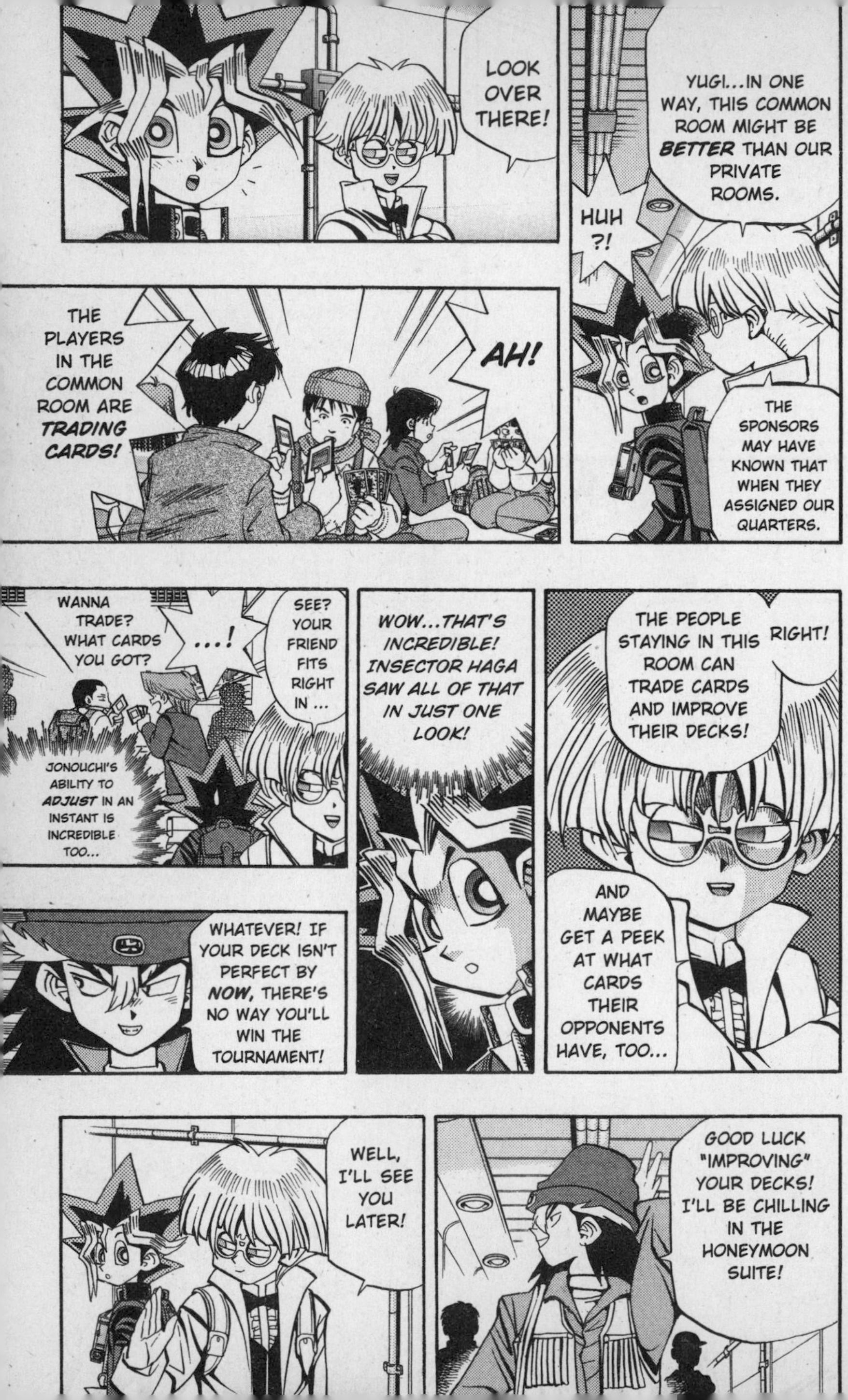
YUGI...IN ONE WAY, THIS COMMON ROOM MIGHT BE BETTER THAN OUR PRIVATE ROOMS.
HUH ?!
THE SPONSORS MAY HAVE KNOWN THAT WHEN THEY ASSIGNED OUR QUARTERS.
LOOK OVER THERE!
AH!
THE PLAYERS IN THE COMMON ROOM ARE TRADING CARDS!
RIGHT!
THE PEOPLE STAYING IN THIS ROOM CAN TRADE CARDS AND IMPROVE THEIR DECKS!
AND MAYBE GET A PEEK AT WHAT CARDS THEIR OPPONENTS HAVE, TOO...
WOW...THAT'S INCREDIBLE! INSECTOR HAGA SAW ALL OF THAT IN JUST ONE LOOK!
SEE? YOUR FRIEND FITS RIGHT IN ...
...!
WANNA TRADE? WHAT CARDS YOU GOT?
JONOUCHI'S ABILITY TO ADJUST IN AN INSTANT IS INCREDIBLE TOO...
WHATEVER! IF YOUR DECK ISN'T PERFECT BY NOW, THERE'S NO WAY YOU'LL WIN THE TOURNAMENT!
GOOD LUCK "IMPROVING" YOUR DECKS! I'LL BE CHILLING IN THE HONEYMOON SUITE!
WELL, I'LL SEE YOU LATER!

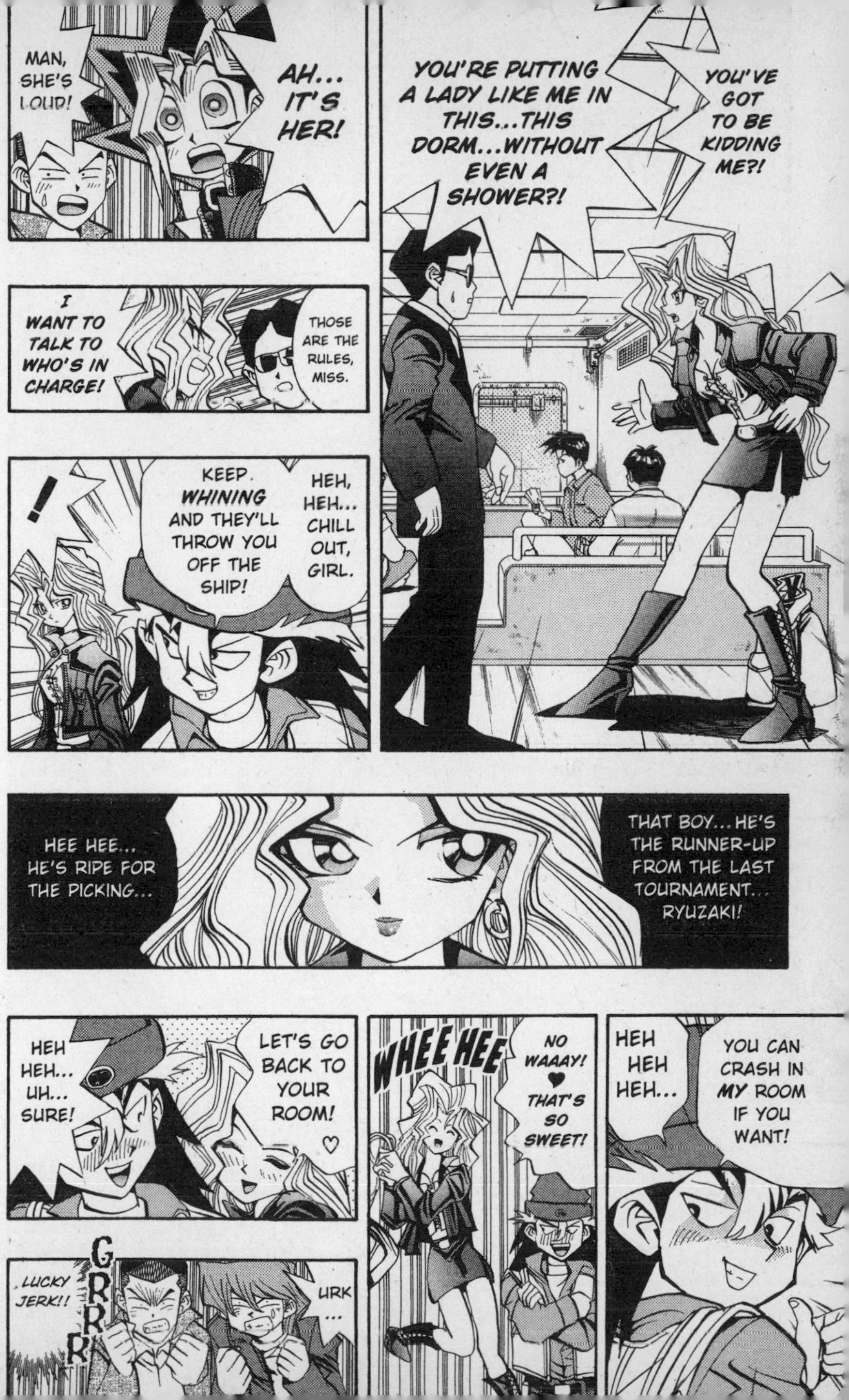
YOU'VE GOT TO BE KIDDING ME?!
YOU'RE PUTTING A LADY LIKE ME IN THIS...THIS DORM...WITHOUT EVEN A SHOWER?!
AH... IT'S HER!
MAN, SHE'S LOUD!
THOSE ARE THE RULES, MISS.
I WANT TO TALK TO WHO'S IN CHARGE!
HEH, HEH... CHILL OUT, GIRL.
KEEP. WHINING AND THEY'LL THROW YOU OFF THE SHIP!
!
THAT BOY...HE'S THE RUNNER-UP FROM THE LAST TOURNAMENT... RYUZAKI!
HEE HEE... HE'S RIPE FOR THE PICKING...
YOU CAN CRASH IN MY ROOM IF YOU WANT!
HEH HEH HEH...
NO WAAAY! ♥ THAT'S SO SWEET!
WHEE HEE
LET'S GO BACK TO YOUR ROOM! ♡
HEH HEH... UH... SURE!
URK ...
GRRR
LUCKY JERK!!

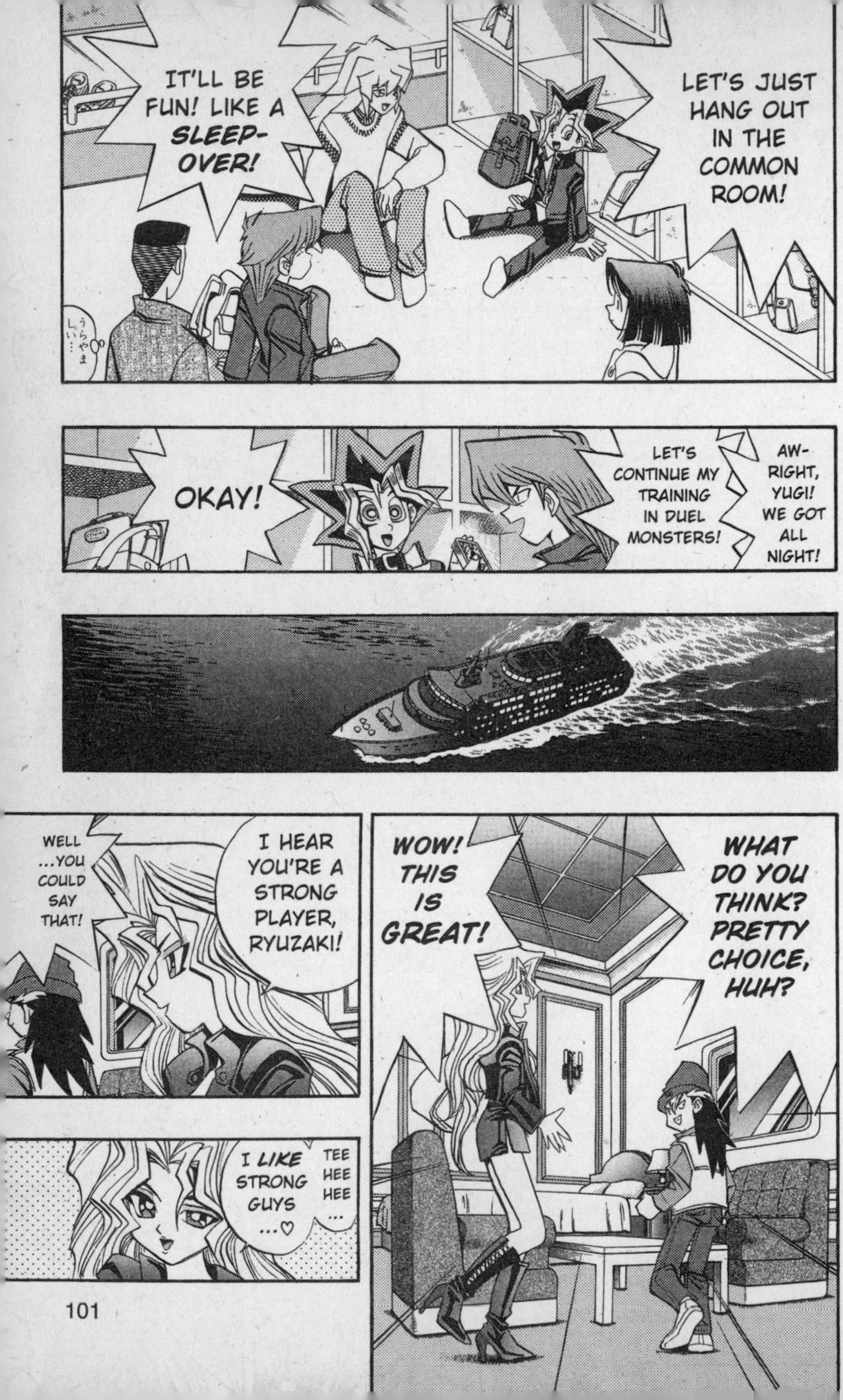
LET'S JUST HANG OUT IN THE COMMON ROOM!
IT'LL BE FUN! LIKE A SLEEP-OVER!
うらやましい…
AW-RIGHT, YUGI! WE GOT ALL NIGHT!
LET'S CONTINUE MY TRAINING IN DUEL MONSTERS!
OKAY!
WHAT DO YOU THINK? PRETTY CHOICE, HUH?
WOW! THIS IS GREAT!
I HEAR YOU'RE A STRONG PLAYER, RYUZAKI!
WELL ...YOU COULD SAY THAT!
TEE HEE HEE ...
I LIKE STRONG GUYS ...♡

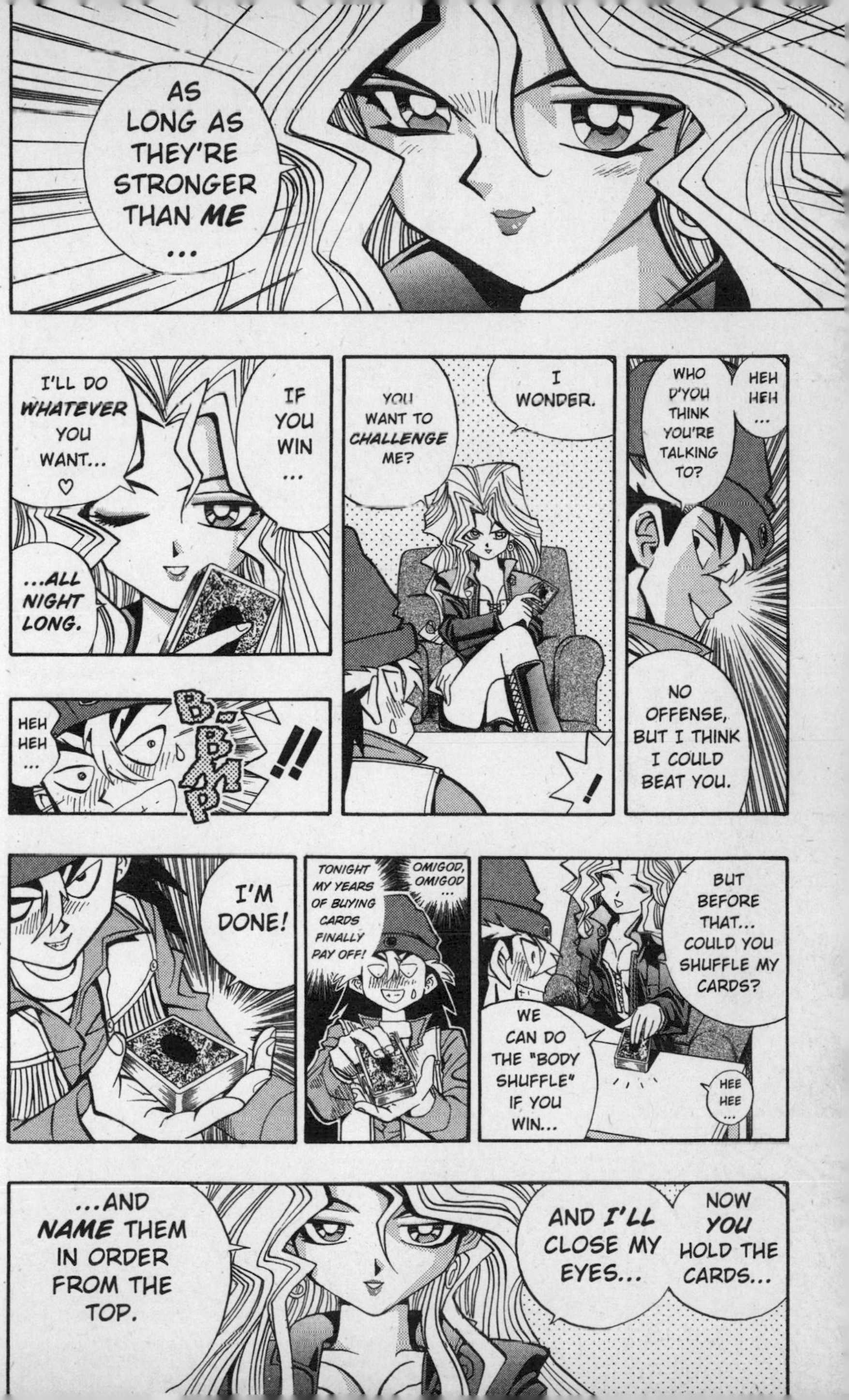
AS LONG AS THEY'RE STRONGER THAN **ME** ...
HEH HEH ...
WHO D'YOU THINK YOU'RE TALKING TO?
NO OFFENSE, BUT I THINK I COULD BEAT YOU.
I WONDER.
YOU WANT TO ***CHALLENGE*** ME?
!
IF YOU WIN ...
I'LL DO ***WHATEVER*** YOU WANT... ♡
...ALL NIGHT LONG.
B-BMP
!!
HEH HEH ...
BUT BEFORE THAT... COULD YOU SHUFFLE MY CARDS?
WE CAN DO THE "BODY SHUFFLE" IF YOU WIN...
HEE HEE ...
OMIGOD, OMIGOD ...
TONIGHT MY YEARS OF BUYING CARDS FINALLY PAY OFF!
I'M DONE!
NOW ***YOU*** HOLD THE CARDS...
AND ***I'LL*** CLOSE MY EYES...
...AND ***NAME*** THEM IN ORDER FROM THE TOP.

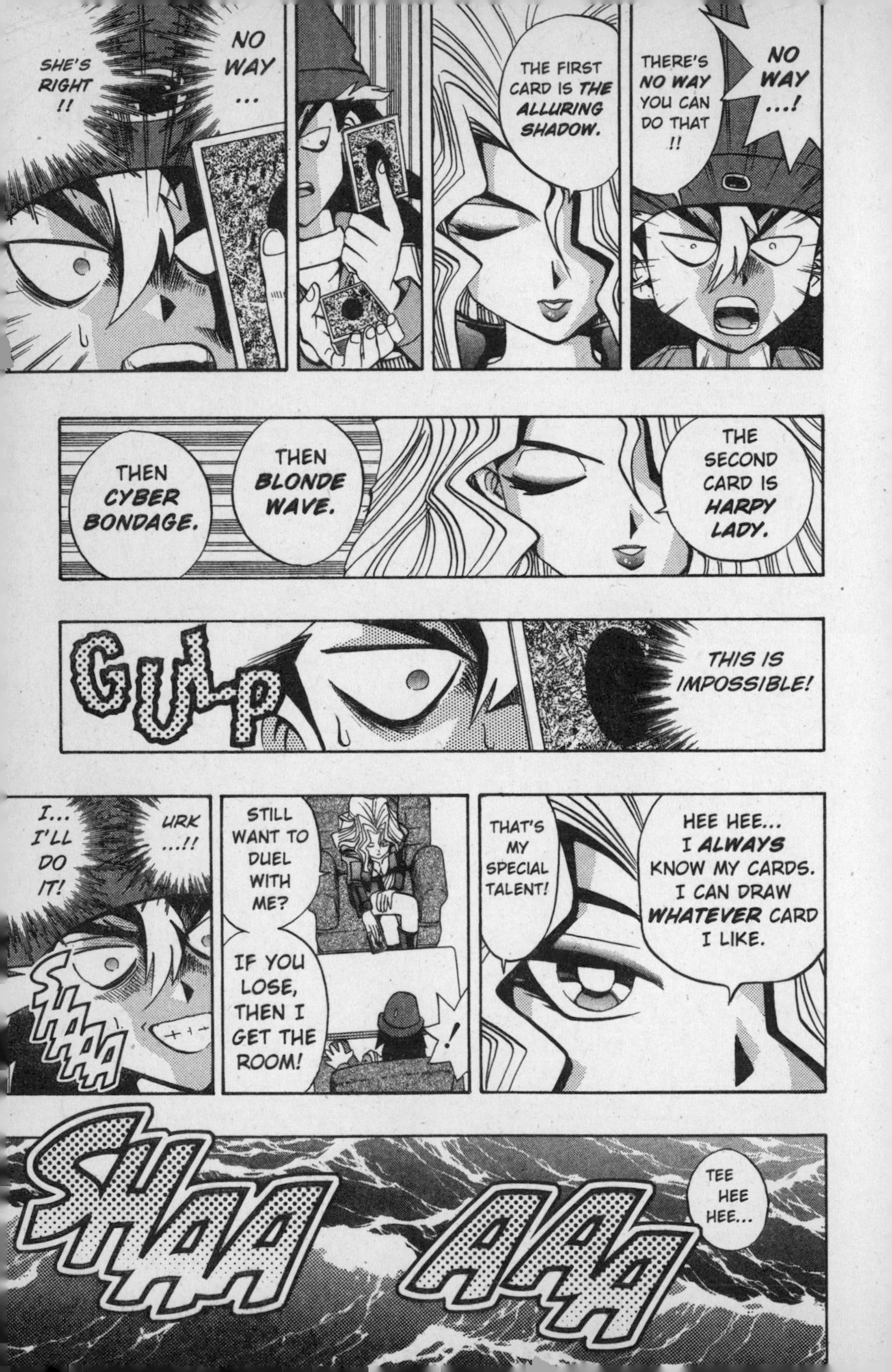
NO WAY ...!
THERE'S NO WAY YOU CAN DO THAT !!
THE FIRST CARD IS THE ALLURING SHADOW.
NO WAY ...
SHE'S RIGHT !!
THE SECOND CARD IS HARPY LADY.
THEN BLONDE WAVE.
THEN CYBER BONDAGE.
THIS IS IMPOSSIBLE!
GULP
HEE HEE... I ALWAYS KNOW MY CARDS. I CAN DRAW WHATEVER CARD I LIKE.
THAT'S MY SPECIAL TALENT!
STILL WANT TO DUEL WITH ME?
IF YOU LOSE, THEN I GET THE ROOM!
!
URK ...!!
I... I'LL DO IT!
SHAAA
TEE HEE HEE...
SHAA AAA

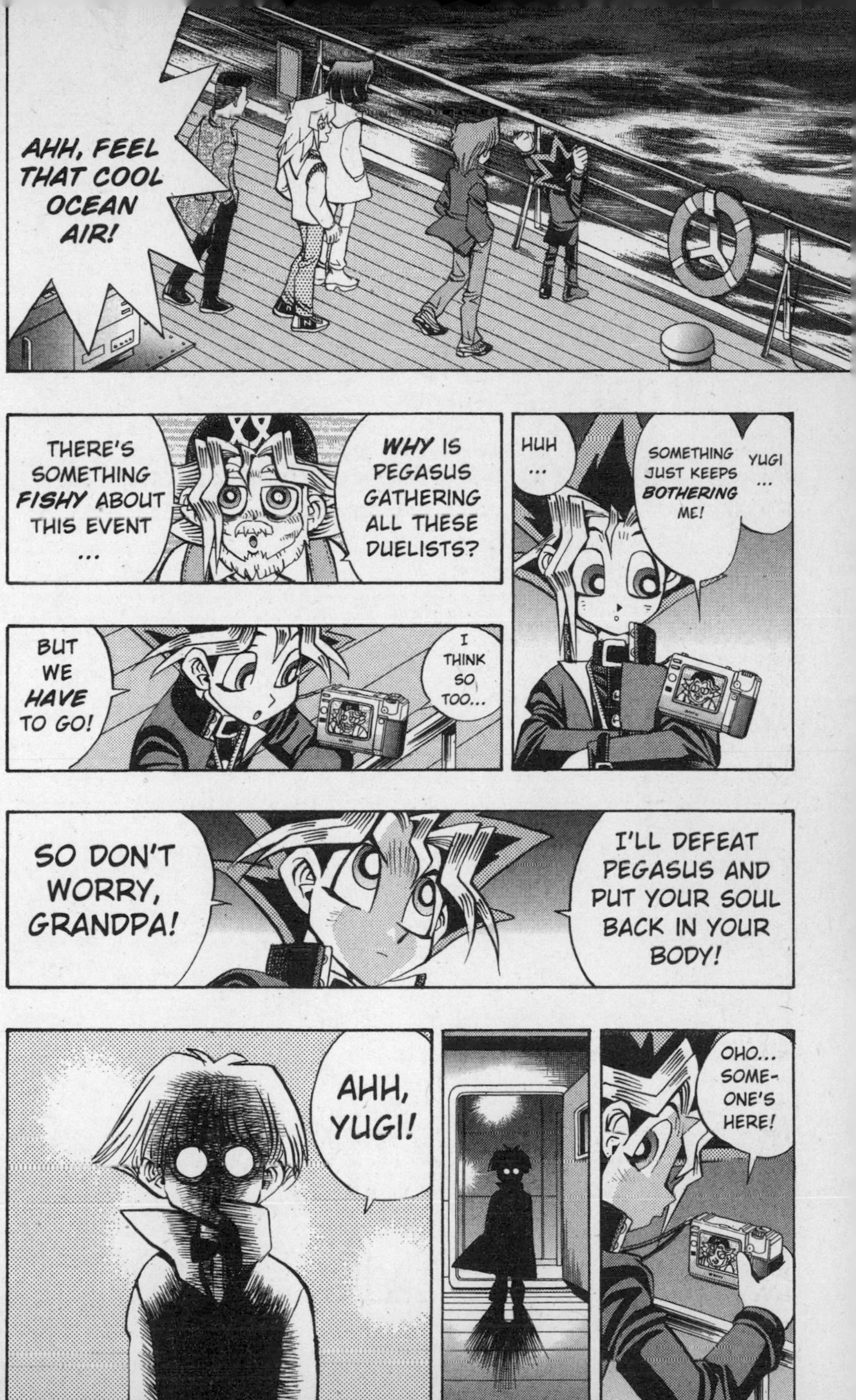
AHH, FEEL THAT COOL OCEAN AIR!
YUGI ...
SOMETHING JUST KEEPS BOTHERING ME!
HUH ...
WHY IS PEGASUS GATHERING ALL THESE DUELISTS?
THERE'S SOMETHING FISHY ABOUT THIS EVENT ...
I THINK SO TOO...
BUT WE HAVE TO GO!
I'LL DEFEAT PEGASUS AND PUT YOUR SOUL BACK IN YOUR BODY!
SO DON'T WORRY, GRANDPA!
OHO... SOME-ONE'S HERE!
AHH, YUGI!

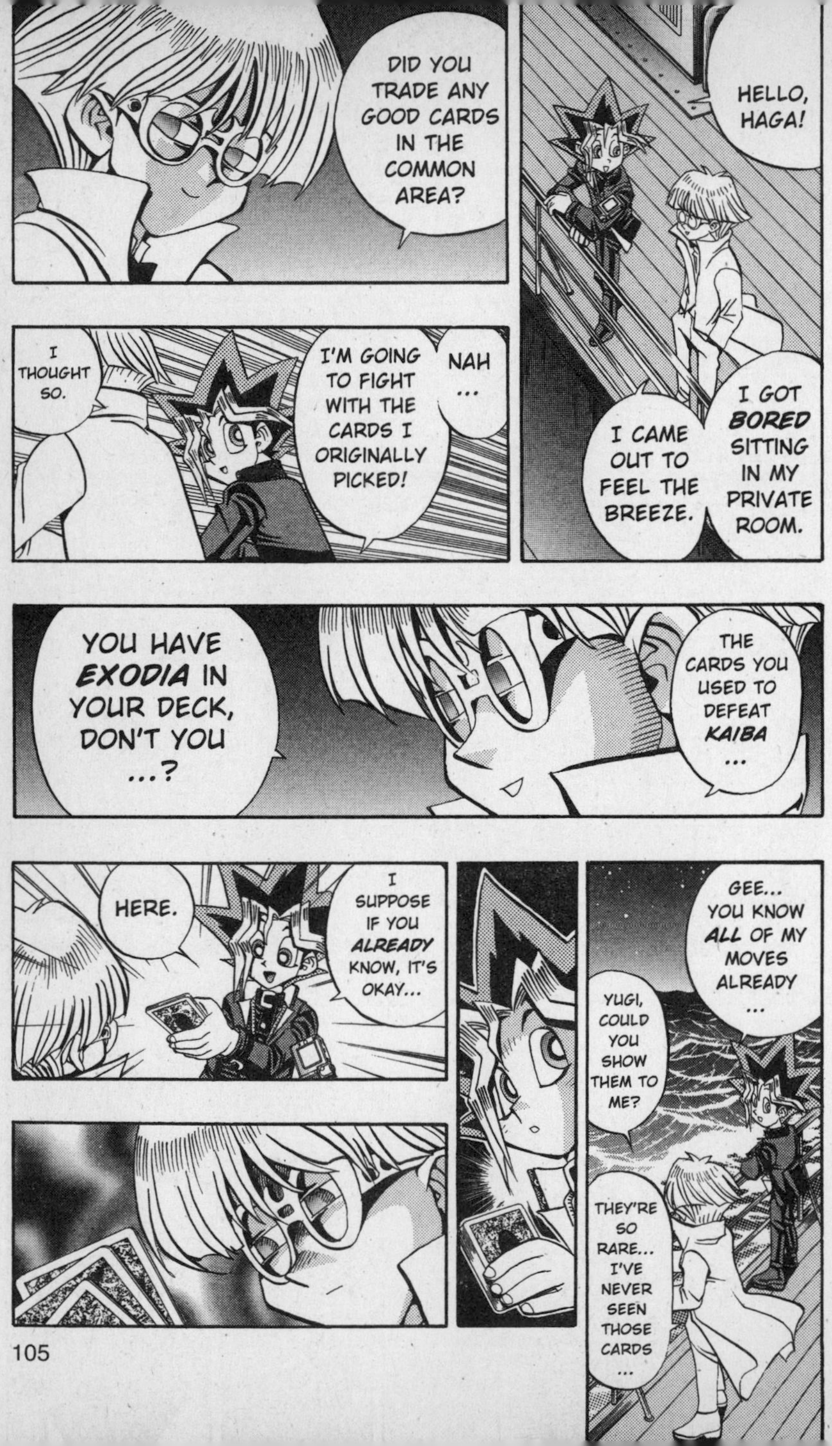
HELLO, HAGA!
I GOT BORED SITTING IN MY PRIVATE ROOM.
I CAME OUT TO FEEL THE BREEZE.
DID YOU TRADE ANY GOOD CARDS IN THE COMMON AREA?
NAH ...
I'M GOING TO FIGHT WITH THE CARDS I ORIGINALLY PICKED!
I THOUGHT SO.
THE CARDS YOU USED TO DEFEAT KAIBA ...
YOU HAVE EXODIA IN YOUR DECK, DON'T YOU ...?
GEE... YOU KNOW ALL OF MY MOVES ALREADY ...
YUGI, COULD YOU SHOW THEM TO ME?
THEY'RE SO RARE... I'VE NEVER SEEN THOSE CARDS ...
I SUPPOSE IF YOU ALREADY KNOW, IT'S OKAY...
HERE.

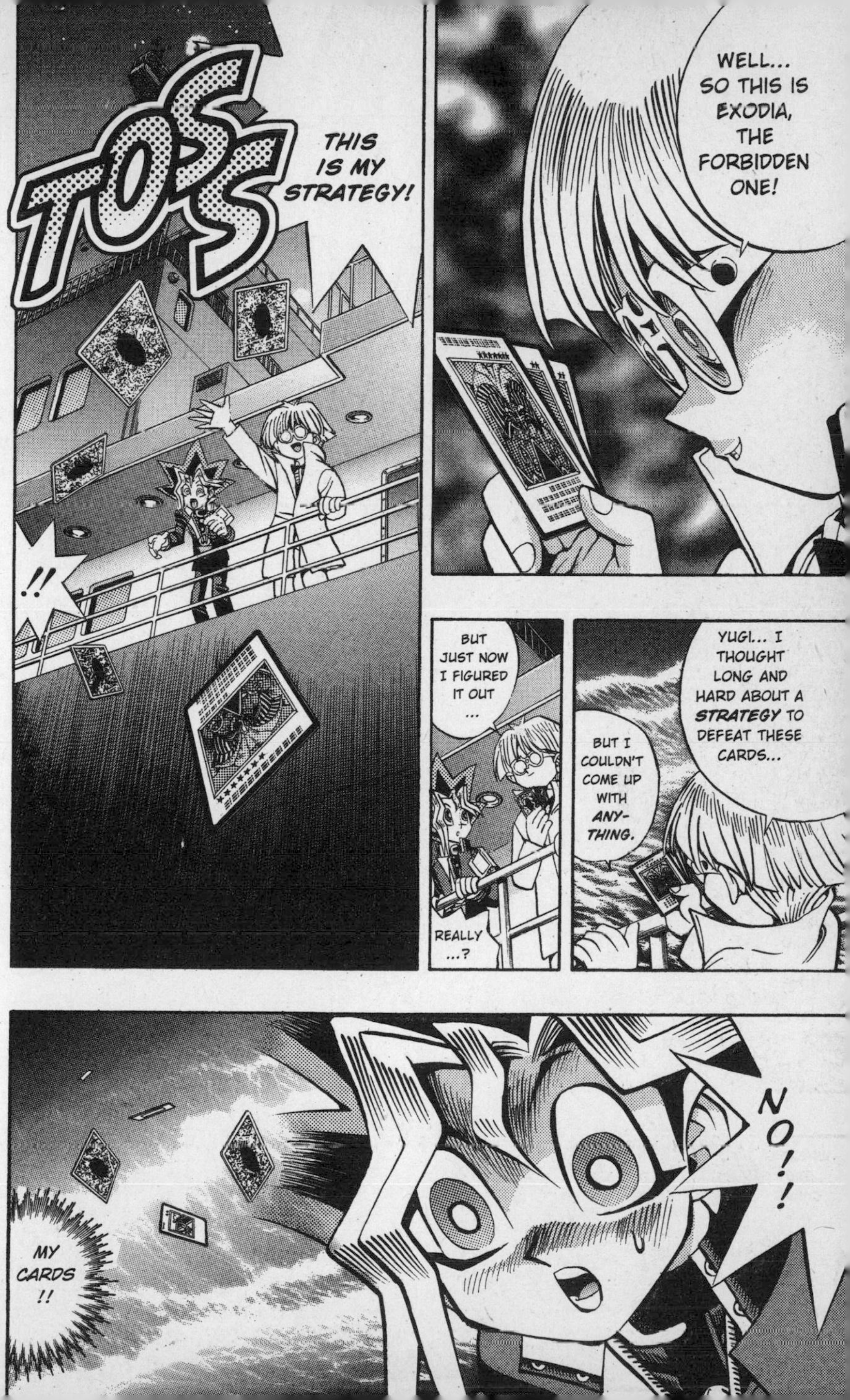
WELL... SO THIS IS EXODIA, THE FORBIDDEN ONE!
YUGI... I THOUGHT LONG AND HARD ABOUT A STRATEGY TO DEFEAT THESE CARDS...
BUT I COULDN'T COME UP WITH ANYTHING.
BUT JUST NOW I FIGURED IT OUT ...
REALLY ...?
TOSS
THIS IS MY STRATEGY!
!!
NO!!
MY CARDS !!

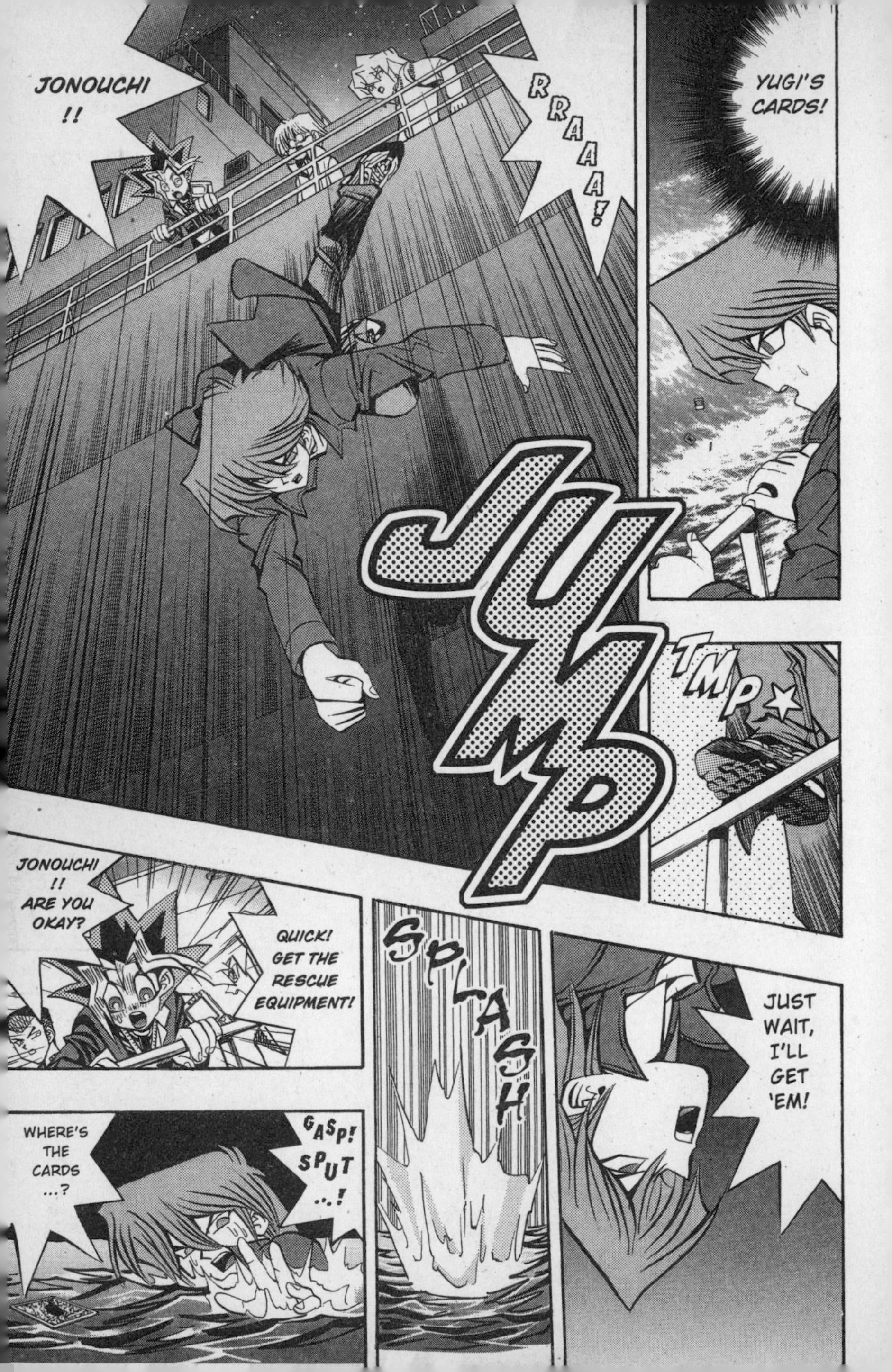
YUGI'S CARDS!
TMP★
RRAAAA!
JONOUCHI !!
JUMP
JUST WAIT, I'LL GET 'EM!
SPLASH!
JONOUCHI !! ARE YOU OKAY?
QUICK! GET THE RESCUE EQUIPMENT!
GASP! SPUT ..!
WHERE'S THE CARDS ...?

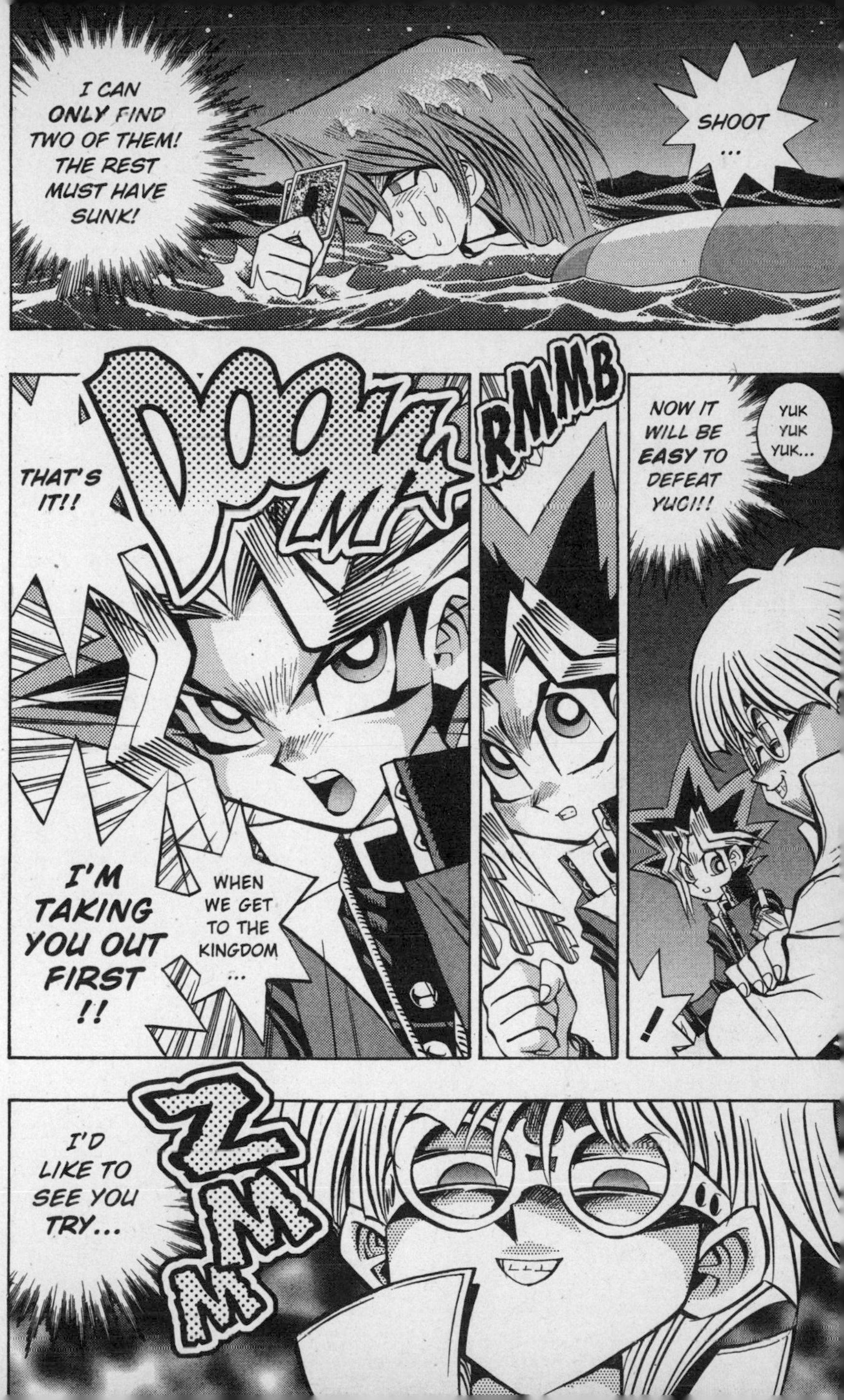
SHOOT ...
I CAN ONLY FIND TWO OF THEM! THE REST MUST HAVE SUNK!
YUK YUK YUK...
NOW IT WILL BE EASY TO DEFEAT YUGI!!
!
RMMB
DOOM
THAT'S IT!!
WHEN WE GET TO THE KINGDOM ...
I'M TAKING YOU OUT FIRST !!
ZMM
I'D LIKE TO SEE YOU TRY...

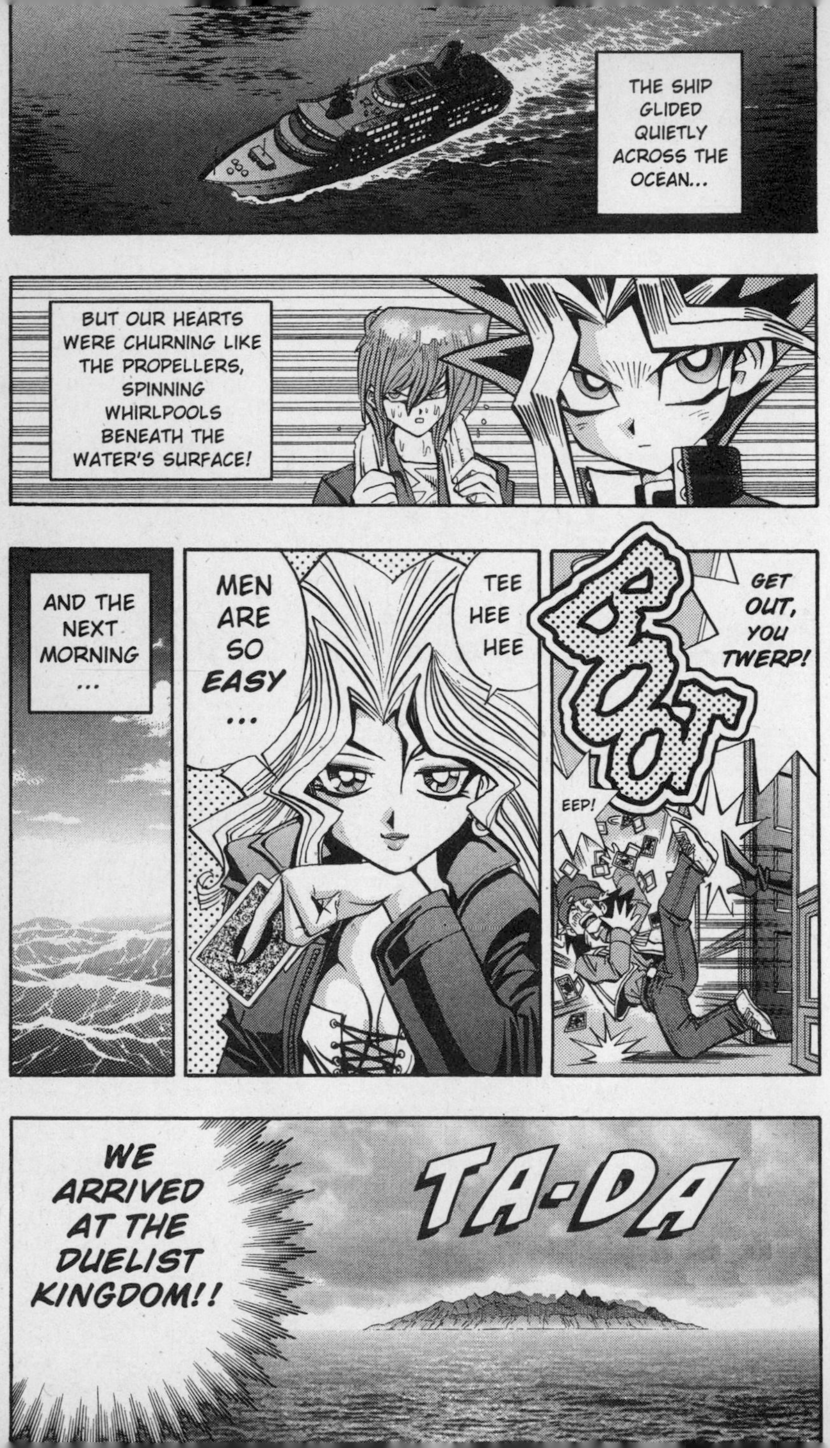

THE SHIP GLIDED QUIETLY ACROSS THE OCEAN...
BUT OUR HEARTS WERE CHURNING LIKE THE PROPELLERS, SPINNING WHIRLPOOLS BENEATH THE WATER'S SURFACE!
GET OUT, YOU TWERP!
BOOT
EEP!
TEE HEE HEE
MEN ARE SO *EASY* ...
AND THE NEXT MORNING ...
TA-DA
WE ARRIVED AT THE DUELIST KINGDOM!!

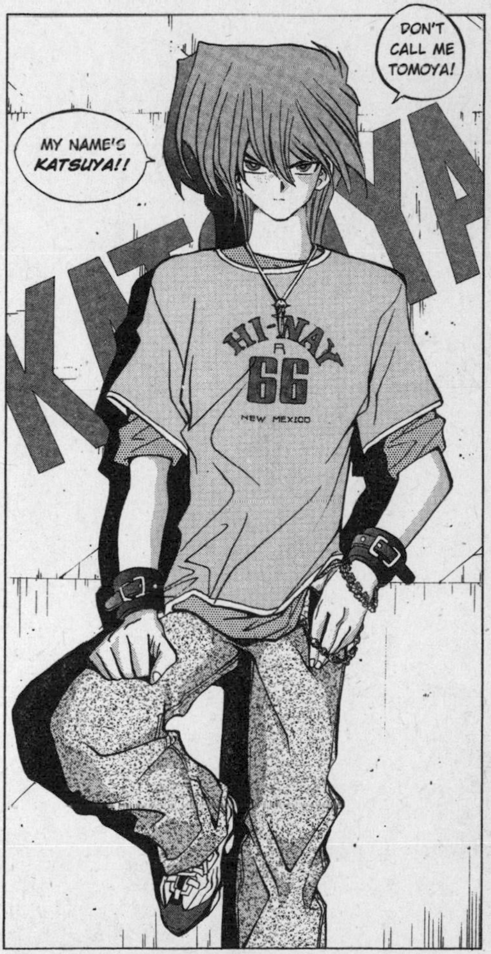
DON'T CALL ME TOMOYA!
MY NAME'S KATSUYA!!
HI-WAY
A
66
NEW MEXICO

Duel 6: Let the Duel Begin!

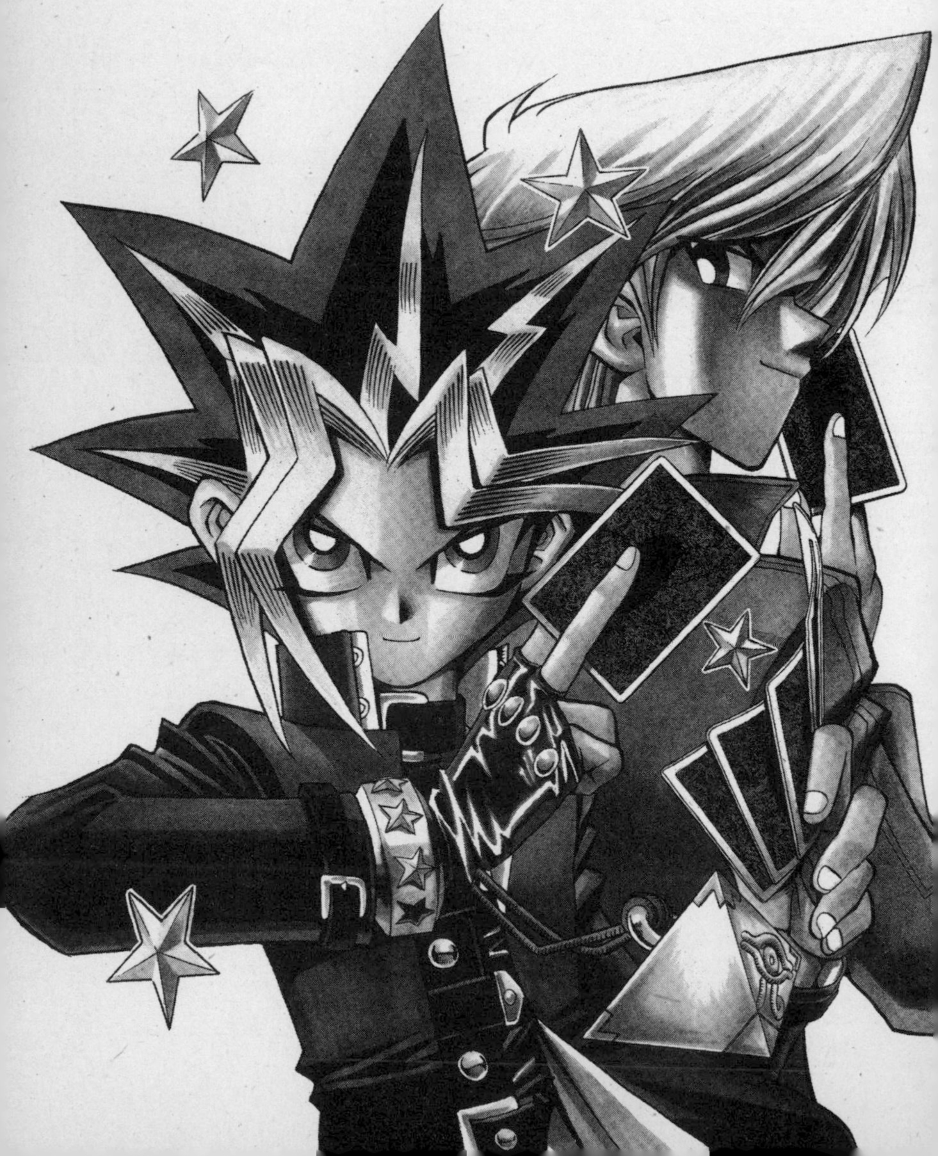

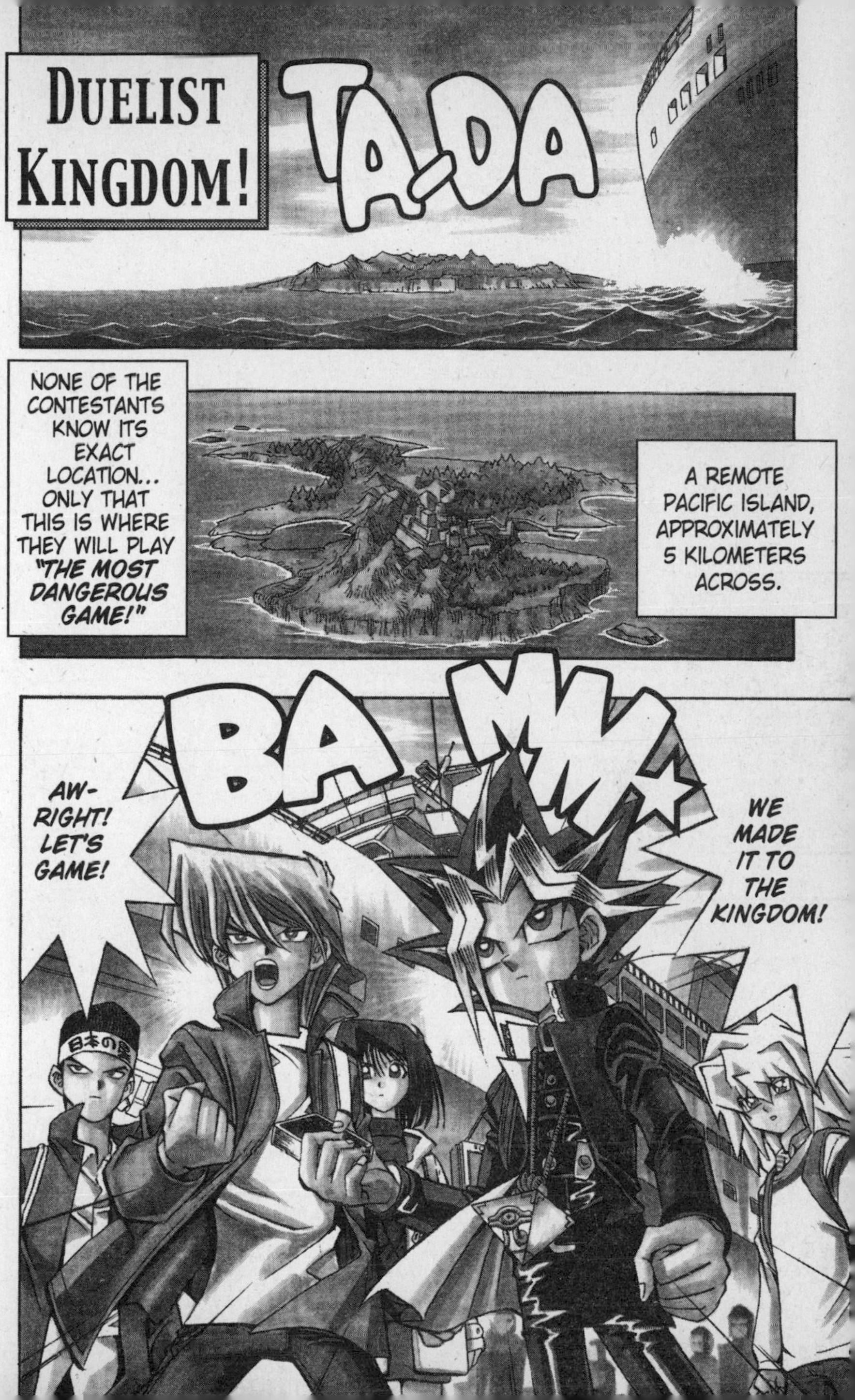
DUELIST KINGDOM!
TA-DA
A REMOTE PACIFIC ISLAND, APPROXIMATELY 5 KILOMETERS ACROSS.
NONE OF THE CONTESTANTS KNOW ITS EXACT LOCATION... ONLY THAT THIS IS WHERE THEY WILL PLAY *"THE MOST DANGEROUS GAME!"*
BA-MM
WE MADE IT TO THE KINGDOM!
AW-RIGHT! LET'S GAME!

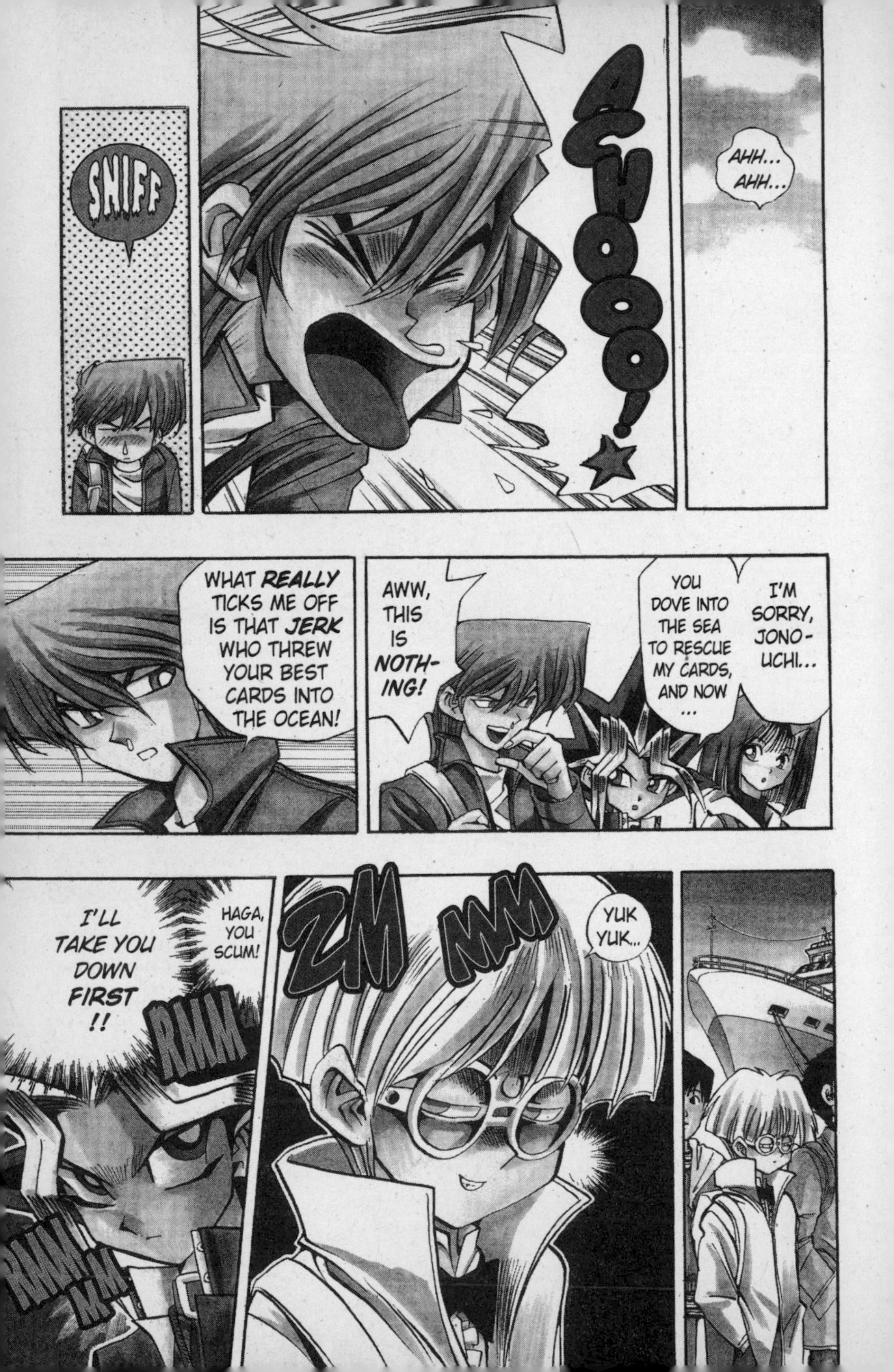
AHH... AHH...
ACHOOO!
SNIFF
I'M SORRY, JONO-UCHI...
YOU DOVE INTO THE SEA TO RESCUE MY CARDS, AND NOW ...
AWW, THIS IS NOTH-ING!
WHAT REALLY TICKS ME OFF IS THAT JERK WHO THREW YOUR BEST CARDS INTO THE OCEAN!
YUK YUK...
ZM MM
HAGA, YOU SCUM!
I'LL TAKE YOU DOWN FIRST !!
RMM
RMMMMM

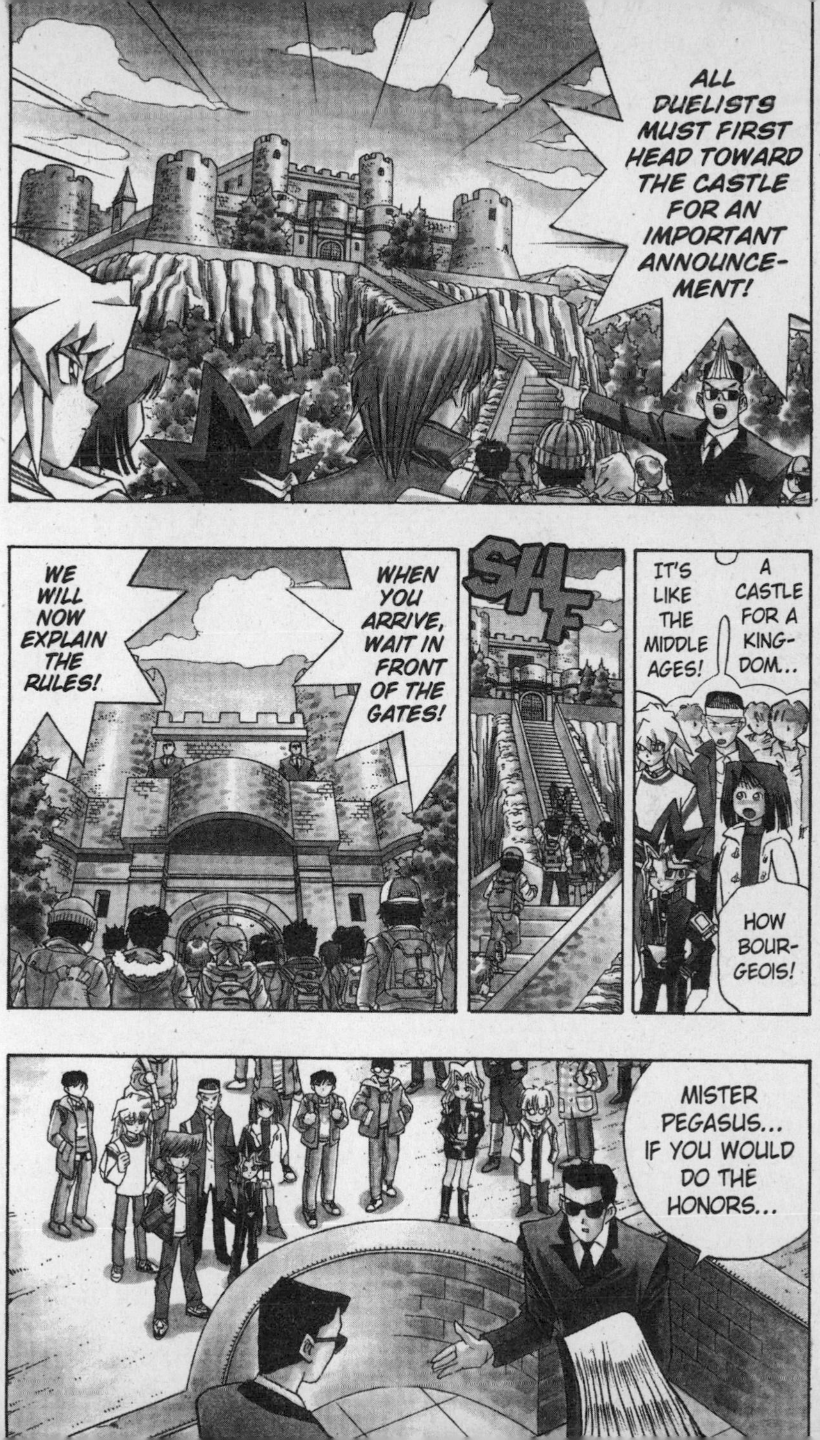
ALL DUELISTS MUST FIRST HEAD TOWARD THE CASTLE FOR AN IMPORTANT ANNOUNCE-MENT!
A CASTLE FOR A KING-DOM...
IT'S LIKE THE MIDDLE AGES!
HOW BOUR-GEOIS!
SHF
WHEN YOU ARRIVE, WAIT IN FRONT OF THE GATES!
WE WILL NOW EXPLAIN THE RULES!
MISTER PEGASUS... IF YOU WOULD DO THE HONORS...

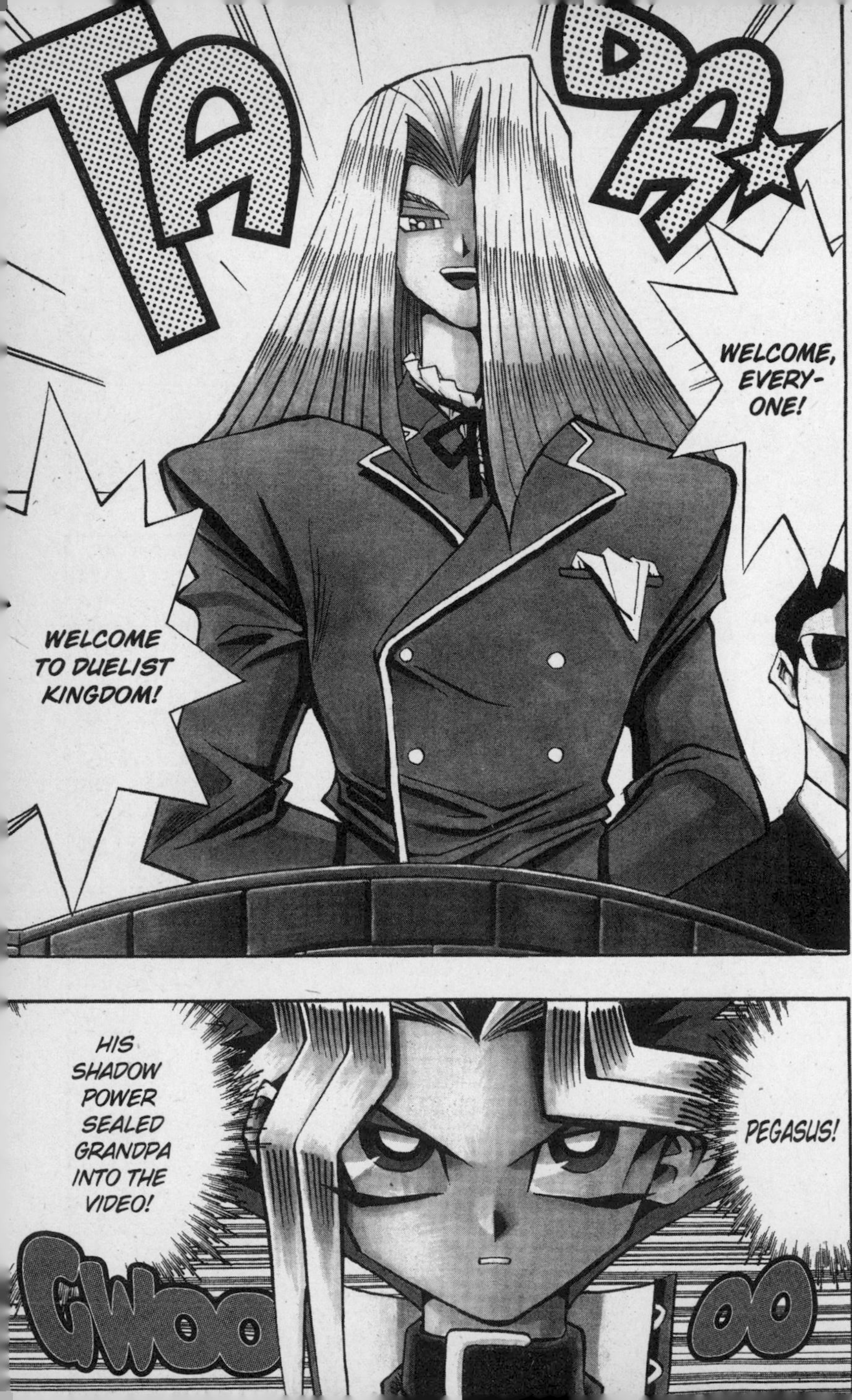
TA-DA☆
WELCOME, EVERY-ONE!
WELCOME TO DUELIST KINGDOM!
PEGASUS!
HIS SHADOW POWER SEALED GRANDPA INTO THE VIDEO!
GWOOOO

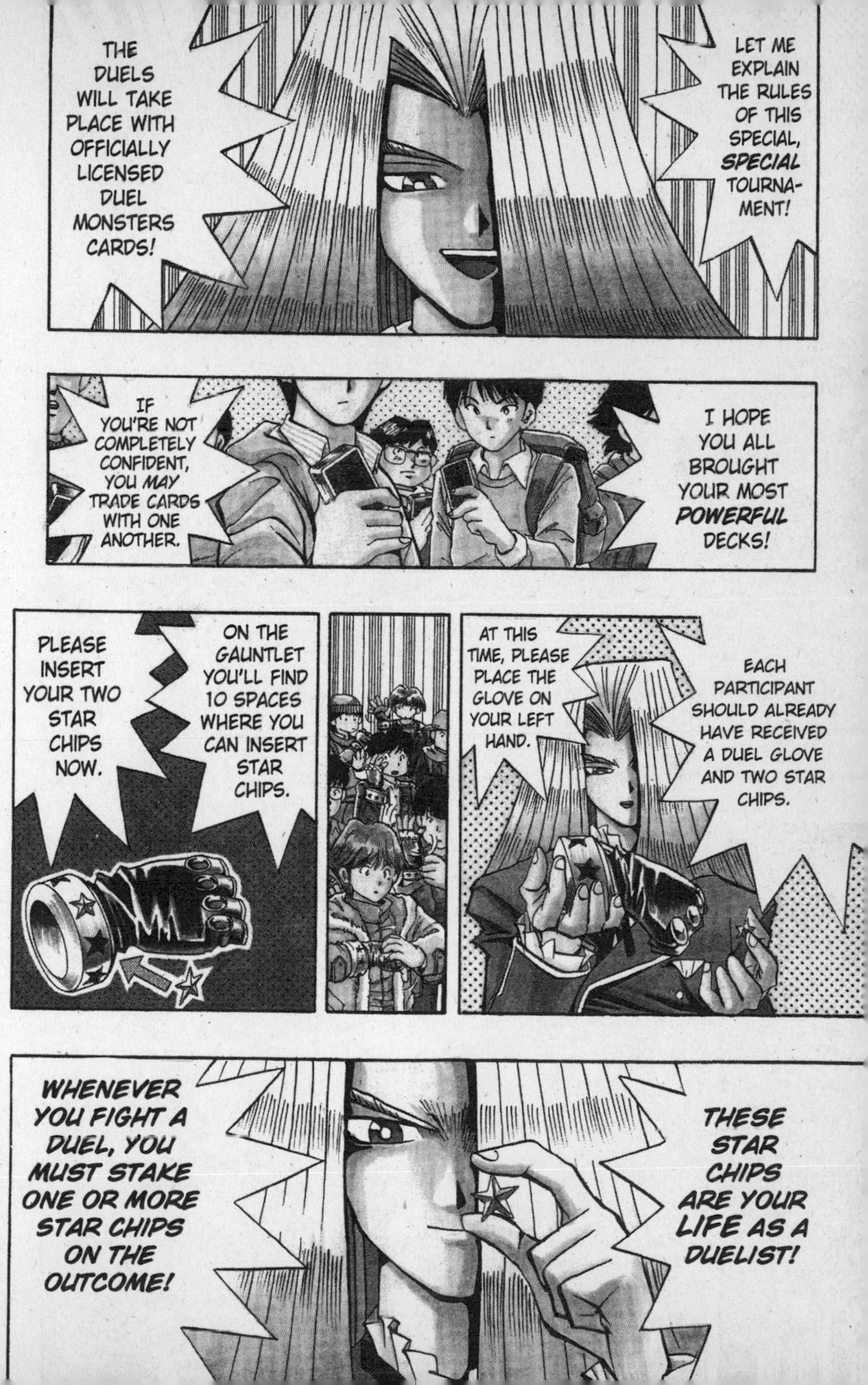
LET ME EXPLAIN THE RULES OF THIS SPECIAL, SPECIAL TOURNAMENT!
THE DUELS WILL TAKE PLACE WITH OFFICIALLY LICENSED DUEL MONSTERS CARDS!
I HOPE YOU ALL BROUGHT YOUR MOST POWERFUL DECKS!
IF YOU'RE NOT COMPLETELY CONFIDENT, YOU MAY TRADE CARDS WITH ONE ANOTHER.
EACH PARTICIPANT SHOULD ALREADY HAVE RECEIVED A DUEL GLOVE AND TWO STAR CHIPS.
AT THIS TIME, PLEASE PLACE THE GLOVE ON YOUR LEFT HAND.
ON THE GAUNTLET YOU'LL FIND 10 SPACES WHERE YOU CAN INSERT STAR CHIPS.
PLEASE INSERT YOUR TWO STAR CHIPS NOW.
THESE STAR CHIPS ARE YOUR LIFE AS A DUELIST!
WHENEVER YOU FIGHT A DUEL, YOU MUST STAKE ONE OR MORE STAR CHIPS ON THE OUTCOME!

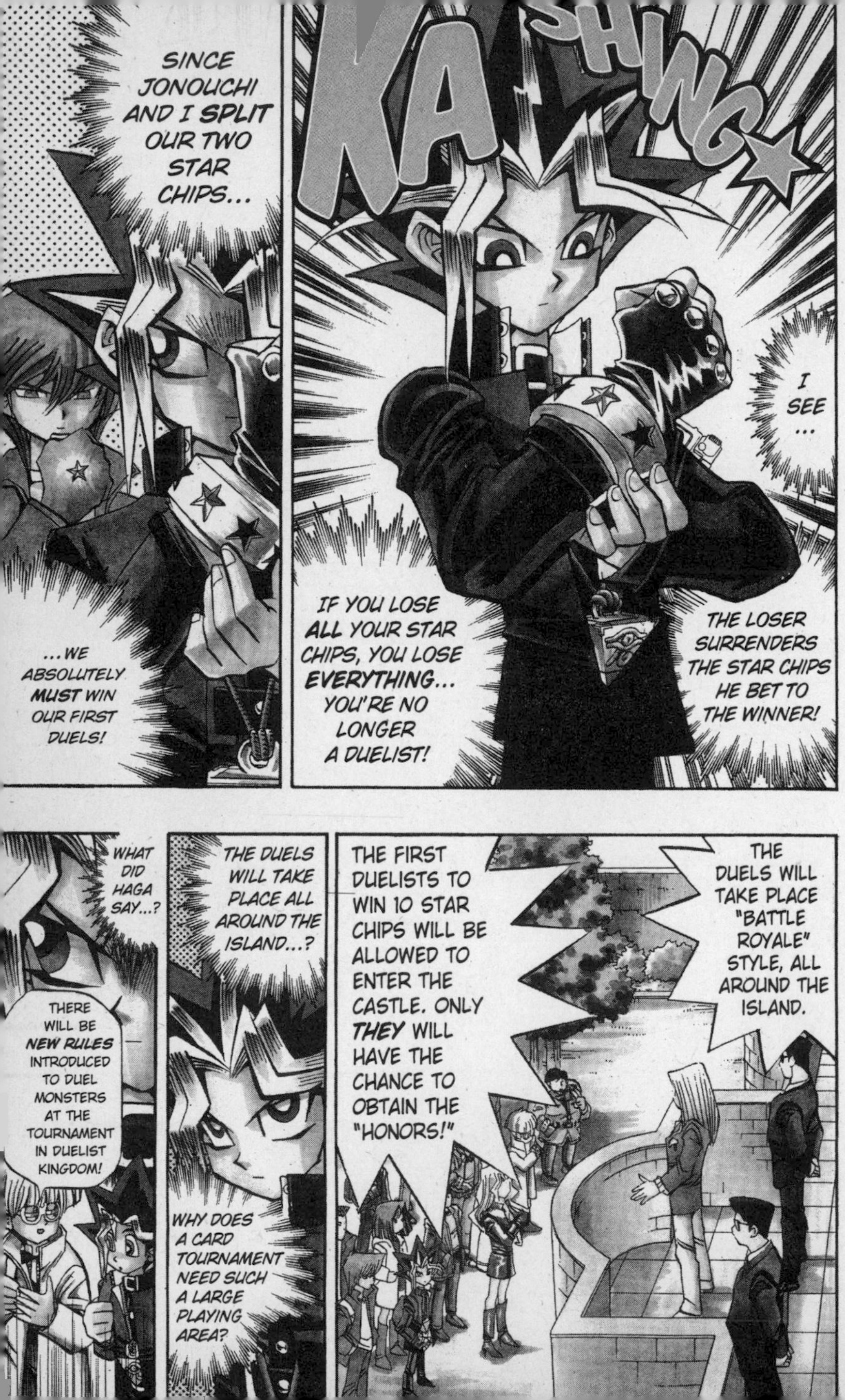
KASHING
I SEE...
THE LOSER SURRENDERS THE STAR CHIPS HE BET TO THE WINNER!
IF YOU LOSE ALL YOUR STAR CHIPS, YOU LOSE EVERYTHING... YOU'RE NO LONGER A DUELIST!
SINCE JONOUCHI AND I SPLIT OUR TWO STAR CHIPS...
...WE ABSOLUTELY MUST WIN OUR FIRST DUELS!
THE DUELS WILL TAKE PLACE "BATTLE ROYALE" STYLE, ALL AROUND THE ISLAND.
THE FIRST DUELISTS TO WIN 10 STAR CHIPS WILL BE ALLOWED TO ENTER THE CASTLE. ONLY THEY WILL HAVE THE CHANCE TO OBTAIN THE "HONORS!"
THE DUELS WILL TAKE PLACE ALL AROUND THE ISLAND...?
WHY DOES A CARD TOURNAMENT NEED SUCH A LARGE PLAYING AREA?
WHAT DID HAGA SAY...?
THERE WILL BE NEW RULES INTRODUCED TO DUEL MONSTERS AT THE TOURNAMENT IN DUELIST KINGDOM!

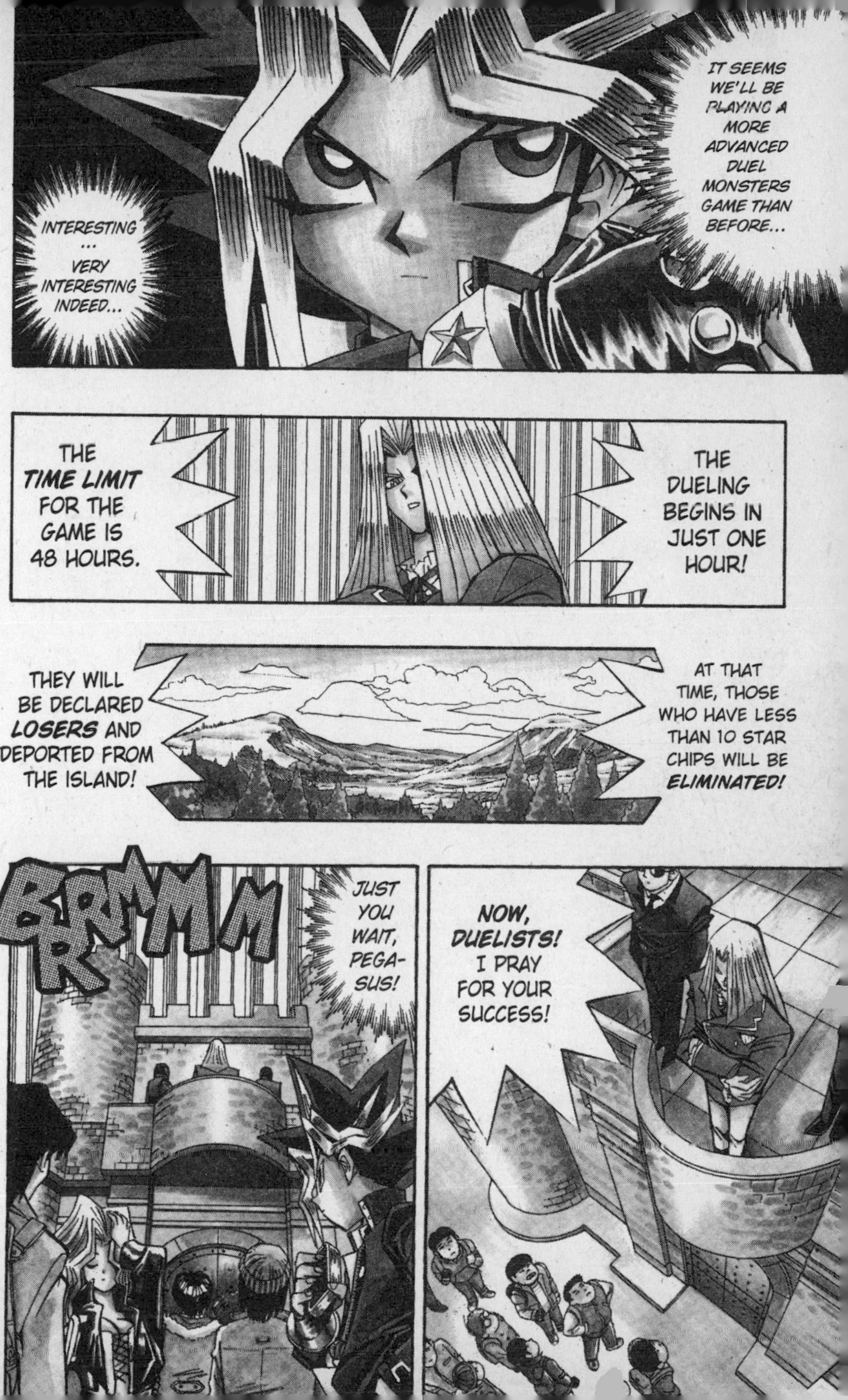
IT SEEMS WE'LL BE PLAYING A MORE ADVANCED DUEL MONSTERS GAME THAN BEFORE...
INTERESTING... VERY INTERESTING INDEED...
THE DUELING BEGINS IN JUST ONE HOUR!
THE TIME LIMIT FOR THE GAME IS 48 HOURS.
AT THAT TIME, THOSE WHO HAVE LESS THAN 10 STAR CHIPS WILL BE ELIMINATED!
THEY WILL BE DECLARED LOSERS AND DEPORTED FROM THE ISLAND!
NOW, DUELISTS! I PRAY FOR YOUR SUCCESS!
JUST YOU WAIT, PEGASUS!
BRRMMMM

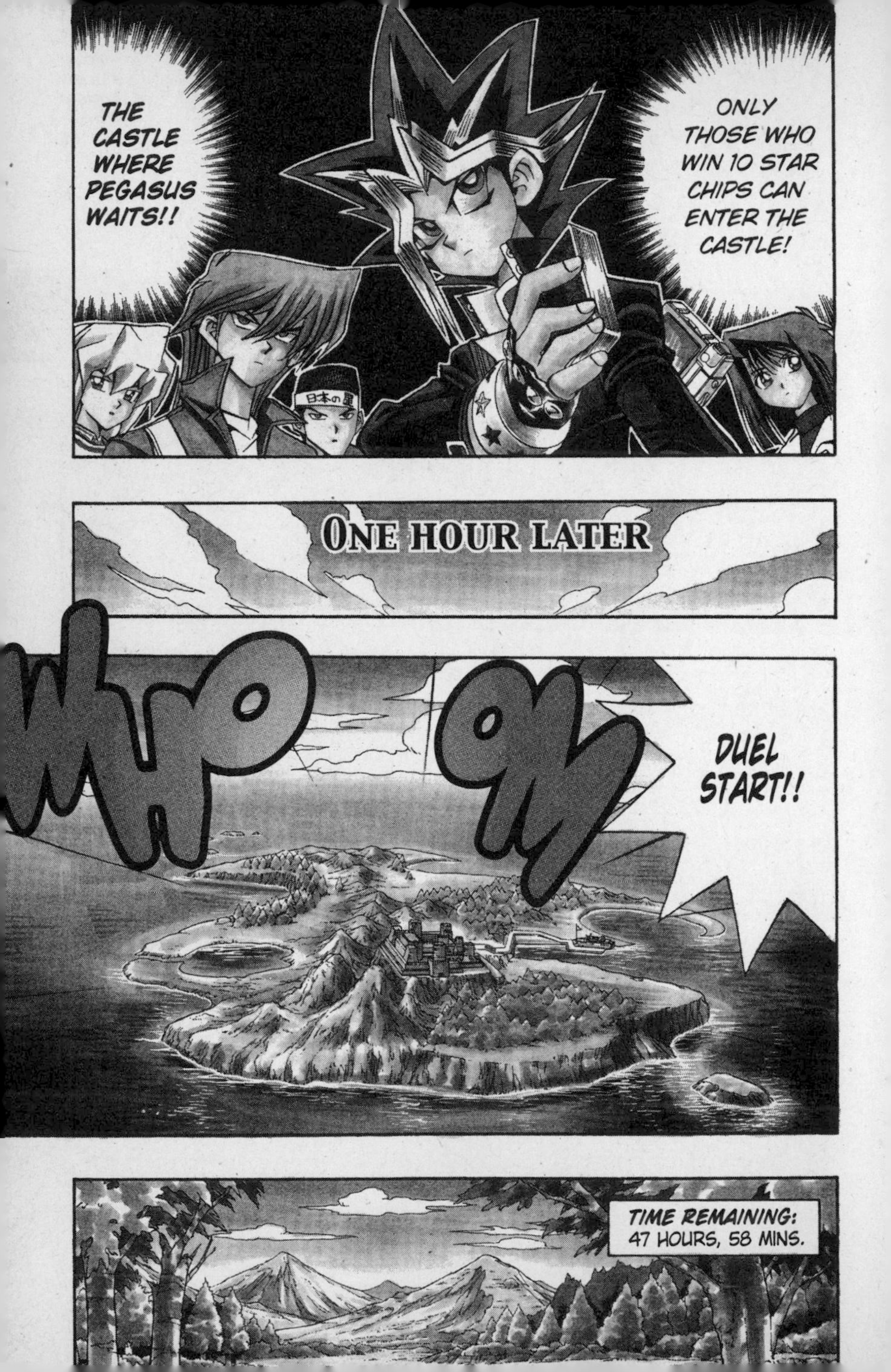
ONLY THOSE WHO WIN 10 STAR CHIPS CAN ENTER THE CASTLE!
THE CASTLE WHERE PEGASUS WAITS!!
ONE HOUR LATER
DUEL START!!
WHOOM
TIME REMAINING: 47 HOURS, 58 MINS.

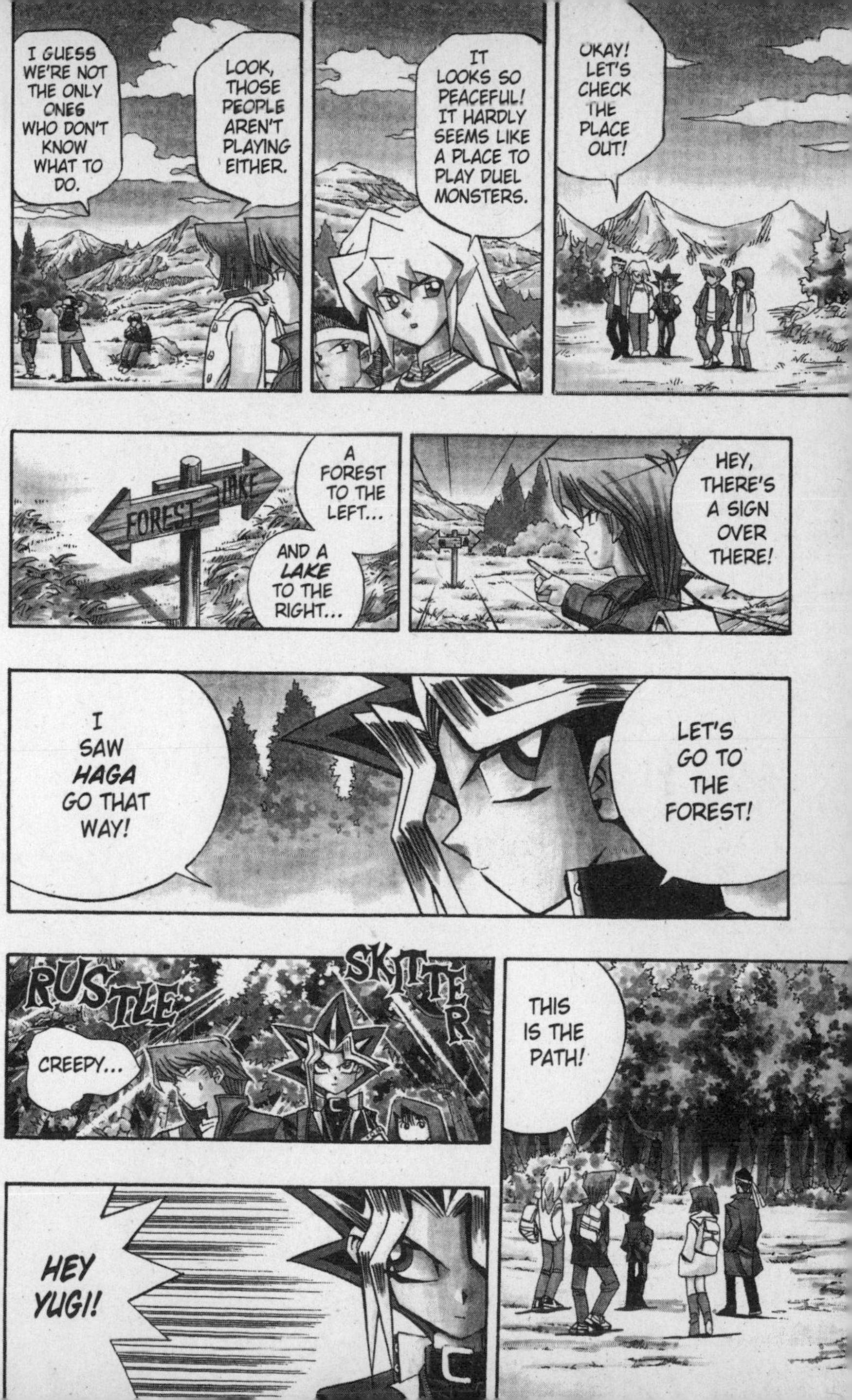

OKAY! LET'S CHECK THE PLACE OUT!
IT LOOKS SO PEACEFUL! IT HARDLY SEEMS LIKE A PLACE TO PLAY DUEL MONSTERS.
LOOK, THOSE PEOPLE AREN'T PLAYING EITHER.
I GUESS WE'RE NOT THE ONLY ONES WHO DON'T KNOW WHAT TO DO.
HEY, THERE'S A SIGN OVER THERE!
A FOREST TO THE LEFT...
AND A *LAKE* TO THE RIGHT...
FOREST
LAKE
LET'S GO TO THE FOREST!
I SAW *HAGA* GO THAT WAY!
THIS IS THE PATH!
SKITTER
RUSTLE
CREEPY...
HEY YUGI!

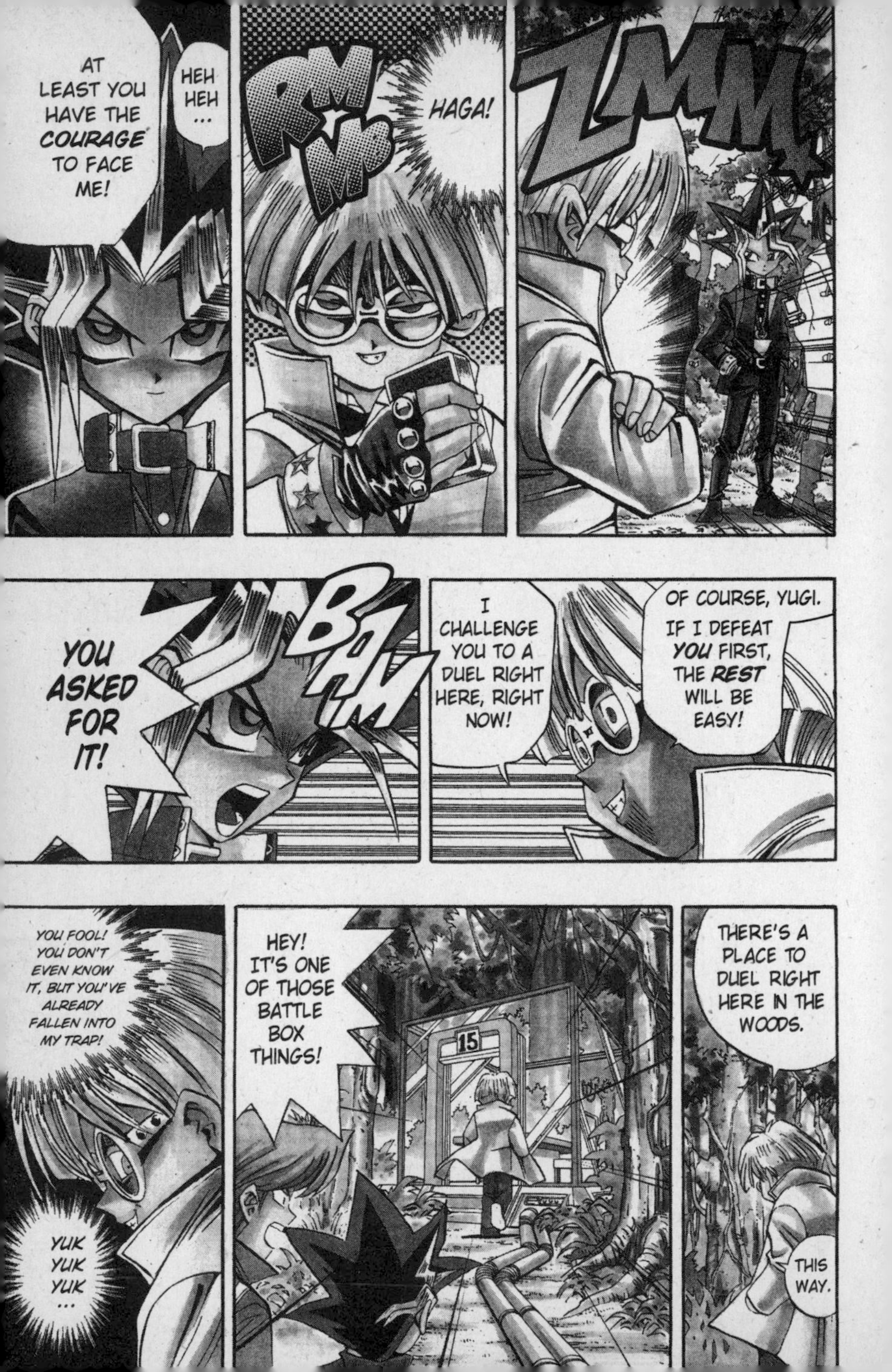
ZMM
HAGA!
HEH HEH ...
AT LEAST YOU HAVE THE COURAGE TO FACE ME!
OF COURSE, YUGI.
IF I DEFEAT YOU FIRST, THE REST WILL BE EASY!
I CHALLENGE YOU TO A DUEL RIGHT HERE, RIGHT NOW!
BAM
YOU ASKED FOR IT!
THERE'S A PLACE TO DUEL RIGHT HERE IN THE WOODS.
THIS WAY.
HEY! IT'S ONE OF THOSE BATTLE BOX THINGS!
15
YOU FOOL! YOU DON'T EVEN KNOW IT, BUT YOU'VE ALREADY FALLEN INTO MY TRAP!
YUK YUK YUK ...

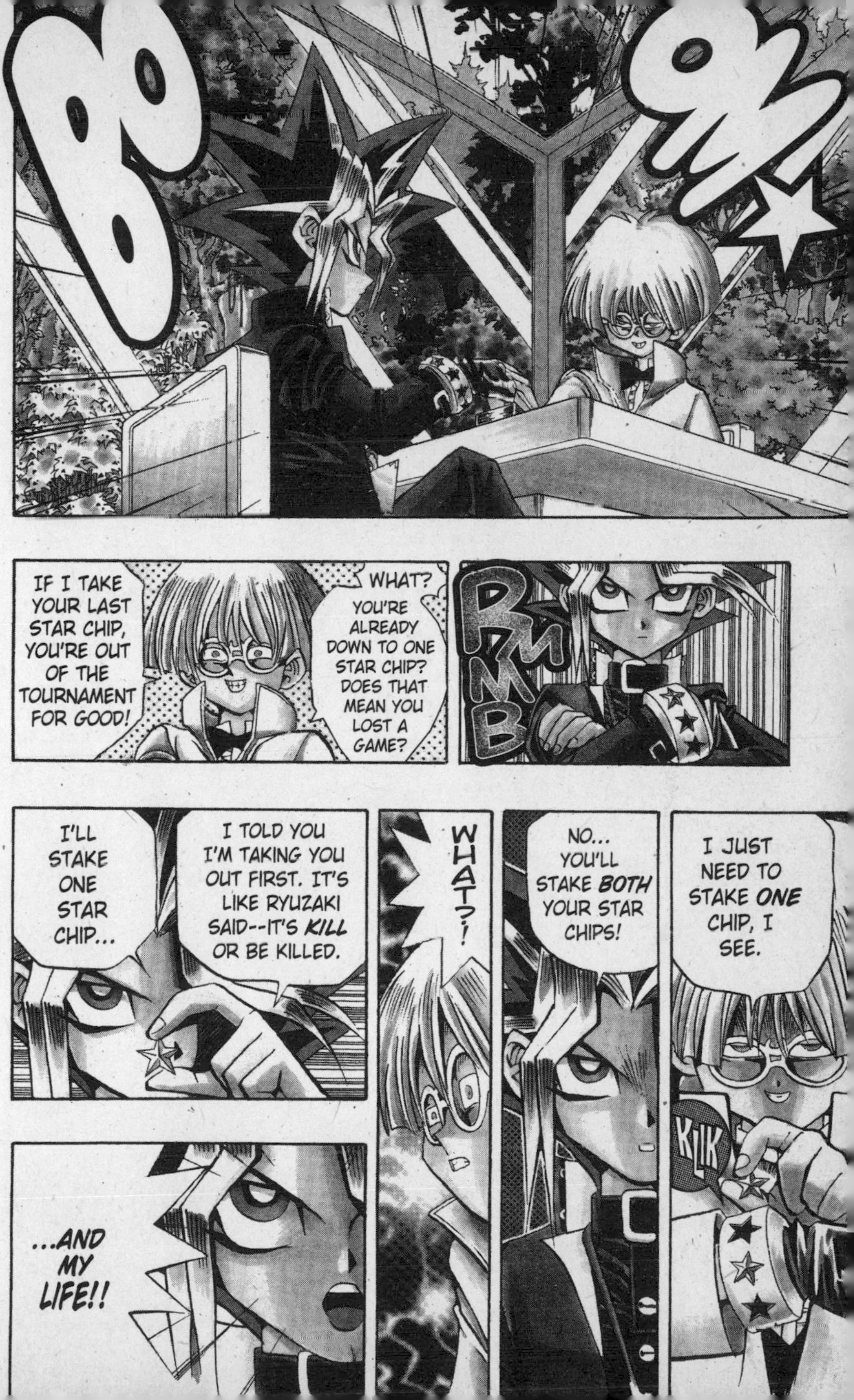
RUMB
WHAT? YOU'RE ALREADY DOWN TO ONE STAR CHIP? DOES THAT MEAN YOU LOST A GAME?
IF I TAKE YOUR LAST STAR CHIP, YOU'RE OUT OF THE TOURNAMENT FOR GOOD!
I JUST NEED TO STAKE *ONE* CHIP, I SEE.
KLIK
NO... YOU'LL STAKE *BOTH* YOUR STAR CHIPS!
WHAT?!
I TOLD YOU I'M TAKING YOU OUT FIRST. IT'S LIKE RYUZAKI SAID--IT'S *KILL* OR BE KILLED.
I'LL STAKE ONE STAR CHIP...
...AND MY LIFE!!

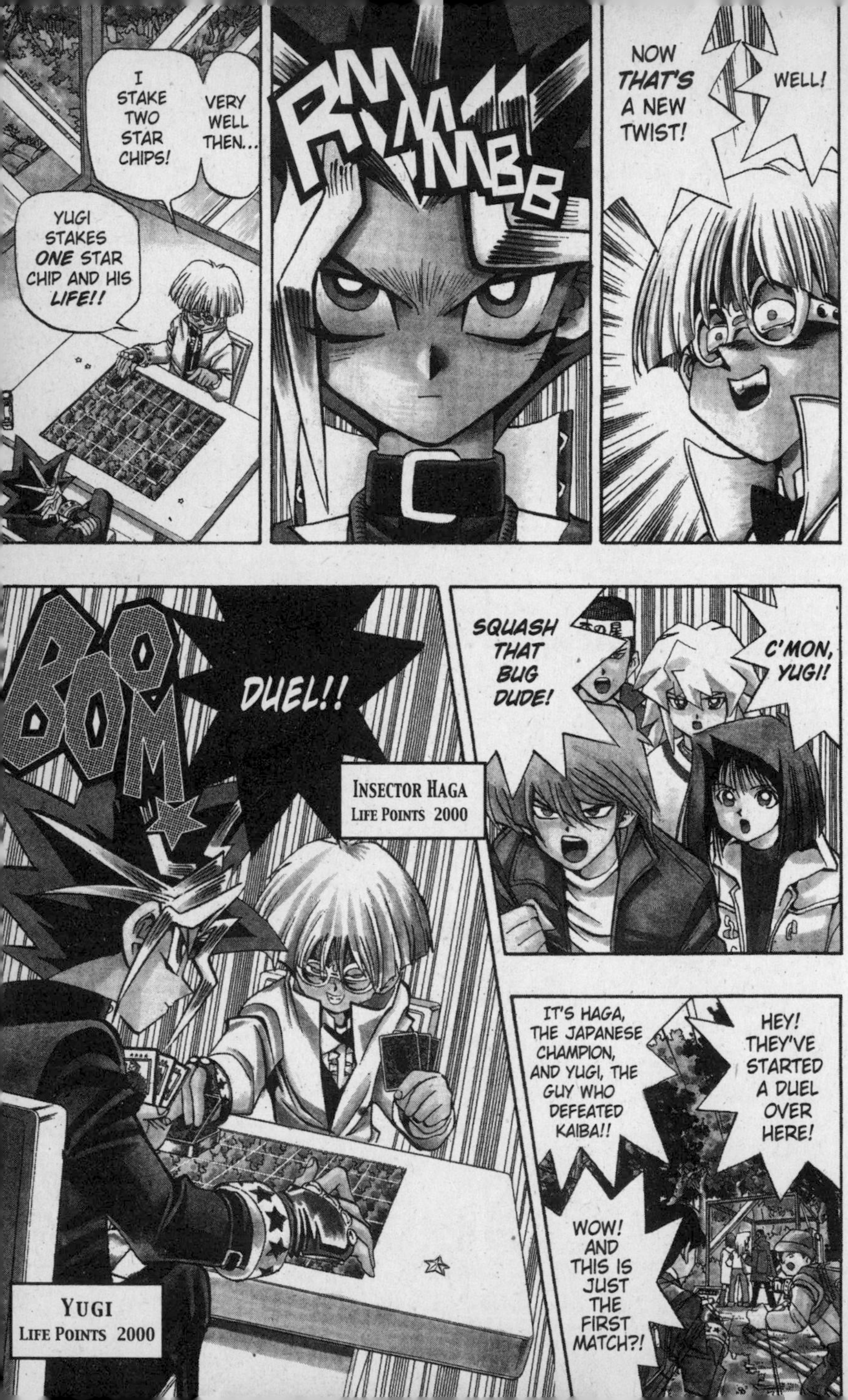
WELL!
NOW THAT'S A NEW TWIST!
RMMBB
VERY WELL THEN...
I STAKE TWO STAR CHIPS!
YUGI STAKES ONE STAR CHIP AND HIS LIFE!!
C'MON, YUGI!
SQUASH THAT BUG DUDE!
HEY! THEY'VE STARTED A DUEL OVER HERE!
IT'S HAGA, THE JAPANESE CHAMPION, AND YUGI, THE GUY WHO DEFEATED KAIBA!!
WOW! AND THIS IS JUST THE FIRST MATCH?!
DUEL!!
BOOM
INSECTOR HAGA LIFE POINTS 2000
YUGI LIFE POINTS 2000

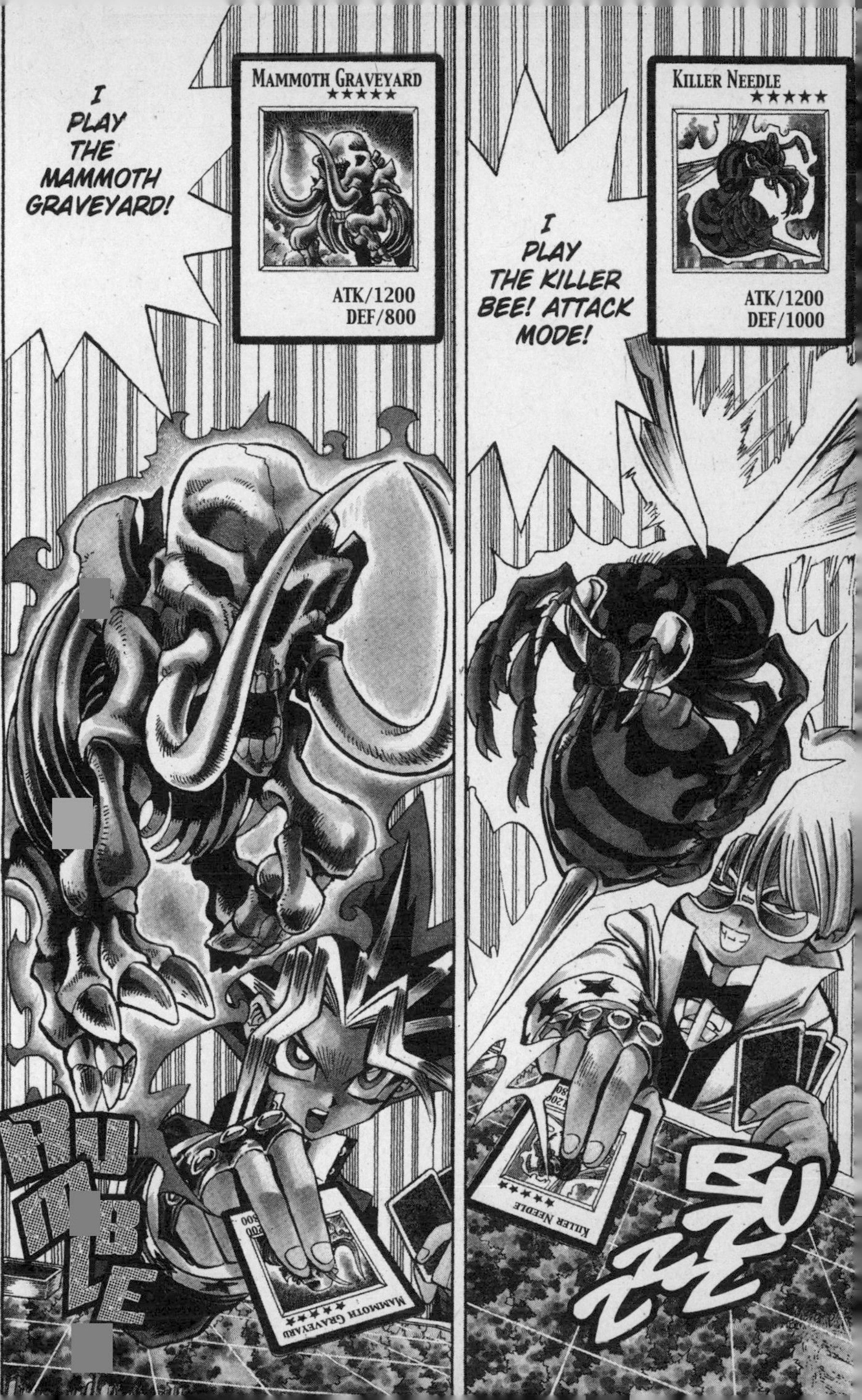
KILLER NEEDLE
ATK/1200
DEF/1000
I PLAY THE KILLER BEE! ATTACK MODE!
MAMMOTH GRAVEYARD
ATK/1200
DEF/800
I PLAY THE MAMMOTH GRAVEYARD!

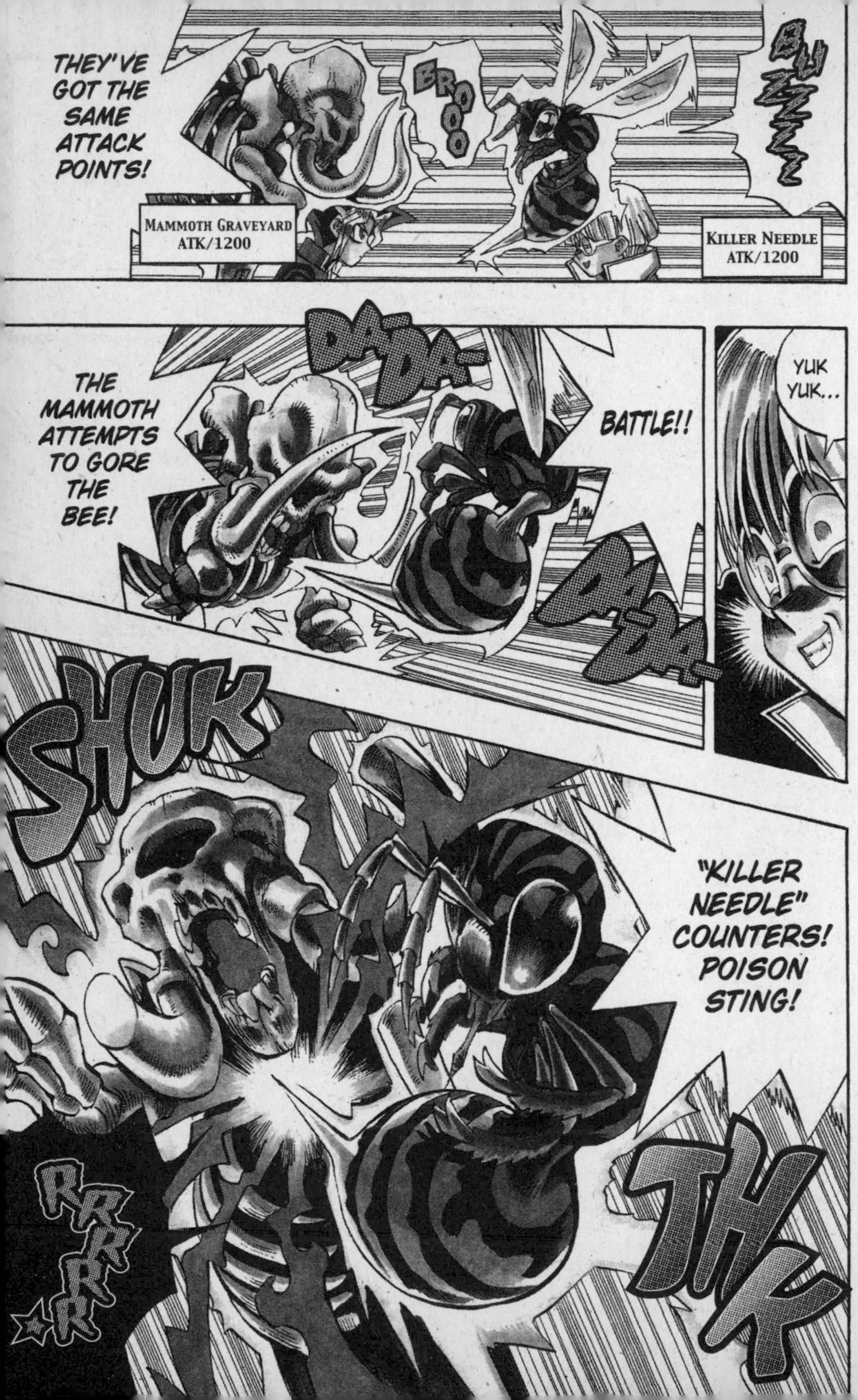
BUZZZZZ
BROOO
Killer Needle
ATK/1200
THEY'VE GOT THE SAME ATTACK POINTS!
Mammoth Graveyard
ATK/1200
YUK YUK...
DA-DA-
BATTLE!!
THE MAMMOTH ATTEMPTS TO GORE THE BEE!
DA-DA-
SHUK
"KILLER NEEDLE" COUNTERS! POISON STING!
THK
RRRRR

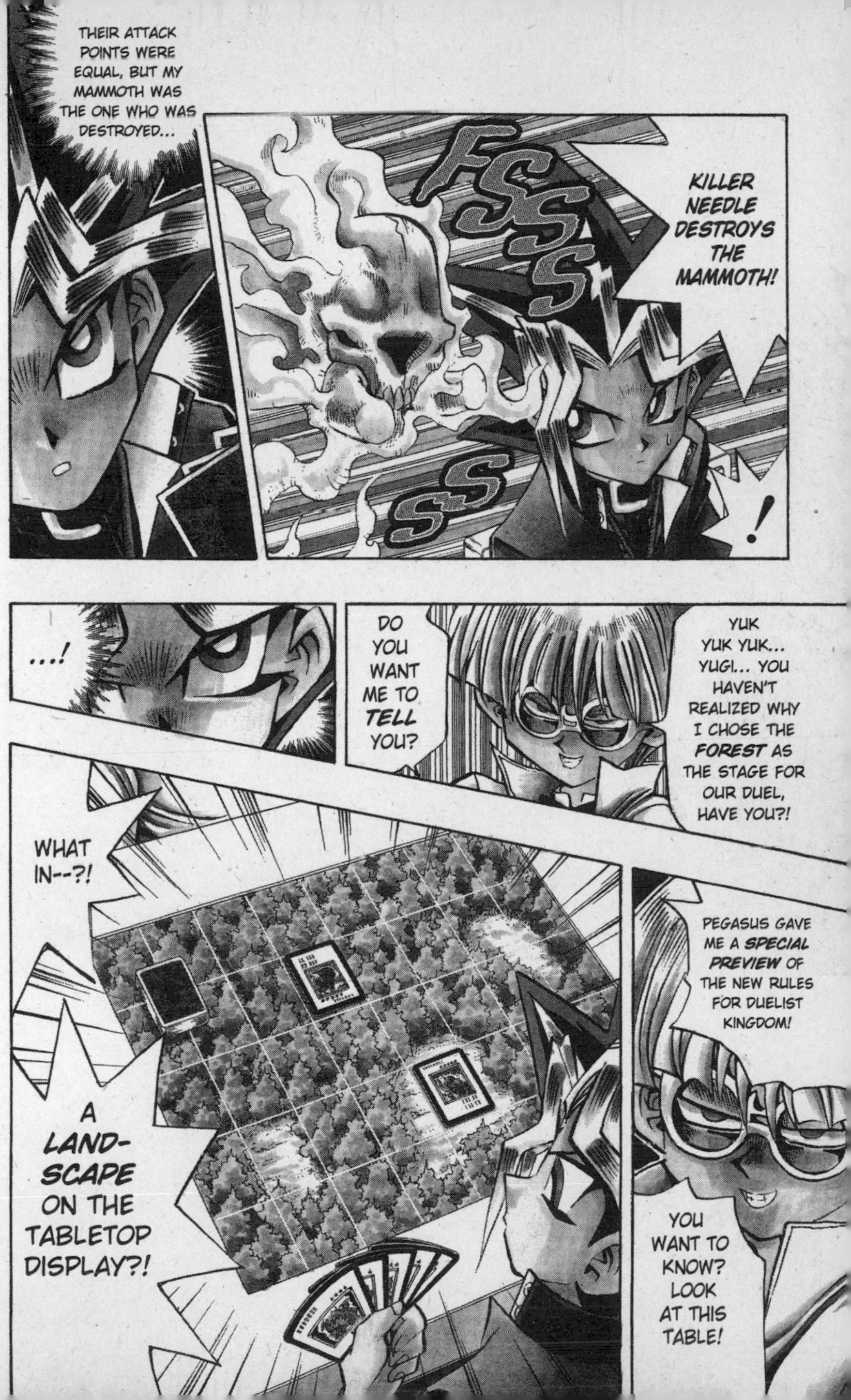

FSSS
KILLER NEEDLE DESTROYS THE MAMMOTH!
SSS
!
THEIR ATTACK POINTS WERE EQUAL, BUT MY MAMMOTH WAS THE ONE WHO WAS DESTROYED...
YUK YUK YUK... YUGI... YOU HAVEN'T REALIZED WHY I CHOSE THE FOREST AS THE STAGE FOR OUR DUEL, HAVE YOU?!
DO YOU WANT ME TO TELL YOU?
...!
PEGASUS GAVE ME A SPECIAL PREVIEW OF THE NEW RULES FOR DUELIST KINGDOM!
YOU WANT TO KNOW? LOOK AT THIS TABLE!
WHAT IN--?!
A LANDSCAPE ON THE TABLETOP DISPLAY?!

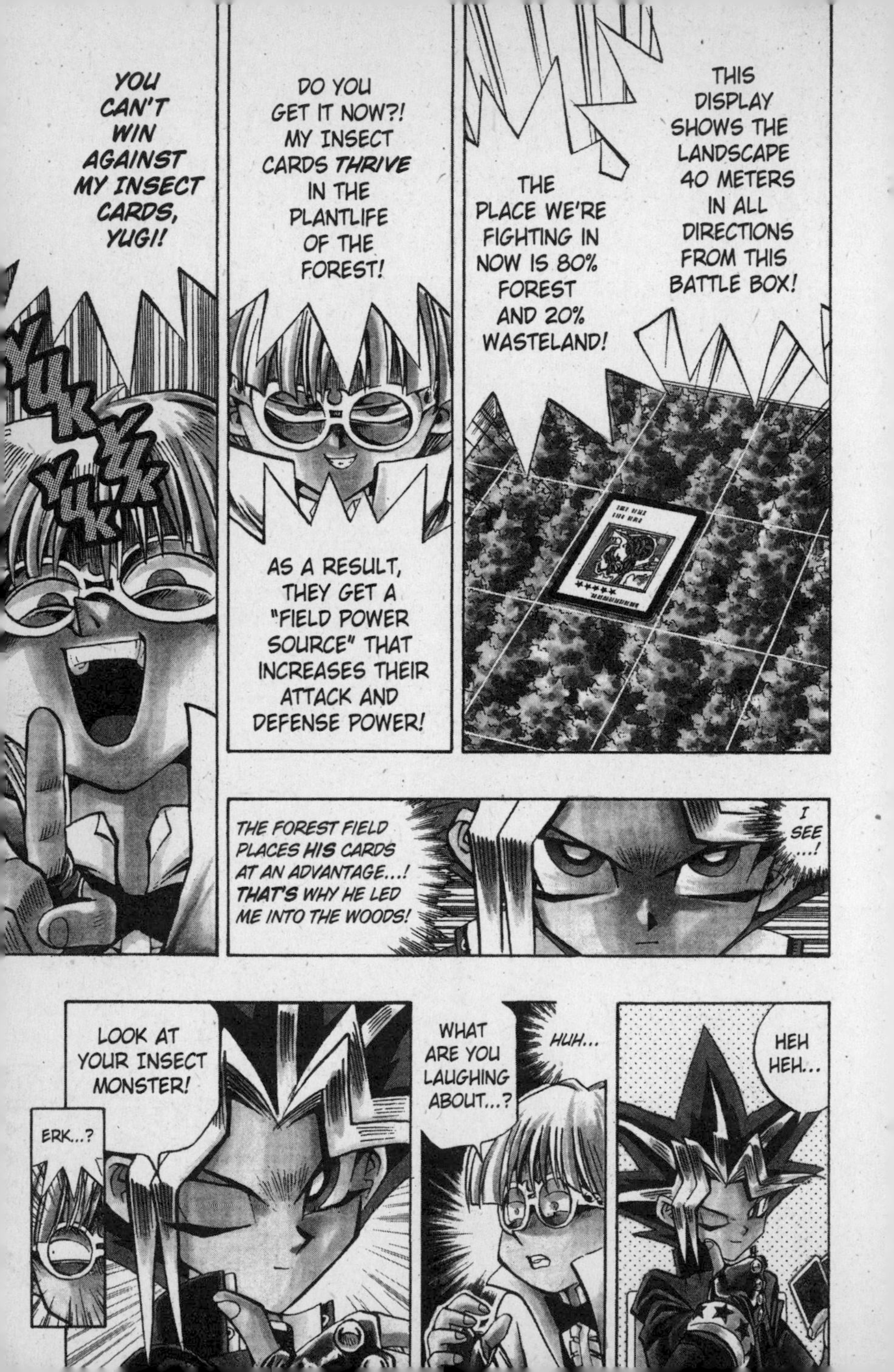

THIS DISPLAY SHOWS THE LANDSCAPE 40 METERS IN ALL DIRECTIONS FROM THIS BATTLE BOX!
THE PLACE WE'RE FIGHTING IN NOW IS 80% FOREST AND 20% WASTELAND!
DO YOU GET IT NOW?! MY INSECT CARDS THRIVE IN THE PLANTLIFE OF THE FOREST!
AS A RESULT, THEY GET A "FIELD POWER SOURCE" THAT INCREASES THEIR ATTACK AND DEFENSE POWER!
I SEE...!
THE FOREST FIELD PLACES HIS CARDS AT AN ADVANTAGE...! THAT'S WHY HE LED ME INTO THE WOODS!
YOU CAN'T WIN AGAINST MY INSECT CARDS, YUGI!
YUK YUK YUK
HEH HEH...
HUH...
WHAT ARE YOU LAUGHING ABOUT...?
LOOK AT YOUR INSECT MONSTER!
ERK...?

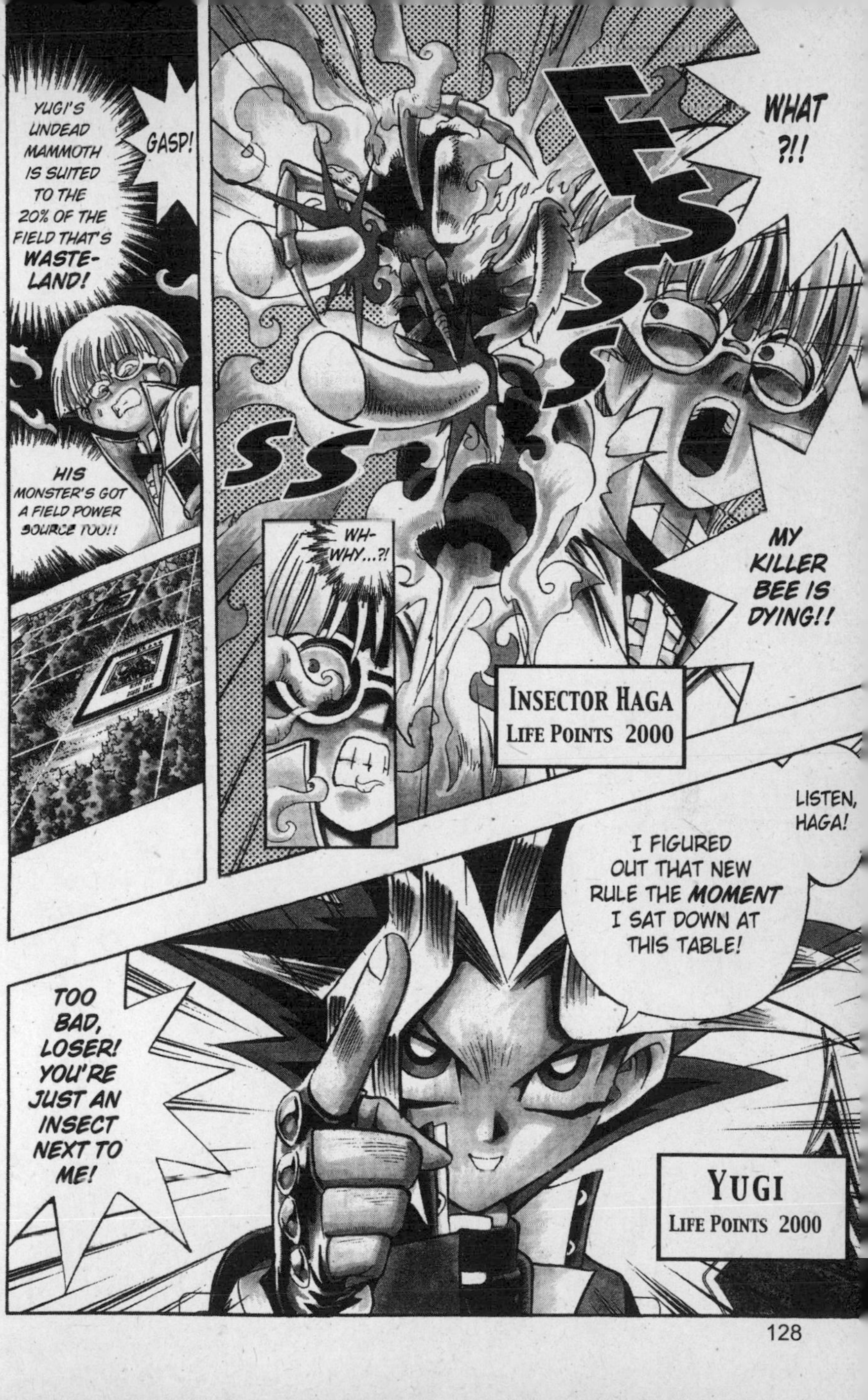
WHAT ?!!
MY KILLER BEE IS DYING!!
WH-WHY...?!
INSECTOR HAGA
LIFE POINTS 2000
GASP!
YUGI'S UNDEAD MAMMOTH IS SUITED TO THE 20% OF THE FIELD THAT'S WASTE-LAND!
HIS MONSTER'S GOT A FIELD POWER SOURCE TOO!!
LISTEN, HAGA!
I FIGURED OUT THAT NEW RULE THE MOMENT I SAT DOWN AT THIS TABLE!
TOO BAD, LOSER! YOU'RE JUST AN INSECT NEXT TO ME!
YUGI
LIFE POINTS 2000

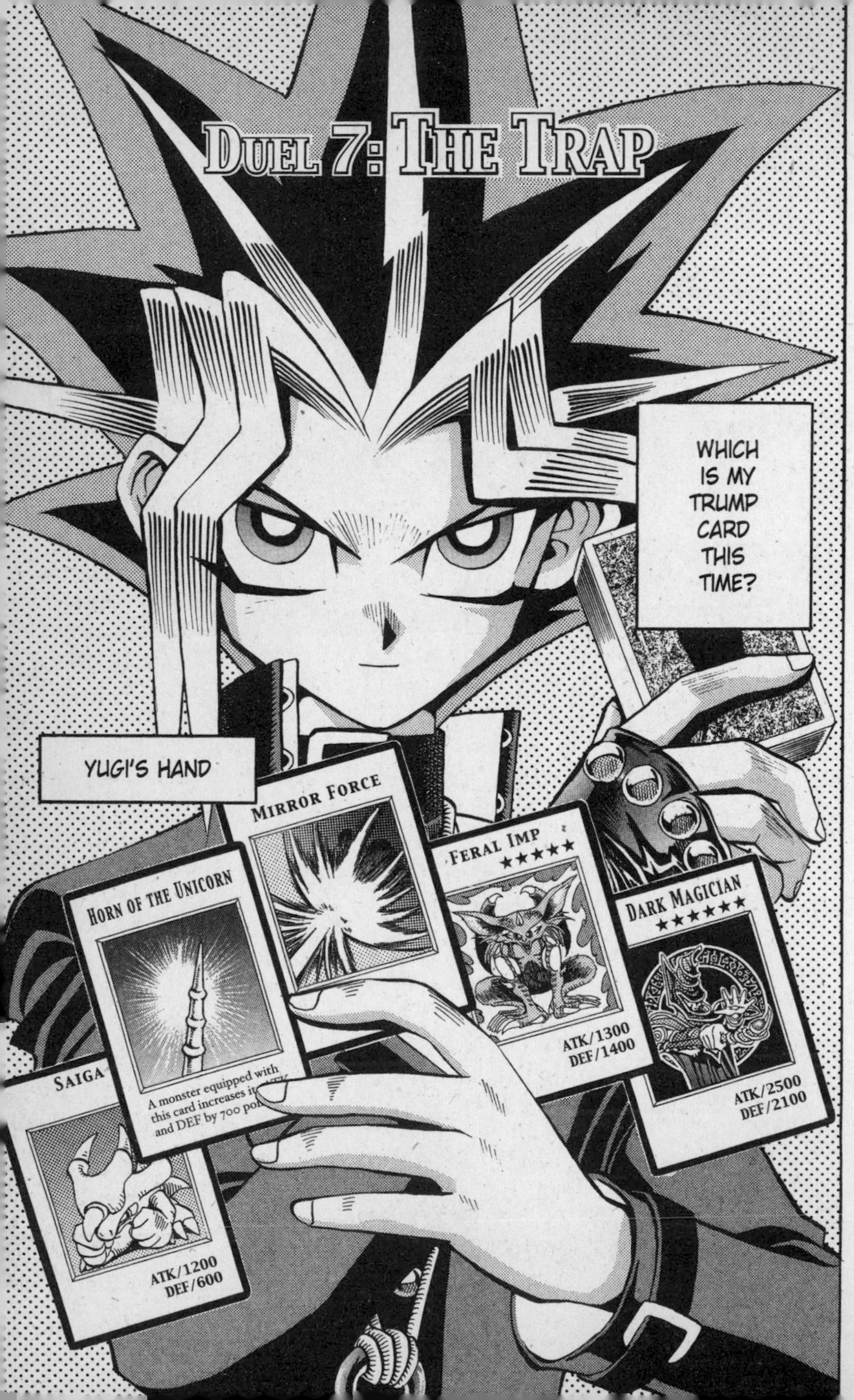
DUEL 7: THE TRAP
WHICH IS MY TRUMP CARD THIS TIME?
YUGI'S HAND
DARK MAGICIAN
ATK/2500 DEF/2100
FERAL IMP
ATK/1300 DEF/1400
MIRROR FORCE
HORN OF THE UNICORN
SAIGA
ATK/1200 DEF/600

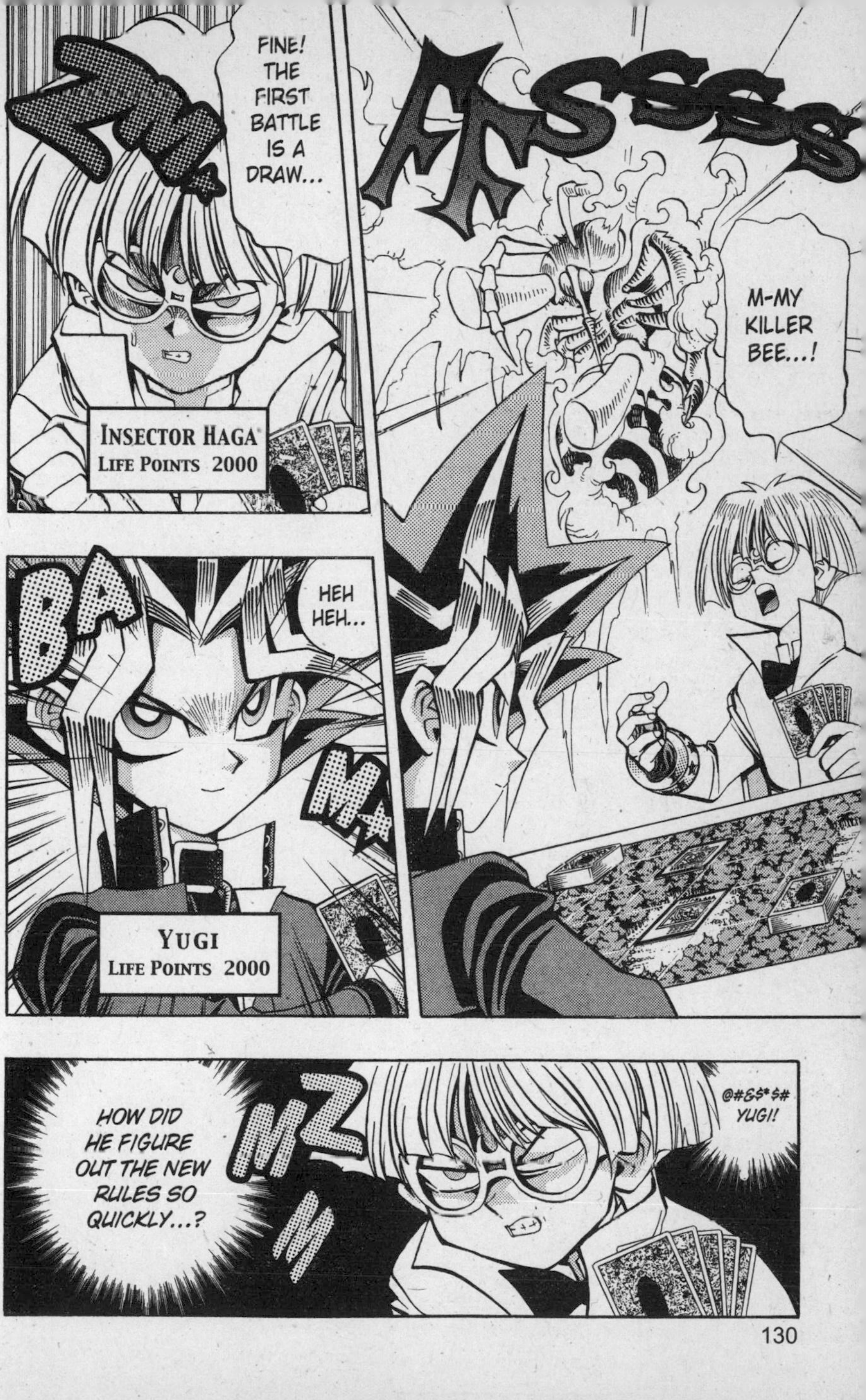
FSSSS
M-MY KILLER BEE...!
FINE! THE FIRST BATTLE IS A DRAW...
INSECTOR HAGA
LIFE POINTS 2000
BA
HEH HEH...
YUGI
LIFE POINTS 2000
@#&$*$# YUGI!
HOW DID HE FIGURE OUT THE NEW RULES SO QUICKLY...?

READ THIS WAY

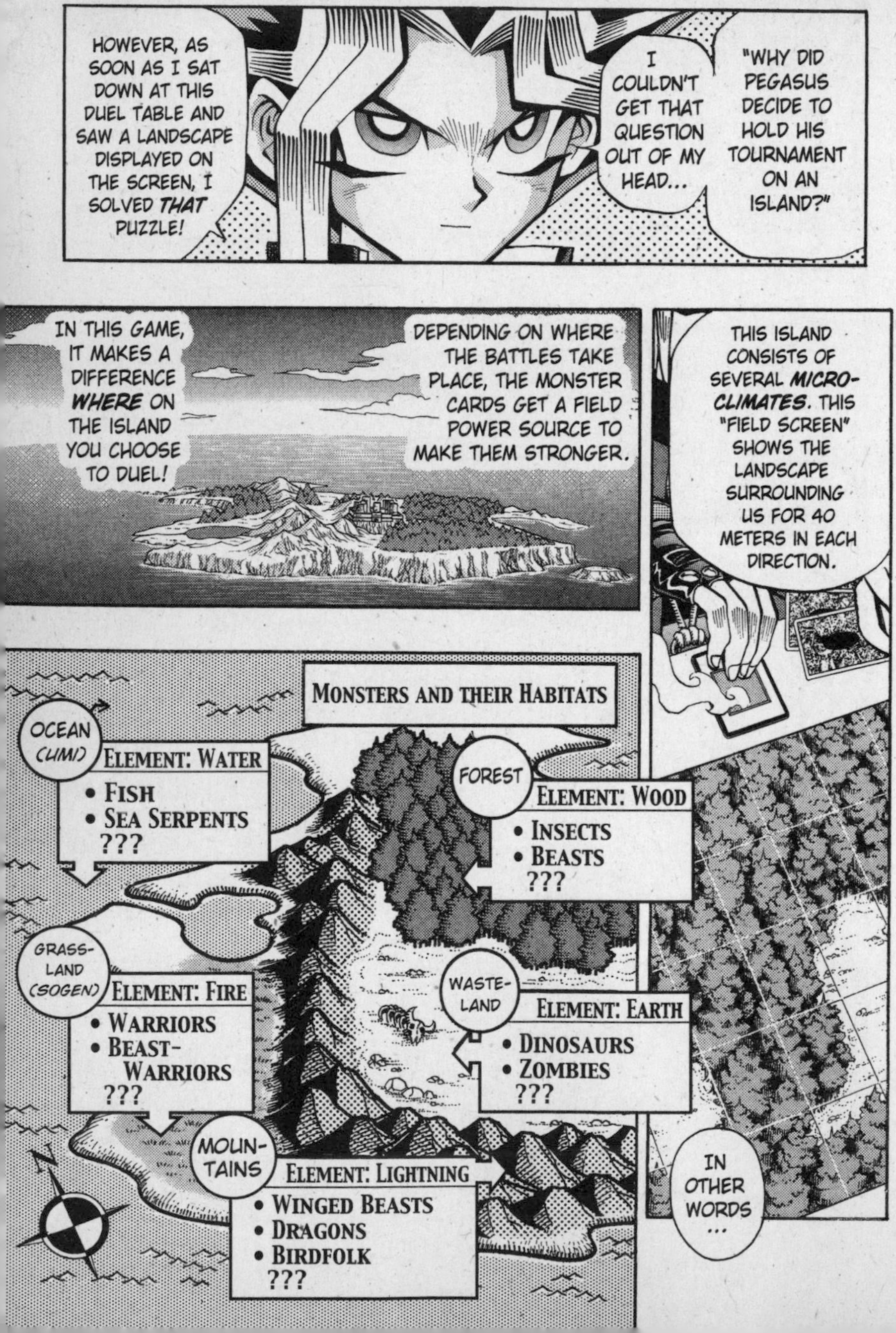

"WHY DID PEGASUS DECIDE TO HOLD HIS TOURNAMENT ON AN ISLAND?"
I COULDN'T GET THAT QUESTION OUT OF MY HEAD...
HOWEVER, AS SOON AS I SAT DOWN AT THIS DUEL TABLE AND SAW A LANDSCAPE DISPLAYED ON THE SCREEN, I SOLVED *THAT* PUZZLE!
THIS ISLAND CONSISTS OF SEVERAL *MICRO-CLIMATES*. THIS "FIELD SCREEN" SHOWS THE LANDSCAPE SURROUNDING US FOR 40 METERS IN EACH DIRECTION.
IN OTHER WORDS...
DEPENDING ON WHERE THE BATTLES TAKE PLACE, THE MONSTER CARDS GET A FIELD POWER SOURCE TO MAKE THEM STRONGER.
IN THIS GAME, IT MAKES A DIFFERENCE *WHERE* ON THE ISLAND YOU CHOOSE TO DUEL!
MONSTERS AND THEIR HABITATS
OCEAN (UMI)
ELEMENT: WATER
• FISH
• SEA SERPENTS
???
FOREST
ELEMENT: WOOD
• INSECTS
• BEASTS
???
GRASS-LAND (SOGEN)
ELEMENT: FIRE
• WARRIORS
• BEAST-WARRIORS
???
WASTE-LAND
ELEMENT: EARTH
• DINOSAURS
• ZOMBIES
???
MOUN-TAINS
ELEMENT: LIGHTNING
• WINGED BEASTS
• DRAGONS
• BIRDFOLK
???

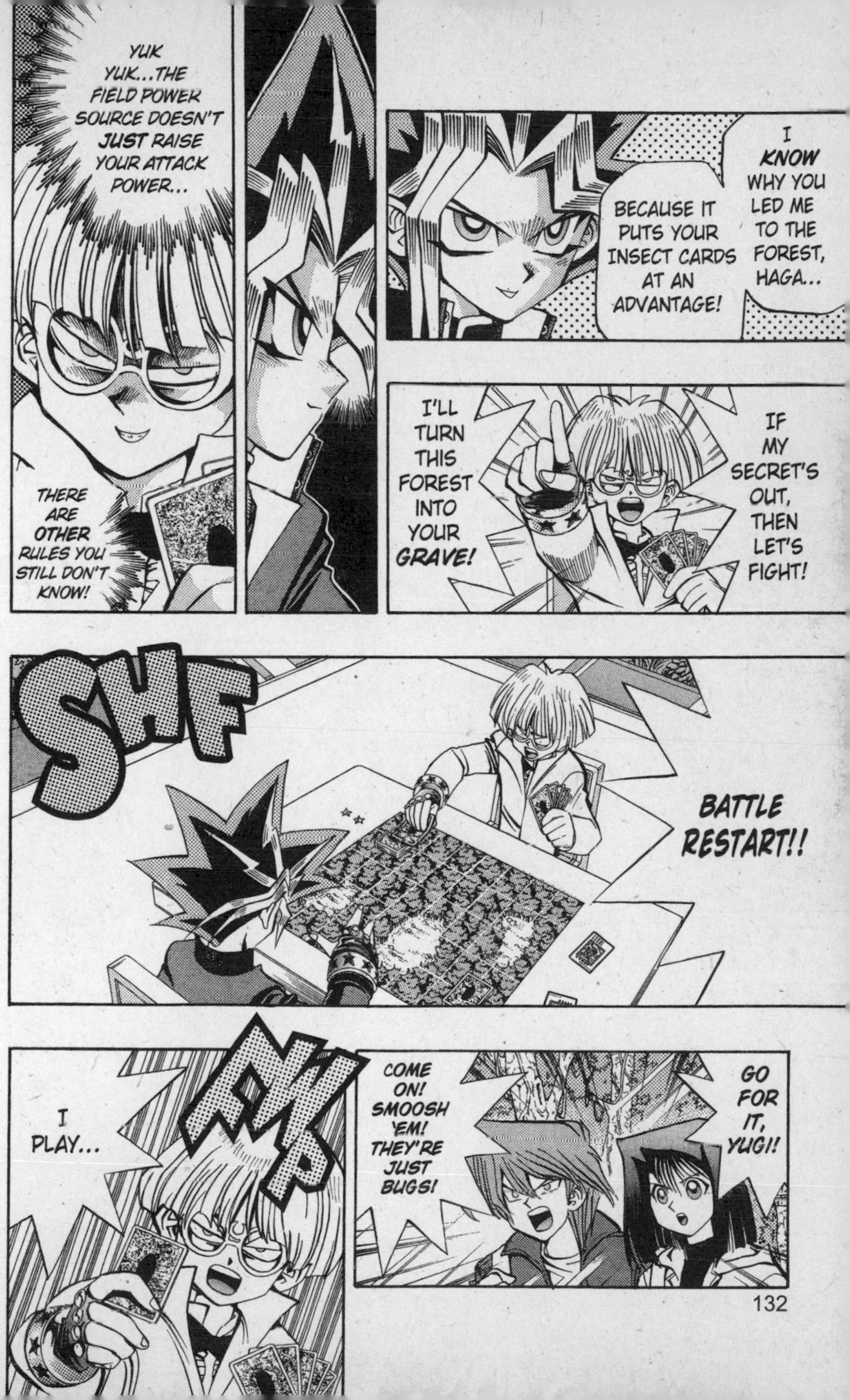
I KNOW WHY YOU LED ME TO THE FOREST, HAGA...
BECAUSE IT PUTS YOUR INSECT CARDS AT AN ADVANTAGE!
IF MY SECRET'S OUT, THEN LET'S FIGHT!
I'LL TURN THIS FOREST INTO YOUR GRAVE!
YUK YUK...THE FIELD POWER SOURCE DOESN'T JUST RAISE YOUR ATTACK POWER...
THERE ARE OTHER RULES YOU STILL DON'T KNOW!
BATTLE RESTART!!
SHF
GO FOR IT, YUGI!
COME ON! SMOOSH 'EM! THEY'RE JUST BUGS!
I PLAY...

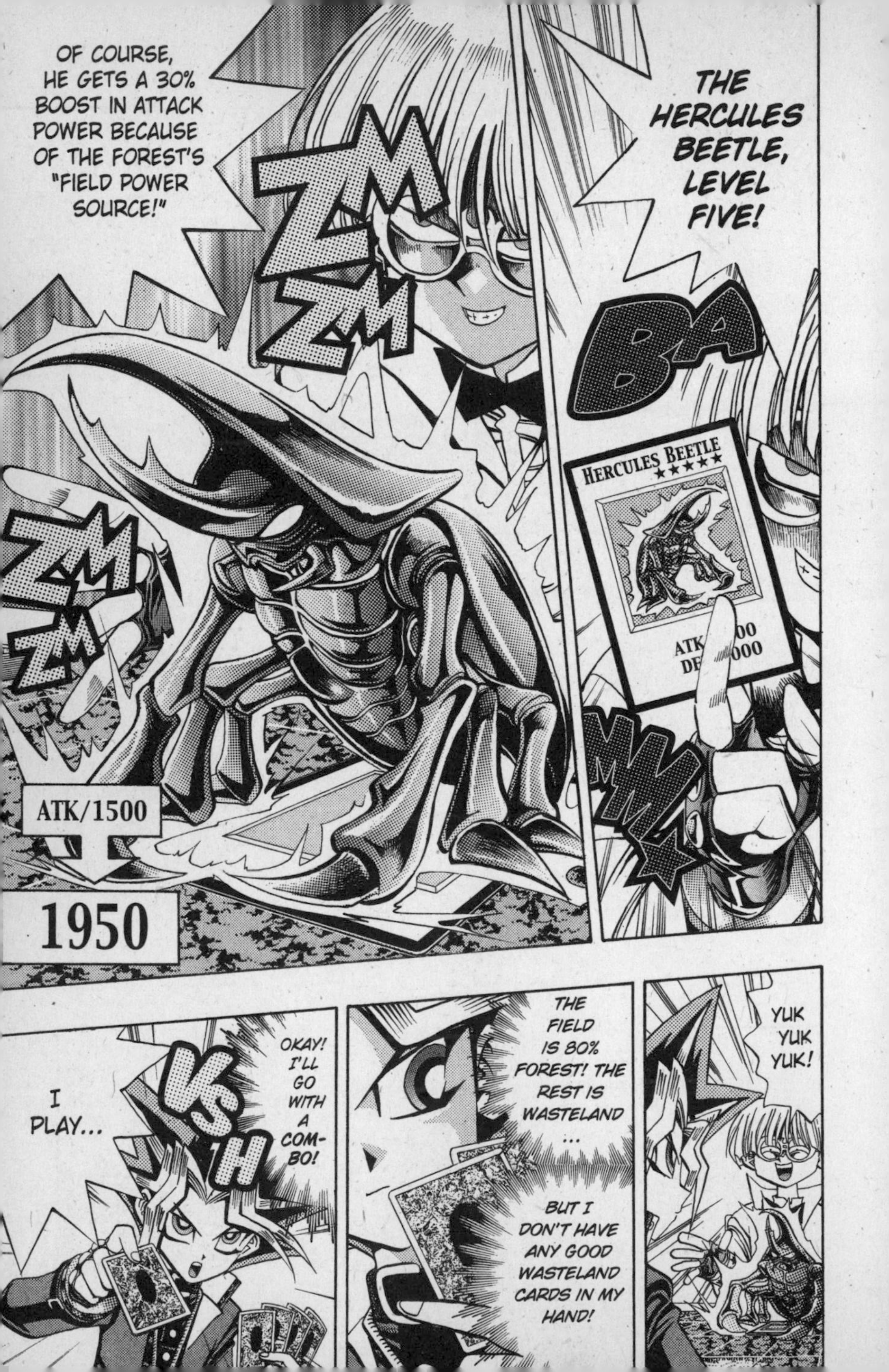
THE HERCULES BEETLE, LEVEL FIVE!
BA
HERCULES BEETLE
MM
OF COURSE, HE GETS A 30% BOOST IN ATTACK POWER BECAUSE OF THE FOREST'S "FIELD POWER SOURCE!"
ZM ZM
ZM ZM
ATK/1500
1950
YUK YUK YUK!
THE FIELD IS 80% FOREST! THE REST IS WASTELAND ...
BUT I DON'T HAVE ANY GOOD WASTELAND CARDS IN MY HAND!
OKAY! I'LL GO WITH A COMBO!
VSH
I PLAY...

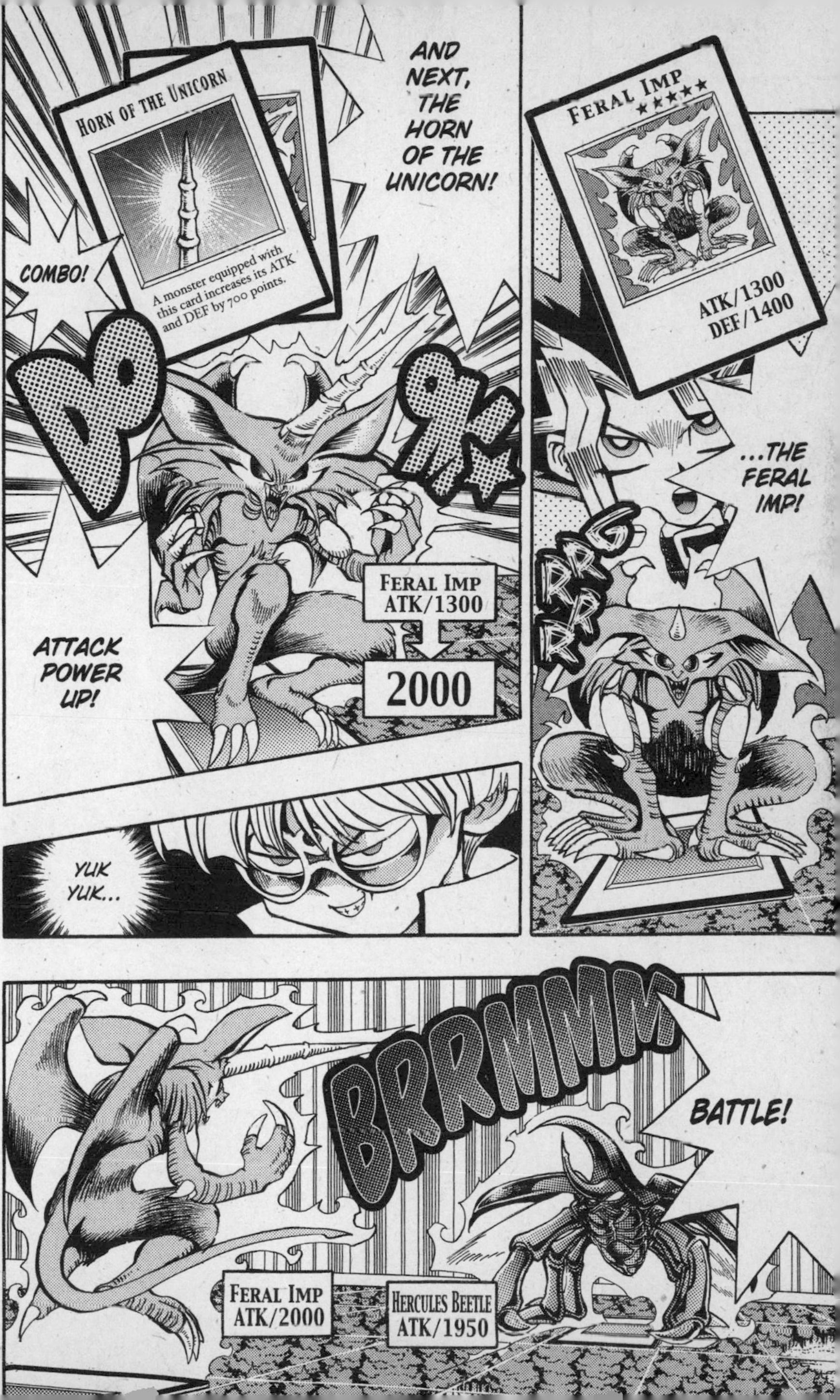

FERAL IMP ★★★★★
ATK/1300 DEF/1400
...THE FERAL IMP!
AND NEXT, THE HORN OF THE UNICORN!
HORN OF THE UNICORN
A monster equipped with this card increases its ATK and DEF by 700 points.
COMBO!
DOOK
FERAL IMP ATK/1300
2000
ATTACK POWER UP!
YUK YUK...
BATTLE!
BRRMMMM
FERAL IMP ATK/2000
HERCULES BEETLE ATK/1950

READ THIS WAY

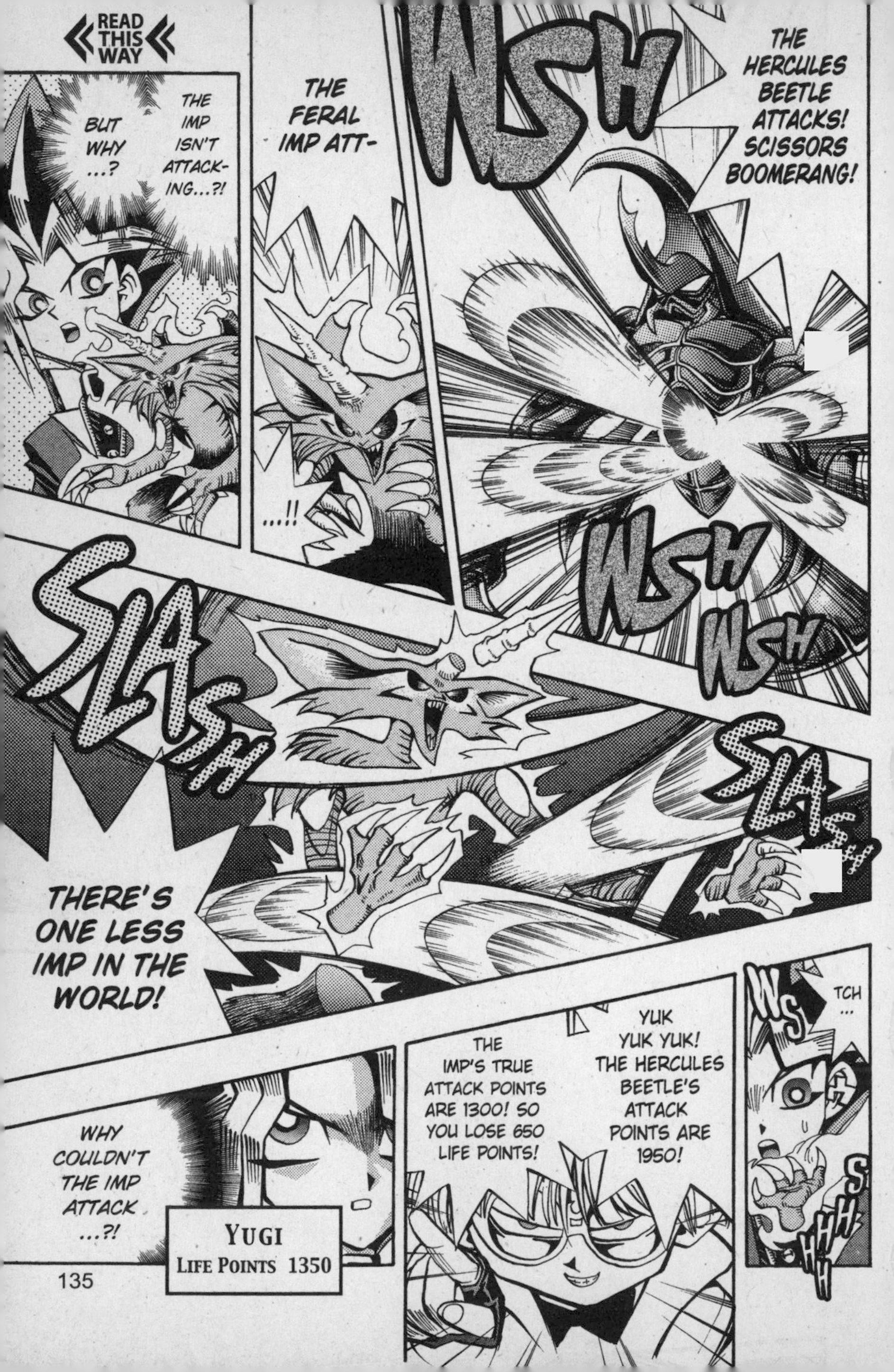
WSH
THE HERCULES BEETLE ATTACKS! SCISSORS BOOMERANG!
WSH
WSH
THE FERAL IMP ATT-
...!!
THE IMP ISN'T ATTACK-ING...?!
BUT WHY ...?
SLASH
SLASH
THERE'S ONE LESS IMP IN THE WORLD!
WS
TCH ...
SHHHH
YUK YUK YUK! THE HERCULES BEETLE'S ATTACK POINTS ARE 1950!
THE IMP'S TRUE ATTACK POINTS ARE 1300! SO YOU LOSE 650 LIFE POINTS!
WHY COULDN'T THE IMP ATTACK ...?!
YUGI
LIFE POINTS 1350

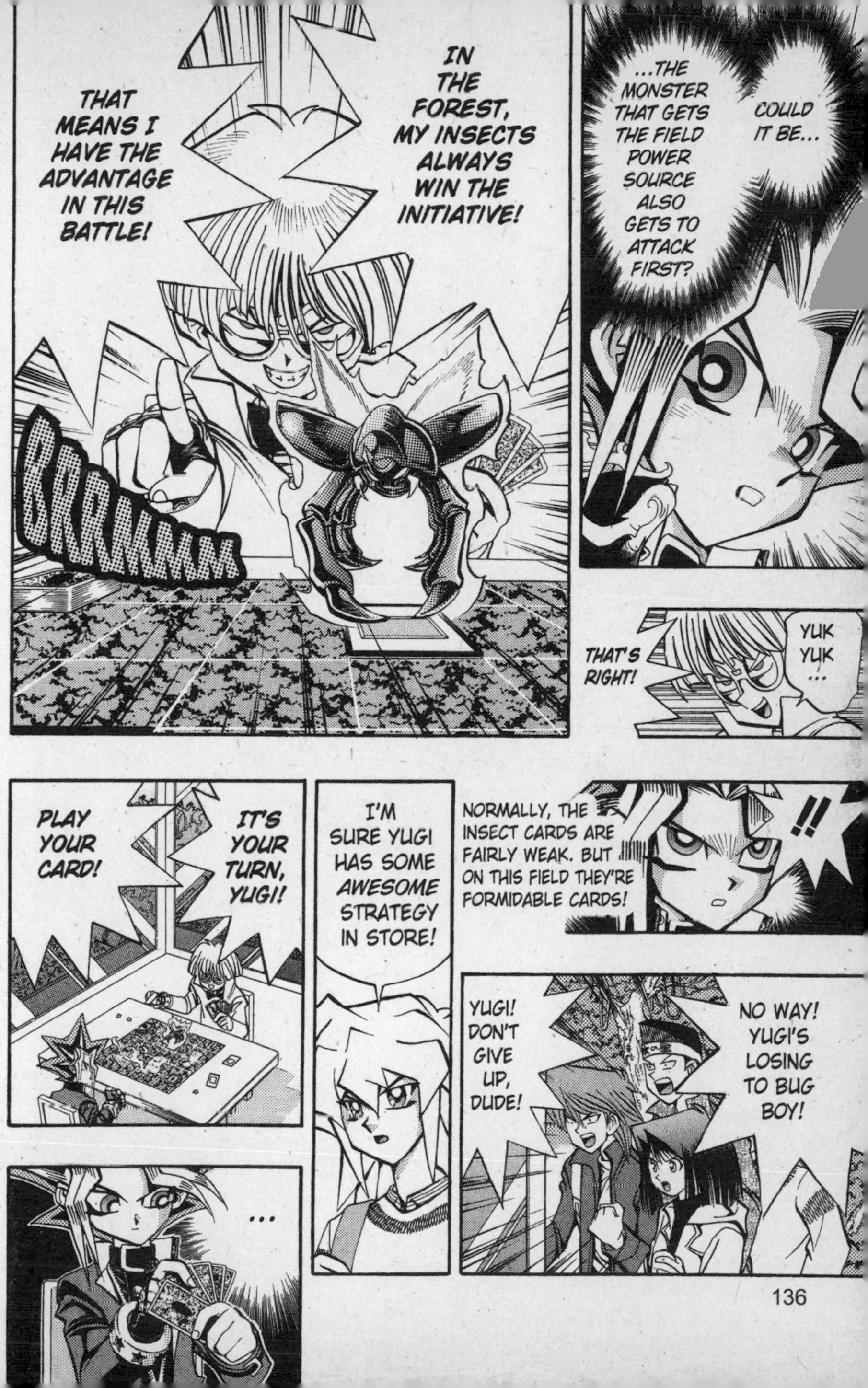
COULD IT BE...
...THE MONSTER THAT GETS THE FIELD POWER SOURCE ALSO GETS TO ATTACK FIRST?
YUK YUK ...
THAT'S RIGHT!
IN THE FOREST, MY INSECTS ALWAYS WIN THE INITIATIVE!
THAT MEANS I HAVE THE ADVANTAGE IN THIS BATTLE!
BRRMMMM
!!
NORMALLY, THE INSECT CARDS ARE FAIRLY WEAK. BUT ON THIS FIELD THEY'RE FORMIDABLE CARDS!
NO WAY! YUGI'S LOSING TO BUG BOY!
YUGI! DON'T GIVE UP, DUDE!
I'M SURE YUGI HAS SOME AWESOME STRATEGY IN STORE!
IT'S YOUR TURN, YUGI!
PLAY YOUR CARD!
...

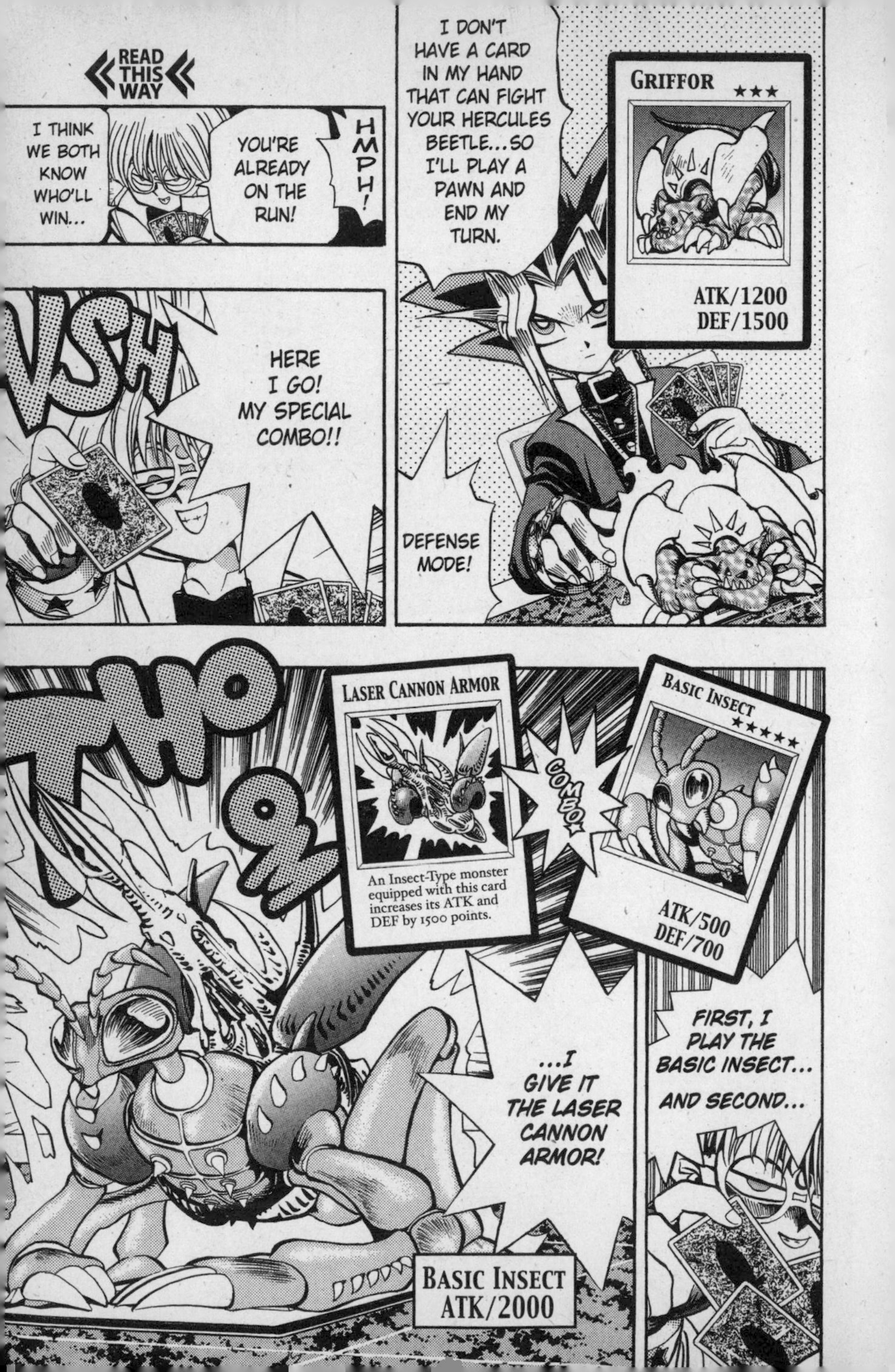
READ THIS WAY
I DON'T HAVE A CARD IN MY HAND THAT CAN FIGHT YOUR HERCULES BEETLE...SO I'LL PLAY A PAWN AND END MY TURN.
GRIFFOR ★★★
ATK/1200 DEF/1500
DEFENSE MODE!
HMPH!
YOU'RE ALREADY ON THE RUN!
I THINK WE BOTH KNOW WHO'LL WIN...
VSH
HERE I GO! MY SPECIAL COMBO!!
FIRST, I PLAY THE BASIC INSECT...
AND SECOND...
...I GIVE IT THE LASER CANNON ARMOR!
BASIC INSECT ★★★★★
ATK/500 DEF/700
COMBO★
LASER CANNON ARMOR
An Insect-Type monster equipped with this card increases its ATK and DEF by 1500 points.
THOOM
BASIC INSECT ATK/2000

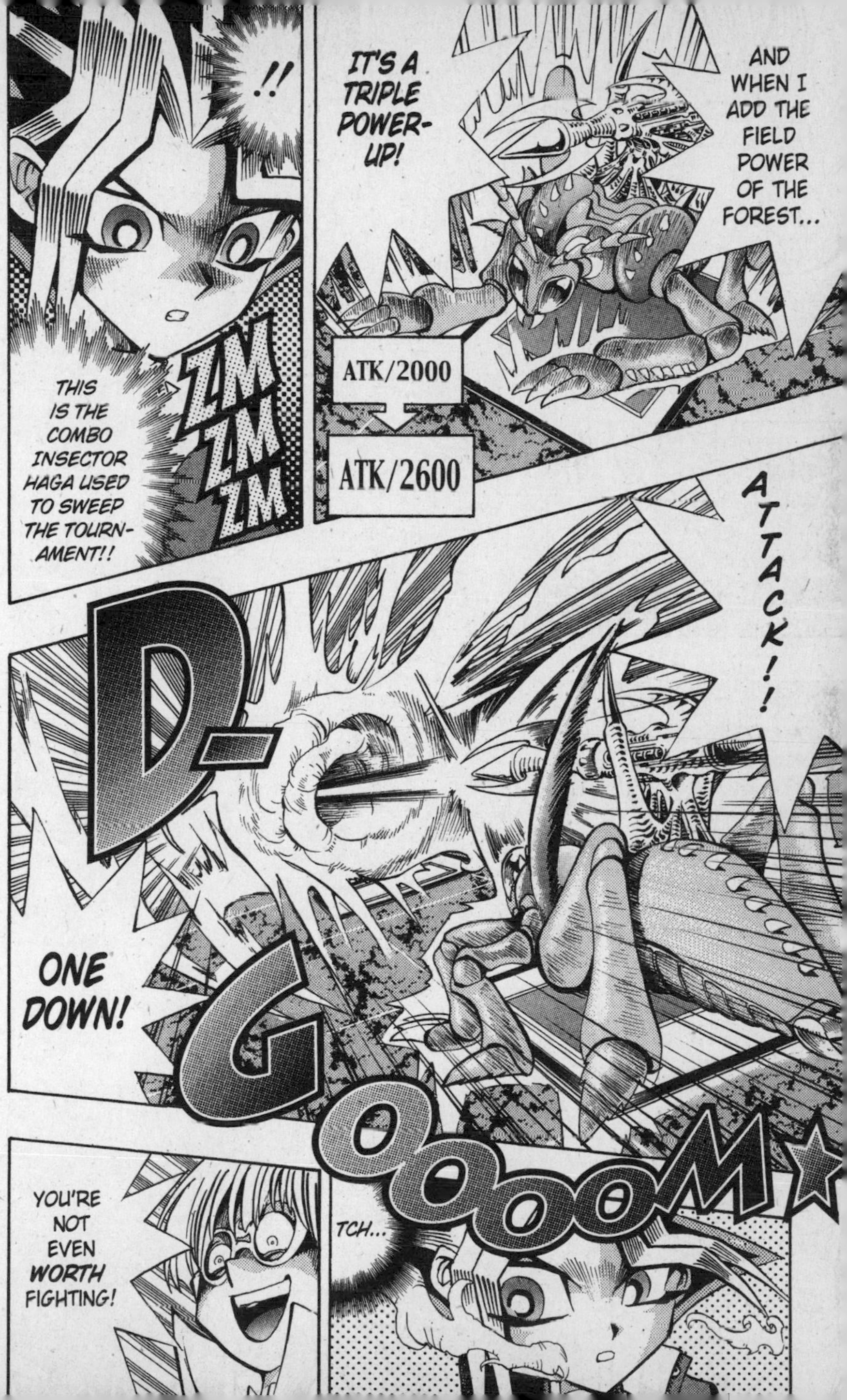
AND WHEN I ADD THE FIELD POWER OF THE FOREST...
IT'S A TRIPLE POWER-UP!
ATK/2000
ATK/2600
!!
ZM ZM ZM
THIS IS THE COMBO INSECTOR HAGA USED TO SWEEP THE TOURNAMENT!!
ATTACK!!
D-GOOOOM★
ONE DOWN!
TCH...
YOU'RE NOT EVEN WORTH FIGHTING!

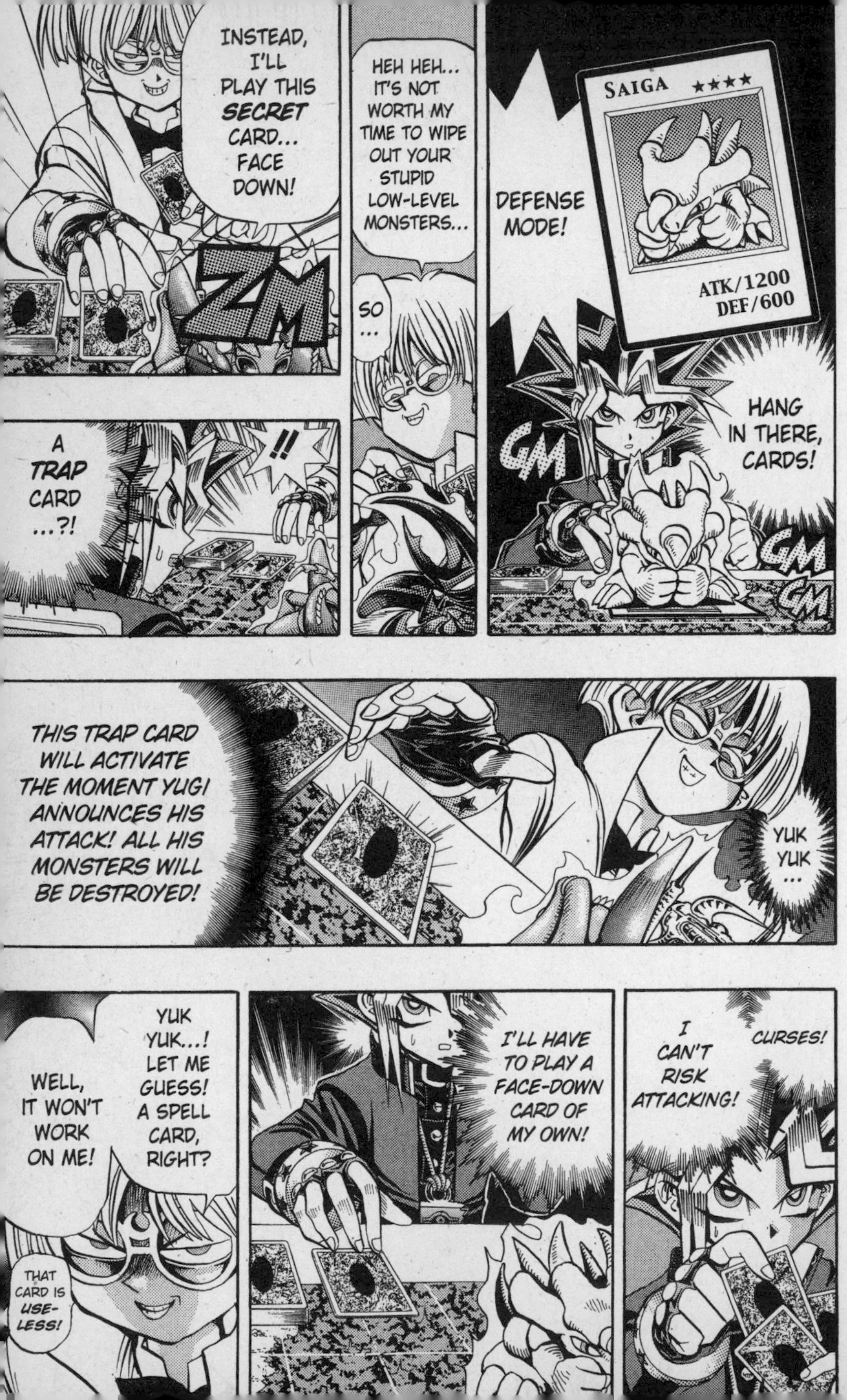
DEFENSE MODE!
SAIGA ★★★★
ATK/1200 DEF/600
HANG IN THERE, CARDS!
GM
GM GM
HEH HEH... IT'S NOT WORTH MY TIME TO WIPE OUT YOUR STUPID LOW-LEVEL MONSTERS...
SO ...
INSTEAD, I'LL PLAY THIS SECRET CARD... FACE DOWN!
ZM
!!
A TRAP CARD ...?!
YUK YUK ...
THIS TRAP CARD WILL ACTIVATE THE MOMENT YUGI ANNOUNCES HIS ATTACK! ALL HIS MONSTERS WILL BE DESTROYED!
CURSES!
I CAN'T RISK ATTACKING!
I'LL HAVE TO PLAY A FACE-DOWN CARD OF MY OWN!
YUK YUK...! LET ME GUESS! A SPELL CARD, RIGHT?
WELL, IT WON'T WORK ON ME!
THAT CARD IS USE-LESS!

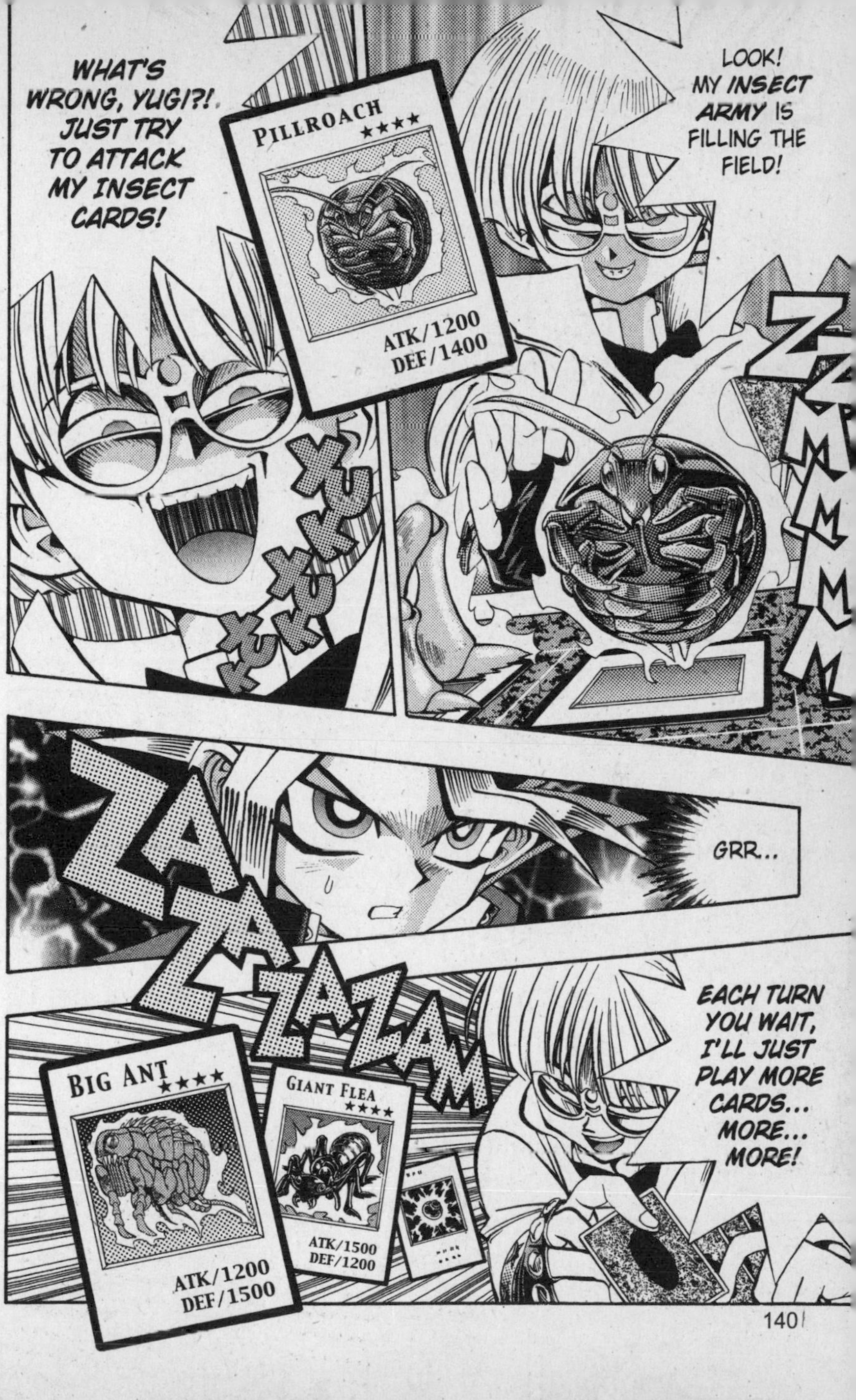
LOOK! MY INSECT ARMY IS FILLING THE FIELD!
WHAT'S WRONG, YUGI?! JUST TRY TO ATTACK MY INSECT CARDS!
PILLROACH ★★★★
ATK/1200
DEF/1400
XUK XUK XUK
GRR...
ZAZAZAM
EACH TURN YOU WAIT, I'LL JUST PLAY MORE CARDS... MORE... MORE!
GIANT FLEA ★★★★
ATK/1500
DEF/1200
BIG ANT ★★★★
ATK/1200
DEF/1500

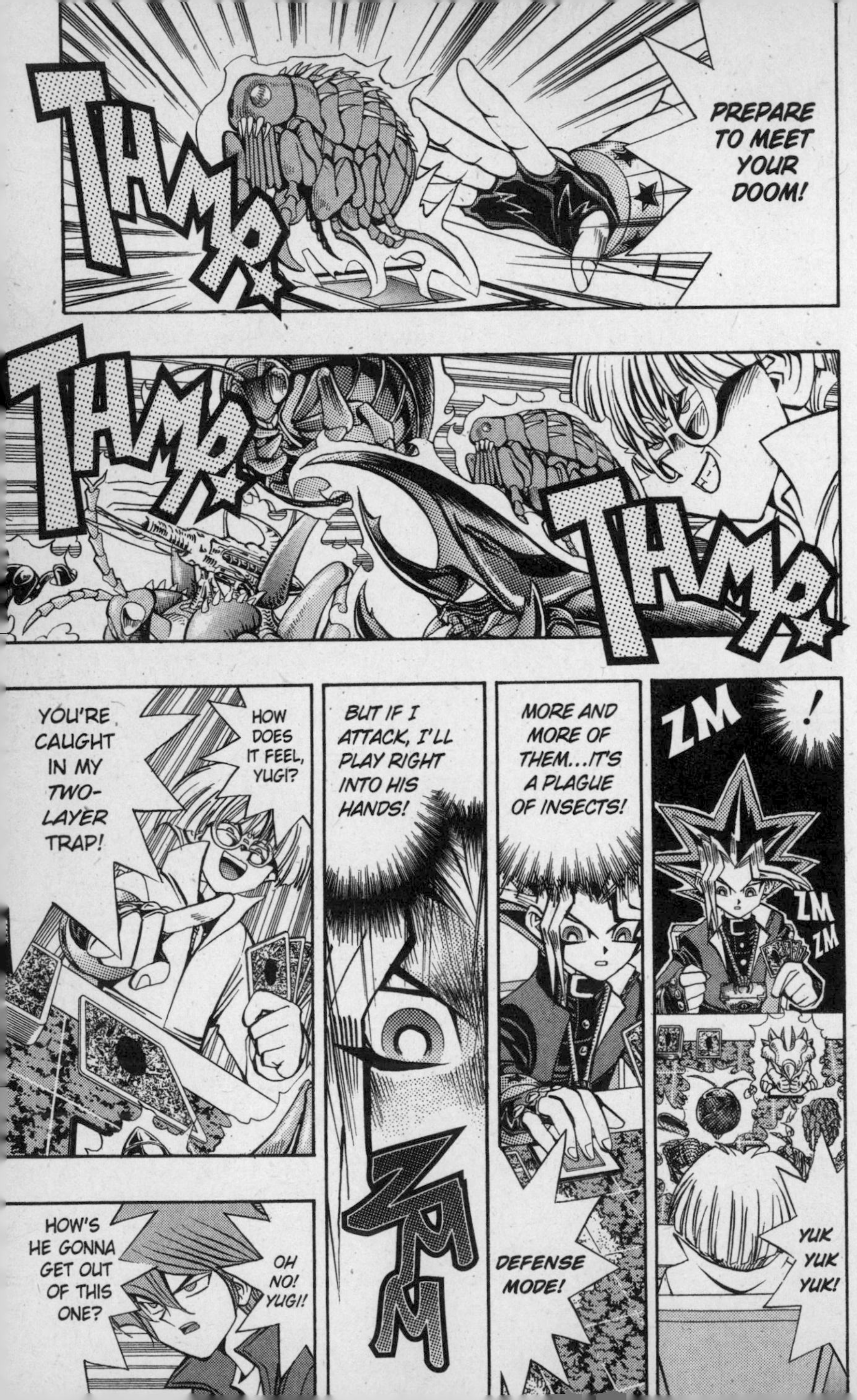
PREPARE TO MEET YOUR DOOM!
THMP
THMP
THMP
!
ZM
ZM ZM
YUK YUK YUK!
MORE AND MORE OF THEM...IT'S A PLAGUE OF INSECTS!
DEFENSE MODE!
BUT IF I ATTACK, I'LL PLAY RIGHT INTO HIS HANDS!
HOW DOES IT FEEL, YUGI?
YOU'RE CAUGHT IN MY TWO-LAYER TRAP!
OH NO! YUGI!
HOW'S HE GONNA GET OUT OF THIS ONE?

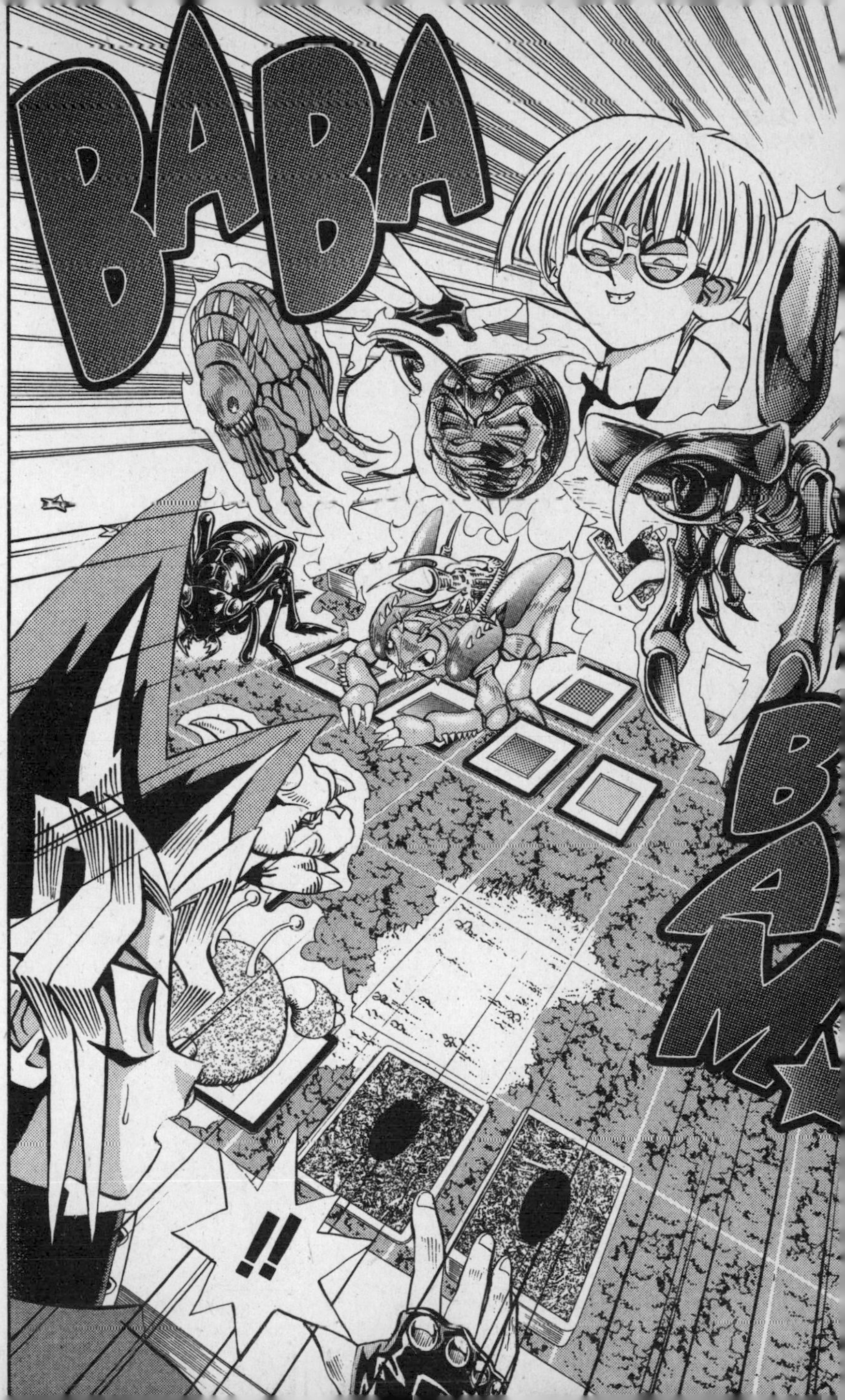
BABA
BAM
!!

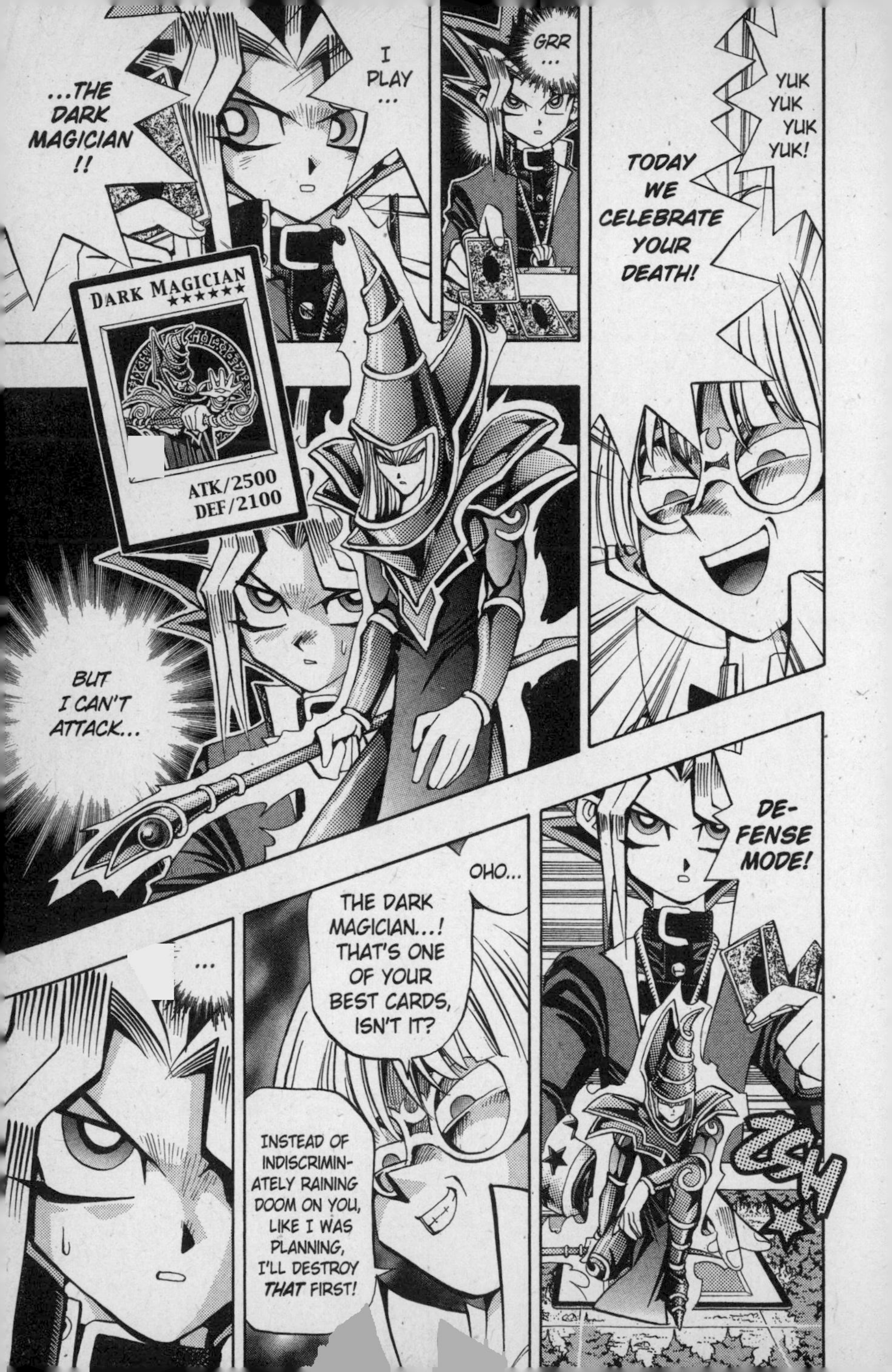
YUK YUK YUK YUK!
TODAY WE CELEBRATE YOUR DEATH!
GRR ...
I PLAY ...
...THE DARK MAGICIAN !!
DARK MAGICIAN
ATK/2500
DEF/2100
BUT I CAN'T ATTACK...
DE-FENSE MODE!
OHO...
THE DARK MAGICIAN...! THAT'S ONE OF YOUR BEST CARDS, ISN'T IT?
INSTEAD OF INDISCRIMIN-ATELY RAINING DOOM ON YOU, LIKE I WAS PLANNING, I'LL DESTROY THAT FIRST!
...

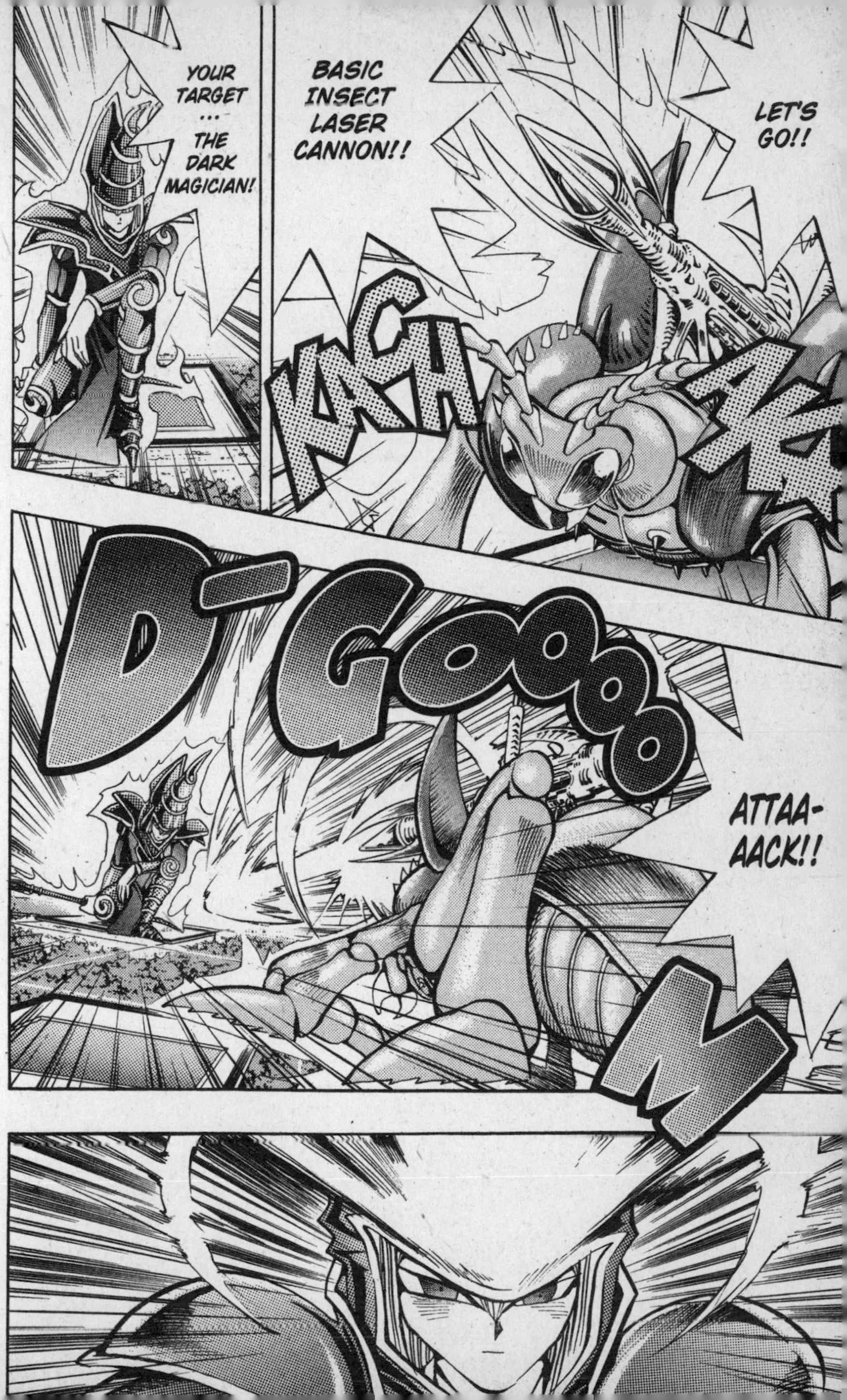
LET'S GO!!
BASIC INSECT LASER CANNON!!
KACHA
YOUR TARGET ... THE DARK MAGICIAN!
ATTAA-AACK!!
D'GOOOOM

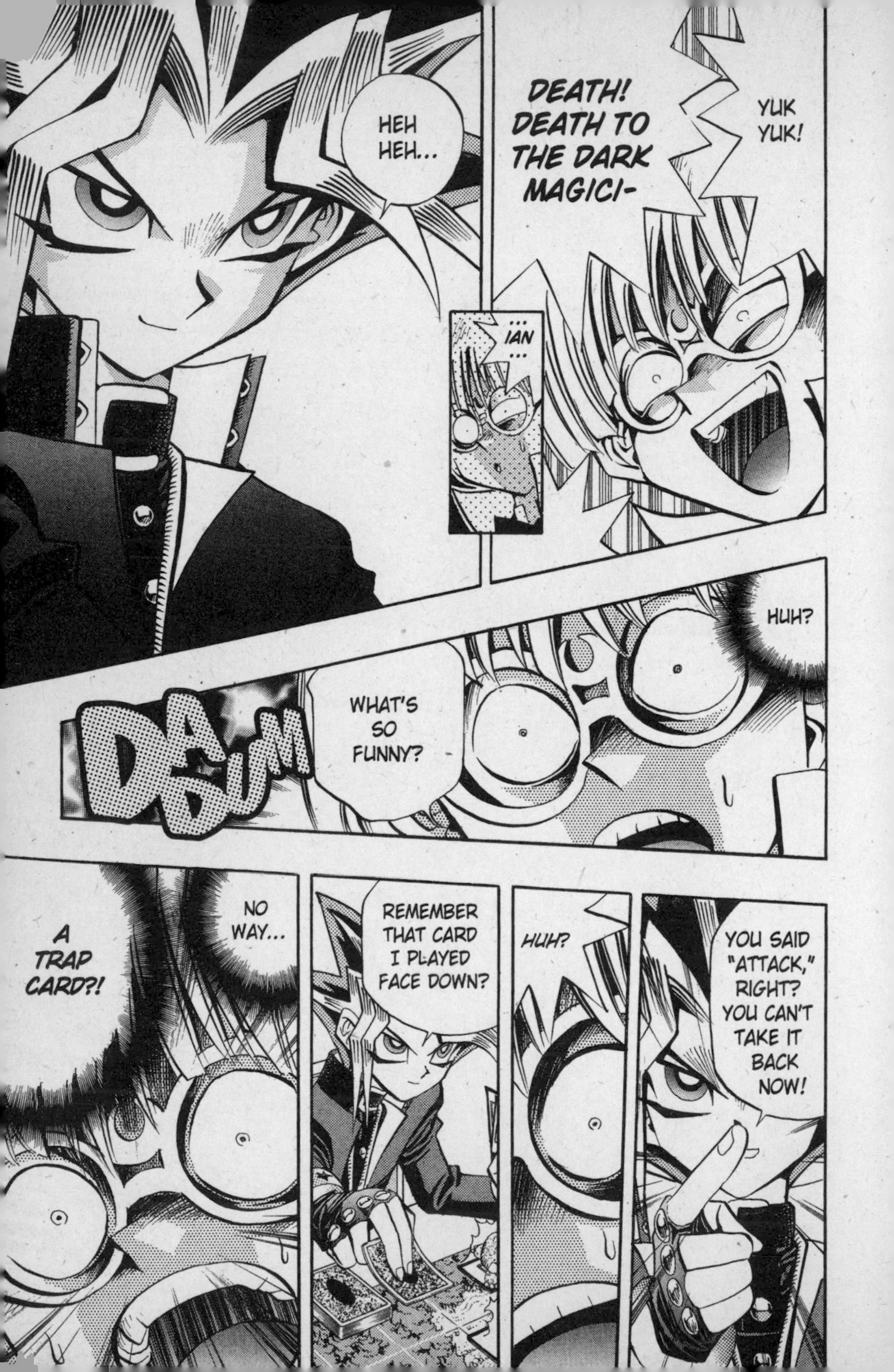
YUK YUK!
DEATH! DEATH TO THE DARK MAGICI-
...IAN...
HEH HEH...
HUH?
WHAT'S SO FUNNY?
DABUM
YOU SAID "ATTACK," RIGHT? YOU CAN'T TAKE IT BACK NOW!
HUH?
REMEMBER THAT CARD I PLAYED FACE DOWN?
NO WAY...
A TRAP CARD?!

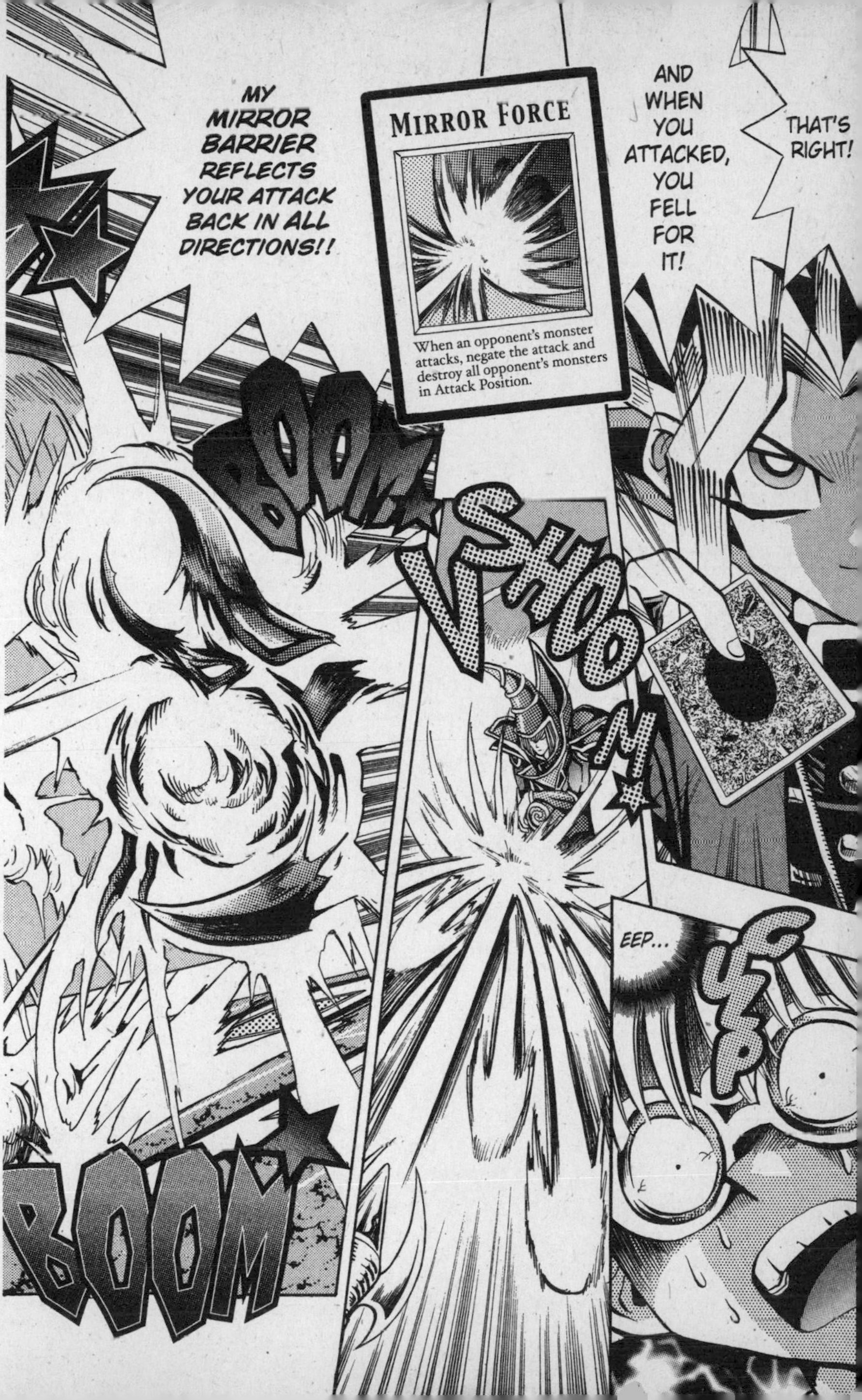
THAT'S RIGHT!
AND WHEN YOU ATTACKED, YOU FELL FOR IT!
MY MIRROR BARRIER REFLECTS YOUR ATTACK BACK IN ALL DIRECTIONS!!
MIRROR FORCE
When an opponent's monster attacks, negate the attack and destroy all opponent's monsters in Attack Position.
BOOM
SHOOM
EEP...
GULP
BOOM

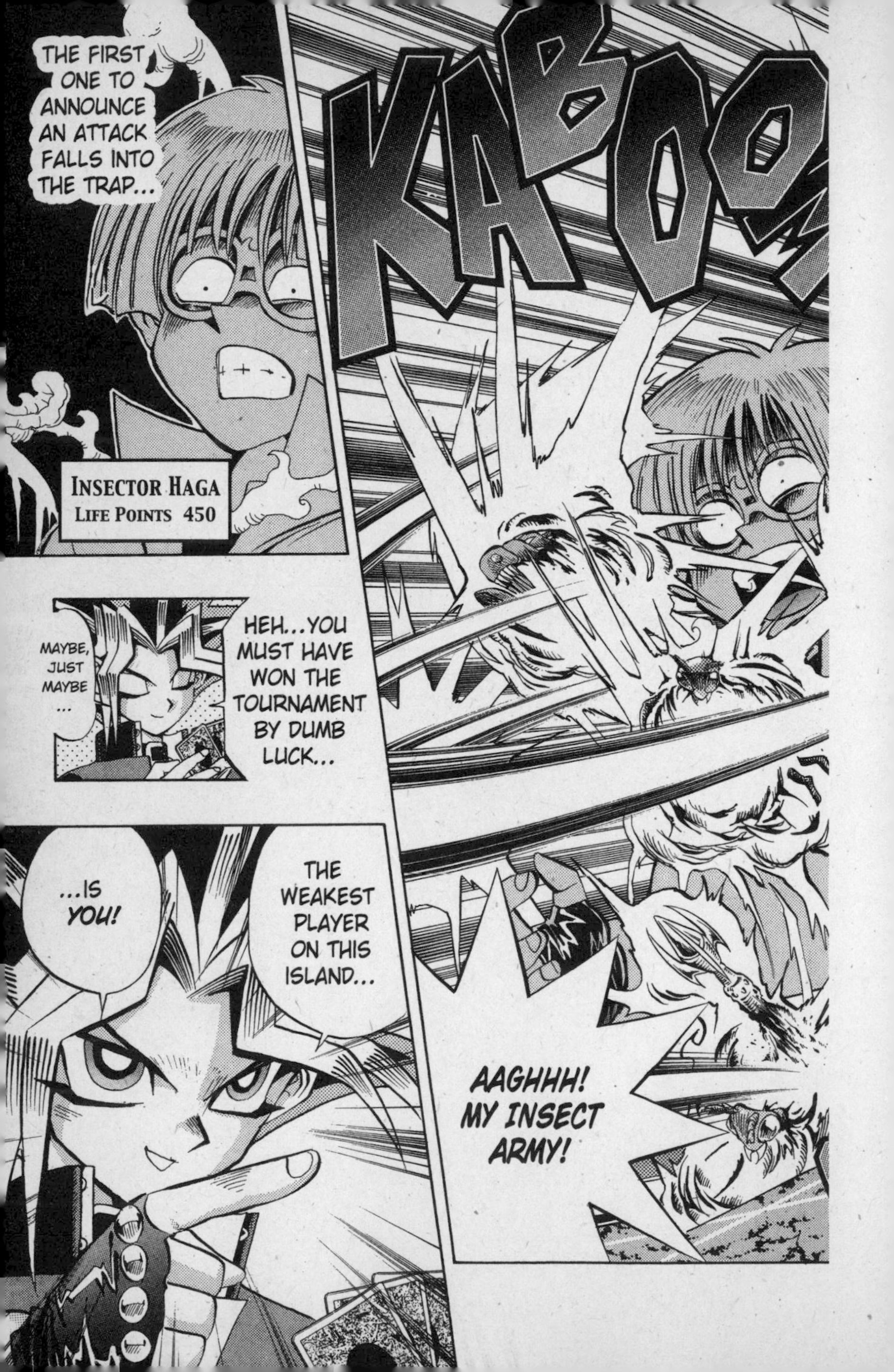

KABOO
AAGHHH! MY INSECT ARMY!
THE FIRST ONE TO ANNOUNCE AN ATTACK FALLS INTO THE TRAP...
INSECTOR HAGA
LIFE POINTS 450
HEH...YOU MUST HAVE WON THE TOURNAMENT BY DUMB LUCK...
MAYBE, JUST MAYBE ...
THE WEAKEST PLAYER ON THIS ISLAND...
...IS YOU!

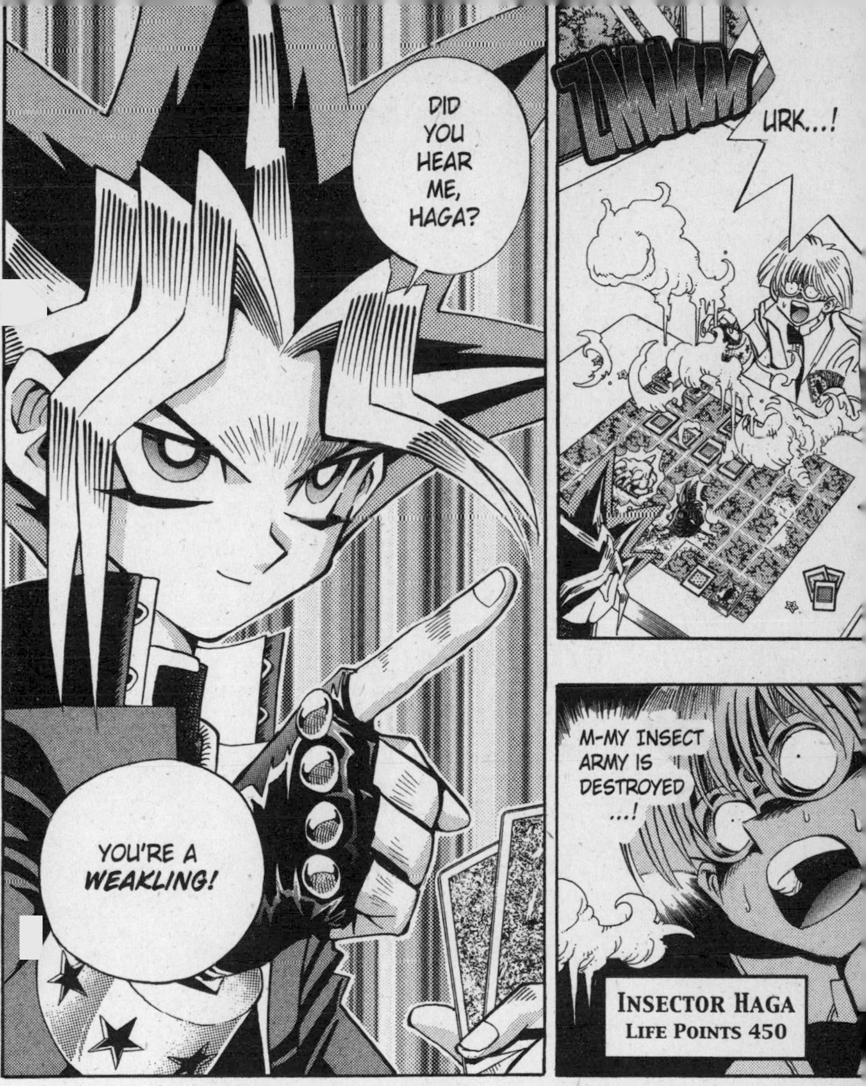
URK...!
M-MY INSECT ARMY IS DESTROYED ...!
INSECTOR HAGA
LIFE POINTS 450
DID YOU HEAR ME, HAGA?
YOU'RE A *WEAKLING!*

Duel 8: The Ultimate Great Moth

READ THIS WAY

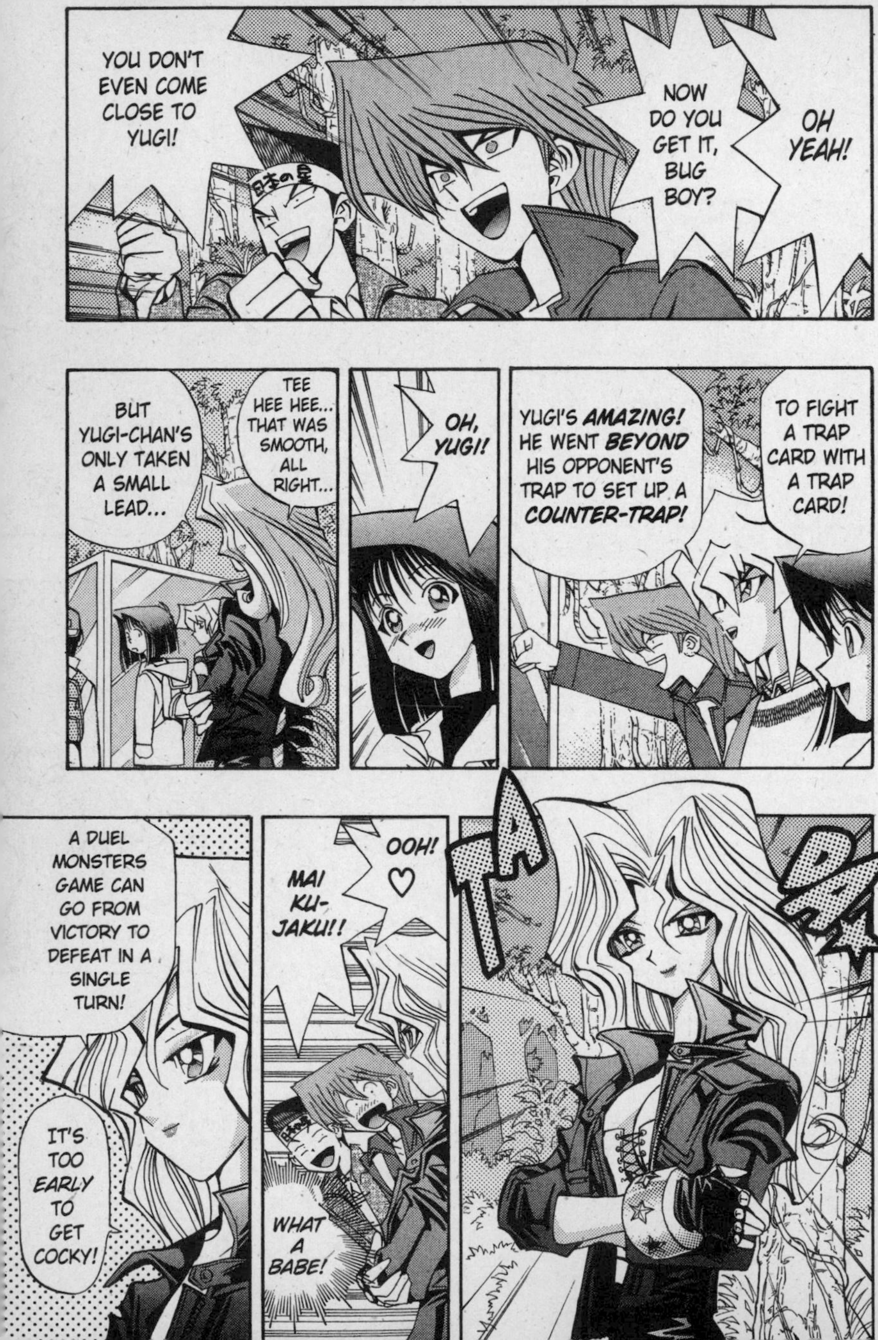

NOW DO YOU GET IT, BUG BOY?
OH YEAH!
YOU DON'T EVEN COME CLOSE TO YUGI!
TO FIGHT A TRAP CARD WITH A TRAP CARD!
YUGI'S AMAZING! HE WENT BEYOND HIS OPPONENT'S TRAP TO SET UP A COUNTER-TRAP!
OH, YUGI!
TEE HEE HEE... THAT WAS SMOOTH, ALL RIGHT...
BUT YUGI-CHAN'S ONLY TAKEN A SMALL LEAD...
TA DA
OOH! ♡
MAI KU-JAKU!!
WHAT A BABE!
A DUEL MONSTERS GAME CAN GO FROM VICTORY TO DEFEAT IN A SINGLE TURN!
IT'S TOO EARLY TO GET COCKY!

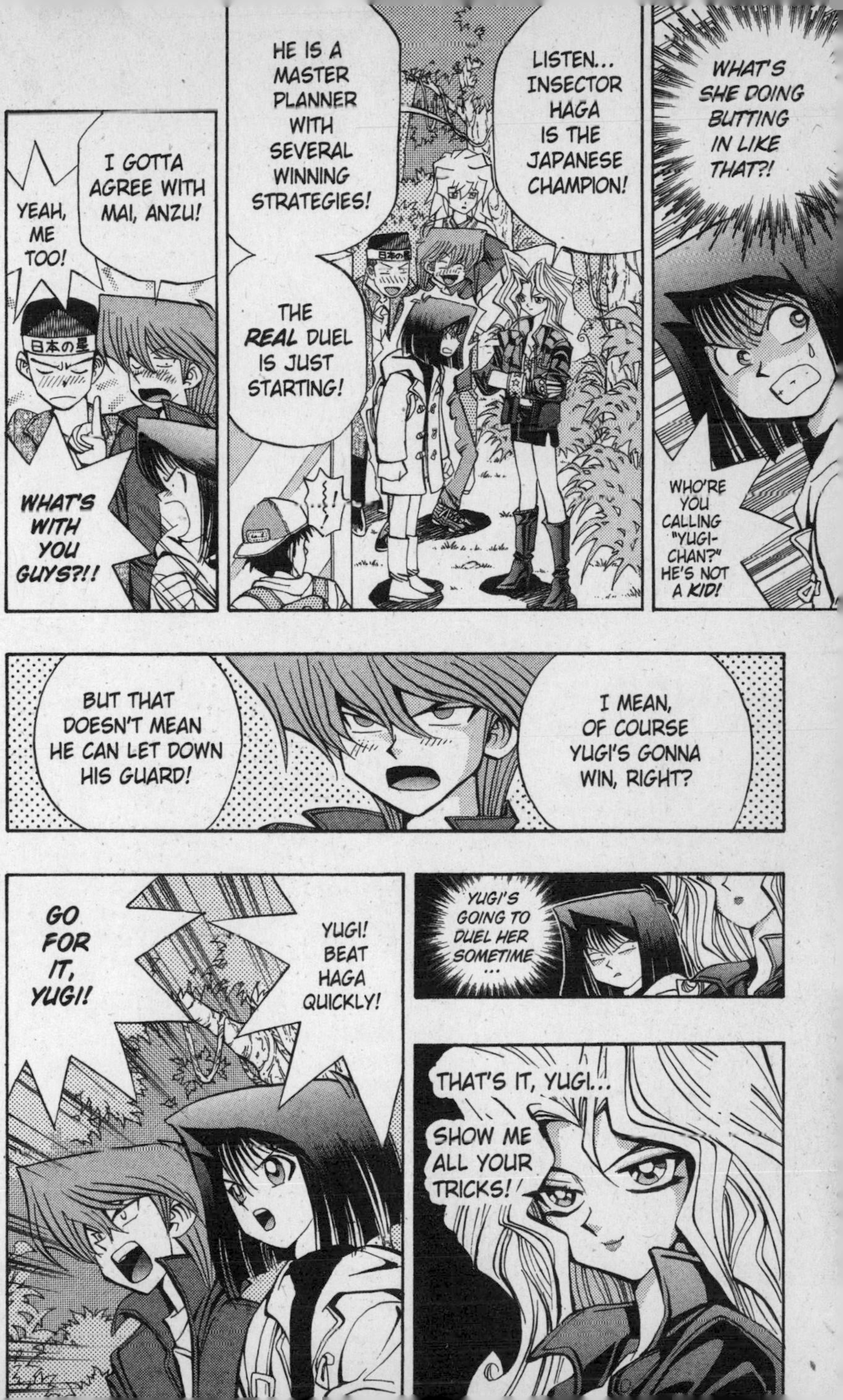
WHAT'S SHE DOING BUTTING IN LIKE THAT?!
WHO'RE YOU CALLING "YUGI-CHAN?" HE'S NOT A KID!
LISTEN... INSECTOR HAGA IS THE JAPANESE CHAMPION!
HE IS A MASTER PLANNER WITH SEVERAL WINNING STRATEGIES!
THE REAL DUEL IS JUST STARTING!
...!
I GOTTA AGREE WITH MAI, ANZU!
YEAH, ME TOO!
WHAT'S WITH YOU GUYS?!!
I MEAN, OF COURSE YUGI'S GONNA WIN, RIGHT?
BUT THAT DOESN'T MEAN HE CAN LET DOWN HIS GUARD!
YUGI'S GOING TO DUEL HER SOMETIME ...
THAT'S IT, YUGI...
SHOW ME ALL YOUR TRICKS!
YUGI! BEAT HAGA QUICKLY!
GO FOR IT, YUGI!

YOU'LL REGRET THIS, YOU BIG-HAIRED FREAK!

NOW YOU'VE REALLY MADE ME MAD!!

B0OOM!

YUGI	INSECTOR HAGA
LIFE POINTS 1350	LIFE POINTS 450

...AND SEND IT TO ME THROUGH YOUR CARDS!

AND I'LL GIVE IT BACK TO YOU!

TALK IS CHEAP. TAKE YOUR FRUSTRATION...

YUGI! YOU CAN'T ESCAPE YOUR DEATH!

IF I CAN PLAY *THAT* CARD, VICTORY IS MINE!

YOU'RE THE ONE WHO TALKS BIG! I STILL HAVE THE *ULTIMATE WEAPON* IN MY INSECT DECK!

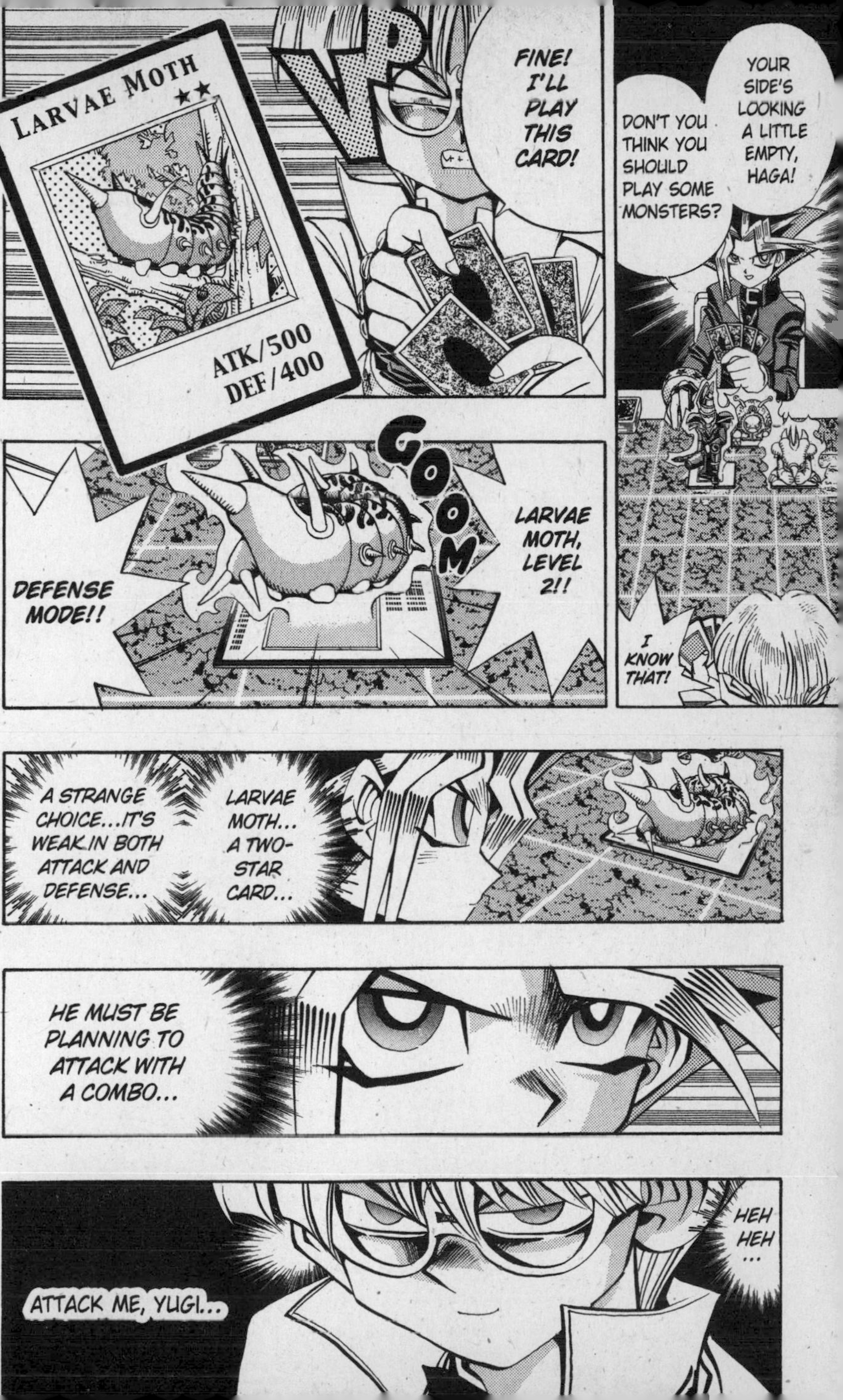
YOUR SIDE'S LOOKING A LITTLE EMPTY, HAGA!
DON'T YOU THINK YOU SHOULD PLAY SOME MONSTERS?
I KNOW THAT!
VP
FINE! I'LL PLAY THIS CARD!
LARVAE MOTH ★★
ATK/500 DEF/400
GOOOM
LARVAE MOTH, LEVEL 2!!
DEFENSE MODE!!
LARVAE MOTH... A TWO-STAR CARD...
A STRANGE CHOICE...IT'S WEAK IN BOTH ATTACK AND DEFENSE...
HE MUST BE PLANNING TO ATTACK WITH A COMBO...
HEH HEH...
ATTACK ME, YUGI...

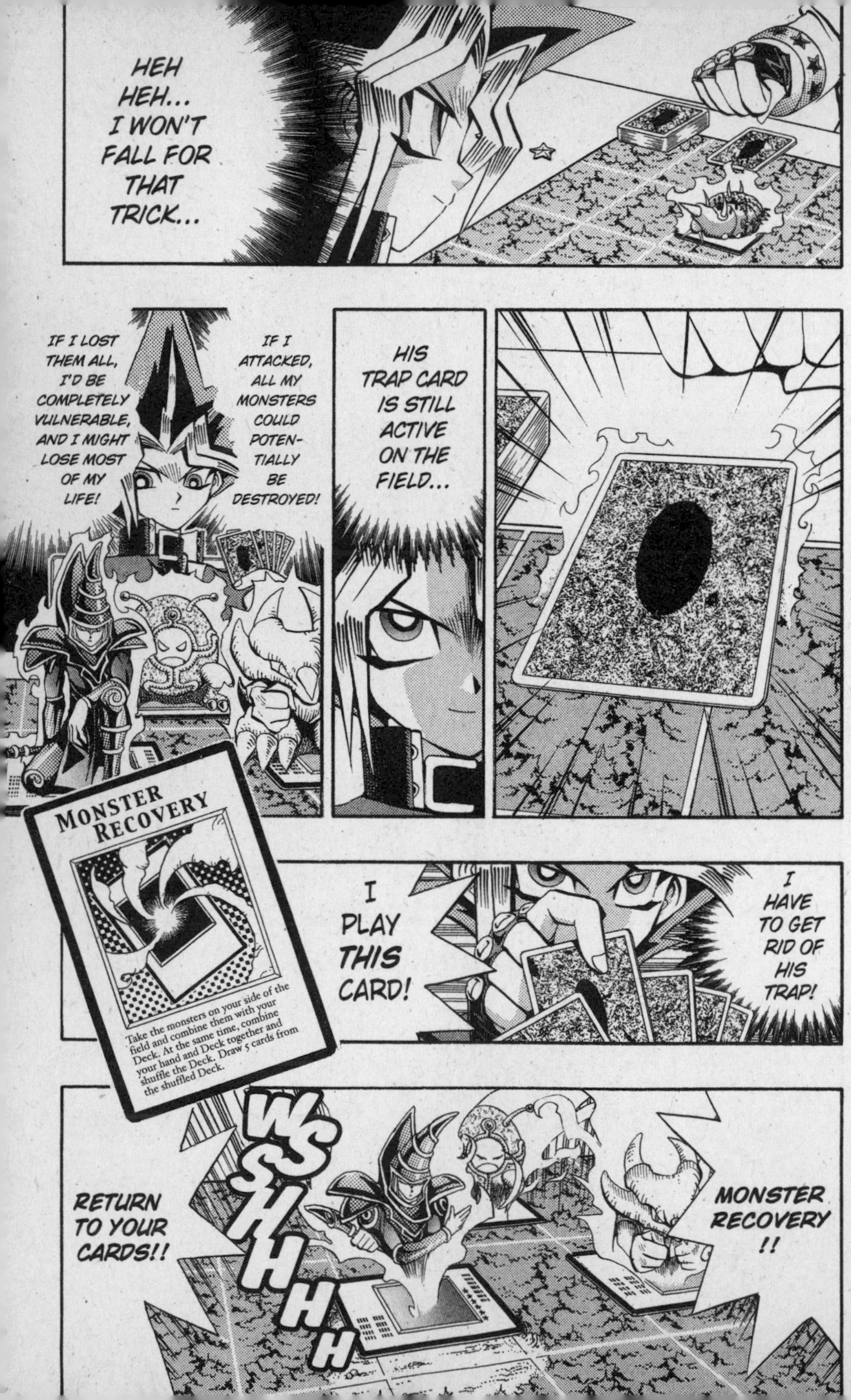
HEH HEH... I WON'T FALL FOR THAT TRICK...
HIS TRAP CARD IS STILL ACTIVE ON THE FIELD...
IF I ATTACKED, ALL MY MONSTERS COULD POTENTIALLY BE DESTROYED!
IF I LOST THEM ALL, I'D BE COMPLETELY VULNERABLE, AND I MIGHT LOSE MOST OF MY LIFE!
I HAVE TO GET RID OF HIS TRAP!
I PLAY THIS CARD!
MONSTER RECOVERY
Take the monsters on your side of the field and combine them with your Deck. At the same time, combine your hand and Deck together and shuffle the Deck. Draw 5 cards from the shuffled Deck.
MONSTER RECOVERY !!
WSSHHHHH
RETURN TO YOUR CARDS!!

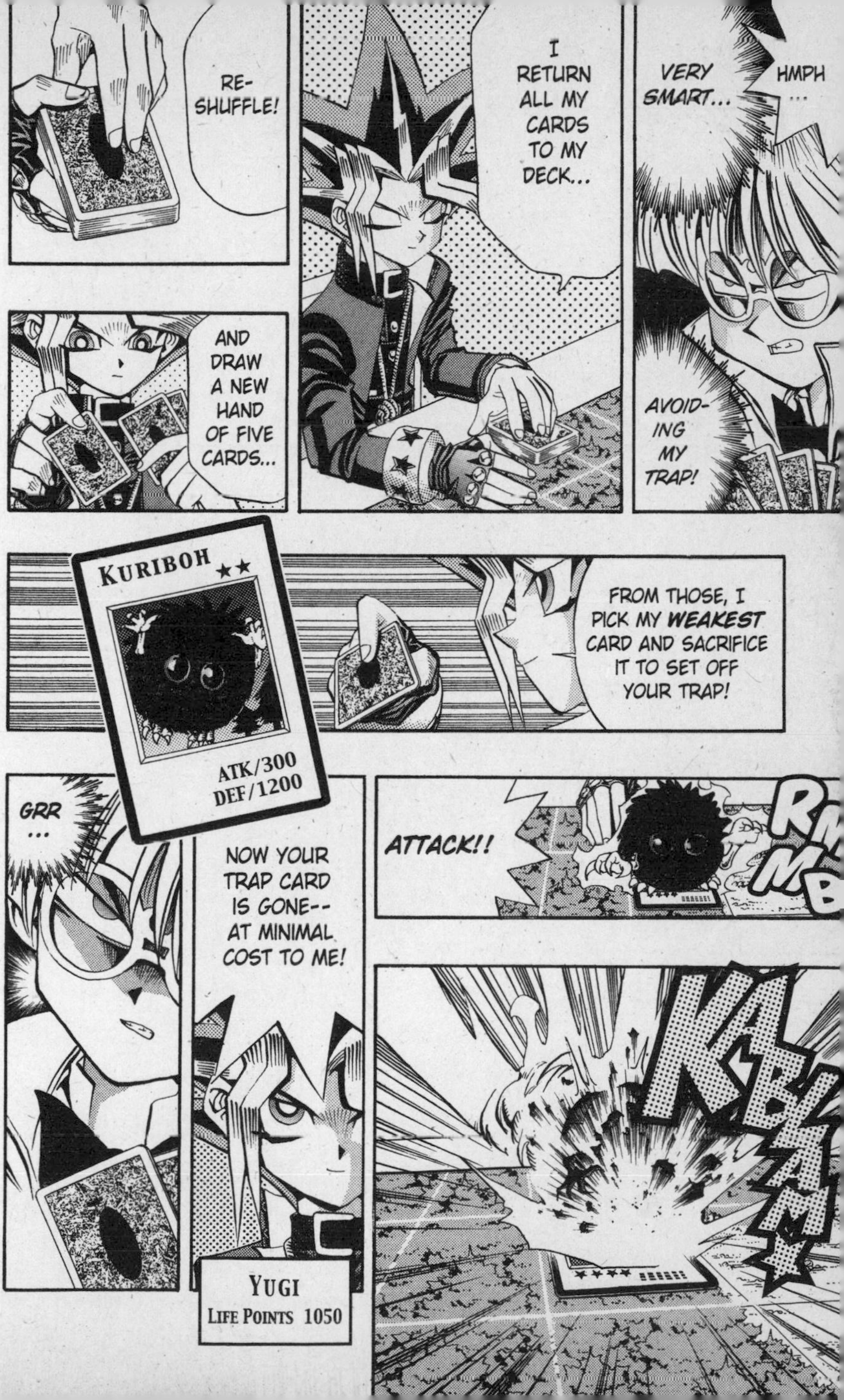
HMPH ...
VERY SMART...
AVOIDING MY TRAP!
I RETURN ALL MY CARDS TO MY DECK...
RE-SHUFFLE!
AND DRAW A NEW HAND OF FIVE CARDS...
FROM THOSE, I PICK MY WEAKEST CARD AND SACRIFICE IT TO SET OFF YOUR TRAP!
KURIBOH
ATK/300
DEF/1200
ATTACK!!
KA-BAM
NOW YOUR TRAP CARD IS GONE-- AT MINIMAL COST TO ME!
YUGI
LIFE POINTS 1050
GRR ...

READ THIS WAY

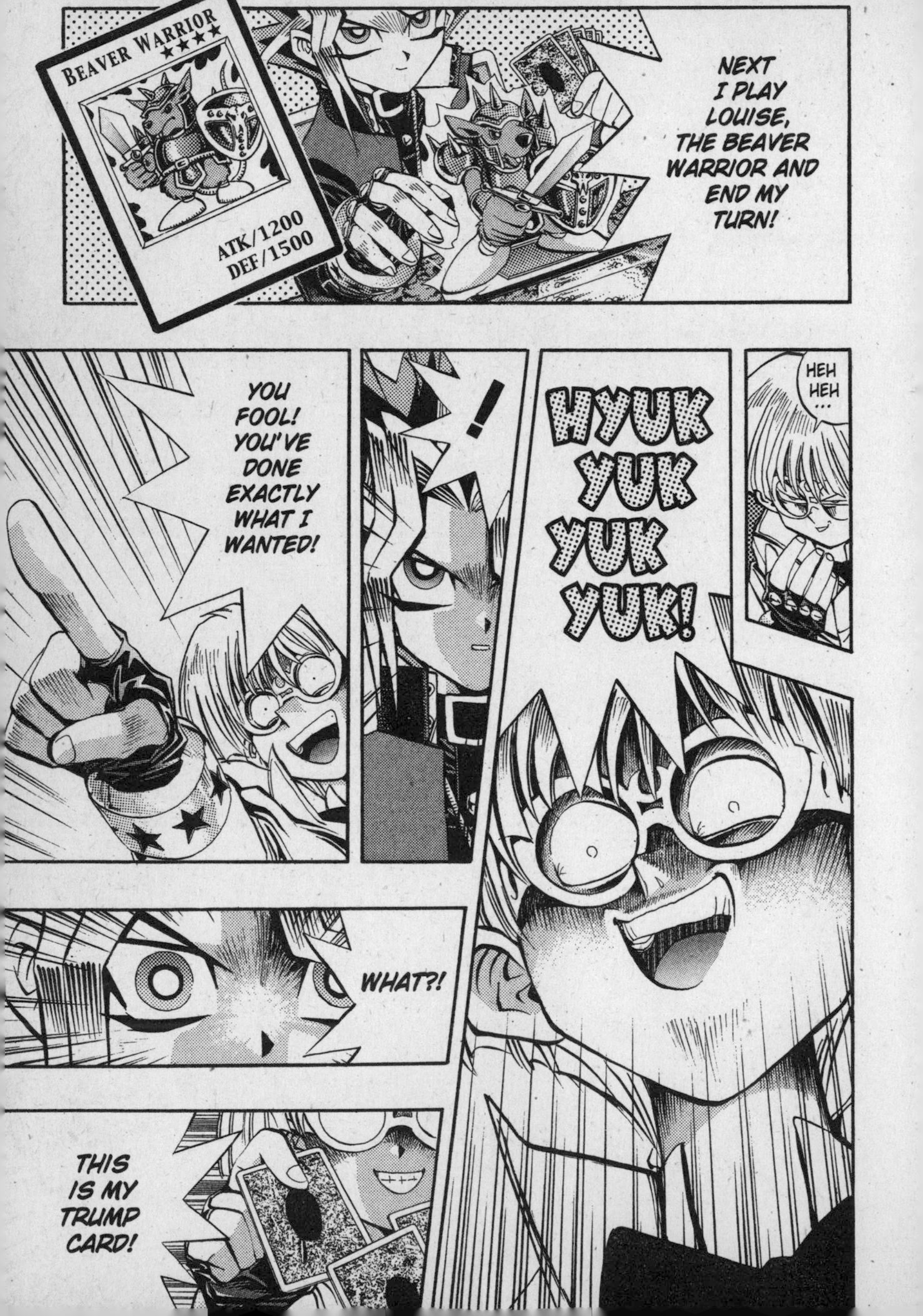

BEAVER WARRIOR ★★★★
ATK/1200
DEF/1500
NEXT I PLAY LOUISE, THE BEAVER WARRIOR AND END MY TURN!
HEH HEH ...
HYUK YUK YUK YUK!
!
YOU FOOL! YOU'VE DONE EXACTLY WHAT I WANTED!
WHAT?!
THIS IS MY TRUMP CARD!

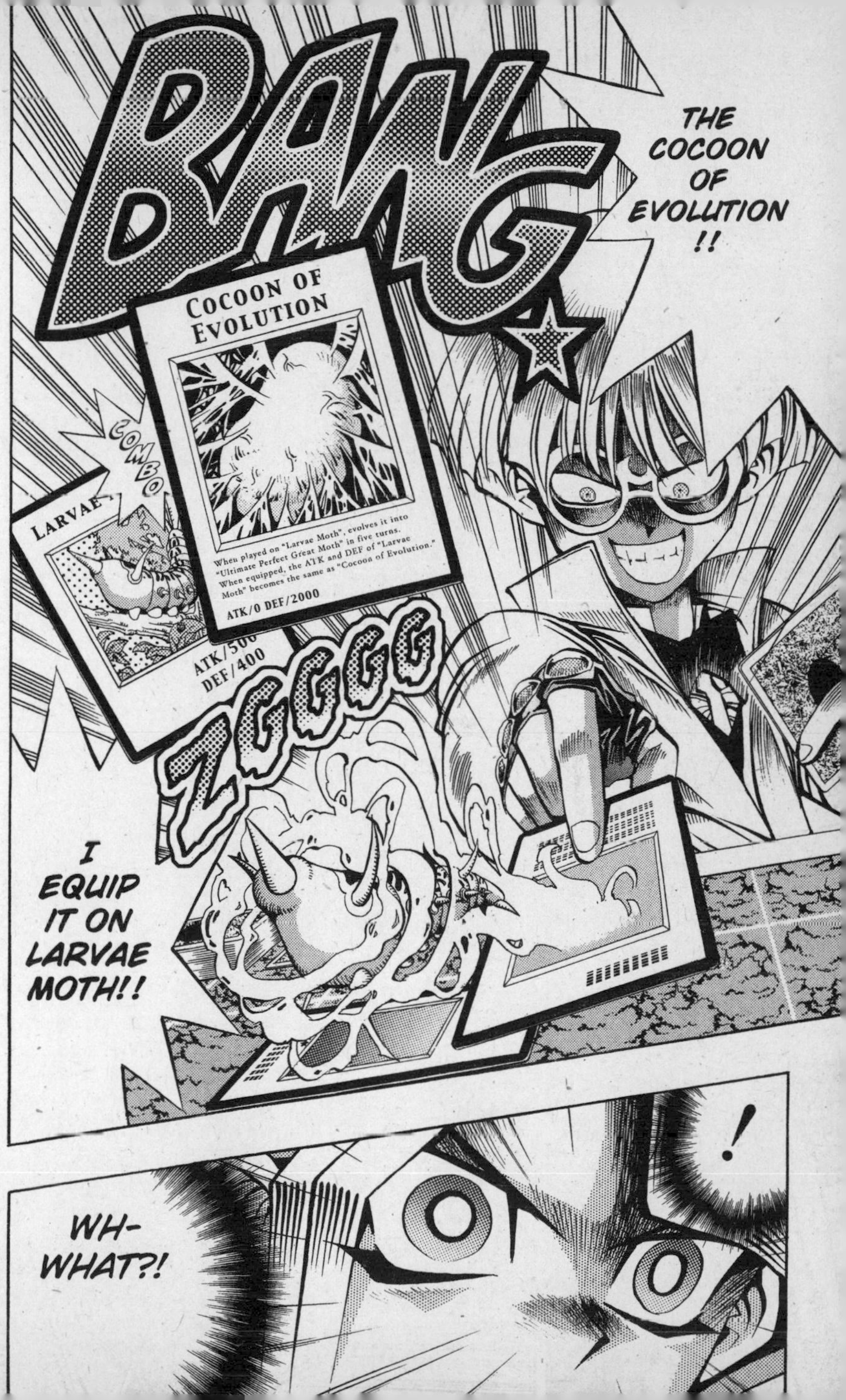
BANG
THE COCOON OF EVOLUTION!!
Cocoon of Evolution
When played on "Larvae Moth", evolves it into "Ultimate Perfect Great Moth" in five turns. When equipped, the ATK and DEF of "Larvae Moth" becomes the same as "Cocoon of Evolution."
ATK/0 DEF/2000
COMBO
LARVAE
ATK/500
DEF/400
ZGGGG
I EQUIP IT ON LARVAE MOTH!!
!
WH-WHAT?!

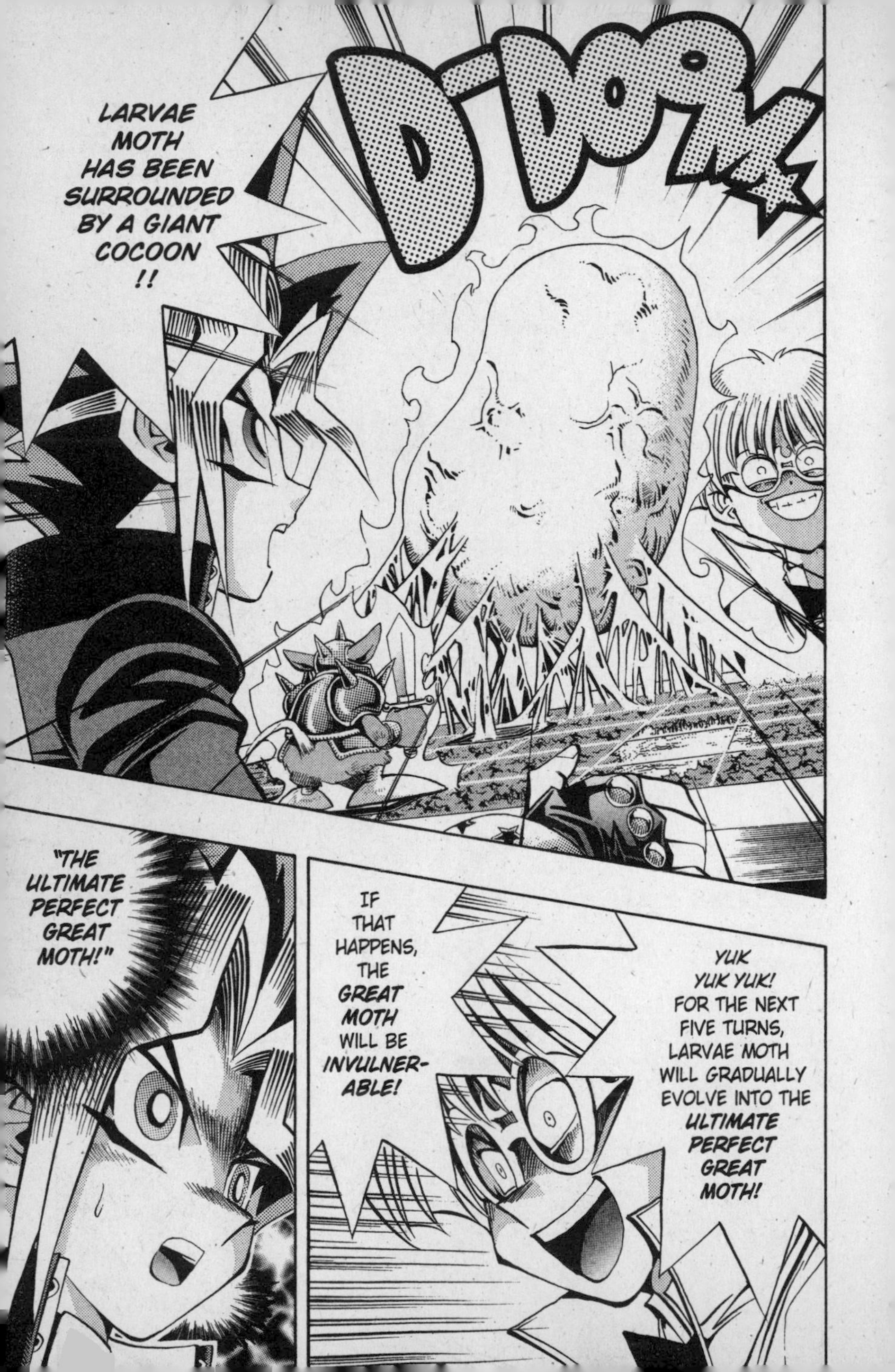
D-DOOM
LARVAE MOTH HAS BEEN SURROUNDED BY A GIANT COCOON !!
YUK YUK YUK! FOR THE NEXT FIVE TURNS, LARVAE MOTH WILL GRADUALLY EVOLVE INTO THE ULTIMATE PERFECT GREAT MOTH!
IF THAT HAPPENS, THE GREAT MOTH WILL BE INVULNER-ABLE!
"THE ULTIMATE PERFECT GREAT MOTH!"

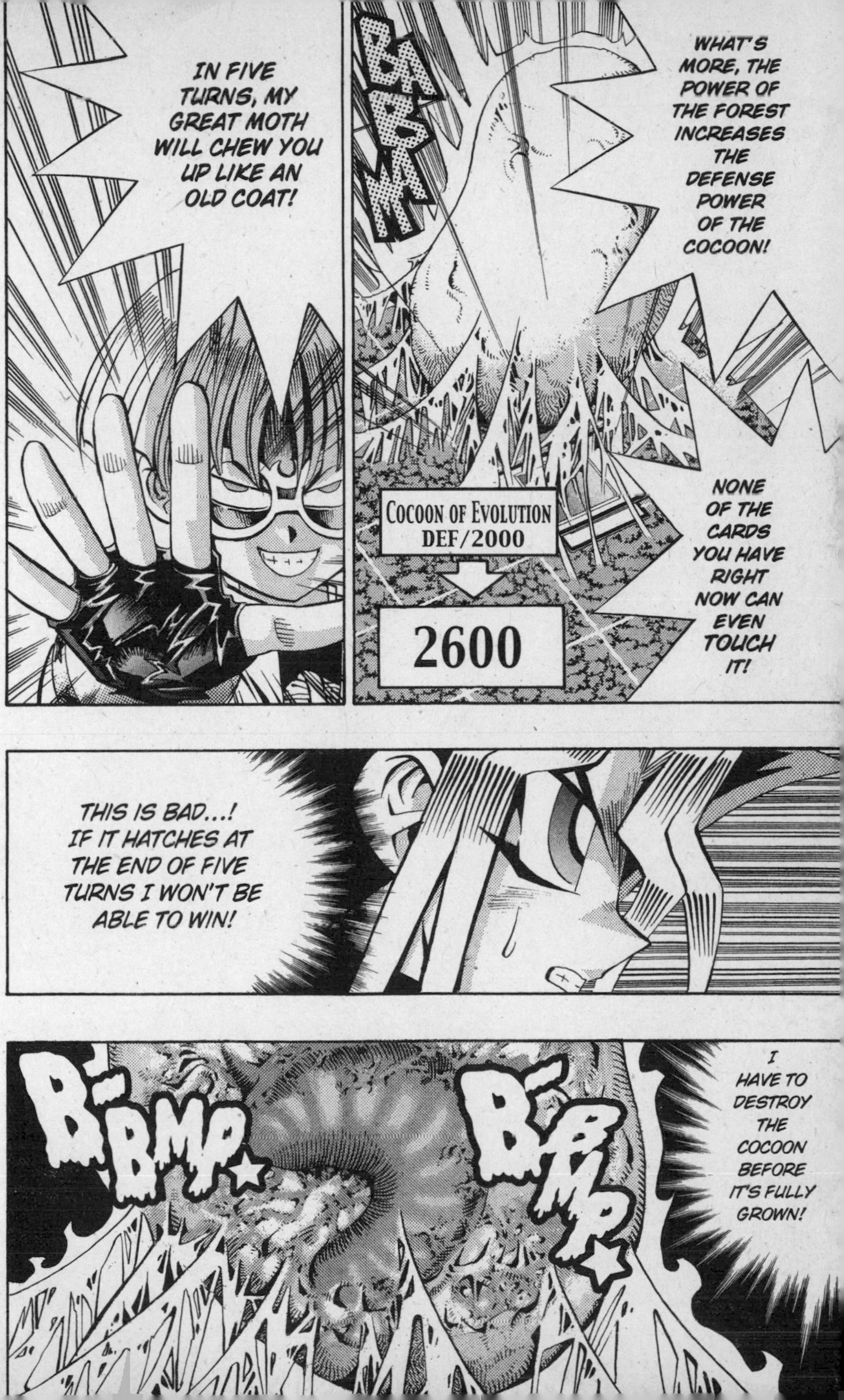

IN FIVE TURNS, MY GREAT MOTH WILL CHEW YOU UP LIKE AN OLD COAT!
WHAT'S MORE, THE POWER OF THE FOREST INCREASES THE DEFENSE POWER OF THE COCOON!
COCOON OF EVOLUTION DEF/2000
2600
NONE OF THE CARDS YOU HAVE RIGHT NOW CAN EVEN TOUCH IT!
THIS IS BAD...! IF IT HATCHES AT THE END OF FIVE TURNS I WON'T BE ABLE TO WIN!
B-BMP
B-BMP
I HAVE TO DESTROY THE COCOON BEFORE IT'S FULLY GROWN!

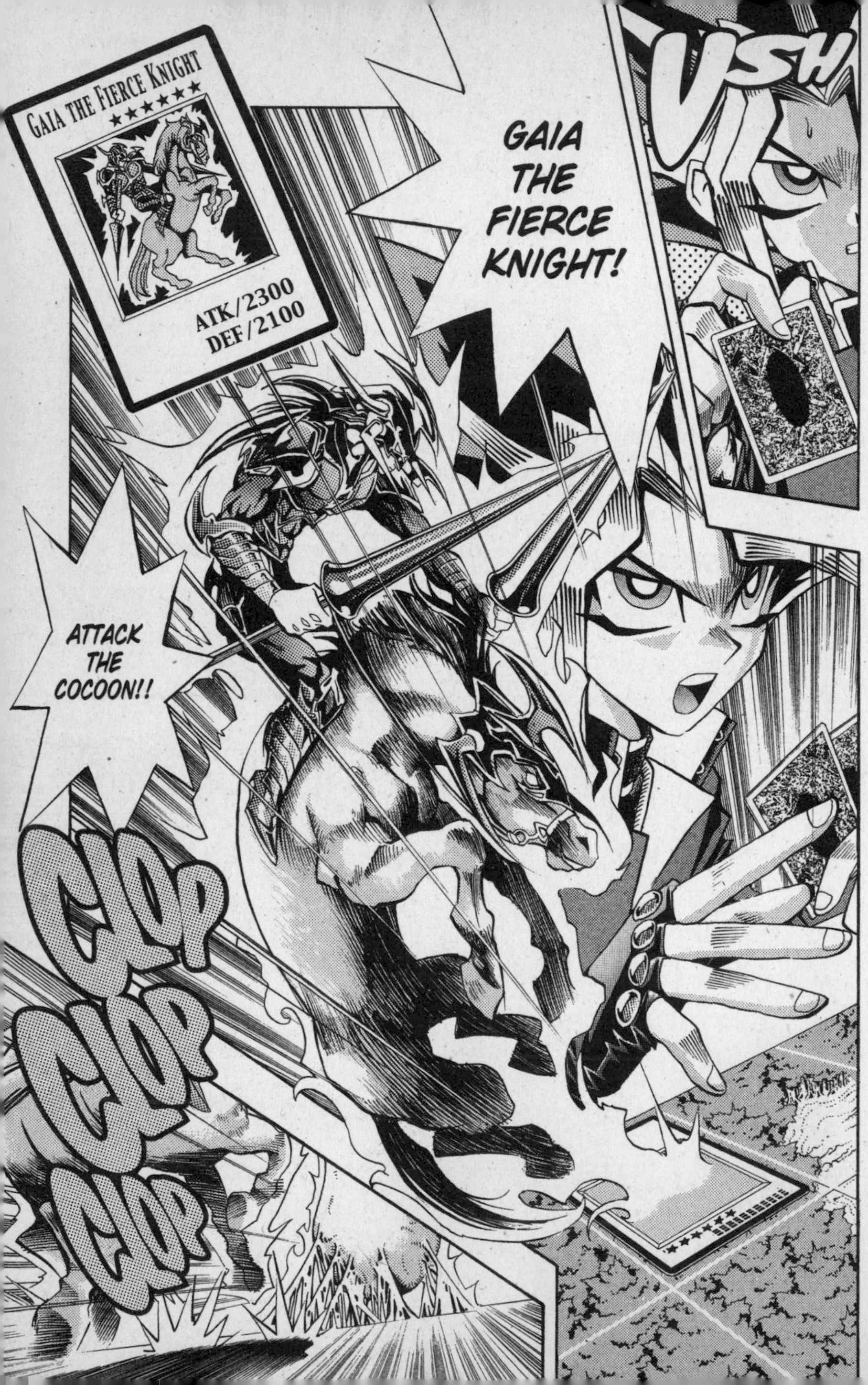

VSH
GAIA THE FIERCE KNIGHT!
GAIA THE FIERCE KNIGHT
ATK/2300
DEF/2100
ATTACK THE COCOON!!
CLOP CLOP CLOP

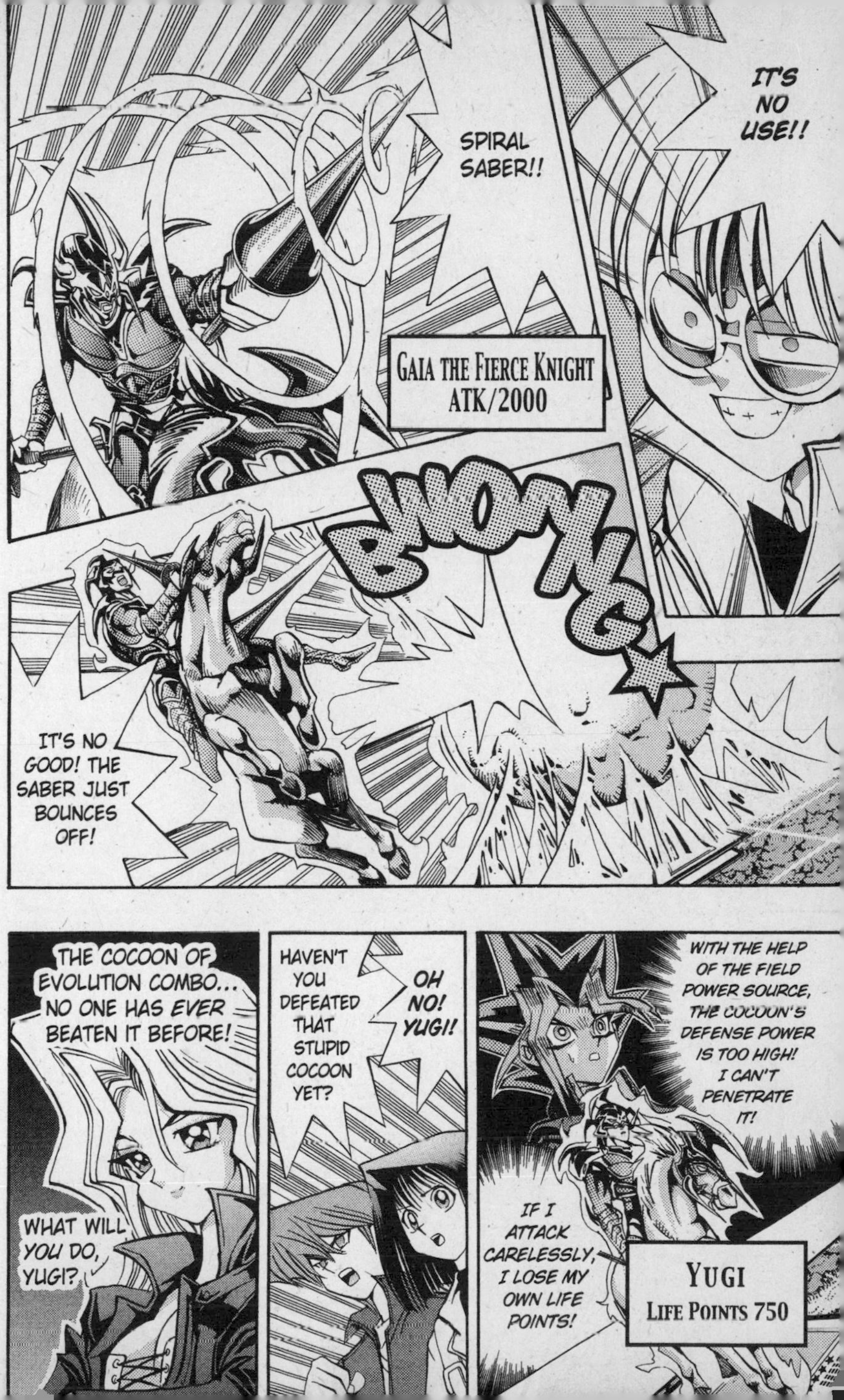

IT'S NO USE!!
SPIRAL SABER!!
GAIA THE FIERCE KNIGHT
ATK/2000
BWONG
IT'S NO GOOD! THE SABER JUST BOUNCES OFF!
WITH THE HELP OF THE FIELD POWER SOURCE, THE COCOON'S DEFENSE POWER IS TOO HIGH! I CAN'T PENETRATE IT!
IF I ATTACK CARELESSLY, I LOSE MY OWN LIFE POINTS!
YUGI
LIFE POINTS 750
OH NO! YUGI!!
HAVEN'T YOU DEFEATED THAT STUPID COCOON YET?
THE COCOON OF EVOLUTION COMBO... NO ONE HAS *EVER* BEATEN IT BEFORE!
WHAT WILL YOU DO, YUGI?

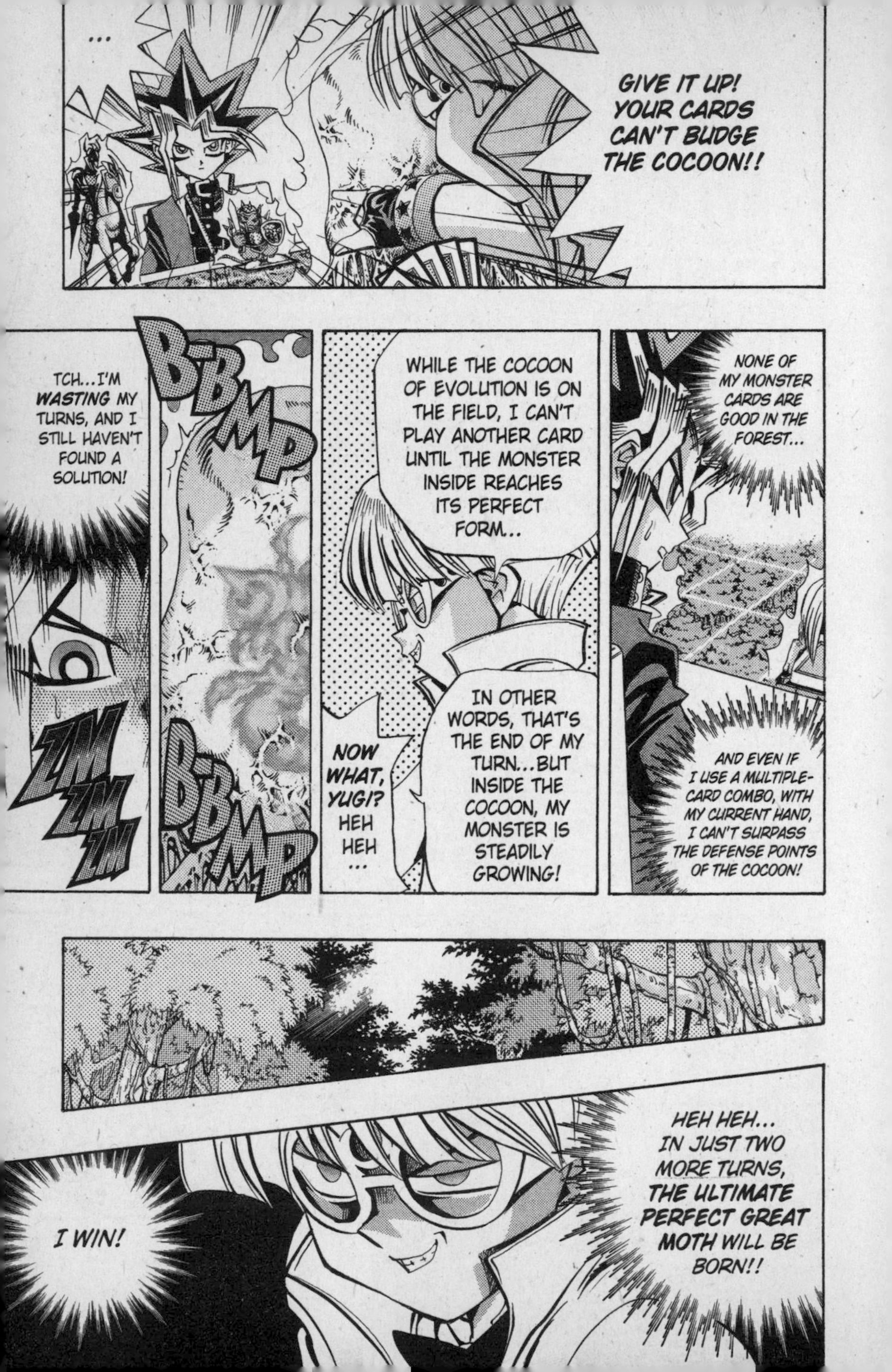
GIVE IT UP! YOUR CARDS CAN'T BUDGE THE COCOON!!
...
NONE OF MY MONSTER CARDS ARE GOOD IN THE FOREST...
AND EVEN IF I USE A MULTIPLE-CARD COMBO, WITH MY CURRENT HAND, I CAN'T SURPASS THE DEFENSE POINTS OF THE COCOON!
WHILE THE COCOON OF EVOLUTION IS ON THE FIELD, I CAN'T PLAY ANOTHER CARD UNTIL THE MONSTER INSIDE REACHES ITS PERFECT FORM...
IN OTHER WORDS, THAT'S THE END OF MY TURN...BUT INSIDE THE COCOON, MY MONSTER IS STEADILY GROWING!
NOW WHAT, YUGI? HEH HEH ...
B-BMP
B-BMP
TCH...I'M WASTING MY TURNS, AND I STILL HAVEN'T FOUND A SOLUTION!
ZM ZM ZM ZM
HEH HEH... IN JUST TWO MORE TURNS, THE ULTIMATE PERFECT GREAT MOTH WILL BE BORN!!
I WIN!

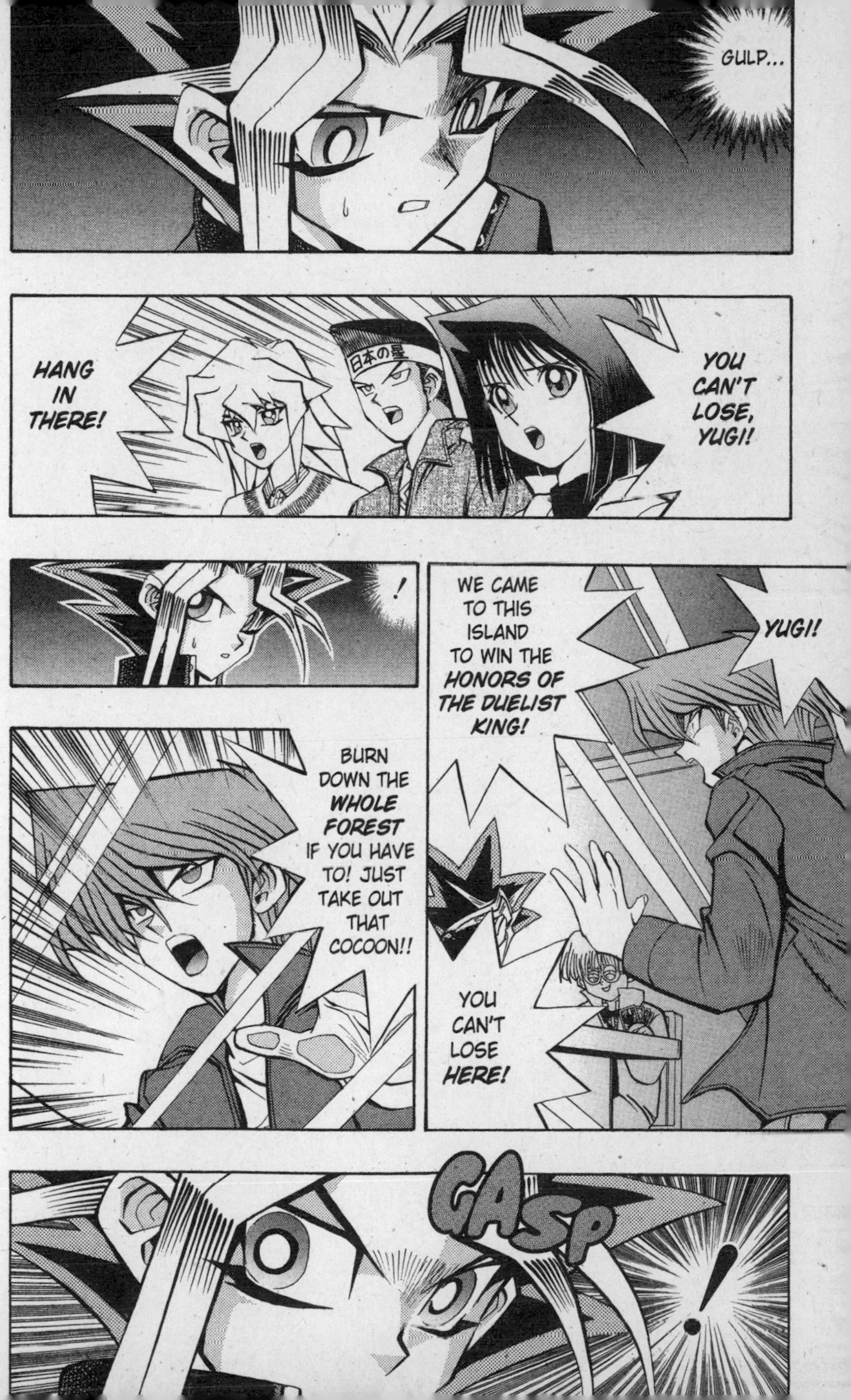

GULP...
YOU CAN'T LOSE, YUGI!
日本の星
HANG IN THERE!
YUGI!
WE CAME TO THIS ISLAND TO WIN THE HONORS OF THE DUELIST KING!
YOU CAN'T LOSE HERE!
!
BURN DOWN THE WHOLE FOREST IF YOU HAVE TO! JUST TAKE OUT THAT COCOON!!
GASP
!

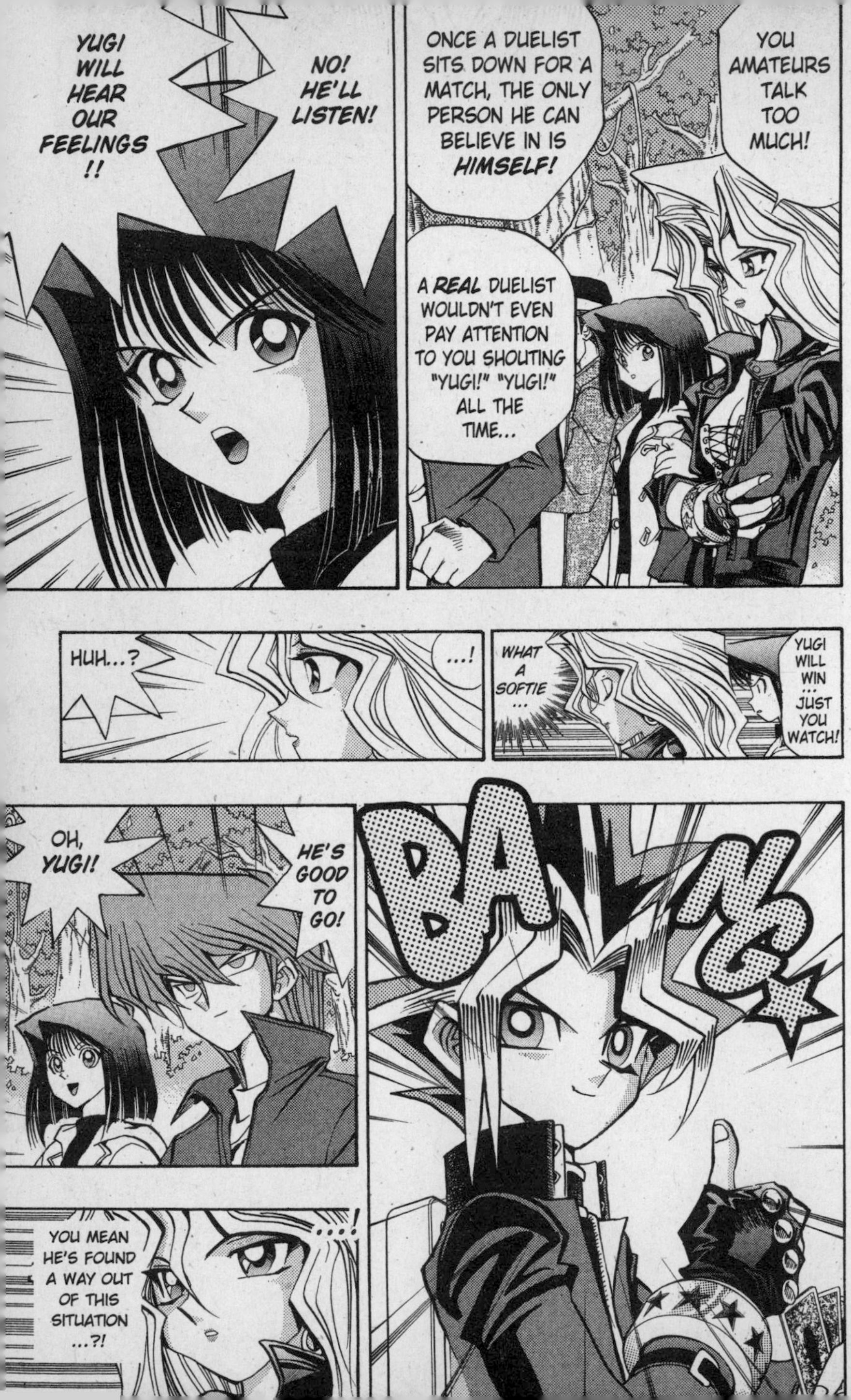

YOU AMATEURS TALK TOO MUCH!
ONCE A DUELIST SITS DOWN FOR A MATCH, THE ONLY PERSON HE CAN BELIEVE IN IS HIMSELF!
A REAL DUELIST WOULDN'T EVEN PAY ATTENTION TO YOU SHOUTING "YUGI!" "YUGI!" ALL THE TIME...
NO! HE'LL LISTEN!
YUGI WILL HEAR OUR FEELINGS !!
YUGI WILL WIN ... JUST YOU WATCH!
WHAT A SOFTIE ...
...!
HUH...?
BANG
HE'S GOOD TO GO!
OH, YUGI!
...!
YOU MEAN HE'S FOUND A WAY OUT OF THIS SITUATION ...?!

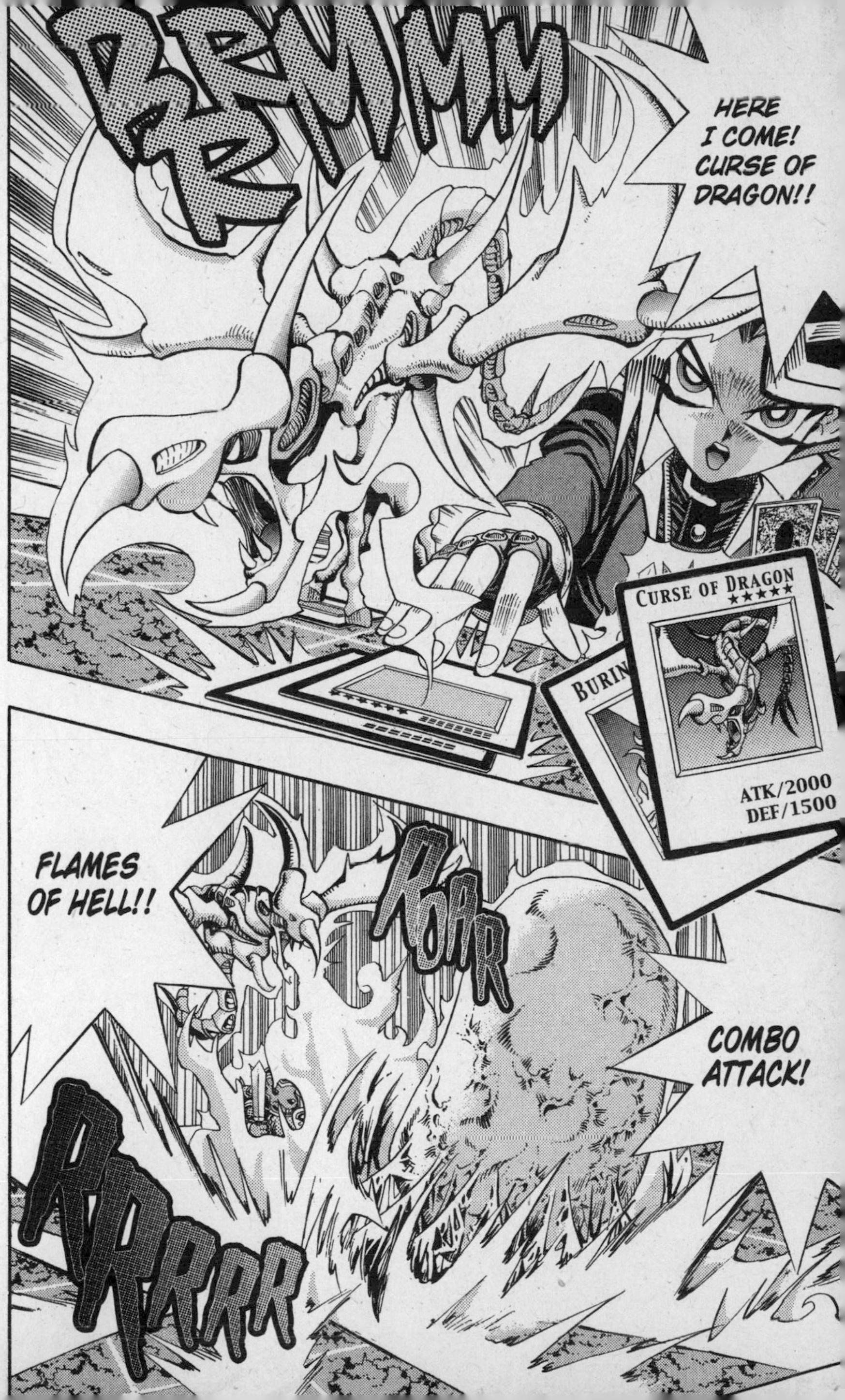
HERE I COME! CURSE OF DRAGON!!
CURSE OF DRAGON ★★★★★
ATK/2000
DEF/1500
COMBO ATTACK!
ROARR
FLAMES OF HELL!!

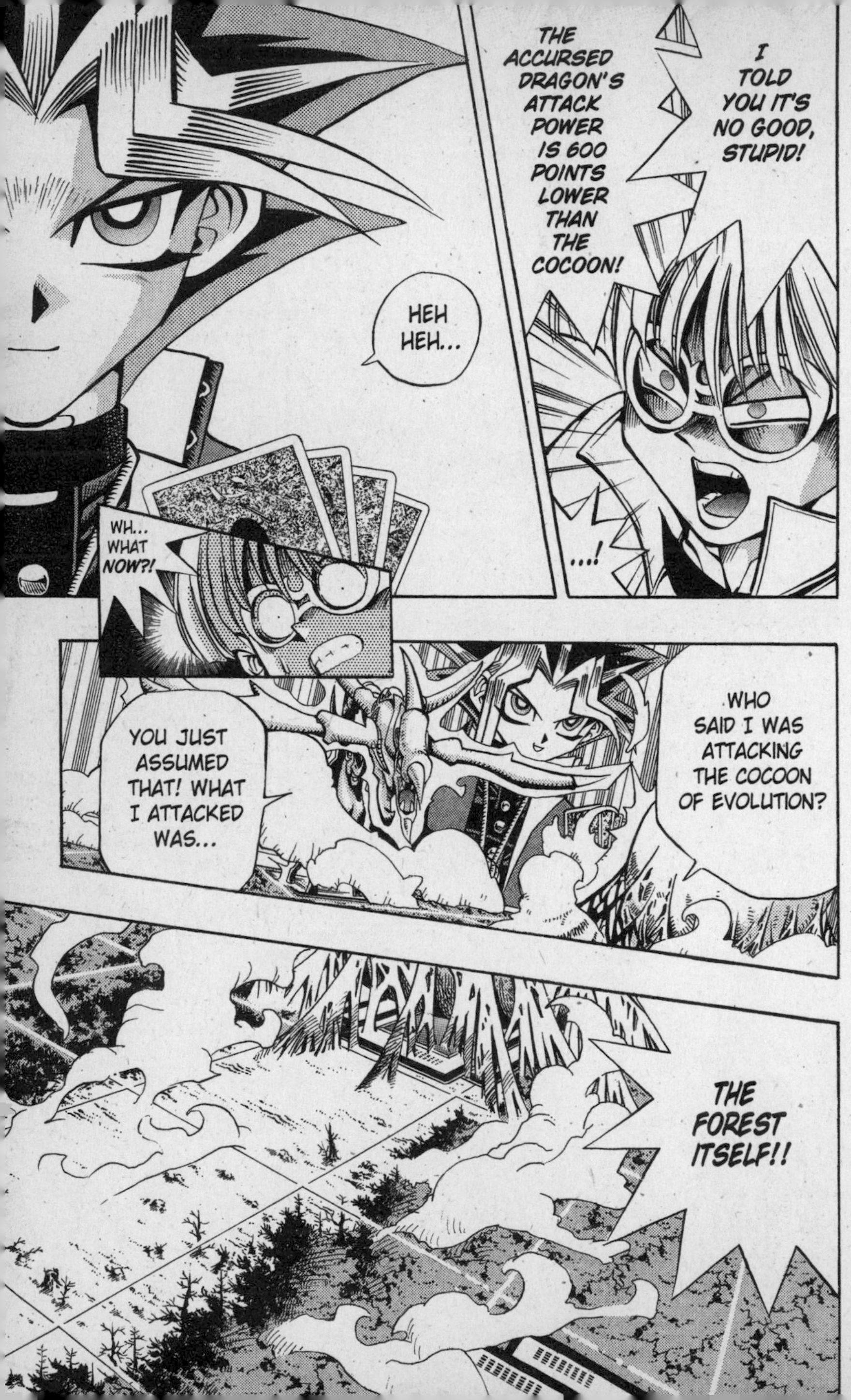
I TOLD YOU IT'S NO GOOD, STUPID!
THE ACCURSED DRAGON'S ATTACK POWER IS 600 POINTS LOWER THAN THE COCOON!
...!
HEH HEH...
WH... WHAT NOW?!
WHO SAID I WAS ATTACKING THE COCOON OF EVOLUTION?
YOU JUST ASSUMED THAT! WHAT I ATTACKED WAS...
THE FOREST ITSELF!!

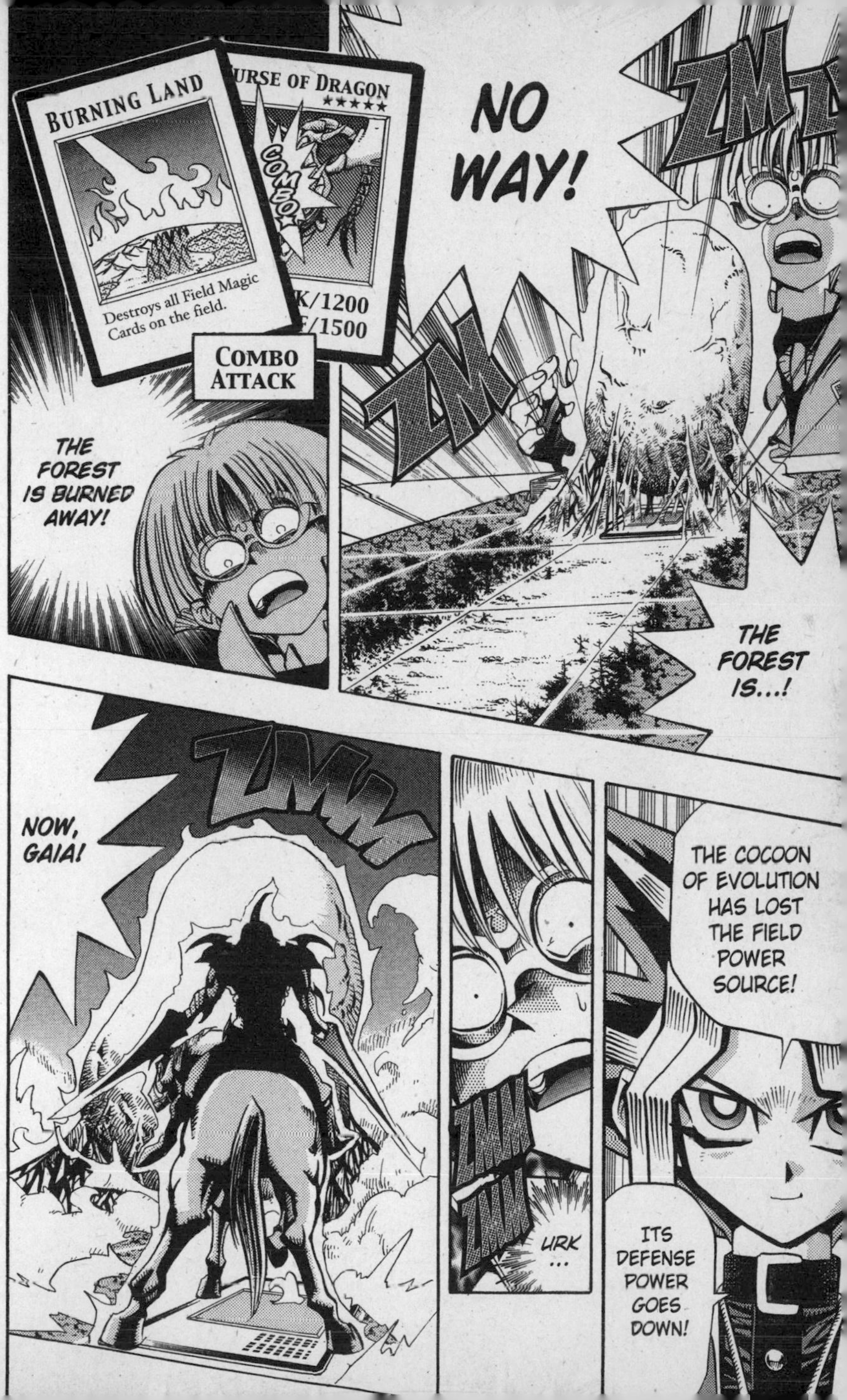
NO WAY!
ZM
THE FOREST IS...!
BURNING LAND
Destroys all Field Magic Cards on the field.
COMBO
COMBO ATTACK
THE FOREST IS BURNED AWAY!
THE COCOON OF EVOLUTION HAS LOST THE FIELD POWER SOURCE!
ITS DEFENSE POWER GOES DOWN!
URK ...
ZMM
NOW, GAIA!

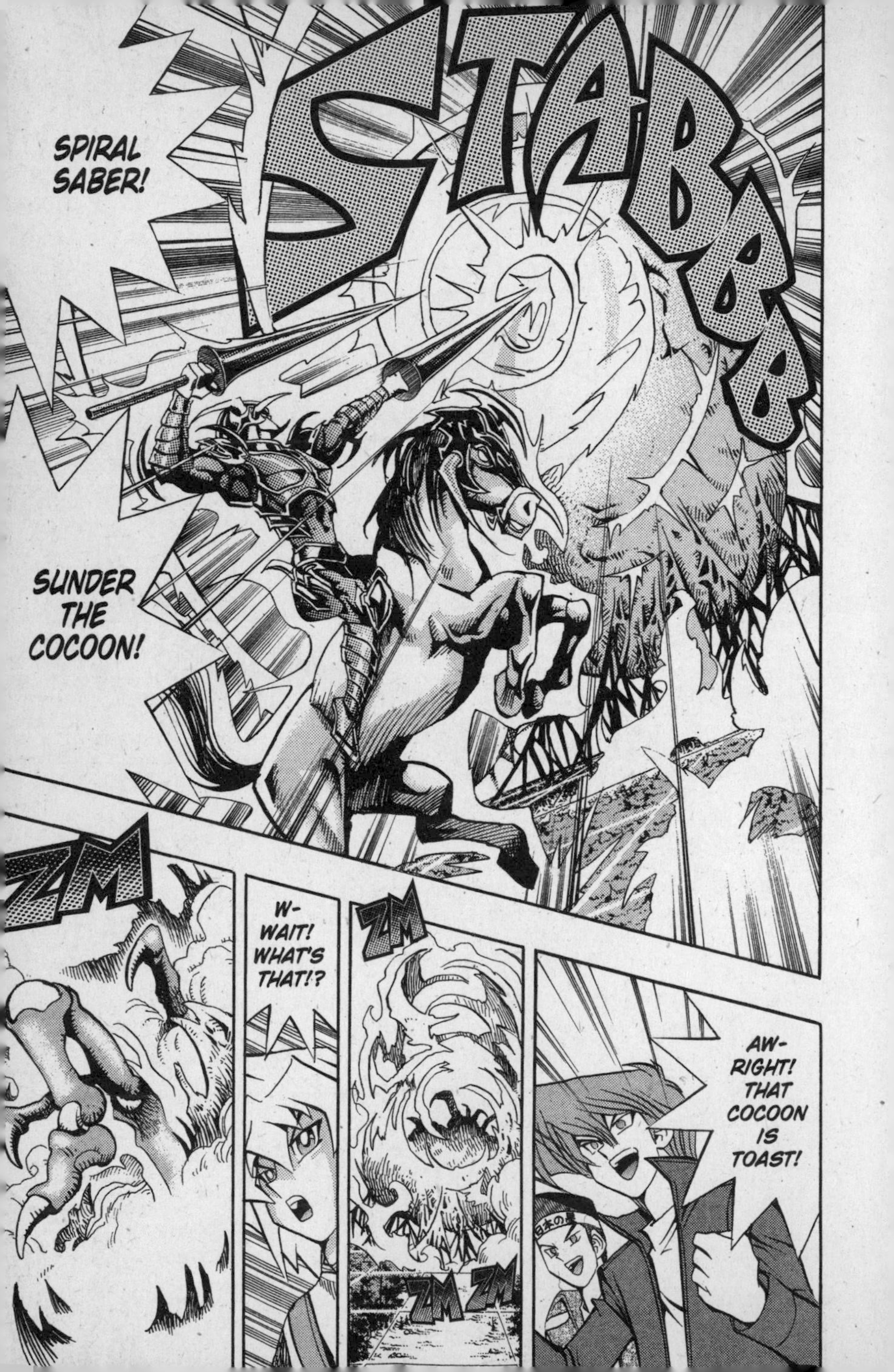
STABBB
SPIRAL SABER!
SUNDER THE COCOON!
AW-RIGHT! THAT COCOON IS TOAST!
ZM
ZM
ZM
W-WAIT! WHAT'S THAT!?
ZM

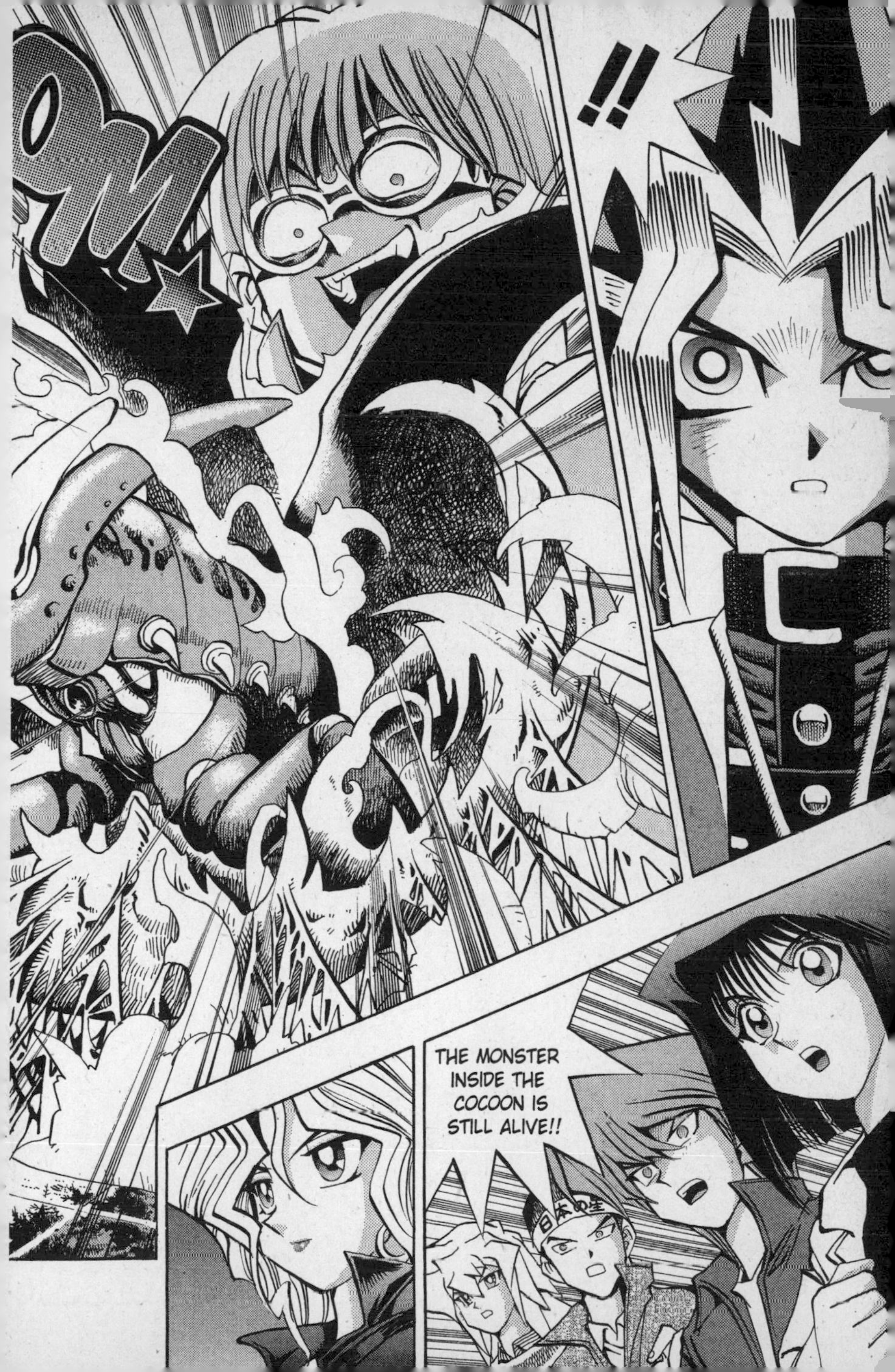
!!
THE MONSTER INSIDE THE COCOON IS STILL ALIVE!!

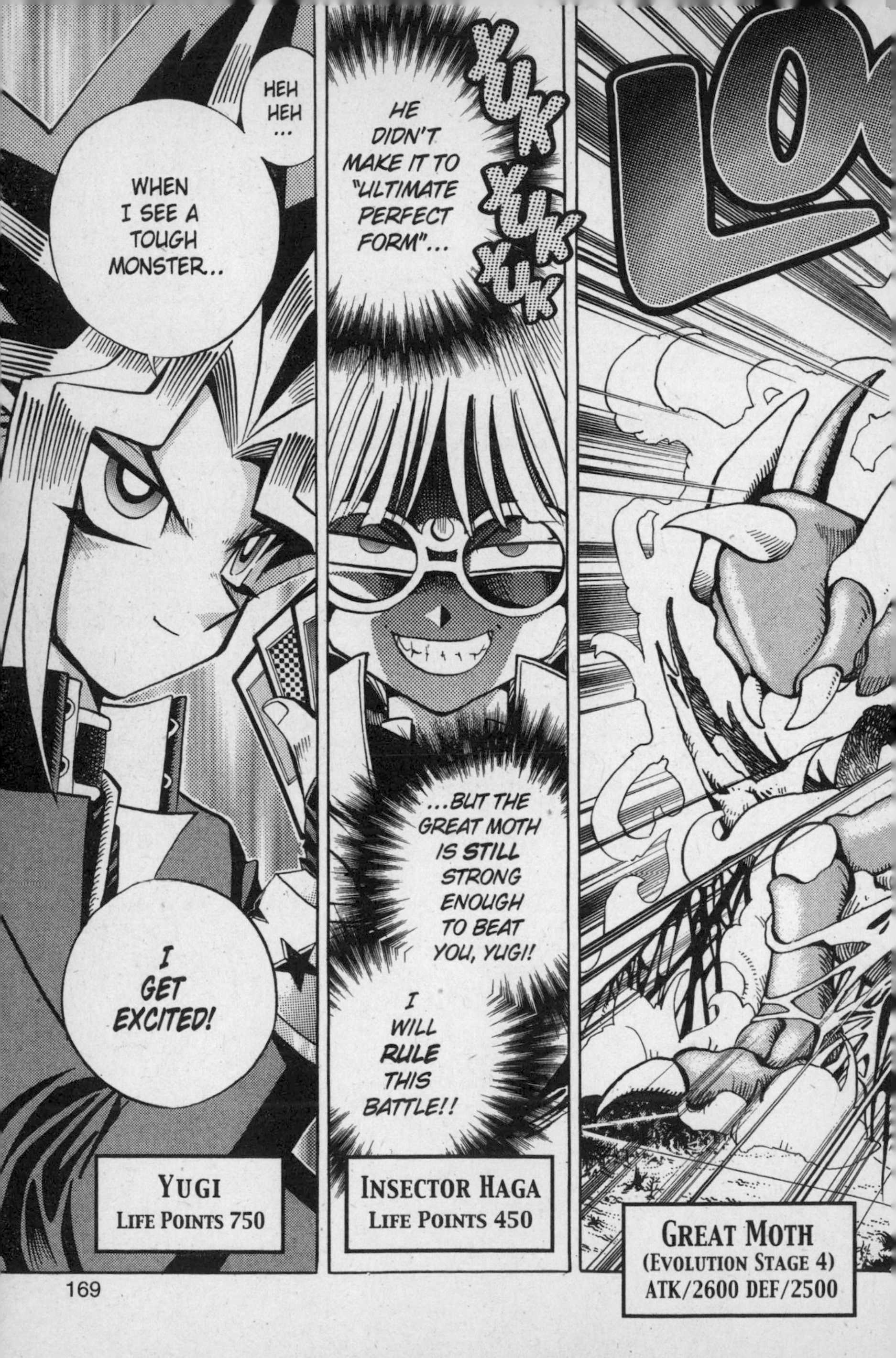
LO
GREAT MOTH
(EVOLUTION STAGE 4)
ATK/2600 DEF/2500
YUK YUK YUK
HE DIDN'T MAKE IT TO "ULTIMATE PERFECT FORM"...
...BUT THE GREAT MOTH IS STILL STRONG ENOUGH TO BEAT YOU, YUGI!
I WILL RULE THIS BATTLE!!
INSECTOR HAGA
LIFE POINTS 450
HEH HEH ...
WHEN I SEE A TOUGH MONSTER...
I GET EXCITED!
YUGI
LIFE POINTS 750

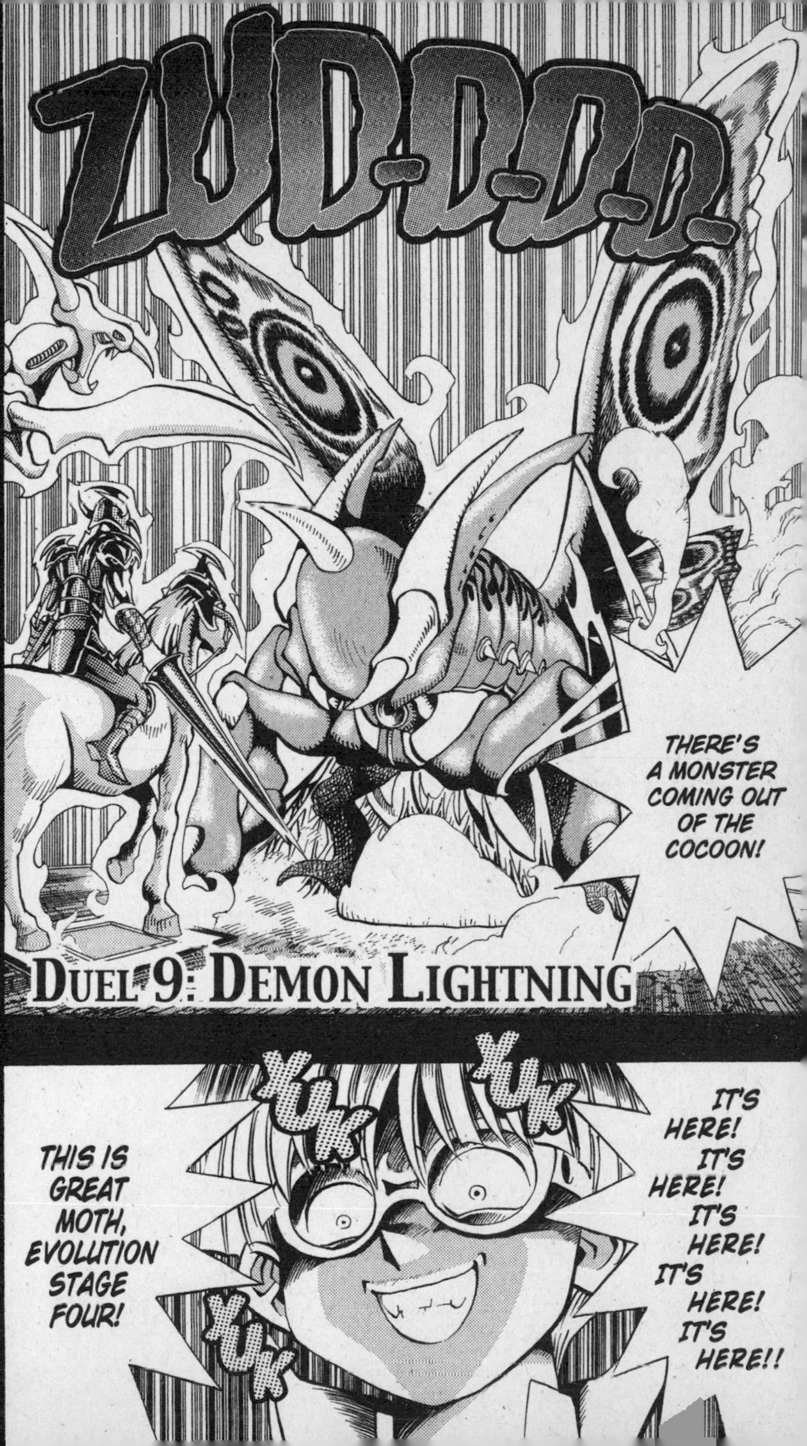
ZUD-D-D-D
THERE'S A MONSTER COMING OUT OF THE COCOON!
DUEL 9: DEMON LIGHTNING
YUK YUK
IT'S HERE! IT'S HERE! IT'S HERE! IT'S HERE! IT'S HERE!!
THIS IS GREAT MOTH, EVOLUTION STAGE FOUR!
YUK

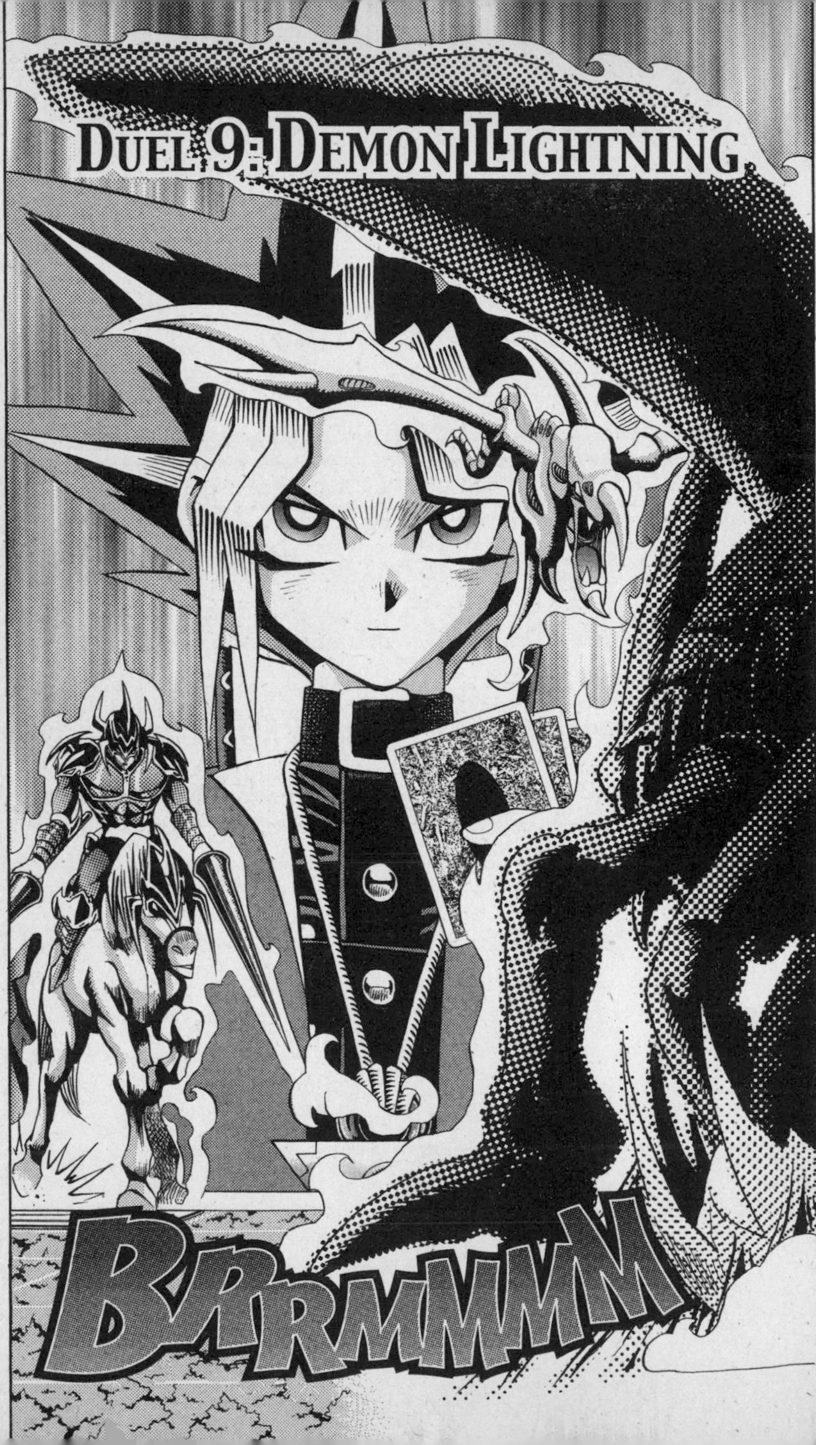
DUEL 9: DEMON LIGHTNING
BRRMMMMM

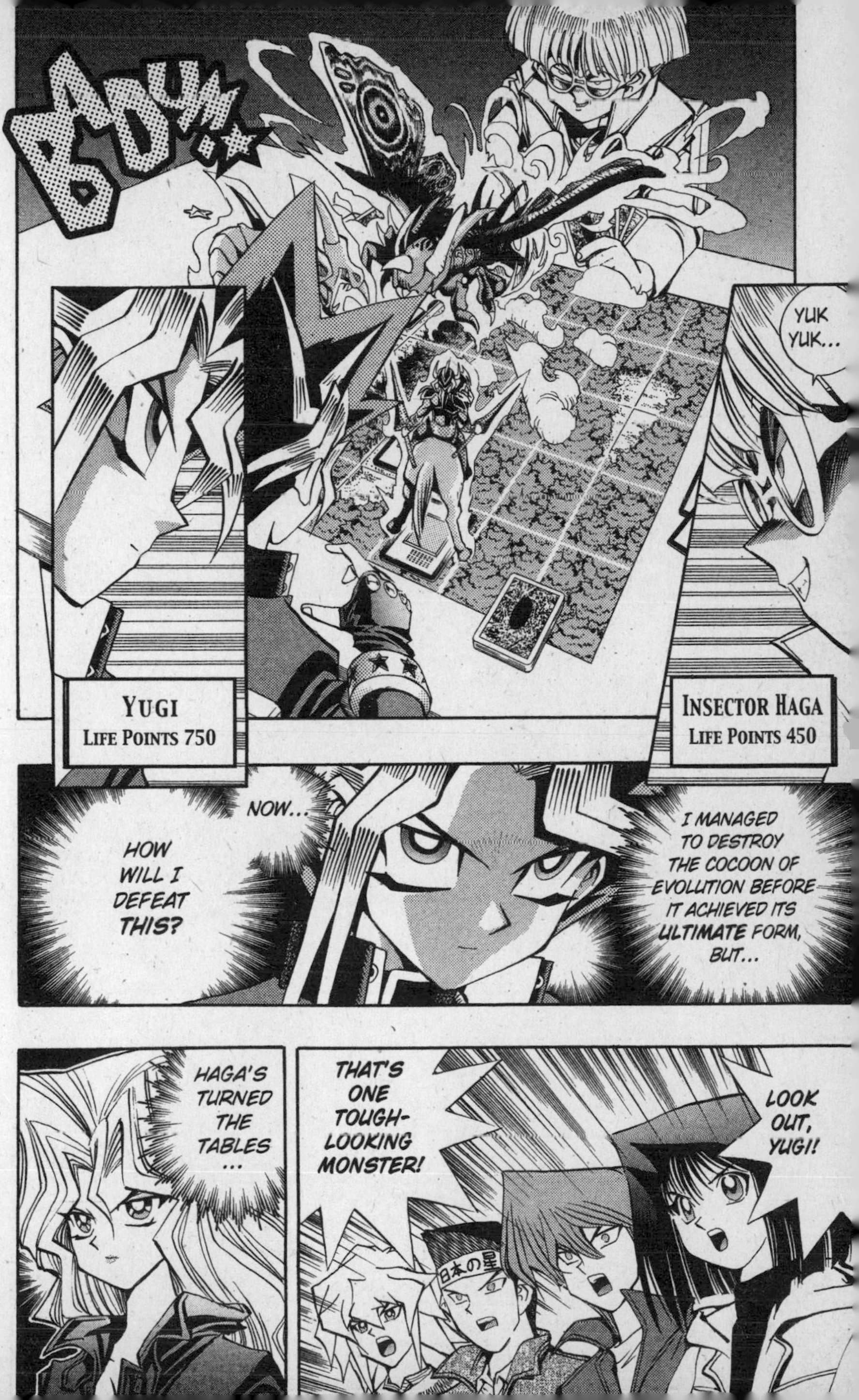
BADUM!
YUK YUK...
INSECTOR HAGA
LIFE POINTS 450
YUGI
LIFE POINTS 750
I MANAGED TO DESTROY THE COCOON OF EVOLUTION BEFORE IT ACHIEVED ITS ULTIMATE FORM, BUT...
NOW...
HOW WILL I DEFEAT THIS?
LOOK OUT, YUGI!
THAT'S ONE TOUGH-LOOKING MONSTER!
日本の星
HAGA'S TURNED THE TABLES ...

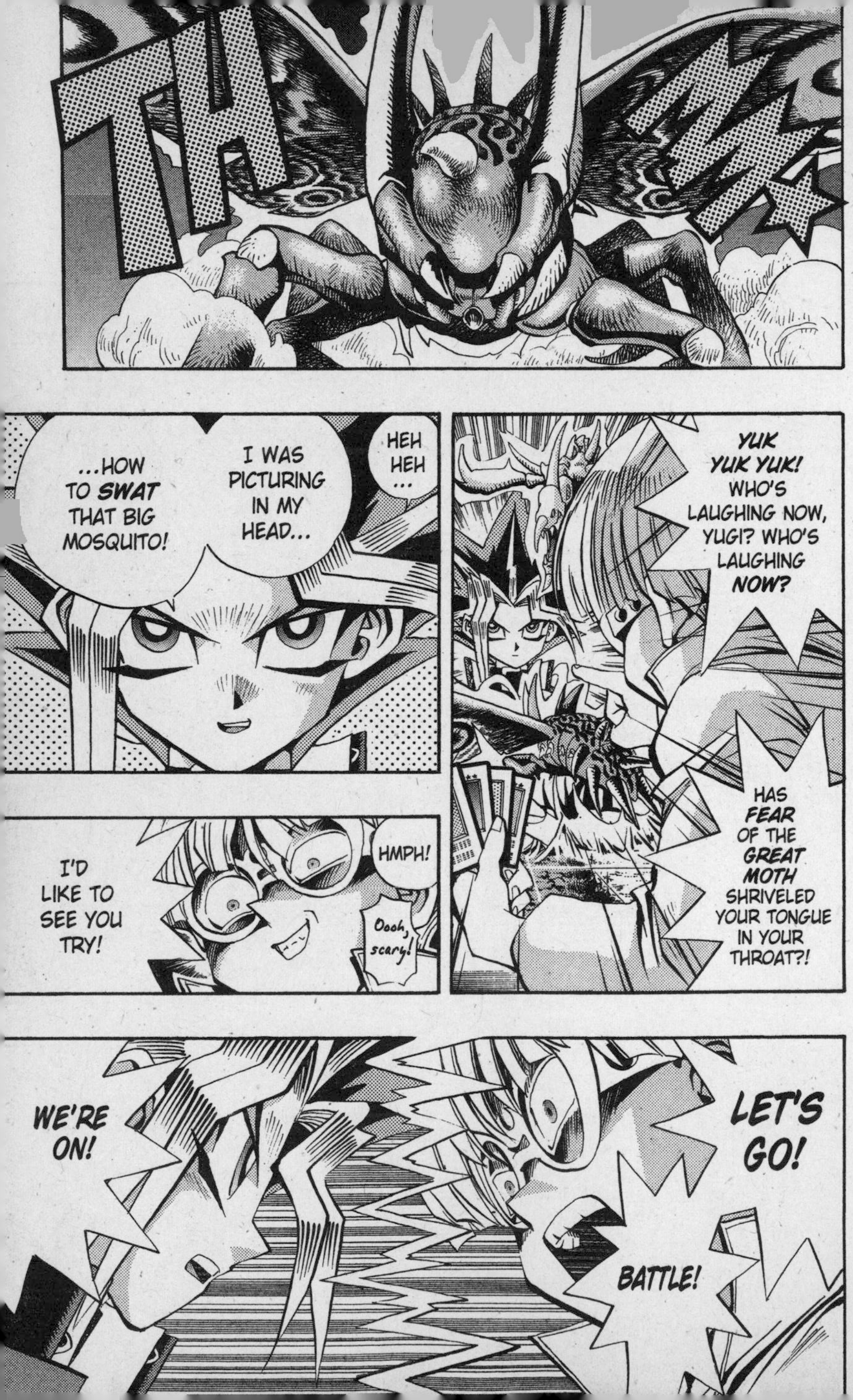
YUK YUK YUK! WHO'S LAUGHING NOW, YUGI? WHO'S LAUGHING NOW?
HAS FEAR OF THE GREAT MOTH SHRIVELED YOUR TONGUE IN YOUR THROAT?!
HEH HEH ...
I WAS PICTURING IN MY HEAD...
...HOW TO SWAT THAT BIG MOSQUITO!
HMPH!
Oooh, scary!
I'D LIKE TO SEE YOU TRY!
LET'S GO!
BATTLE!
WE'RE ON!

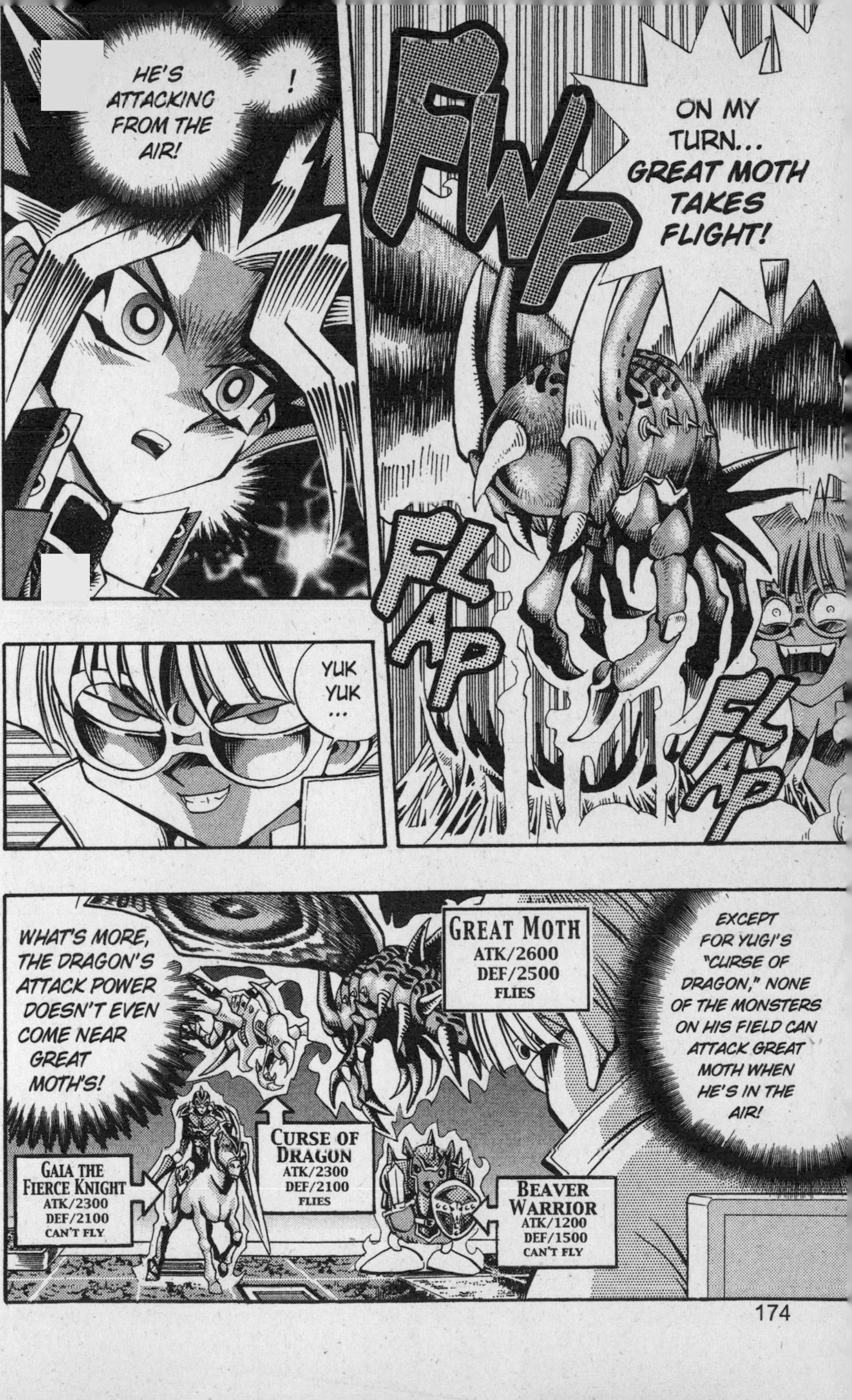
FWP
ON MY TURN... GREAT MOTH TAKES FLIGHT!
FLAP
FLAP
!
HE'S ATTACKING FROM THE AIR!
YUK YUK ...
EXCEPT FOR YUGI'S "CURSE OF DRAGON," NONE OF THE MONSTERS ON HIS FIELD CAN ATTACK GREAT MOTH WHEN HE'S IN THE AIR!
GREAT MOTH ATK/2600 DEF/2500 FLIES
BEAVER WARRIOR ATK/1200 DEF/1500 CAN'T FLY
CURSE OF DRAGON ATK/2300 DEF/2100 FLIES
GAIA THE FIERCE KNIGHT ATK/2300 DEF/2100 CAN'T FLY
WHAT'S MORE, THE DRAGON'S ATTACK POWER DOESN'T EVEN COME NEAR GREAT MOTH'S!

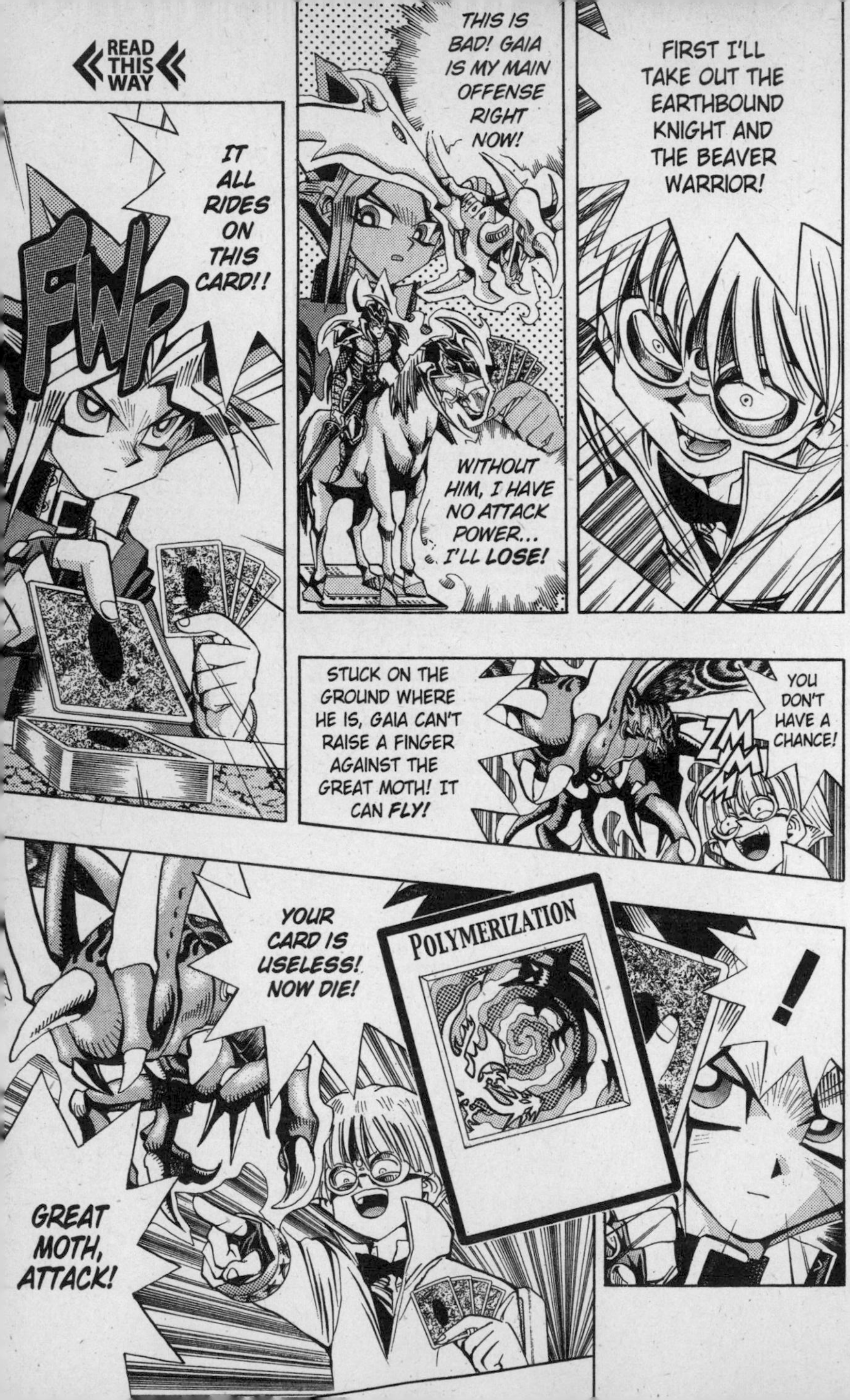
READ THIS WAY
FIRST I'LL TAKE OUT THE EARTHBOUND KNIGHT AND THE BEAVER WARRIOR!
THIS IS BAD! GAIA IS MY MAIN OFFENSE RIGHT NOW!
WITHOUT HIM, I HAVE NO ATTACK POWER... I'LL LOSE!
YOU DON'T HAVE A CHANCE!
ZMMM
STUCK ON THE GROUND WHERE HE IS, GAIA CAN'T RAISE A FINGER AGAINST THE GREAT MOTH! IT CAN FLY!
FWP
IT ALL RIDES ON THIS CARD!!
!
POLYMERIZATION
YOUR CARD IS USELESS! NOW DIE!
GREAT MOTH, ATTACK!

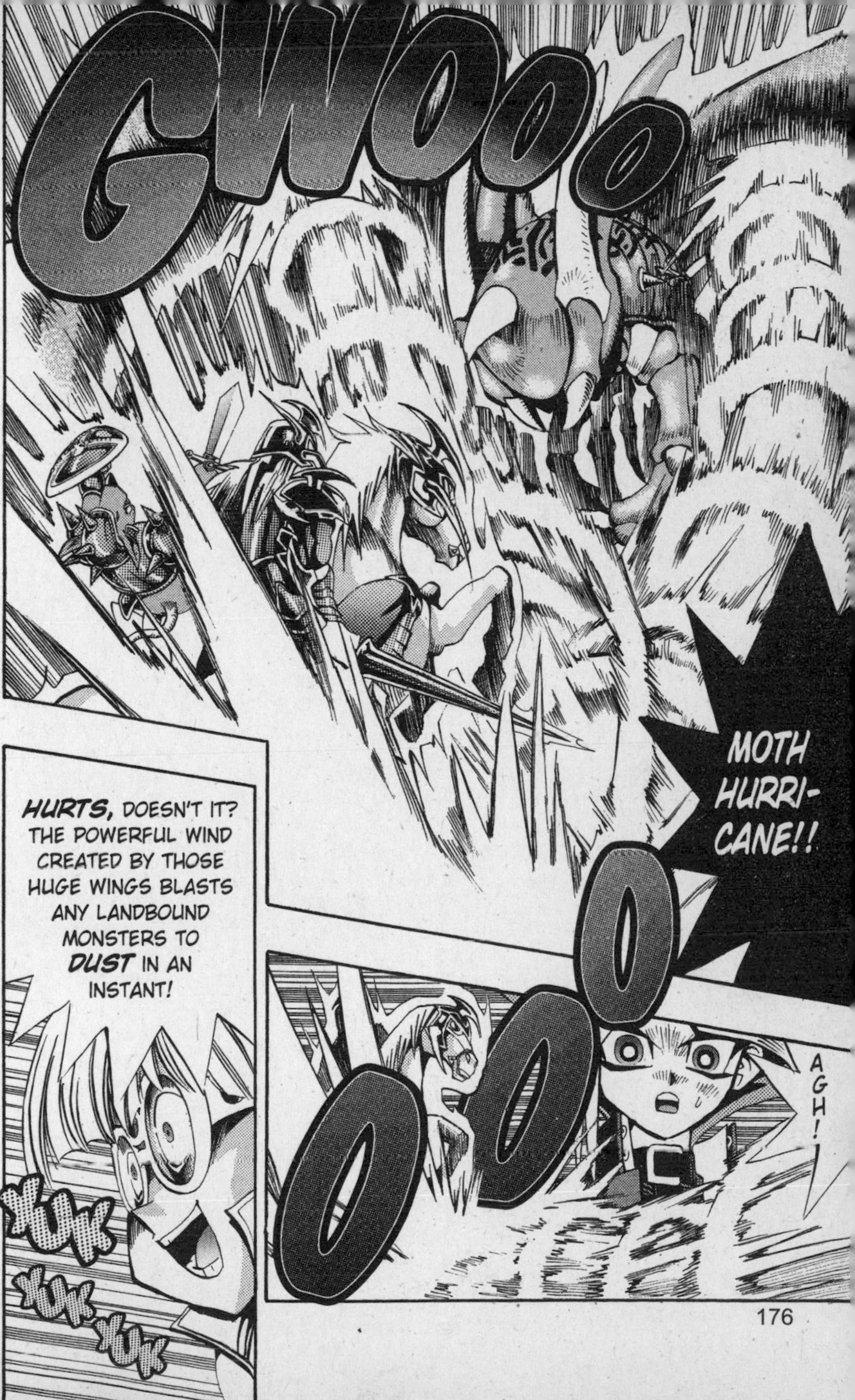
GWOOOO
MOTH HURRI-CANE!!
OOOO
AGH!
HURTS, DOESN'T IT? THE POWERFUL WIND CREATED BY THOSE HUGE WINGS BLASTS ANY LANDBOUND MONSTERS TO DUST IN AN INSTANT!
YUK
YUK
YUK

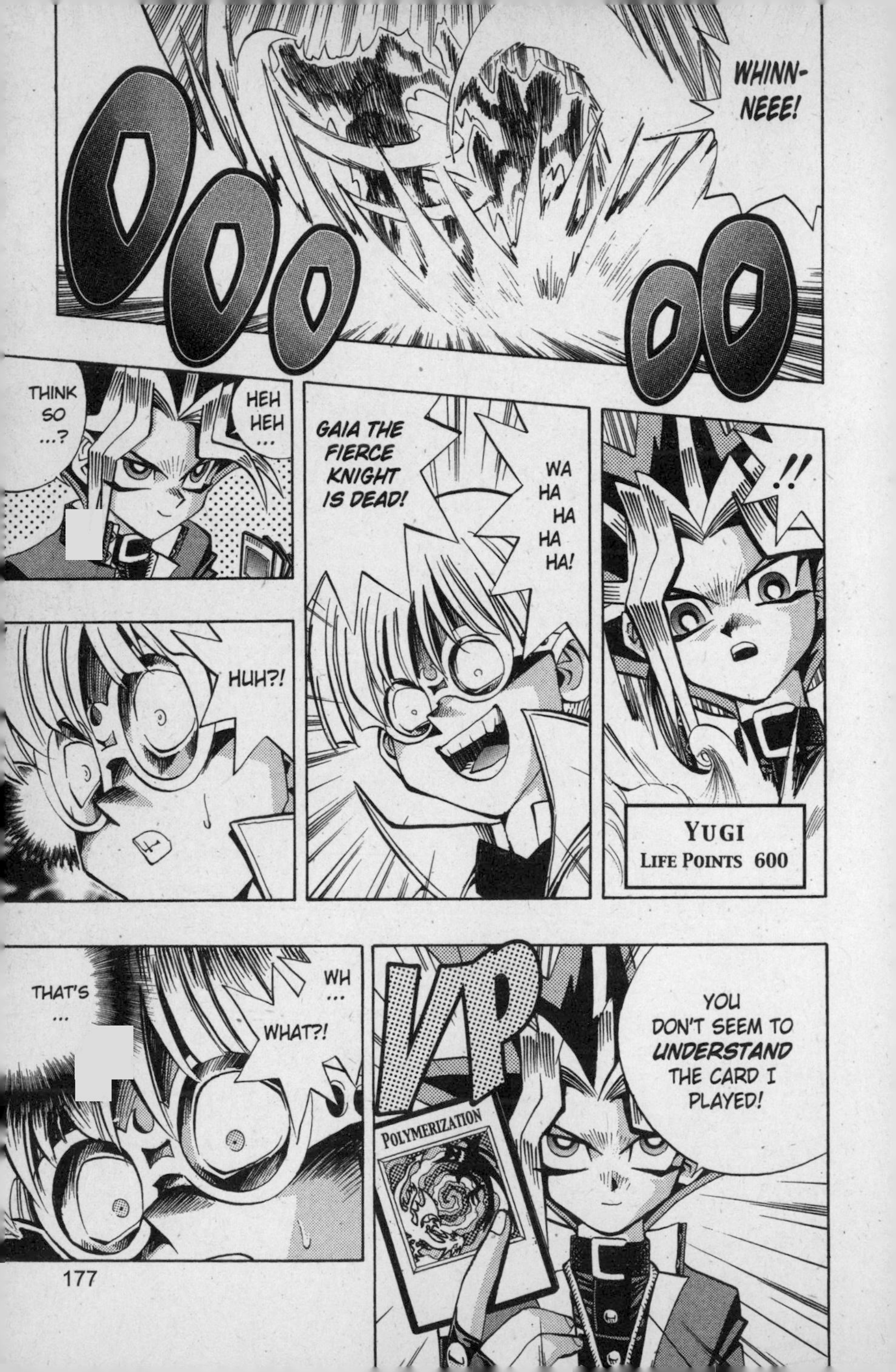
WHINN-NEEE!
OOOOOO
!!
YUGI
LIFE POINTS 600
GAIA THE FIERCE KNIGHT IS DEAD!
WA HA HA HA HA!
HEH HEH ...
THINK SO ...?
HUH?!
VP
YOU DON'T SEEM TO UNDERSTAND THE CARD I PLAYED!
POLYMERIZATION
WH ...
WHAT?!
THAT'S ...

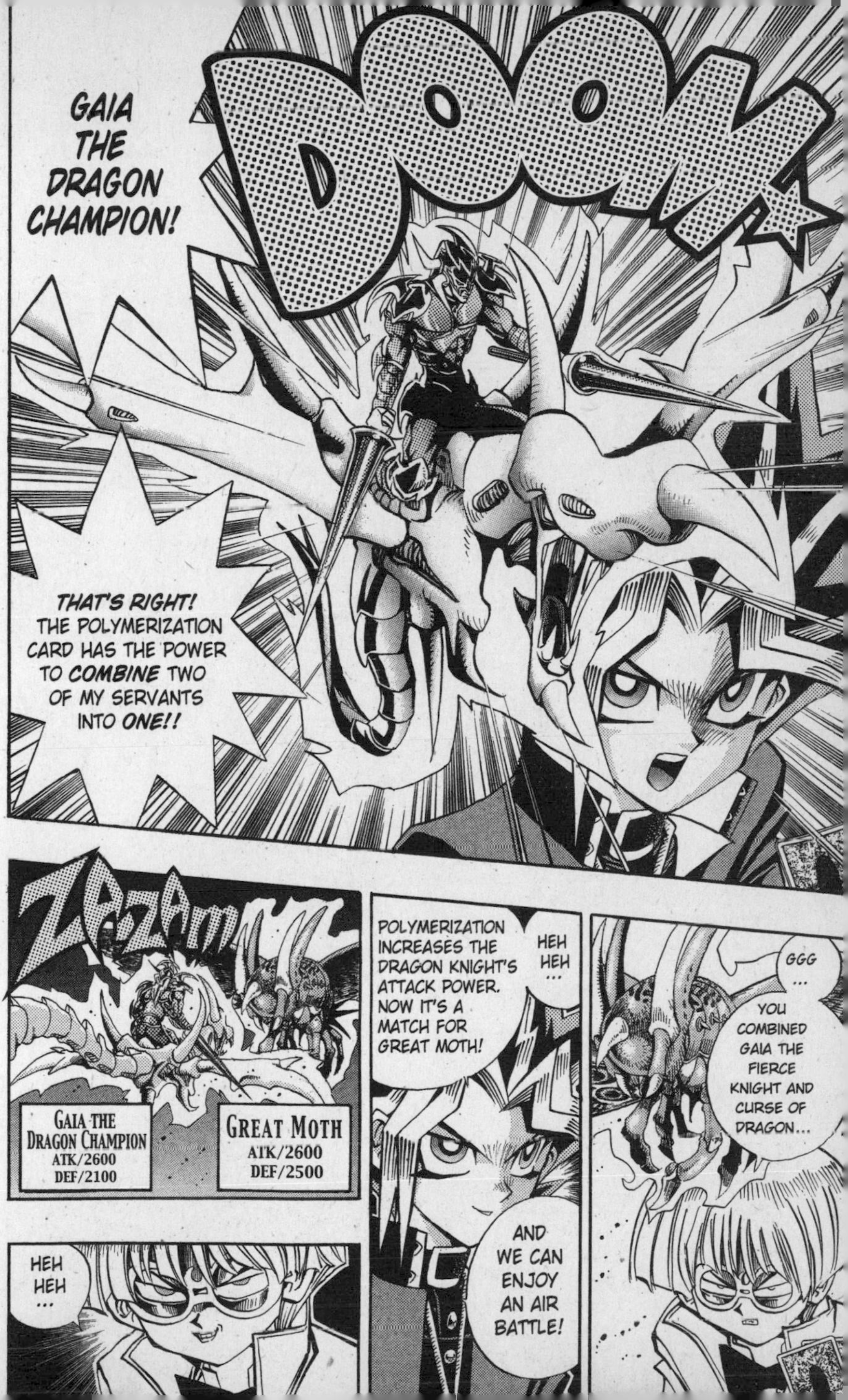
DOOM
GAIA THE DRAGON CHAMPION!
THAT'S RIGHT! THE POLYMERIZATION CARD HAS THE POWER TO COMBINE TWO OF MY SERVANTS INTO ONE!!
GGG ...
YOU COMBINED GAIA THE FIERCE KNIGHT AND CURSE OF DRAGON...
HEH HEH ...
POLYMERIZATION INCREASES THE DRAGON KNIGHT'S ATTACK POWER. NOW IT'S A MATCH FOR GREAT MOTH!
AND WE CAN ENJOY AN AIR BATTLE!
ZAZAM
GREAT MOTH ATK/2600 DEF/2500
GAIA THE DRAGON CHAMPION ATK/2600 DEF/2100
HEH HEH ...

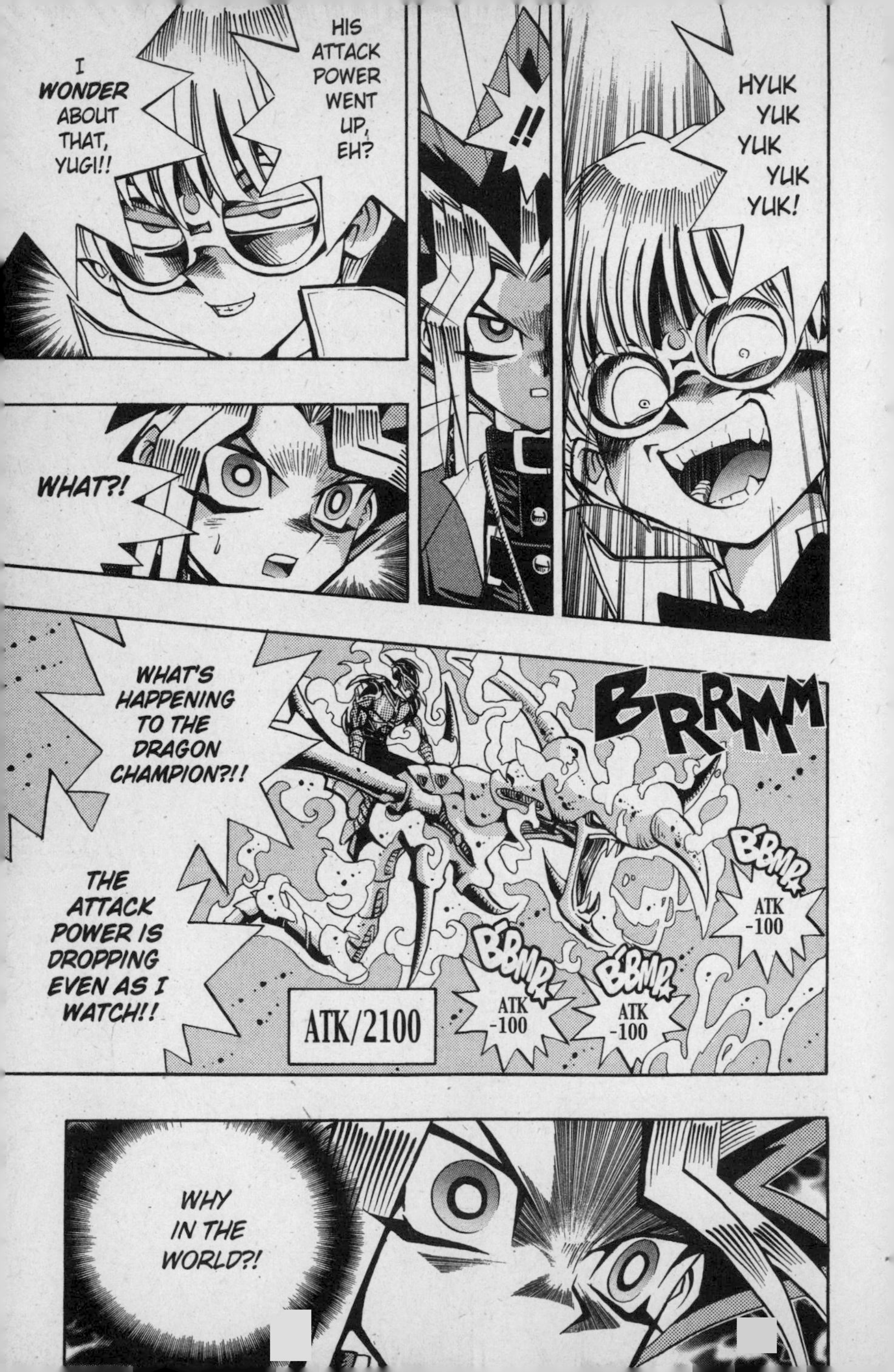
HYUK YUK YUK YUK YUK!
!!
HIS ATTACK POWER WENT UP, EH?
I WONDER ABOUT THAT, YUGI!!
WHAT?!
BRRMM
BBMP
ATK -100
WHAT'S HAPPENING TO THE DRAGON CHAMPION?!!
BBMP
ATK -100
BBMP
ATK -100
ATK/2100
THE ATTACK POWER IS DROPPING EVEN AS I WATCH!!
WHY IN THE WORLD?!

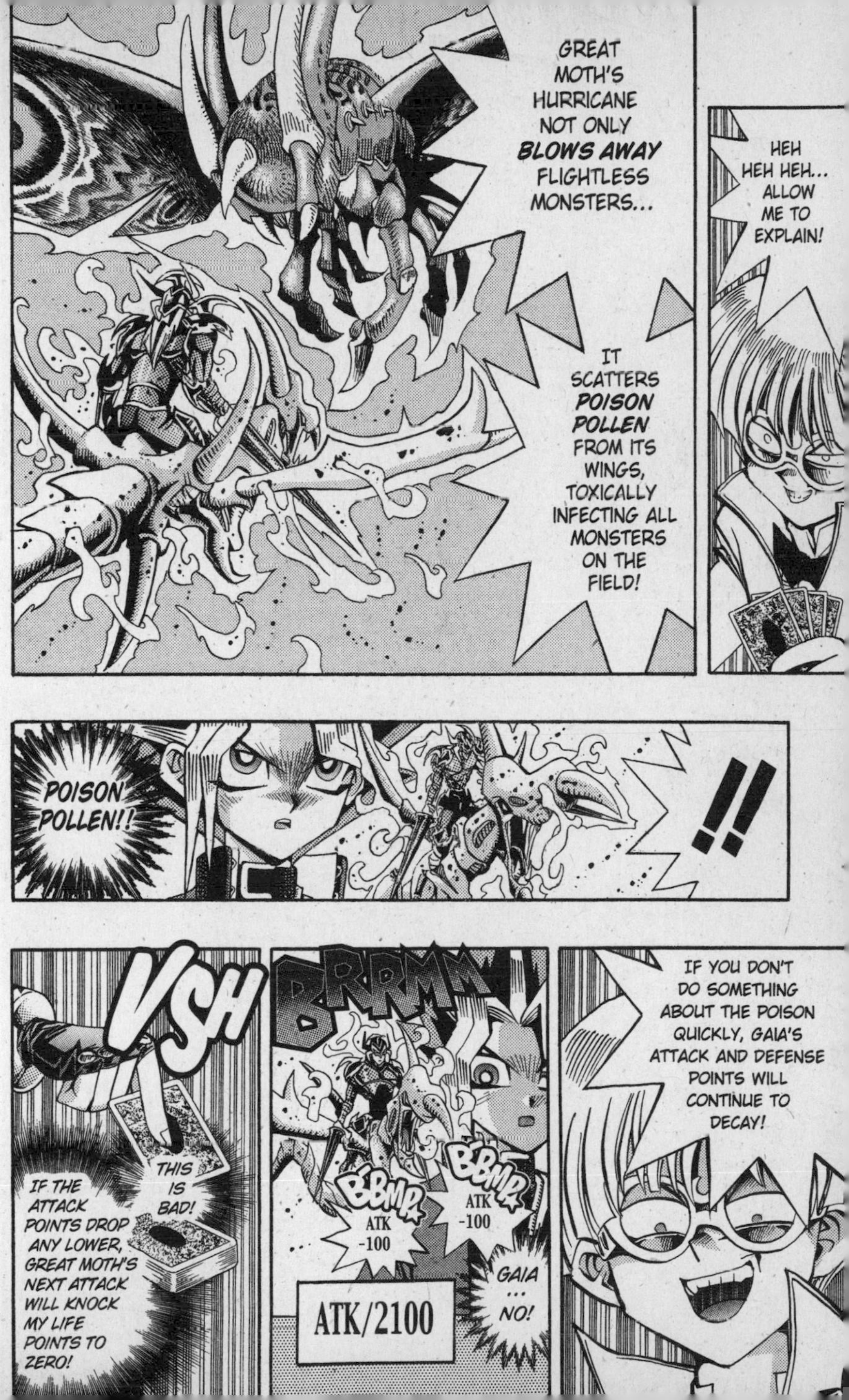
HEH HEH HEH... ALLOW ME TO EXPLAIN!
GREAT MOTH'S HURRICANE NOT ONLY **BLOWS AWAY** FLIGHTLESS MONSTERS...
IT SCATTERS **POISON POLLEN** FROM ITS WINGS, TOXICALLY INFECTING ALL MONSTERS ON THE FIELD!
!!
POISON POLLEN!!
IF YOU DON'T DO SOMETHING ABOUT THE POISON QUICKLY, GAIA'S ATTACK AND DEFENSE POINTS WILL CONTINUE TO DECAY!
BRRMM
BBMP
ATK -100
BBMP
ATK -100
GAIA... NO!
ATK/2100
VSH
THIS IS BAD!
IF THE ATTACK POINTS DROP ANY LOWER, GREAT MOTH'S NEXT ATTACK WILL KNOCK MY LIFE POINTS TO ZERO!

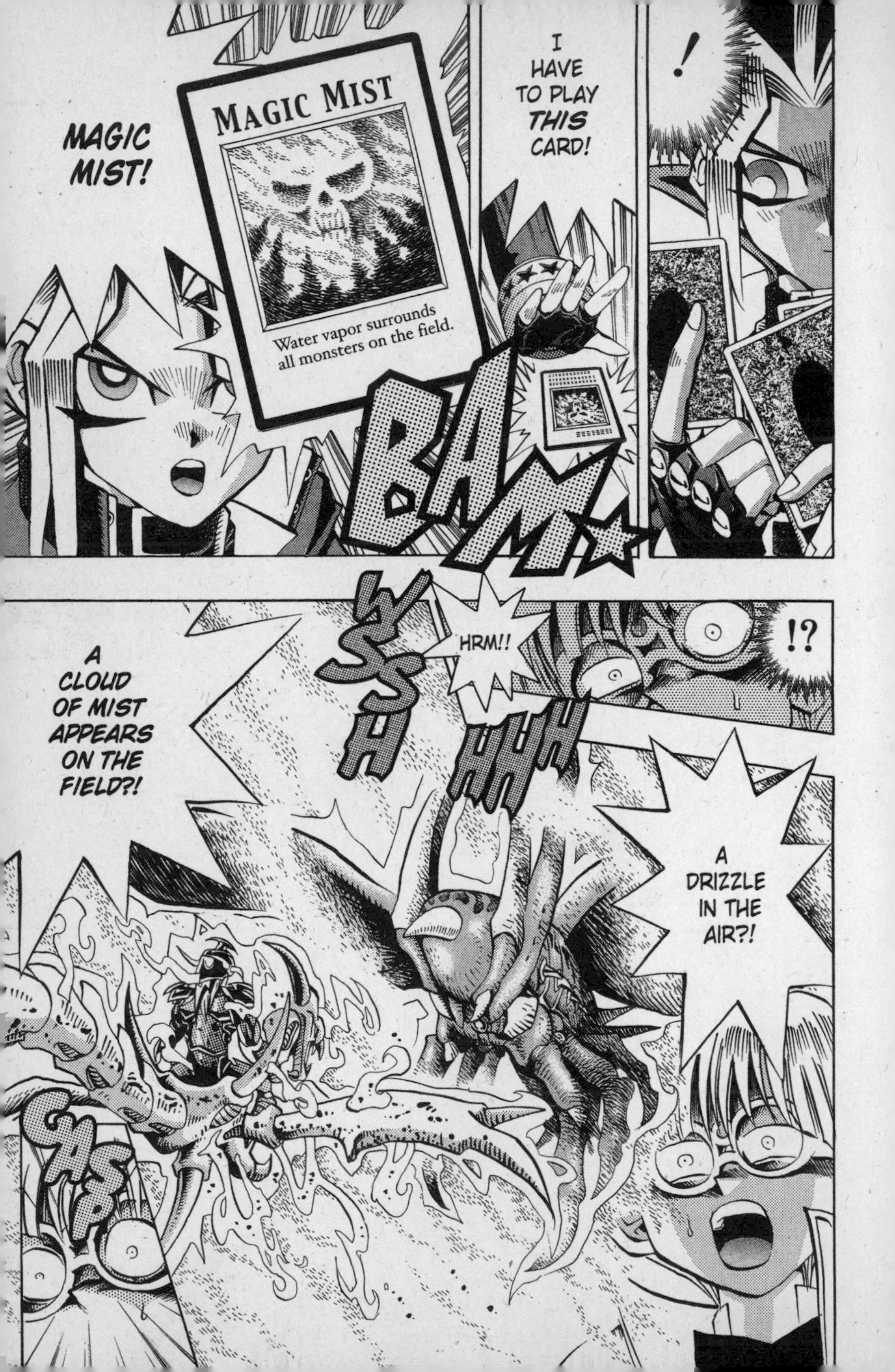
!
I HAVE TO PLAY THIS CARD!
MAGIC MIST!
MAGIC MIST
Water vapor surrounds all monsters on the field.
BAM
!?
HRM!!
A DRIZZLE IN THE AIR?!
A CLOUD OF MIST APPEARS ON THE FIELD?!

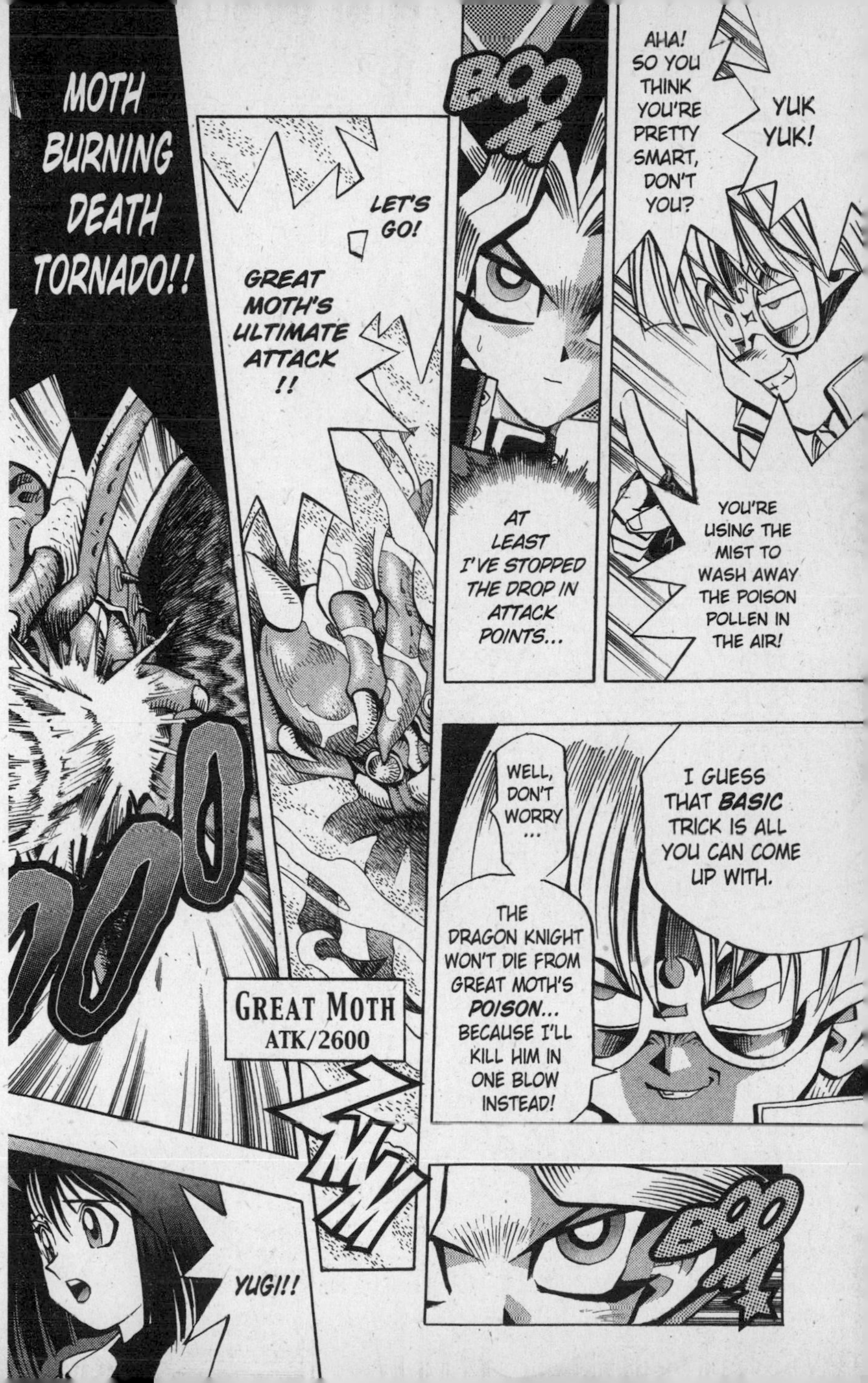
AHA! SO YOU THINK YOU'RE PRETTY SMART, DON'T YOU?
YUK YUK!
YOU'RE USING THE MIST TO WASH AWAY THE POISON POLLEN IN THE AIR!
BOO
AT LEAST I'VE STOPPED THE DROP IN ATTACK POINTS...
I GUESS THAT BASIC TRICK IS ALL YOU CAN COME UP WITH.
WELL, DON'T WORRY...
THE DRAGON KNIGHT WON'T DIE FROM GREAT MOTH'S POISON... BECAUSE I'LL KILL HIM IN ONE BLOW INSTEAD!
LET'S GO!
GREAT MOTH'S ULTIMATE ATTACK!!
GREAT MOTH
ATK/2600
MOTH BURNING DEATH TORNADO!!
YUGI!!

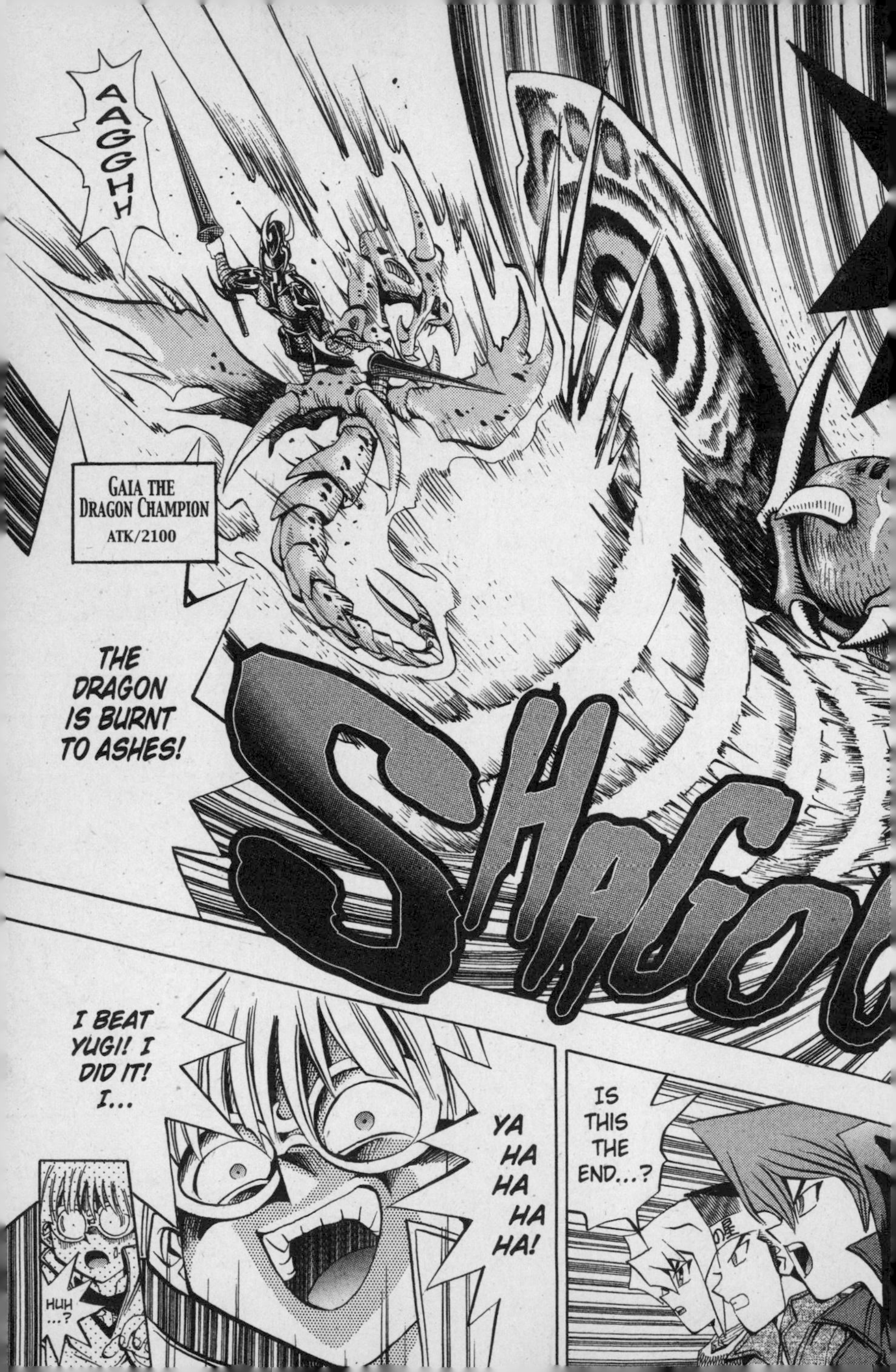
AAGGHH
GAIA THE DRAGON CHAMPION
ATK/2100
THE DRAGON IS BURNT TO ASHES!
SHAGOO
IS THIS THE END...?
I BEAT YUGI! I DID IT! I...
YA HA HA HA HA!
HUH ...?

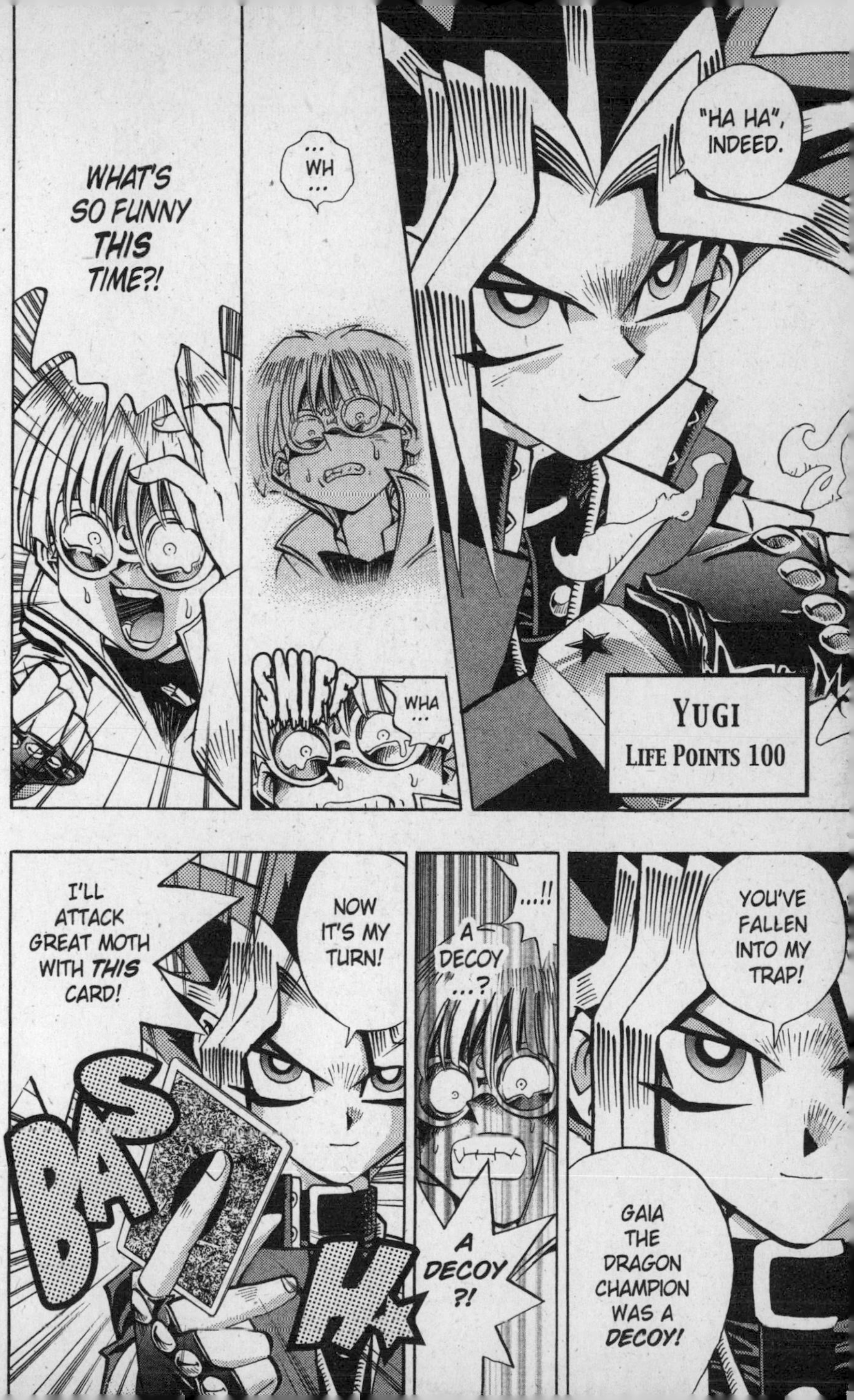
"HA HA", INDEED.
YUGI
LIFE POINTS 100
... WH ...
SNIFF
WHA ...
WHAT'S SO FUNNY THIS TIME?!
YOU'VE FALLEN INTO MY TRAP!
GAIA THE DRAGON CHAMPION WAS A DECOY!
...!!
A DECOY ...?
A DECOY ?!
NOW IT'S MY TURN!
I'LL ATTACK GREAT MOTH WITH THIS CARD!
BASH

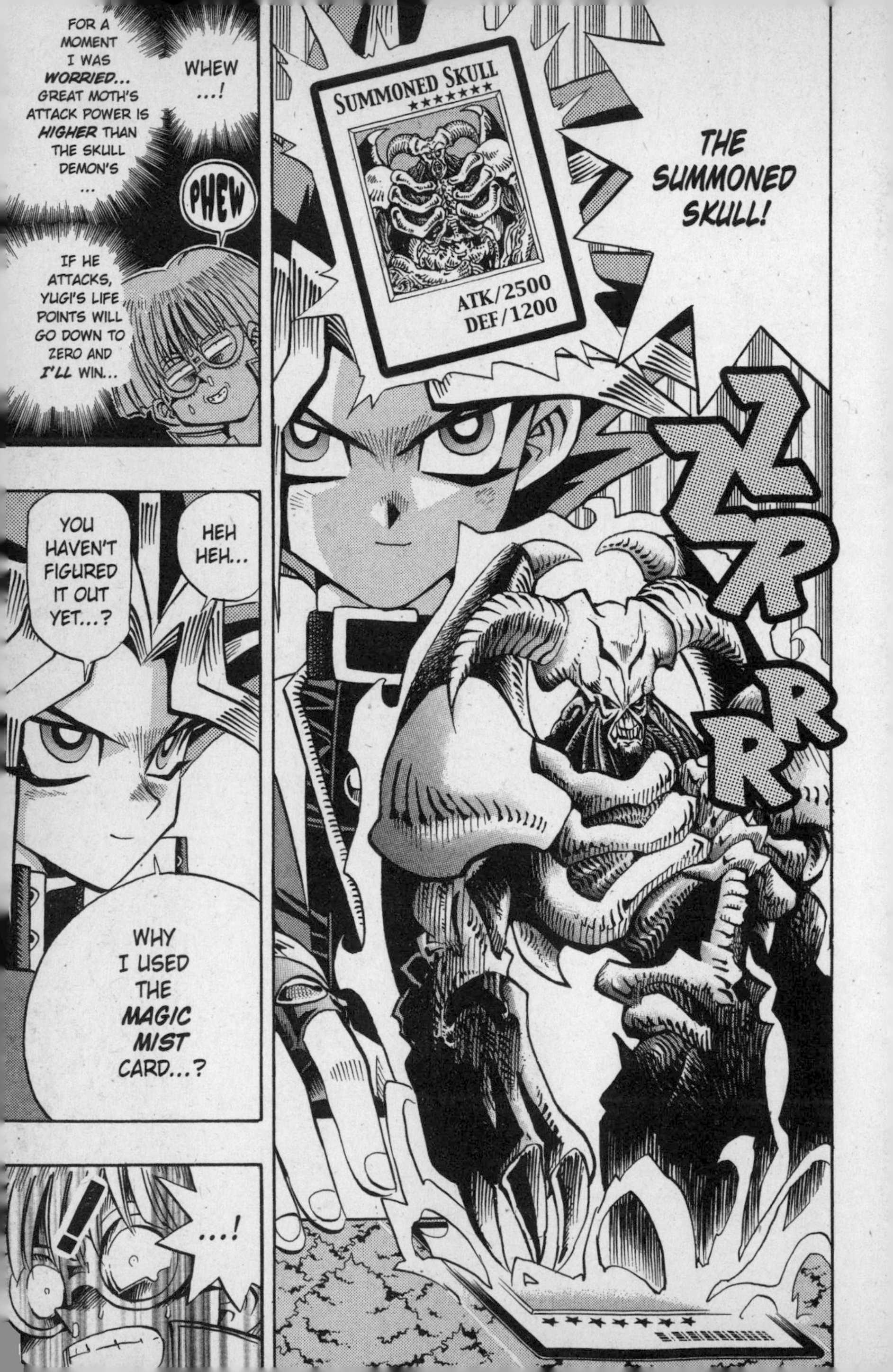
Summoned Skull
ATK/2500
DEF/1200
THE SUMMONED SKULL!
ZRRR
WHEW ...!
FOR A MOMENT I WAS WORRIED... GREAT MOTH'S ATTACK POWER IS HIGHER THAN THE SKULL DEMON'S ...
PHEW
IF HE ATTACKS, YUGI'S LIFE POINTS WILL GO DOWN TO ZERO AND I'LL WIN...
HEH HEH...
YOU HAVEN'T FIGURED IT OUT YET...?
WHY I USED THE MAGIC MIST CARD...?
...!
!

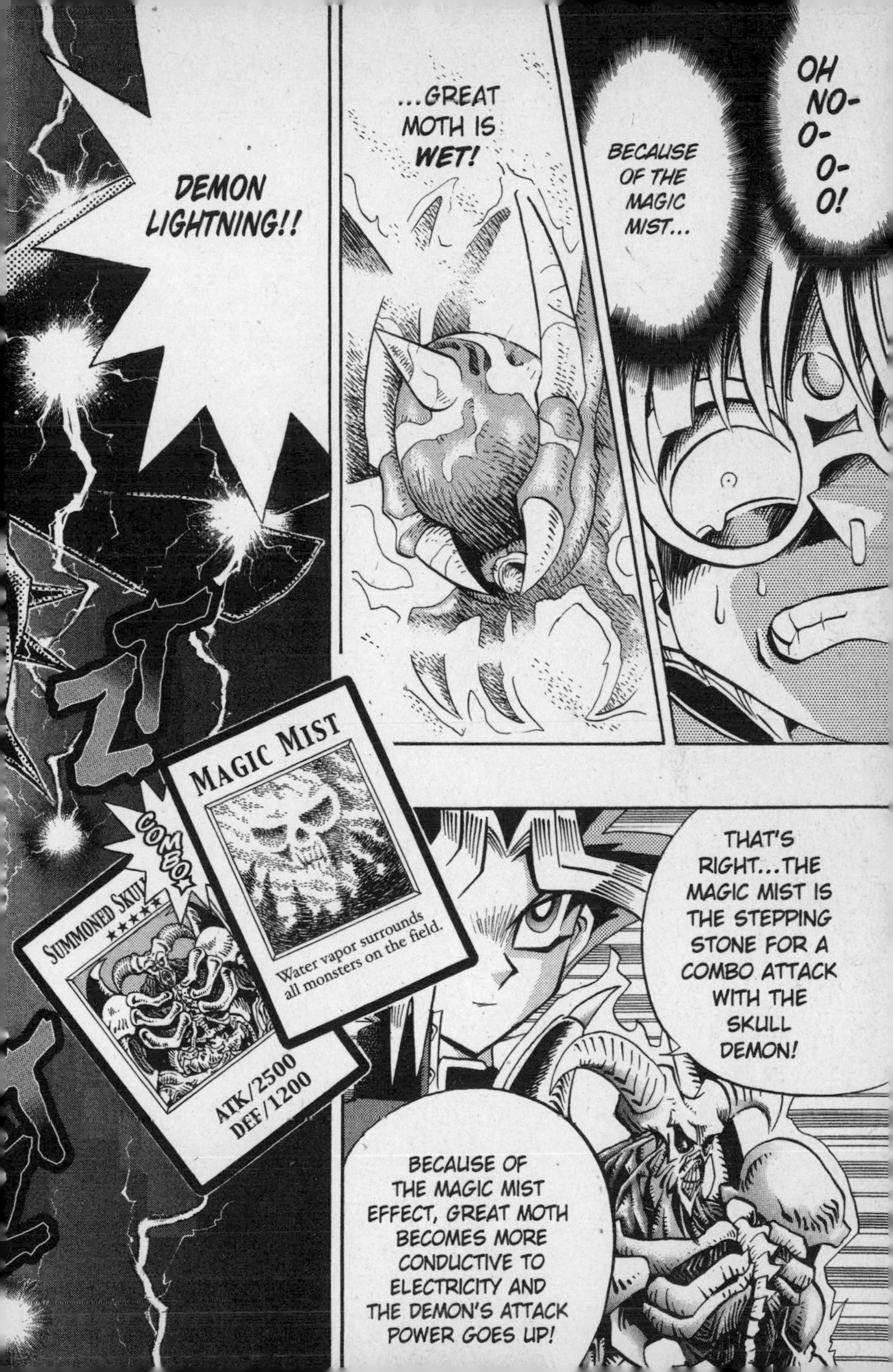

OH NO-O-O-O!
BECAUSE OF THE MAGIC MIST...
...GREAT MOTH IS WET!
THAT'S RIGHT...THE MAGIC MIST IS THE STEPPING STONE FOR A COMBO ATTACK WITH THE SKULL DEMON!
BECAUSE OF THE MAGIC MIST EFFECT, GREAT MOTH BECOMES MORE CONDUCTIVE TO ELECTRICITY AND THE DEMON'S ATTACK POWER GOES UP!
DEMON LIGHTNING!!
ZT
MAGIC MIST
Water vapor surrounds all monsters on the field.
COMBO
SUMMONED SKUL
ATK/2500
DEF/1200

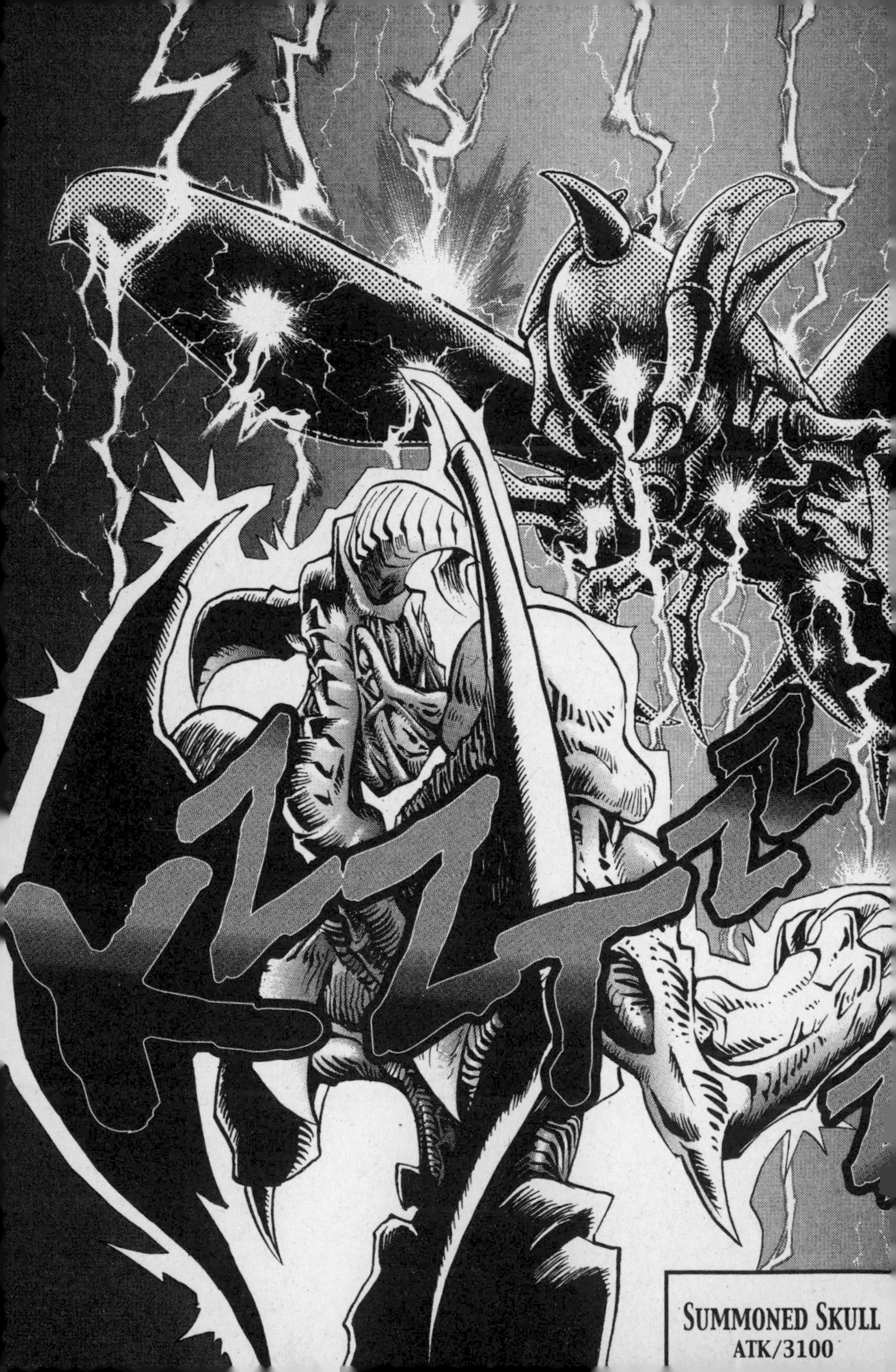

SUMMONED SKULL
ATK/3100

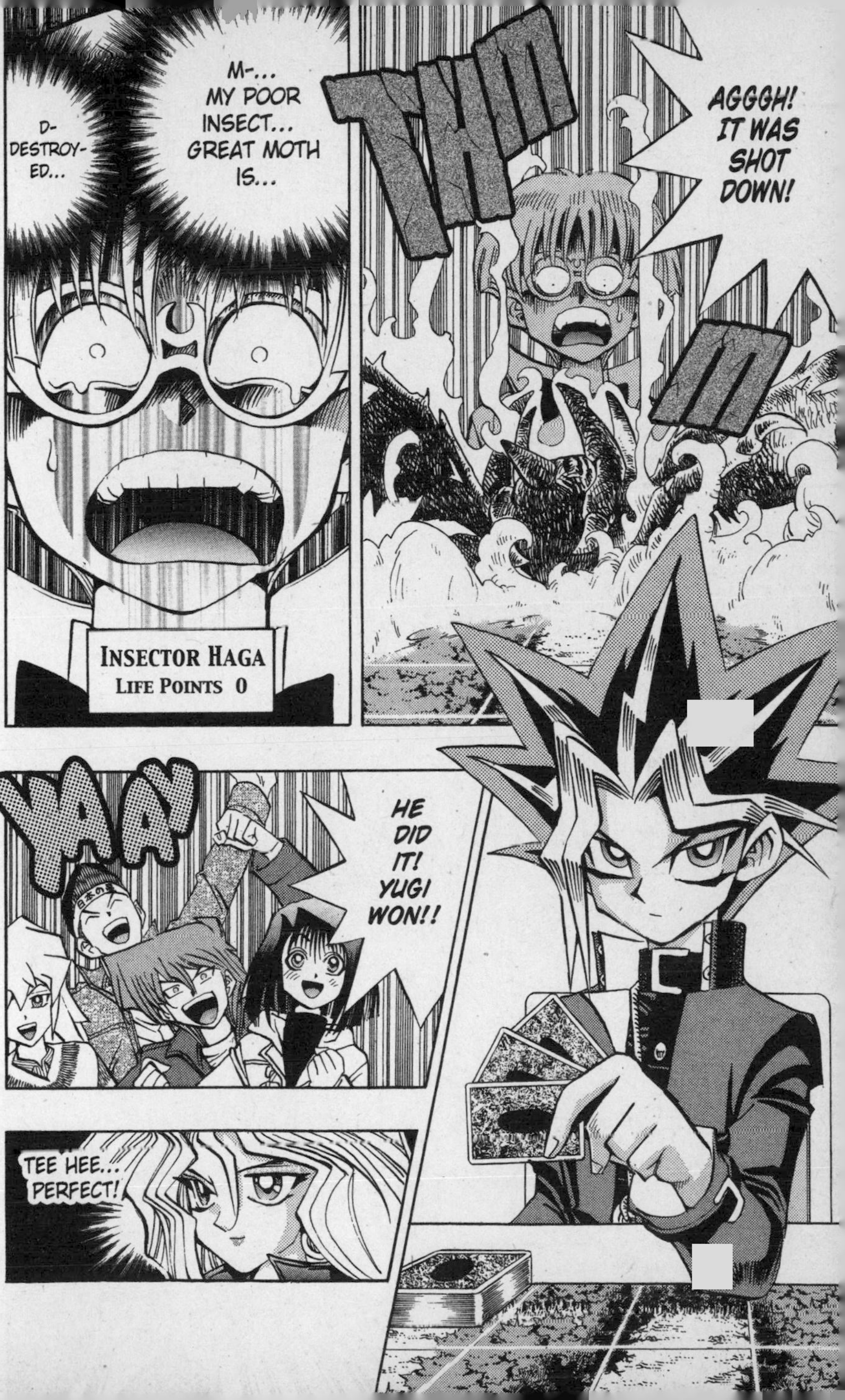
AGGGH! IT WAS SHOT DOWN!
M-... MY POOR INSECT... GREAT MOTH IS...
D-DESTROY-ED...
INSECTOR HAGA
LIFE POINTS 0
HE DID IT! YUGI WON!!
TEE HEE... PERFECT!

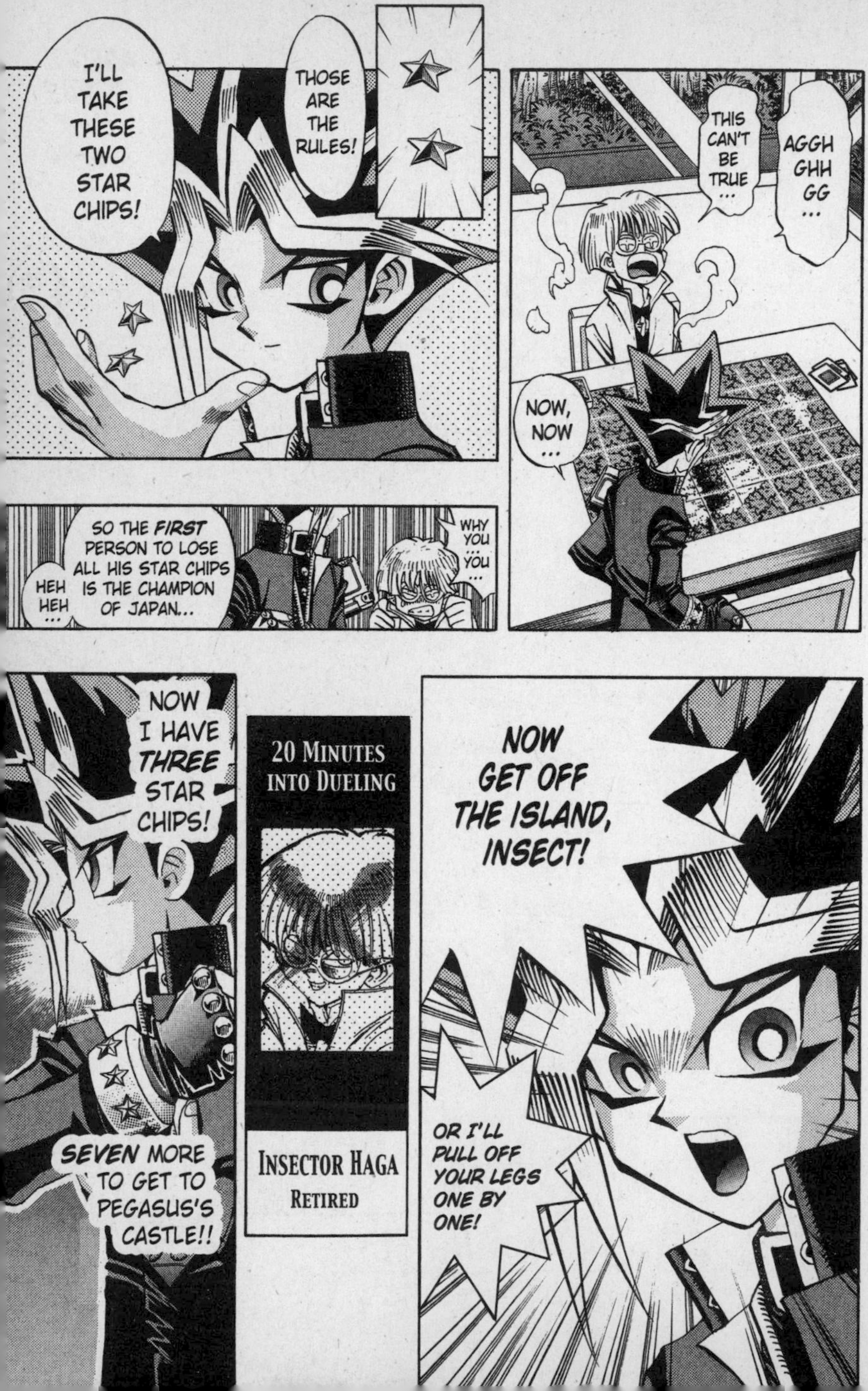
AGGH GHH GG...
THIS CAN'T BE TRUE...
NOW, NOW...
THOSE ARE THE RULES!
I'LL TAKE THESE TWO STAR CHIPS!
WHY YOU... YOU...
SO THE FIRST PERSON TO LOSE ALL HIS STAR CHIPS IS THE CHAMPION OF JAPAN...
HEH HEH...
NOW GET OFF THE ISLAND, INSECT!
OR I'LL PULL OFF YOUR LEGS ONE BY ONE!
20 MINUTES INTO DUELING
INSECTOR HAGA RETIRED
NOW I HAVE THREE STAR CHIPS!
SEVEN MORE TO GET TO PEGASUS'S CASTLE!!

DUELING RULES

- THE DUELS TAKE PLACE IN THE VIRTUAL-REALITY BATTLE BOXES THAT ARE SCATTERED ACROSS THE ISLAND. THE PLAYERS MAY WAGER ANY NUMBER OF THE STAR CHIPS THEY HOLD. HOWEVER, IF A PLAYER LOSES ALL OF HIS STAR CHIPS, HE LOSES HIS STATUS AS A DUELIST AND MUST LEAVE THE ISLAND.
- ONLY PLAYERS WHO GATHER 10 STAR CHIPS ARE ALLOWED TO ENTER PEGASUS'S CASTLE FOR A CHANCE TO WIN THE HONORS.
- THE TIME LIMIT IS 48 HOURS.

THE DUELIST KINGDOM

DUEL 10 : THE SIREN

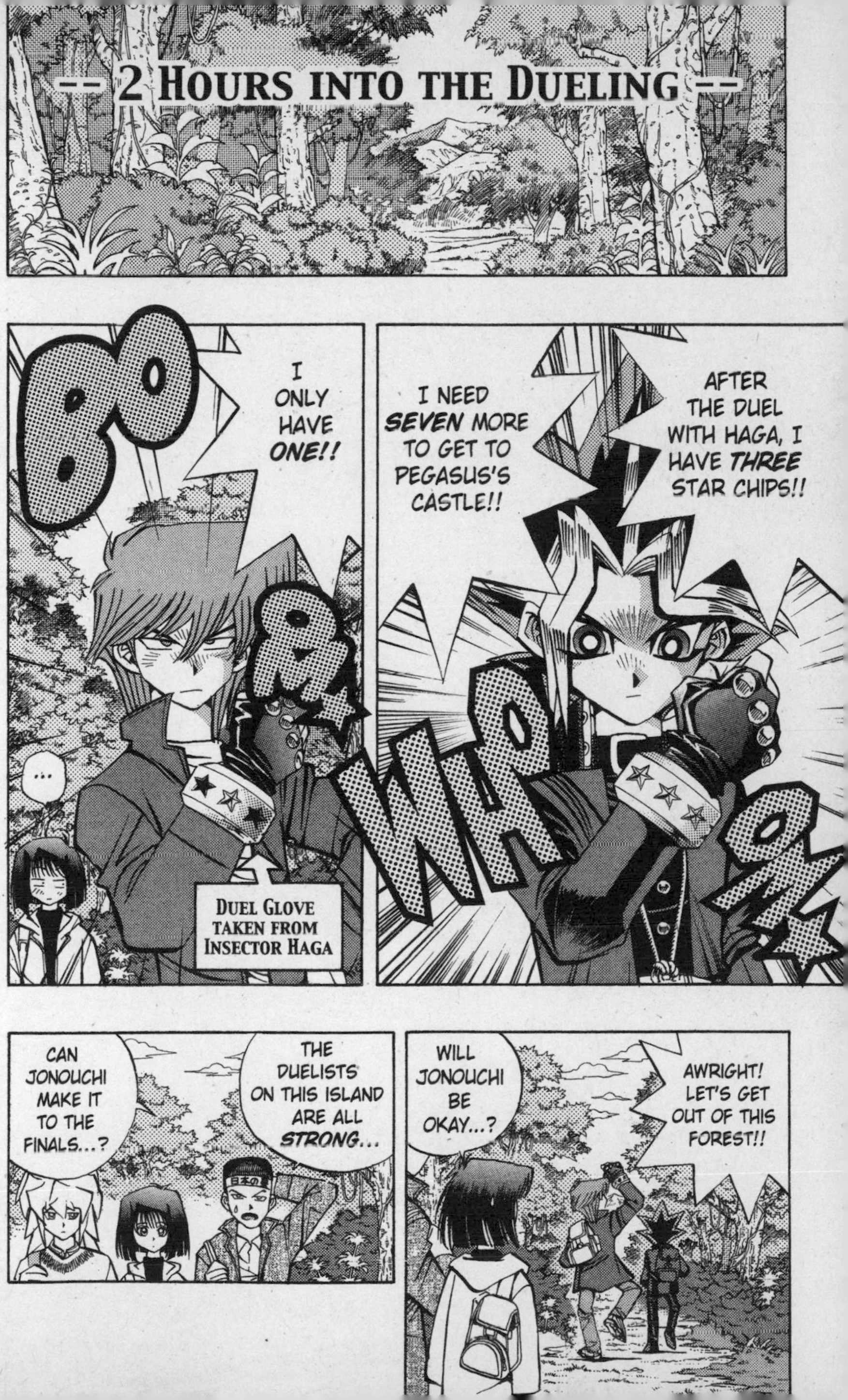
-- 2 Hours into the Dueling --
AFTER THE DUEL WITH HAGA, I HAVE THREE STAR CHIPS!!
I NEED SEVEN MORE TO GET TO PEGASUS'S CASTLE!!
I ONLY HAVE ONE!!
...
DUEL GLOVE TAKEN FROM INSECTOR HAGA
AWRIGHT! LET'S GET OUT OF THIS FOREST!!
WILL JONOUCHI BE OKAY...?
THE DUELISTS ON THIS ISLAND ARE ALL STRONG...
CAN JONOUCHI MAKE IT TO THE FINALS...?

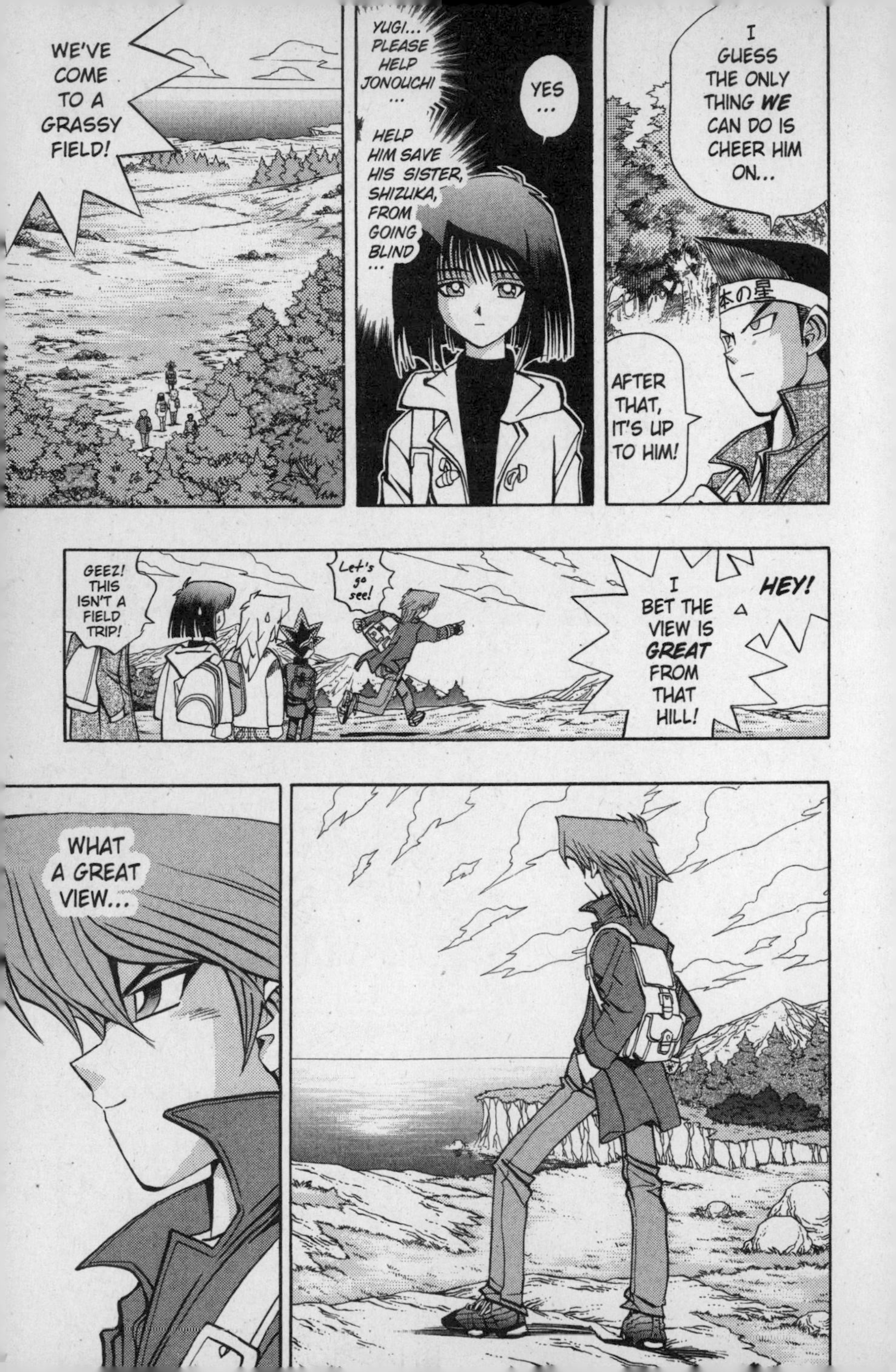
I GUESS THE ONLY THING **WE** CAN DO IS CHEER HIM ON...
AFTER THAT, IT'S UP TO HIM!
YUGI... PLEASE HELP JONOUCHI ...
HELP HIM SAVE HIS SISTER, SHIZUKA, FROM GOING BLIND ...
YES ...
WE'VE COME TO A GRASSY FIELD!
HEY!
I BET THE VIEW IS **GREAT** FROM THAT HILL!
Let's go see!
GEEZ! THIS ISN'T A FIELD TRIP!
WHAT A GREAT VIEW...

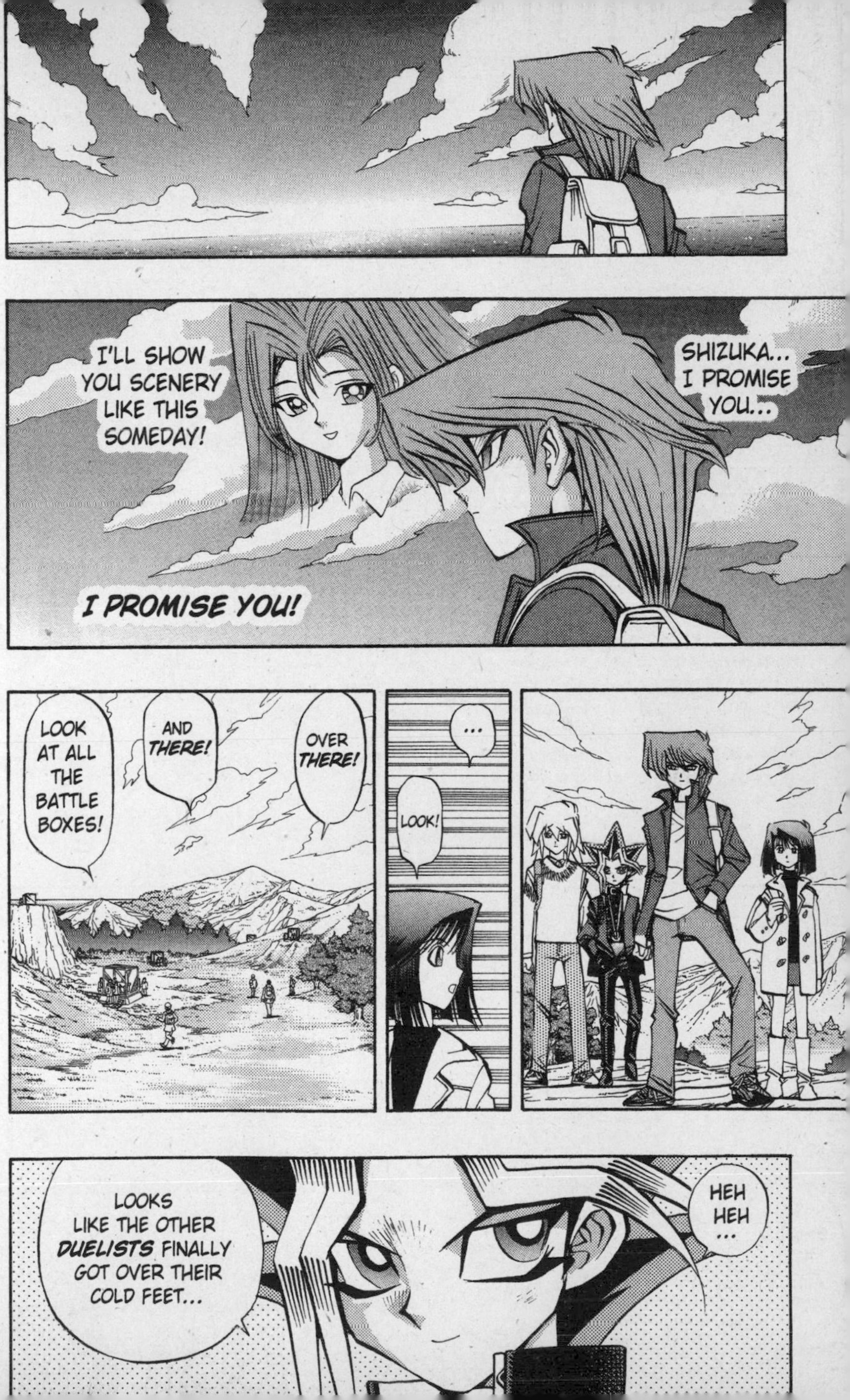
SHIZUKA... I PROMISE YOU...
I'LL SHOW YOU SCENERY LIKE THIS SOMEDAY!
I PROMISE YOU!
...
LOOK!
OVER THERE!
AND THERE!
LOOK AT ALL THE BATTLE BOXES!
HEH HEH ...
LOOKS LIKE THE OTHER DUELISTS FINALLY GOT OVER THEIR COLD FEET...

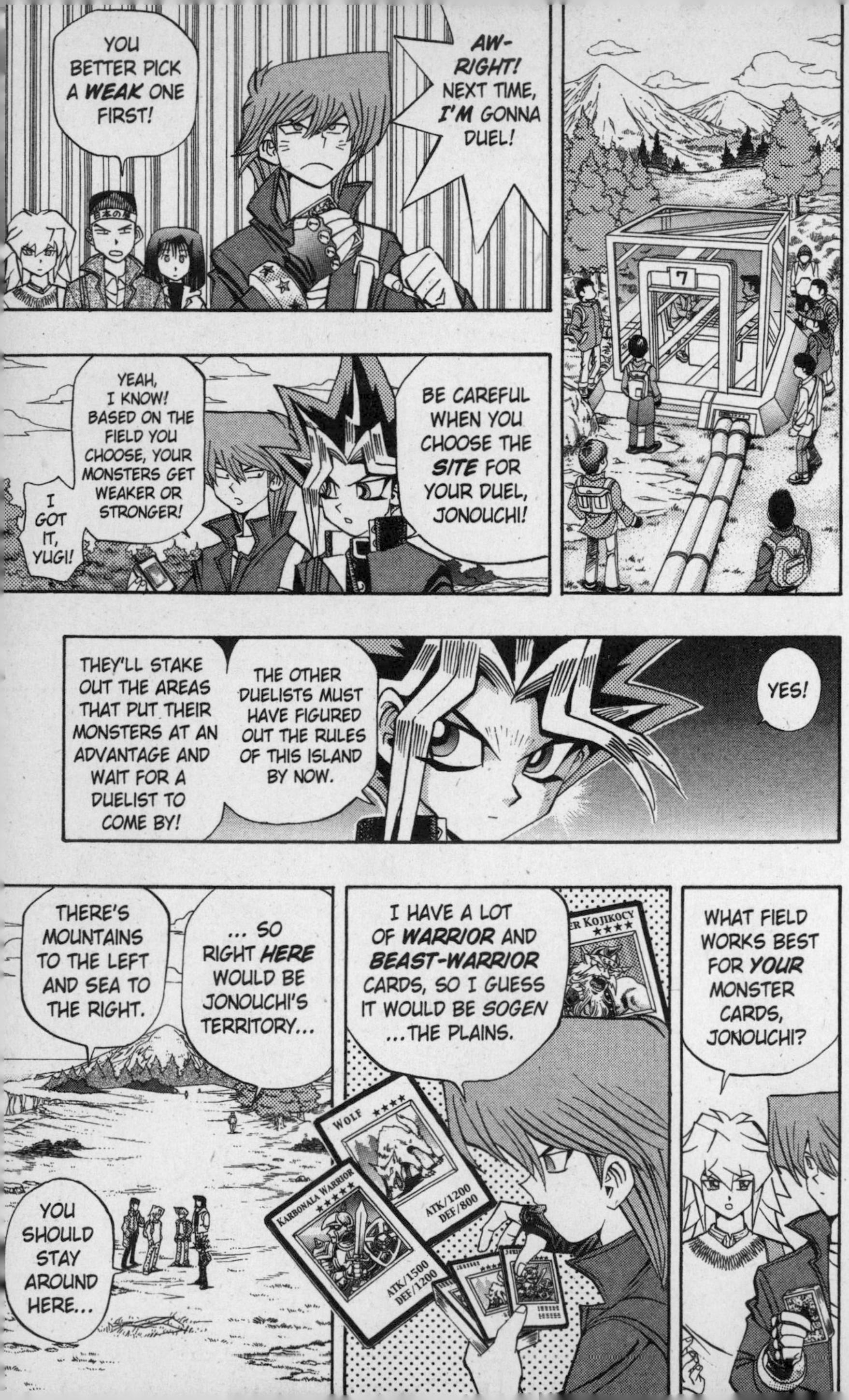
AW-RIGHT! NEXT TIME, I'M GONNA DUEL!
YOU BETTER PICK A WEAK ONE FIRST!
BE CAREFUL WHEN YOU CHOOSE THE SITE FOR YOUR DUEL, JONOUCHI!
YEAH, I KNOW! BASED ON THE FIELD YOU CHOOSE, YOUR MONSTERS GET WEAKER OR STRONGER!
I GOT IT, YUGI!
YES!
THE OTHER DUELISTS MUST HAVE FIGURED OUT THE RULES OF THIS ISLAND BY NOW.
THEY'LL STAKE OUT THE AREAS THAT PUT THEIR MONSTERS AT AN ADVANTAGE AND WAIT FOR A DUELIST TO COME BY!
WHAT FIELD WORKS BEST FOR YOUR MONSTER CARDS, JONOUCHI?
I HAVE A LOT OF WARRIOR AND BEAST-WARRIOR CARDS, SO I GUESS IT WOULD BE SOGEN ...THE PLAINS.
WOLF
ATK/1200 DEF/800
KARBONALA WARRIOR
ATK/1500 DEF/1200
... SO RIGHT HERE WOULD BE JONOUCHI'S TERRITORY...
THERE'S MOUNTAINS TO THE LEFT AND SEA TO THE RIGHT.
YOU SHOULD STAY AROUND HERE...

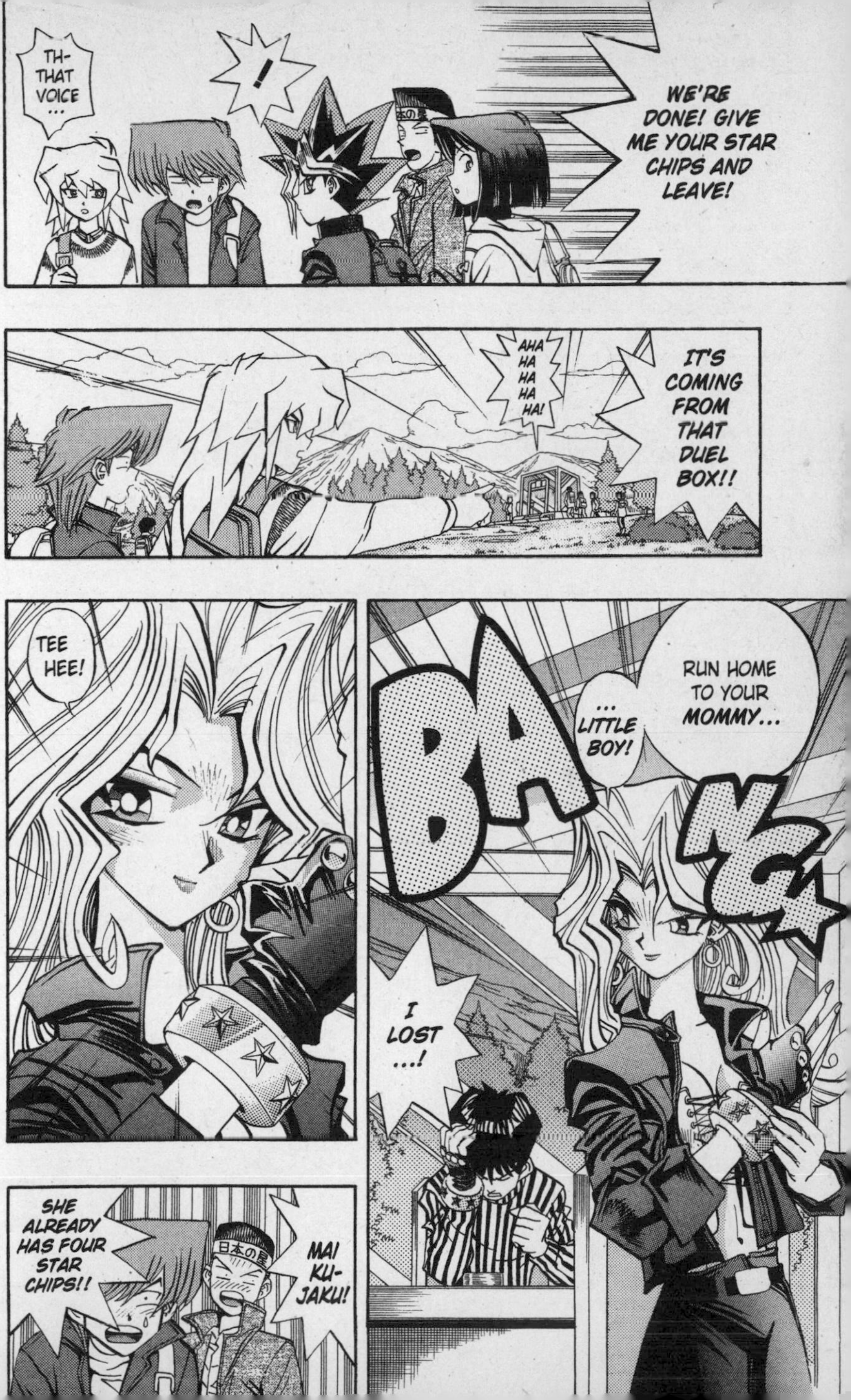
WE'RE DONE! GIVE ME YOUR STAR CHIPS AND LEAVE!
!
TH-THAT VOICE...
IT'S COMING FROM THAT DUEL BOX!!
AHA HA HA HA HA!
RUN HOME TO YOUR MOMMY...
...LITTLE BOY!
BANG
I LOST...!
TEE HEE!
MAI KU-JAKU!
日本の星
SHE ALREADY HAS FOUR STAR CHIPS!!

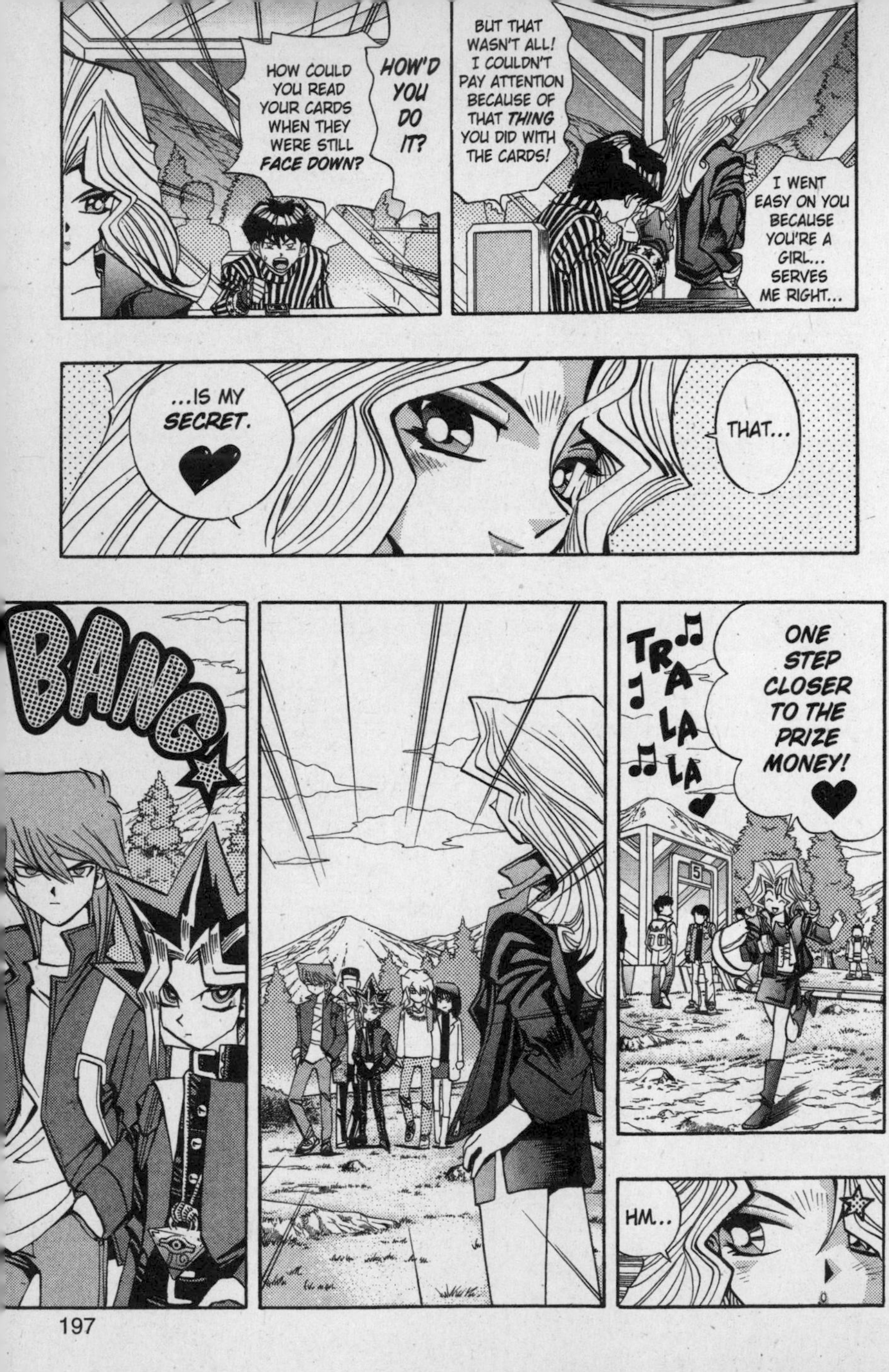
BUT THAT WASN'T ALL! I COULDN'T PAY ATTENTION BECAUSE OF THAT *THING* YOU DID WITH THE CARDS!
I WENT EASY ON YOU BECAUSE YOU'RE A GIRL... SERVES ME RIGHT...
HOW'D YOU DO IT?
HOW COULD YOU READ YOUR CARDS WHEN THEY WERE STILL *FACE DOWN?*
THAT...
...IS MY *SECRET.* ♥
TRA LA LA LA ♥
ONE STEP CLOSER TO THE PRIZE MONEY! ♥
HM...
BANG

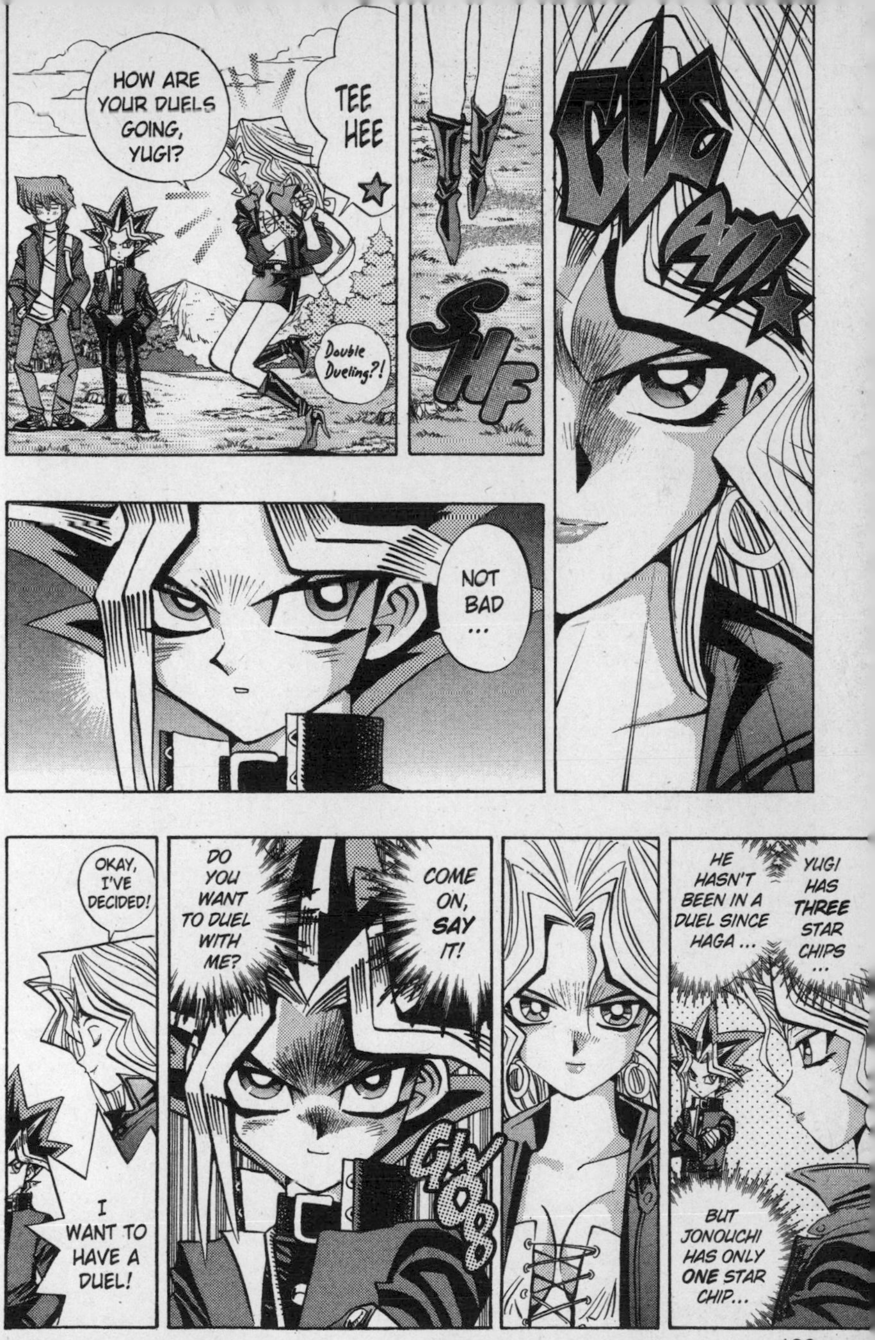
GLEAM
SHF
TEE HEE
HOW ARE YOUR DUELS GOING, YUGI?
Double Dueling?!
NOT BAD ...
YUGI HAS THREE STAR CHIPS ...
HE HASN'T BEEN IN A DUEL SINCE HAGA ...
BUT JONOUCHI HAS ONLY ONE STAR CHIP...
COME ON, SAY IT!
DO YOU WANT TO DUEL WITH ME?
OKAY, I'VE DECIDED!
I WANT TO HAVE A DUEL!

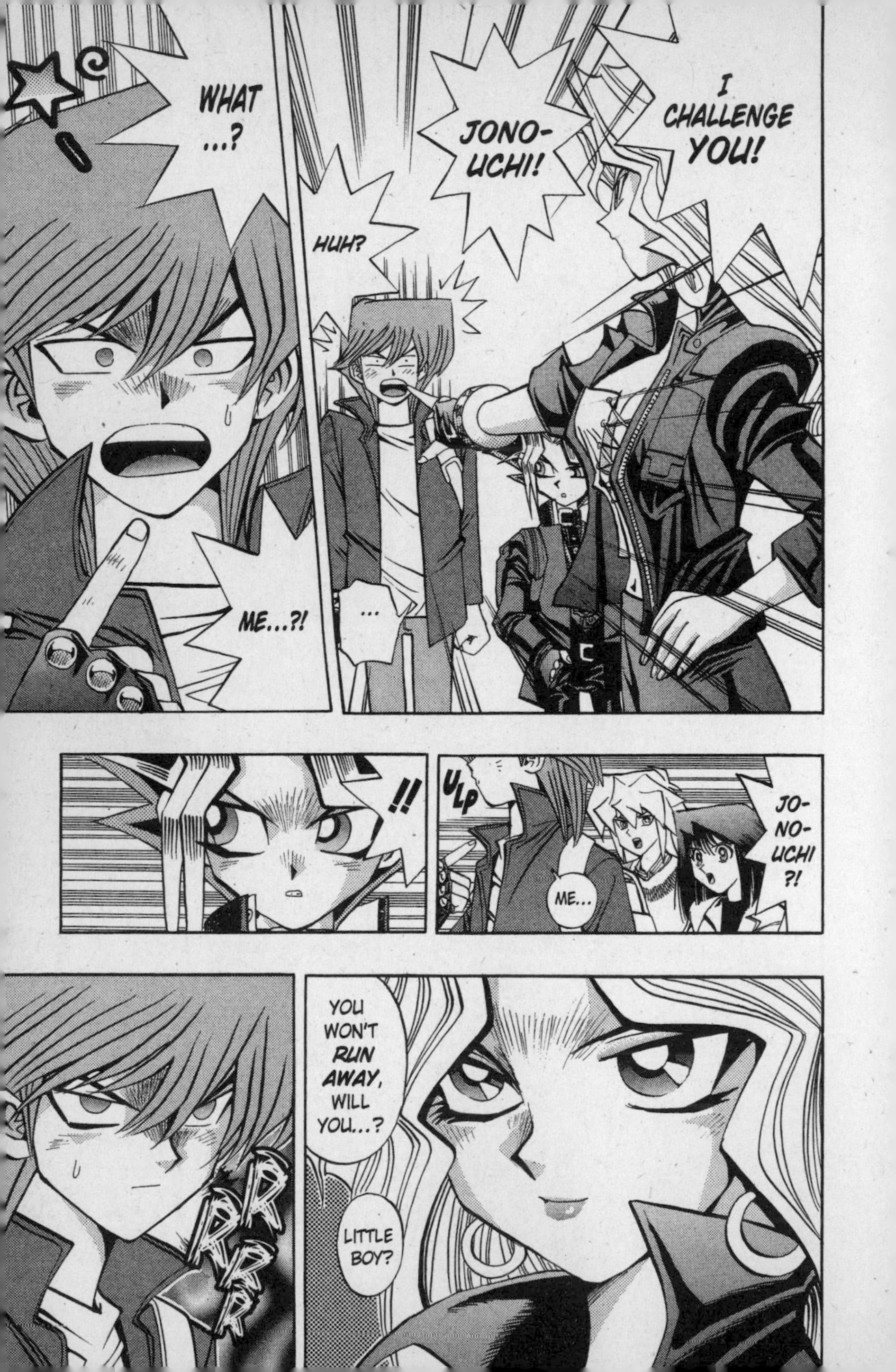
I CHALLENGE YOU!
JONO-UCHI!
HUH?
...
WHAT ...?
ME...?!
JO-NO-UCHI ?!
ULP
ME...
!!
YOU WON'T RUN AWAY, WILL YOU...?
LITTLE BOY?

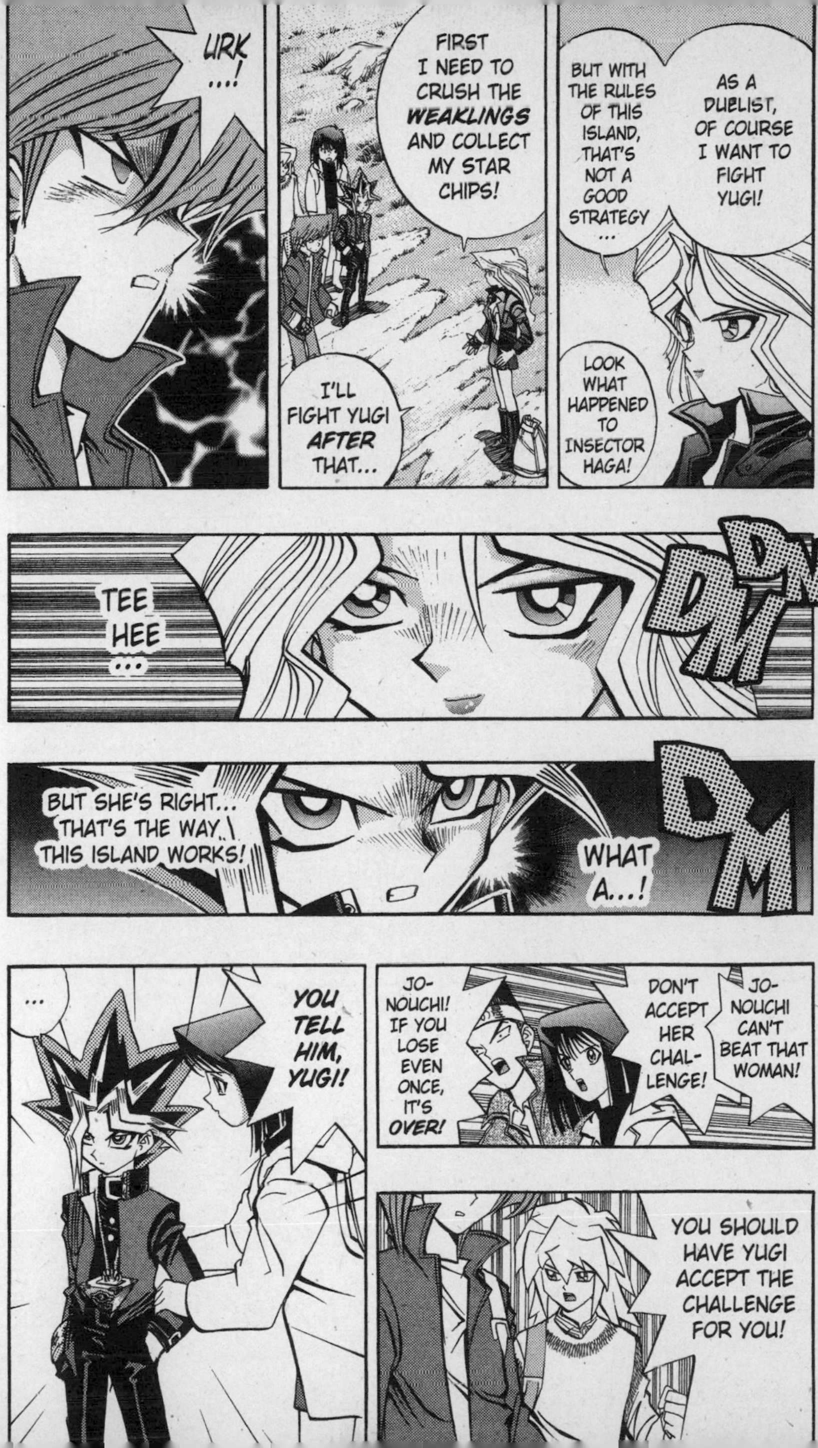
AS A DUELIST, OF COURSE I WANT TO FIGHT YUGI!
BUT WITH THE RULES OF THIS ISLAND, THAT'S NOT A GOOD STRATEGY...
LOOK WHAT HAPPENED TO INSECTOR HAGA!
FIRST I NEED TO CRUSH THE **WEAKLINGS** AND COLLECT MY STAR CHIPS!
I'LL FIGHT YUGI **AFTER** THAT...
URK ...!
DM DM
TEE HEE ...
DM
WHAT A...!
BUT SHE'S RIGHT... THAT'S THE WAY THIS ISLAND WORKS!
JO-NOUCHI CAN'T BEAT THAT WOMAN!
DON'T ACCEPT HER CHAL-LENGE!
JO-NOUCHI! IF YOU LOSE EVEN ONCE, IT'S **OVER!**
YOU SHOULD HAVE YUGI ACCEPT THE CHALLENGE FOR YOU!
YOU TELL HIM, YUGI!
...

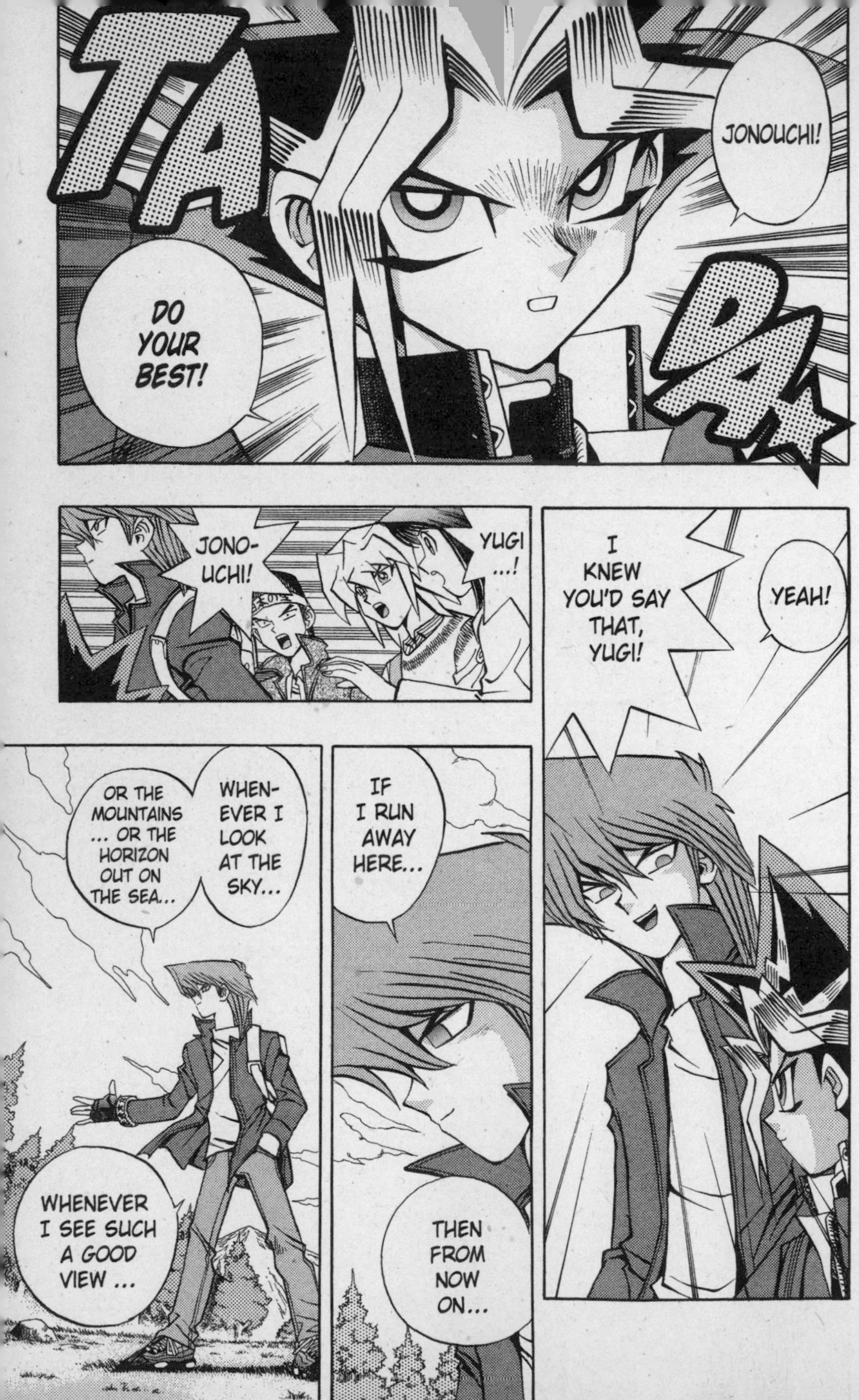
TA DA
JONOUCHI!
DO YOUR BEST!
I KNEW YOU'D SAY THAT, YUGI!
YEAH!
YUGI ...!
JONO-UCHI!
IF I RUN AWAY HERE...
THEN FROM NOW ON...
WHEN-EVER I LOOK AT THE SKY...
OR THE MOUNTAINS ... OR THE HORIZON OUT ON THE SEA...
WHENEVER I SEE SUCH A GOOD VIEW ...

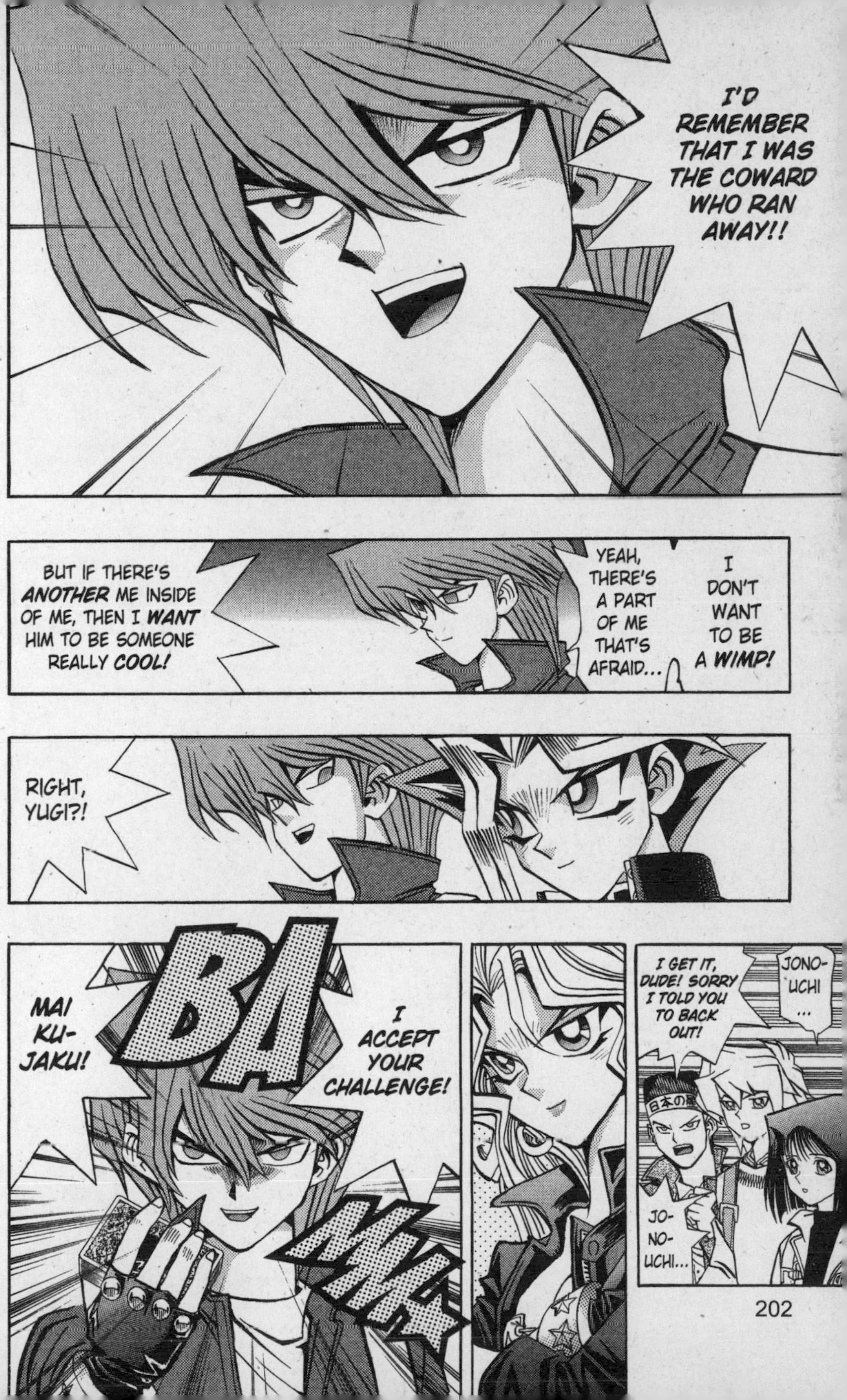

I'D REMEMBER THAT I WAS THE COWARD WHO RAN AWAY!!
I DON'T WANT TO BE A WIMP!
YEAH, THERE'S A PART OF ME THAT'S AFRAID...
BUT IF THERE'S ANOTHER ME INSIDE OF ME, THEN I WANT HIM TO BE SOMEONE REALLY COOL!
RIGHT, YUGI?!
JONO-UCHI ...
I GET IT, DUDE! SORRY I TOLD YOU TO BACK OUT!
JO-NO-UCHI...
I ACCEPT YOUR CHALLENGE!
BA
MAI KU-JAKU!

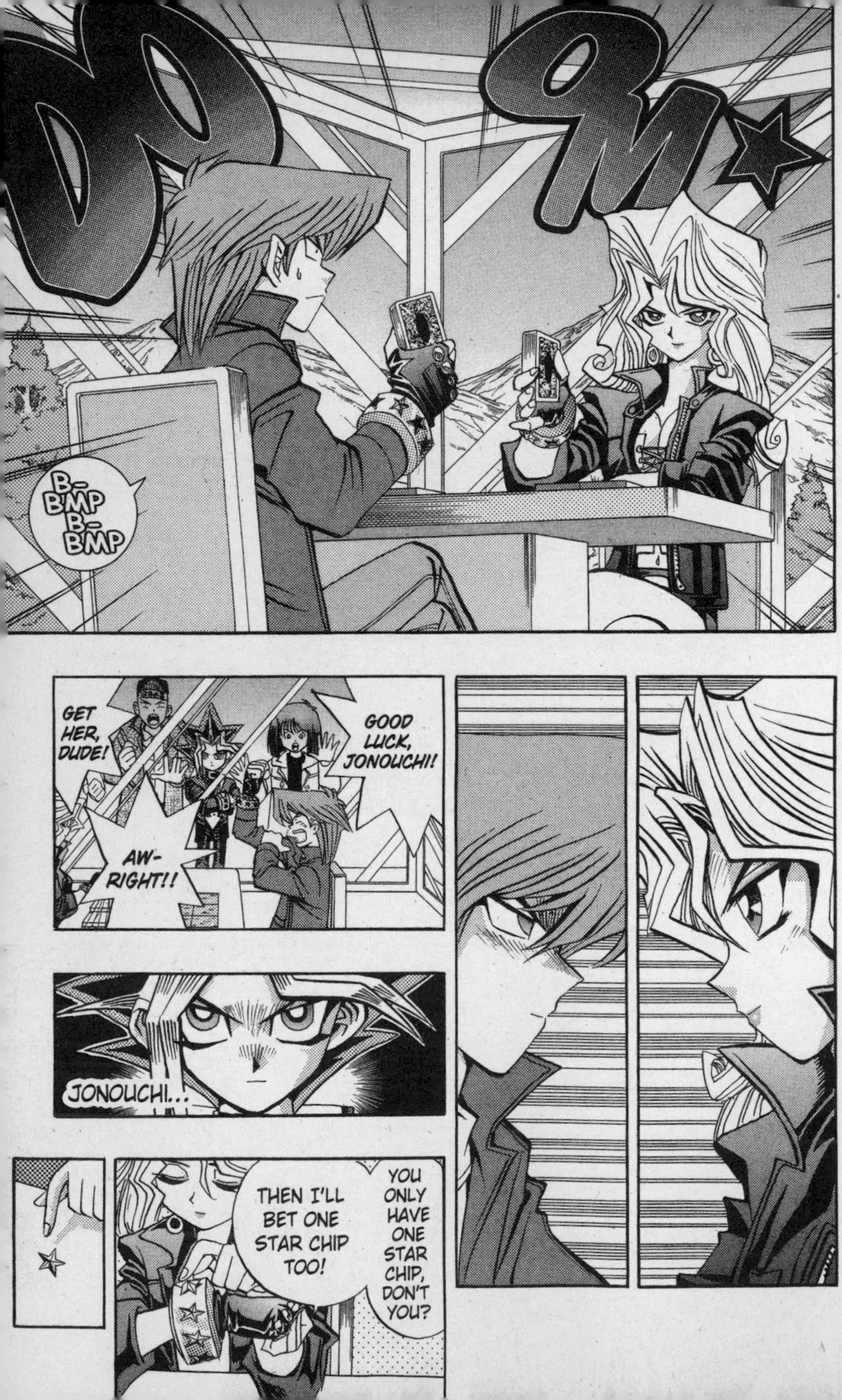
B-B'MP B-B'MP
GOOD LUCK, JONOUCHI!
GET HER, DUDE!
AW-RIGHT!!
JONOUCHI...
YOU ONLY HAVE ONE STAR CHIP, DON'T YOU?
THEN I'LL BET ONE STAR CHIP TOO!

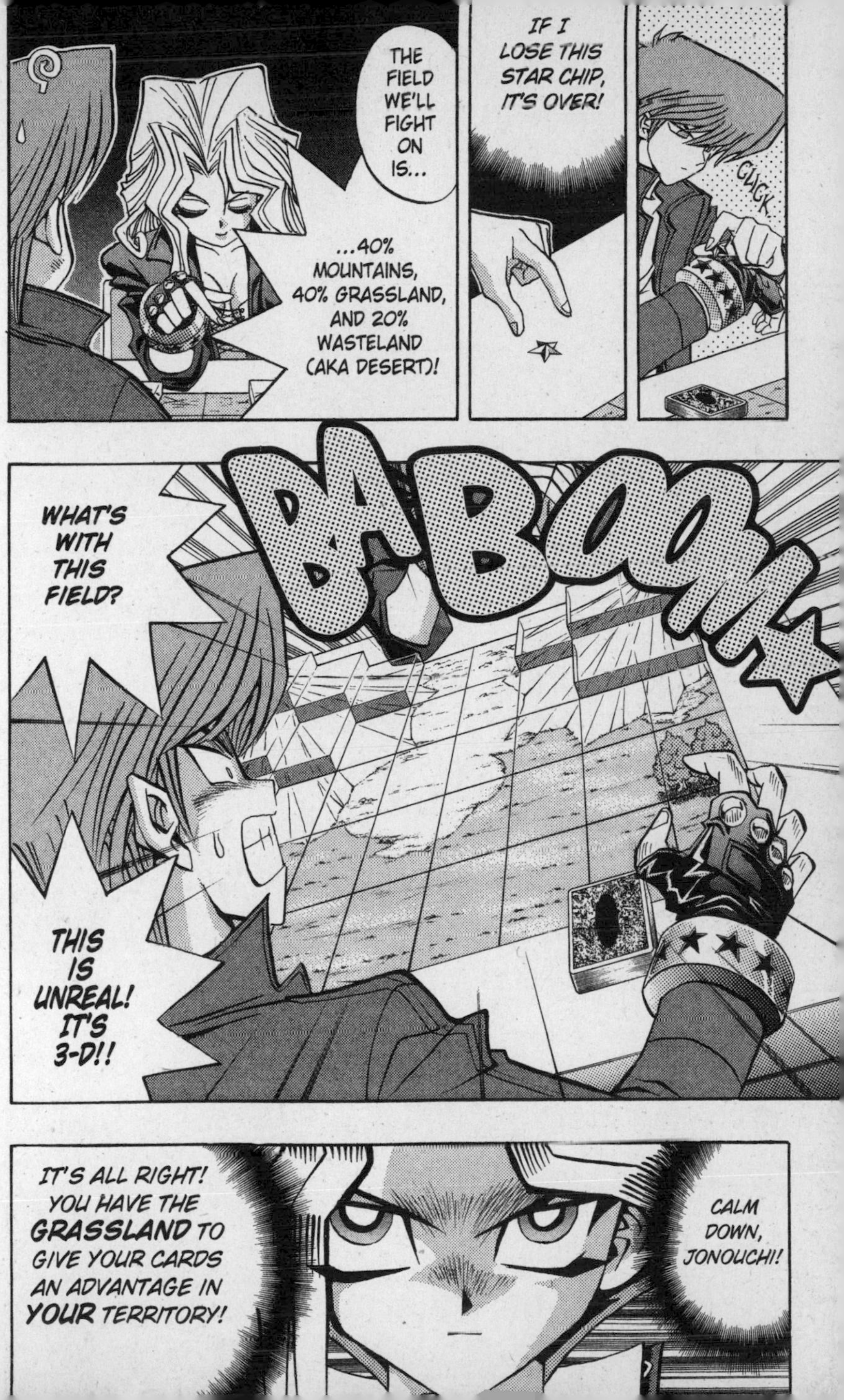
CLICK
IF I LOSE THIS STAR CHIP, IT'S OVER!
THE FIELD WE'LL FIGHT ON IS...
...40% MOUNTAINS, 40% GRASSLAND, AND 20% WASTELAND (AKA DESERT)!
BABOOM
WHAT'S WITH THIS FIELD?
THIS IS UNREAL! IT'S 3-D!!
CALM DOWN, JONOUCHI!
IT'S ALL RIGHT! YOU HAVE THE GRASSLAND TO GIVE YOUR CARDS AN ADVANTAGE IN YOUR TERRITORY!

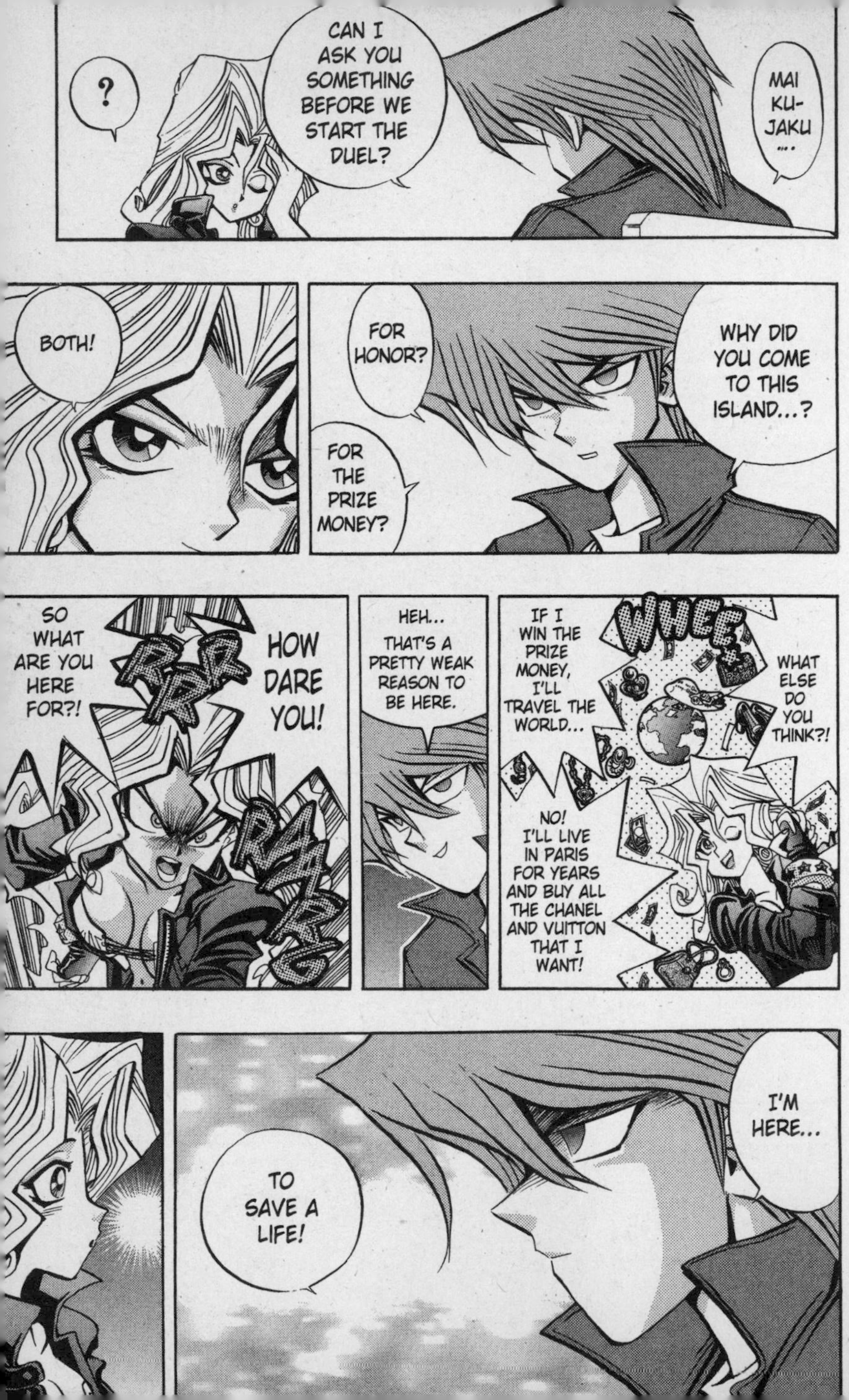
MAI KU-JAKU ....
CAN I ASK YOU SOMETHING BEFORE WE START THE DUEL?
?
WHY DID YOU COME TO THIS ISLAND...?
FOR HONOR?
FOR THE PRIZE MONEY?
BOTH!
WHAT ELSE DO YOU THINK?!
WHEE
IF I WIN THE PRIZE MONEY, I'LL TRAVEL THE WORLD...
NO! I'LL LIVE IN PARIS FOR YEARS AND BUY ALL THE CHANEL AND VUITTON THAT I WANT!
HEH... THAT'S A PRETTY WEAK REASON TO BE HERE.
HOW DARE YOU!
SO WHAT ARE YOU HERE FOR?!
I'M HERE...
TO SAVE A LIFE!

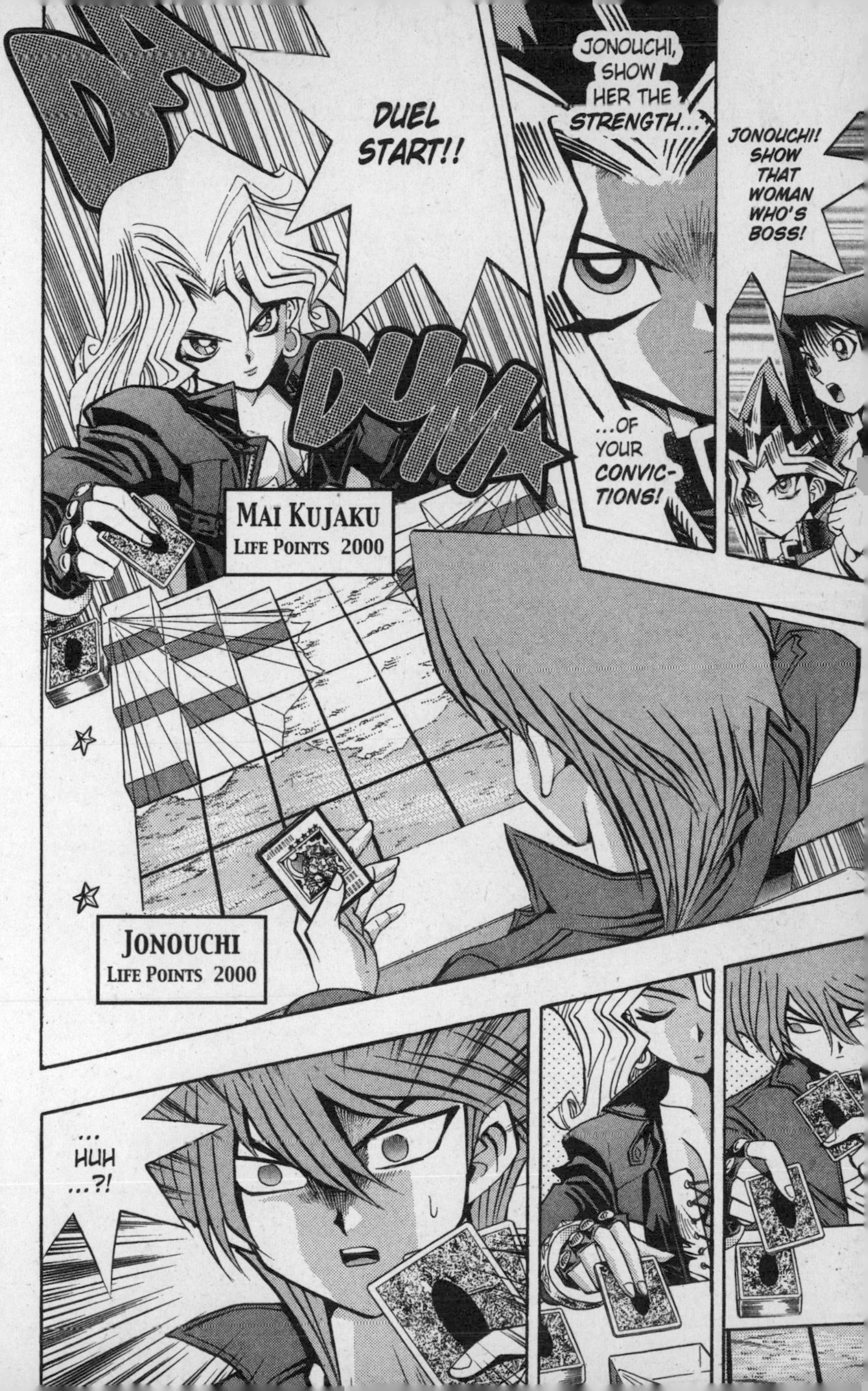
JONOUCHI! SHOW THAT WOMAN WHO'S BOSS!
JONOUCHI, SHOW HER THE STRENGTH...
...OF YOUR CONVICTIONS!
DA
DUEL START!!
MAI KUJAKU
LIFE POINTS 2000
JONOUCHI
LIFE POINTS 2000
... HUH ...?!

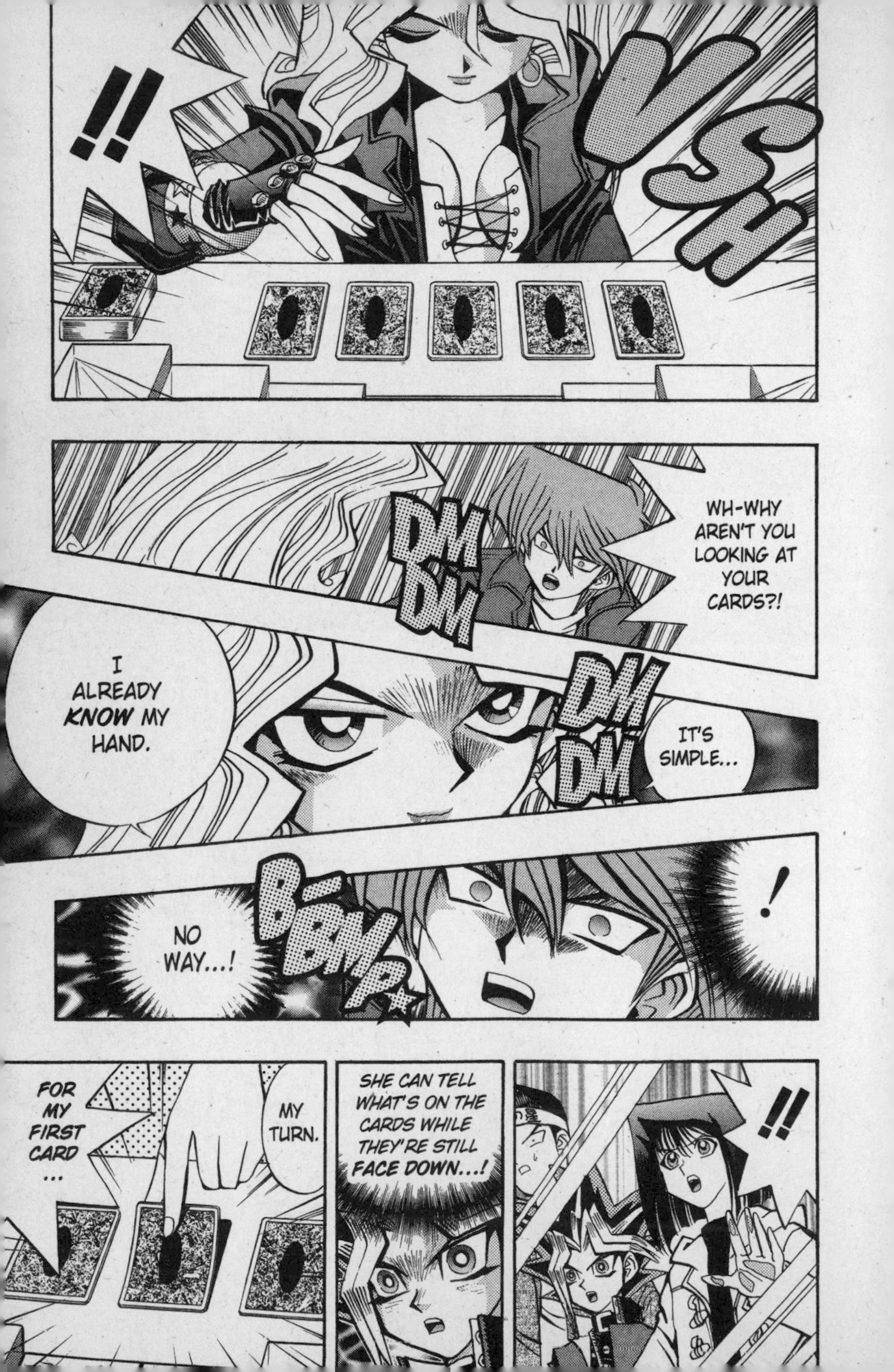
VSH
!!
WH-WHY AREN'T YOU LOOKING AT YOUR CARDS?!
DM DM
DM DM
IT'S SIMPLE...
I ALREADY *KNOW* MY HAND.
!
BBMP
NO WAY...!
!!
SHE CAN TELL WHAT'S ON THE CARDS WHILE THEY'RE STILL FACE DOWN...!
MY TURN.
FOR MY FIRST CARD...

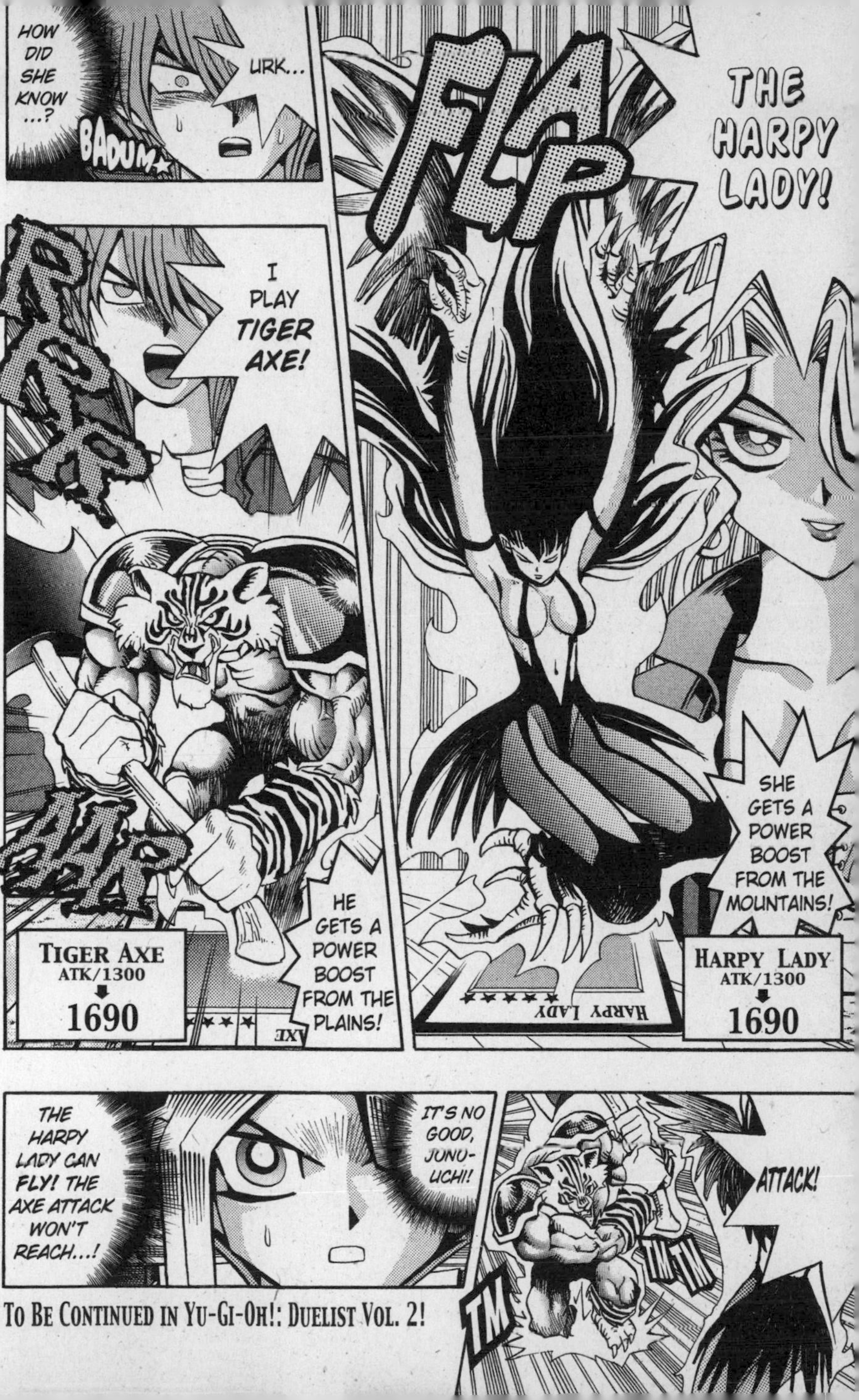
FLAP
THE HARPY LADY!
SHE GETS A POWER BOOST FROM THE MOUNTAINS!
HARPY LADY
ATK/1300
1690
HARPY LADY
URK...
HOW DID SHE KNOW ...?
BADUM★
I PLAY TIGER AXE!
HE GETS A POWER BOOST FROM THE PLAINS!
TIGER AXE
ATK/1300
1690
ATTACK!
IT'S NO GOOD, JUNU-UCHI!
THE HARPY LADY CAN FLY! THE AXE ATTACK WON'T REACH...!

TO BE CONTINUED IN YU-GI-OH!: DUELIST VOL. 2!

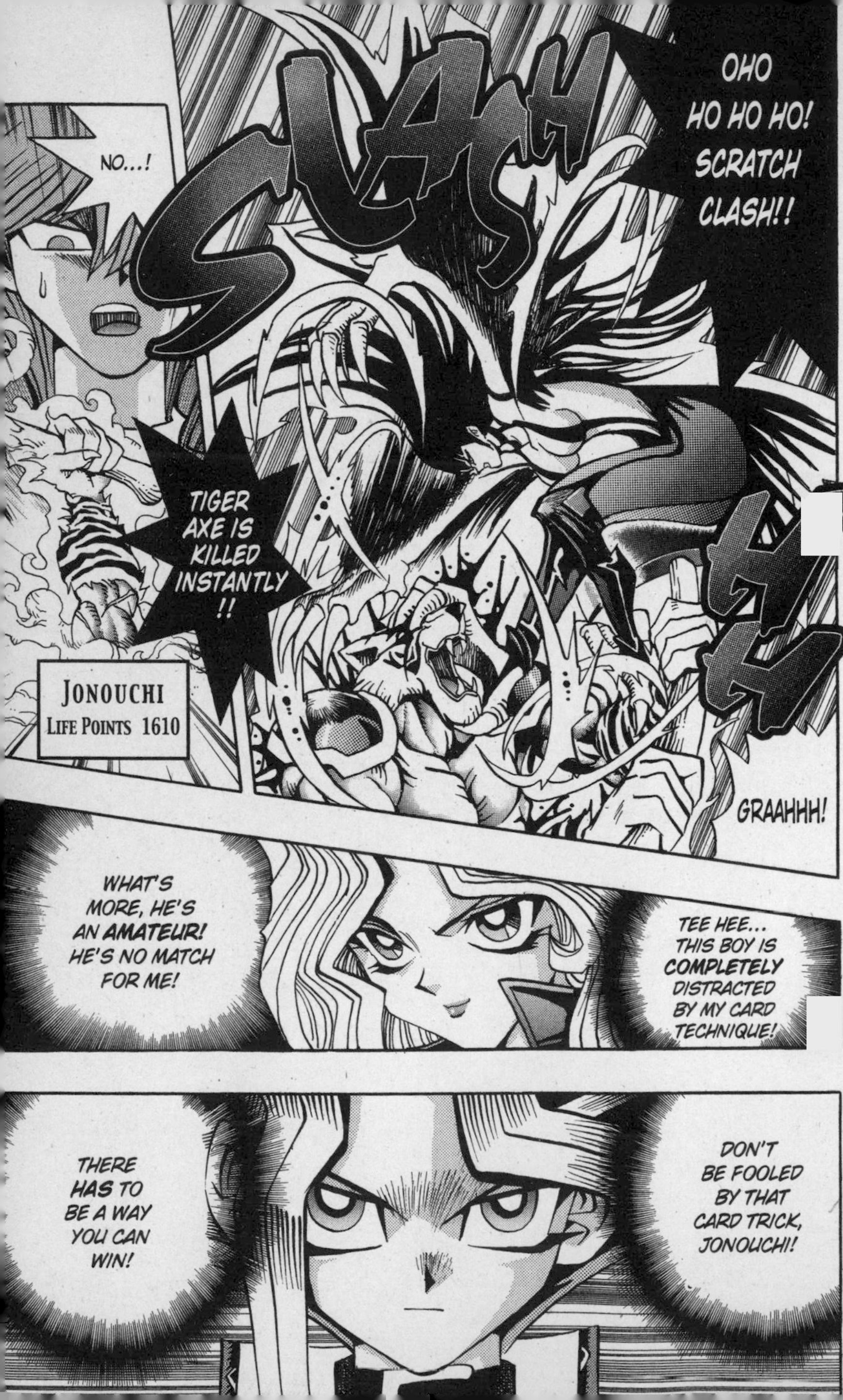
OHO HO HO HO! SCRATCH CLASH!!
SLASH
TIGER AXE IS KILLED INSTANTLY!!
GRAAHHH!
NO...!
JONOUCHI
LIFE POINTS 1610
TEE HEE... THIS BOY IS COMPLETELY DISTRACTED BY MY CARD TECHNIQUE!
WHAT'S MORE, HE'S AN AMATEUR! HE'S NO MATCH FOR ME!
DON'T BE FOOLED BY THAT CARD TRICK, JONOUCHI!
THERE HAS TO BE A WAY YOU CAN WIN!

MASTER OF THE CARDS

The "Duel Monsters" card game first appeared in volume two of the original **Yu-Gi-Oh!** graphic novel series, but it's in **Yu-Gi-Oh!: Duelist** (originally printed in Japan as volumes 8-31 of **Yu-Gi-Oh!**) that it becomes really important. As many fans know, some of the card names are different between the English and Japanese versions. In case you play the game, or you're interested in playing, here's a rundown of some of the cards in this graphic novel.

Some cards only appear in the **Yu-Gi-Oh!** video games, not in the actual collectible card game. There are other differences too: the Field Cards (Forest, Sogen, Wasteland, Umi and Mountain) aren't actually cards in the manga! Check out page 131 of this graphic novel for an explanation of the Field Cards.

FIRST APPEARANCE IN THIS VOLUME	JAPANESE CARD NAME	ENGLISH CARD NAME
p.8	Mountain Warrior	Mountain Warrior (NOTE: Not a real game card.)
p.8	*Gankutsu Majin Ogre Rock* (Grotto/Cave Golem/Djinn Ogre Rock)	Rock Ogre Grotto #1
p.8	*Kami no Ibuki* (Breath of the Gods)	Wind of the Gods (NOTE: Not a real game card. Called "Breath of Life" in the video games.)
p.15	*Nitô o Motsu King Rex* (Two-Headed King Rex)	Two-Headed King Rex
p.16	Basic Insect	Basic Insect
p.16	*Messiah no Arijigoku* (Ant Lion/Sand Trap of the Messiah)	Infinite Dismissal

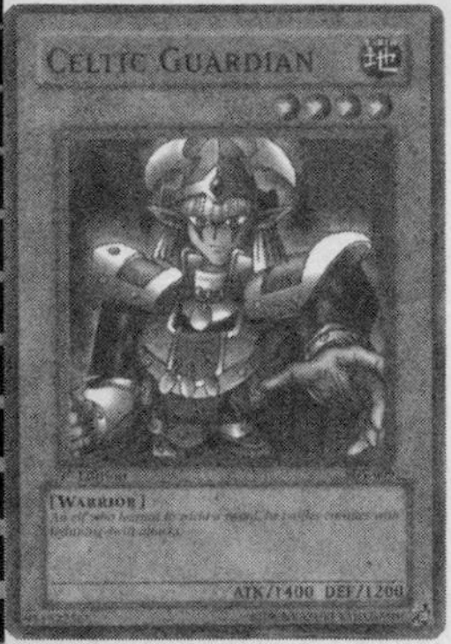
Celtic Guardian
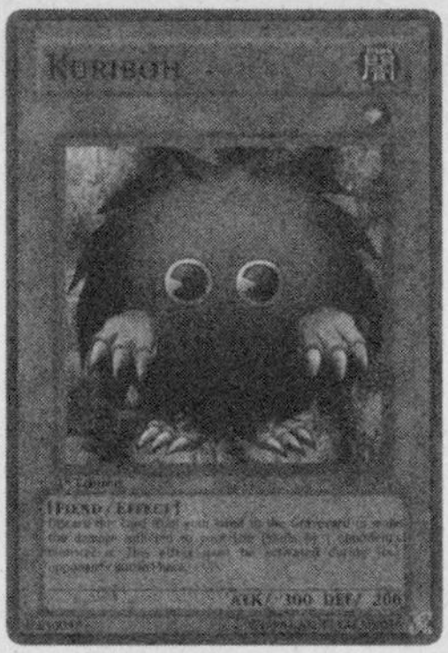
Kuriboh
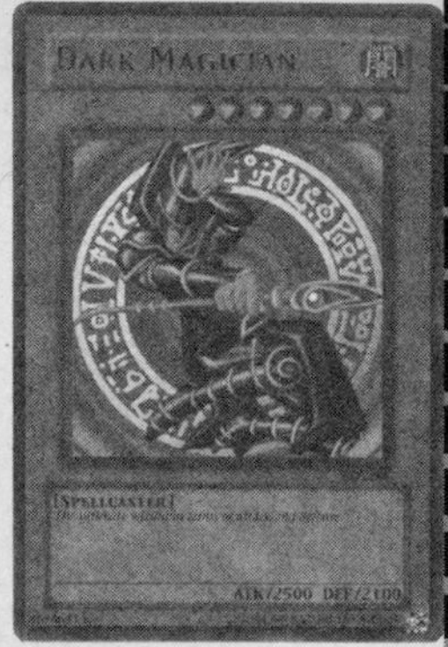
Dark Magician

FIRST APPEARANCE IN THIS VOLUME	JAPANESE CARD NAME	ENGLISH CARD NAME
p.17	*Kakitsuki Insect Armor* (Firearms Insect Armor)	Insect Gun Armor (NOTE: Not a real game card. Called "Insect Armor with Fire" in the video games.)
p.23	*Devil Dragon*	Koumori Dragon (NOTE: "Koumori" means "bat" in Japanese)
p.24	*Dragonzoku Fûin no Tsubo* (Dragon Clan Sealing Jar)	Dragon Capture Jar
p.30	*Baby Dragon*	Baby Dragon
p.31	*Silver Fang*	Silver Fang
p.32	*Tsubo Majin* (Jar Golem/Djinn)	Dragon Piper
p.35	*Great White*	Great White
p.35	*Elekids*	Oscillo Hero #2
p.39	*Undead Warrior*	Undead Warrior (NOTE: Not a real game card. Called "Zombie Warrior" in the video games.)
p.42	*Holy Doll*	Rogue Doll
p.44	*Black Magician*	Dark Magician

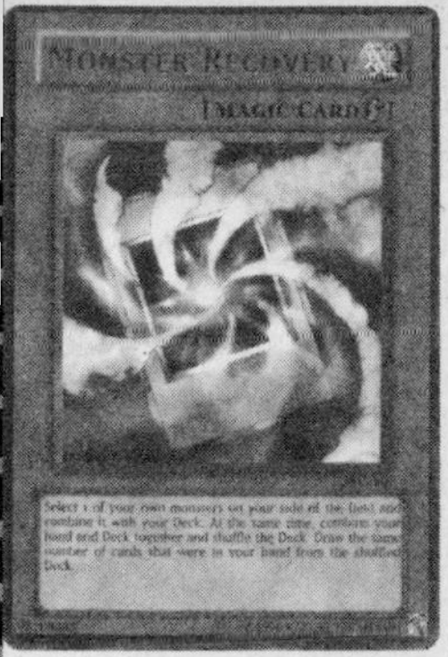
Monster Recovery
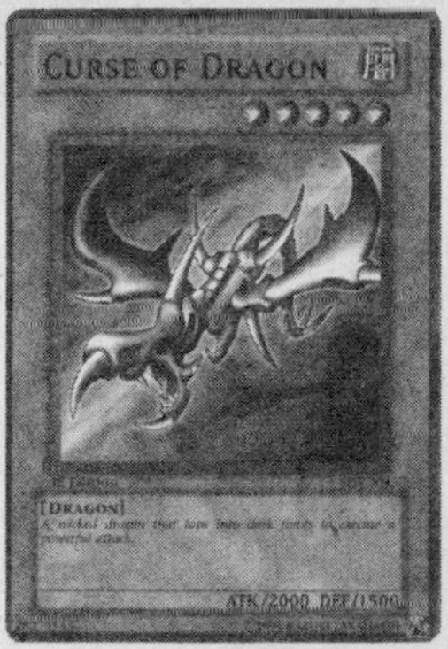
Curse of Dragon
[DRAGON]
ATK/2000 DEF/1500
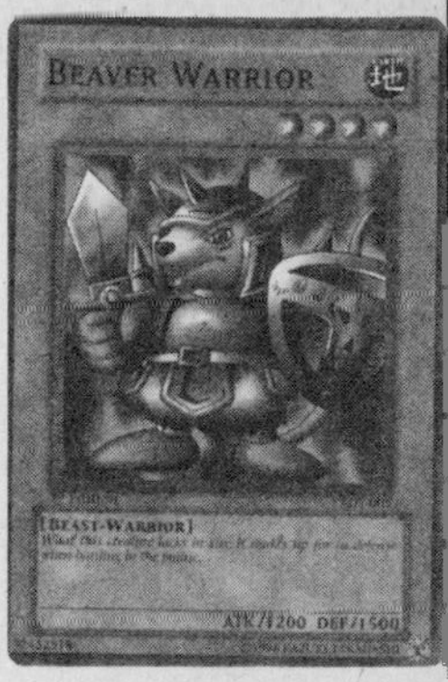
Beaver Warrior
[BEAST-WARRIOR]
ATK/1200 DEF/1500

FIRST APPEARANCE IN THIS VOLUME	JAPANESE CARD NAME	ENGLISH CARD NAME
p.52	*Illusionist No Face*	Illusionist Faceless Mage
p.54	*Genwaku no Manako* (Eye of Enchantment)	Eye of Deception (NOTE: Not a real game card. Called "Eye of Illusion" in the anime.)
p.57	*Elf no Senshi* (Elf Soldier)	Celtic Guardian
p.61	*Demon no Shôkan* (Demon Summoning)	Summoned Skull
p.124	*Killer Bee*	Killer Needle
p.124	*Mammoth no Hakaba* (Mammoth's Graveyard)	Mammoth Graveyard
p.129	*Saiga*	Saiga (NOTE: Not a real game card. Called "Torike" in the video games.)
p.129	*Sei naru Barrier Mirror Force* (Holy Barrier Mirror Force)	Mirror Force
p.129	*Gremlin*	Feral Imp
p.129	*Ikkakujû no Horn* (Unicorn's Horn)	Horn of the Unicorn
p.133	*Hercules Beetle*	Hercules Beetle

FIRST APPEARANCE IN THIS VOLUME	JAPANESE CARD NAME	ENGLISH CARD NAME
p.137	*Guriforu*	Griffor (NOTE: Not a real game card. Called "Griffore" in the video games.)
p.137	*Laser Cannon Armor*	Laser Cannon Armor
p.140	*Gokiboru (Roach Ball)*	Pillroach (NOTE: Not a real game card. Called "Gokibore" in the video games.)
p.140	*Kyuketsunomi (Blood-drinking Flea)*	Giant Flea
p.140	*Big Ant*	Big Ant (NOTE: Not a real game card. Called "Big Insect" in the video games.)
p.152	*Larvae Moth*	Larvae Moth
p.153	*Monster Kaishū (Monster Withdrawal)*	Monster Recovery
p.154	*Kuribo*	Kuriboh
p.155	*Ruizu (NOTE: Sounds like "Louise")*	Beaver Warrior
p.156	*Shinka no Mayu (Cocoon of Evolution)*	Cocoon of Evolution
p.159	*Ankoku Kishi Gaia (Dark Knight Gaia)*	Gaia the Fierce Knight
p.164	*Curse of Dragon*	Curse of Dragon
p.166	*Moesakaru Daichi (Burning Land)*	Burning Land
p.168	*Great Moth Yondanshinka (Great Moth Fourth-Stage Evolution)*	Great Moth
p.175	*Yûgô (Fusion)*	Polymerization
p.178	*Ryûkishi Gaia (Dragon Knight Gaia)*	Gaia the Dragon Champion
p.181	*Makiu (Magic Mist)*	Magic Mist (NOTE: Not a real game card. Called "Magical Mist" in the video games.)
p.195	*Carbonara Senshi (Carbonara Warrior)*	Karbonala Warrior
p.195	*Ookami (Wolf)*	Wolf
p.195	*Guard (NOTE: Full name is covered up)*	Kojikocy
p.208	*Harpie Lady*	Harpy Lady
p.208	*Tiger Axe*	Tiger Axe

IN THE NEXT VOLUME...

Jonouchi has finally learned some strategy, but will it be enough to beat Mai Kujaku's harpies? Then, Yugi must face the fisherman Ryota Kajiki, the "duelist of the sea!" Finally, Yugi must face the spirit of his old enemy, Kaiba, in his most terrifying match yet! Even though Kaiba's body is in a coma, his deck still lives…in the hands of a deadly new enemy!

COMING MARCH 2005!

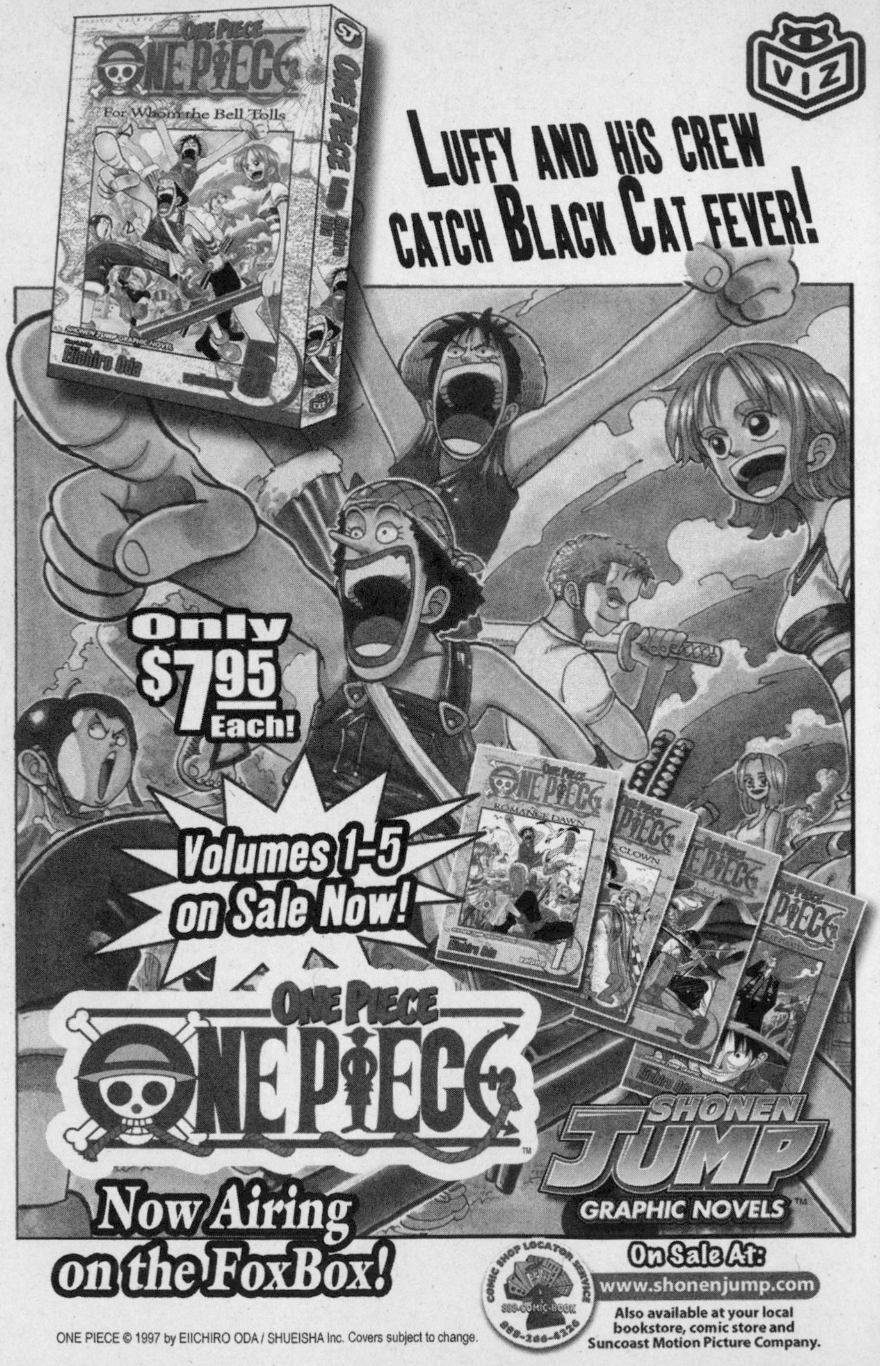
LUFFY AND HIS CREW CATCH BLACK CAT FEVER!
VIZ
Only $7.95 Each!
Volumes 1-5 on Sale Now!
ONE PIECE
ONE PIECE
SHONEN JUMP GRAPHIC NOVELS
Now Airing on the FoxBox!
On Sale At:
www.shonenjump.com
Also available at your local bookstore, comic store and Suncoast Motion Picture Company.
COMIC SHOP LOCATOR SERVICE
888-COMIC-BOOK
888-266-4226

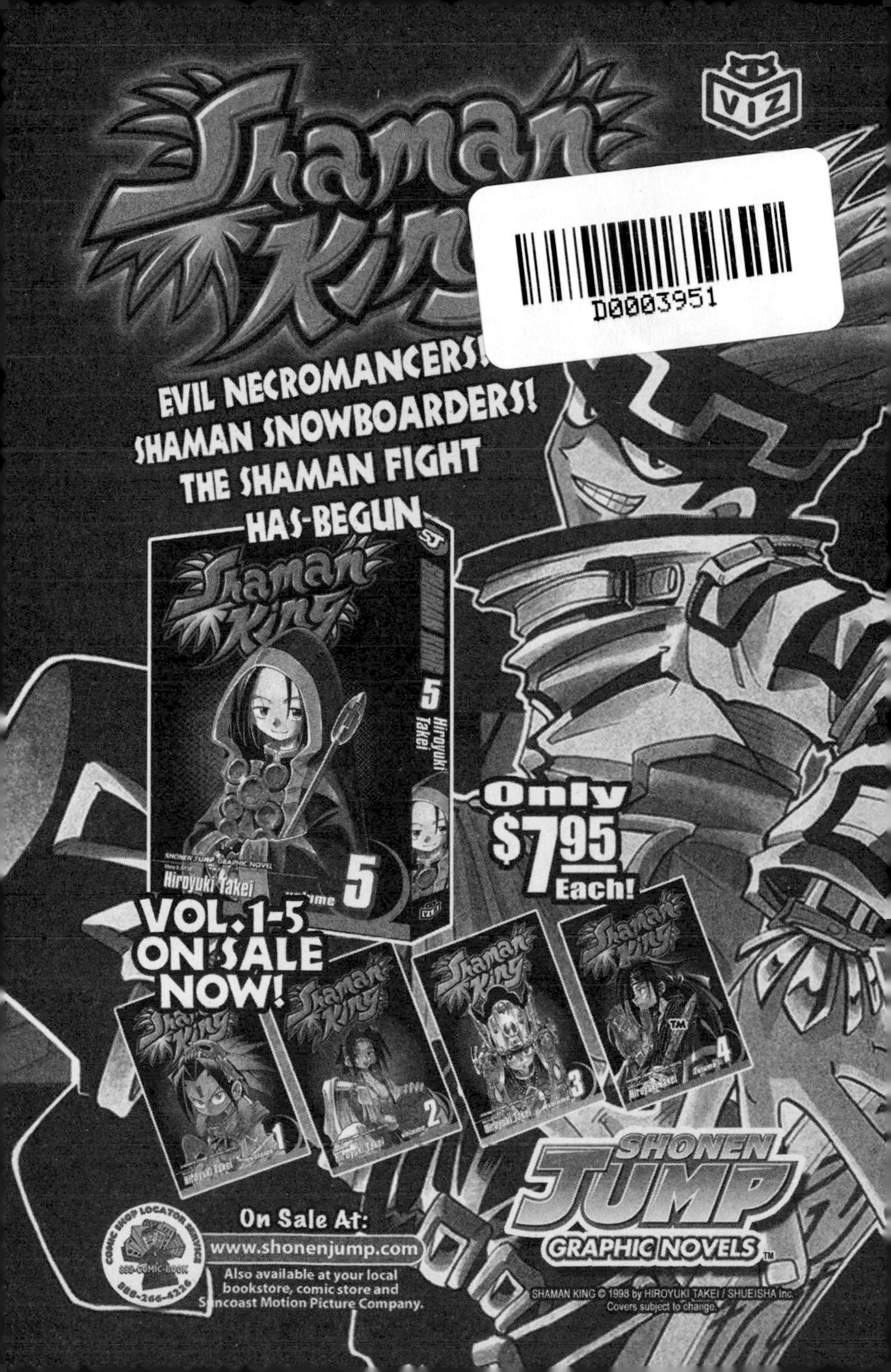

Shaman King
VIZ
EVIL NECROMANCERS!
SHAMAN SNOWBOARDERS!
THE SHAMAN FIGHT
HAS BEGUN
Only $7.95 Each!
VOL. 1-5
ON SALE
NOW!
SHONEN JUMP
GRAPHIC NOVELS
On Sale At:
www.shonenjump.com
Also available at your local
bookstore, comic store and
Suncoast Motion Picture Company.
SHAMAN KING © 1998 by HIROYUKI TAKEI / SHUEISHA Inc.
Covers subject to change.